D1616122

All Honor to Jefferson?

All Honor to Jefferson?

The Virginia Slavery Debates and the Positive Good Thesis

ERIK S. ROOT

LEXINGTON BOOKS

A division of
ROWMAN & LITTLEFIELD PUBLISHERS, INC.
Lanham • Boulder • New York • Toronto • Plymouth, UK

LEXINGTON BOOKS

A division of Rowman & Littlefield Publishers, Inc.
A wholly owned subsidiary of The Rowman & Littlefield Publishing Group, Inc.
4501 Forbes Boulevard, Suite 200
Lanham, MD 20706

Estover Road
Plymouth PL6 7PY
United Kingdom

British Library Cataloguing in Publication Information Available

Library of Congress Cataloging-in-Publication Data

Root, Erik S.
   All honor to Jefferson? : the Virginia slavery debates and the positive good thesis / Erik
S. Root.
     p. cm.
   Includes bibliographical references and index.
   ISBN-13: 978-0-7391-2217-4 (cloth : alk. paper)
   ISBN-10: 0-7391-2217-7 (cloth : alk. paper)
   ISBN-13: 978-0-7391-2218-1 (pbk. : alk. paper)
   ISBN-10: 0-7391-2218-5 (pbk. : alk. paper)
   1. Slavery—Political aspects—Virginia—History—19th century. 2. Slavery—
Virginia—Justification. 3. Virginia—Politics and government—1775–1865. 4. United
States. Declaration of Independence. 5. Slavery—Political aspects—United States—
History—19th century. 6. United States—Politics and government—1815–1861. 7.
Jefferson, Thomas, 1743–1826—Political and social views. 8. Dew, Thomas R. (Thomas
Roderick), 1802–1846—Political and social views. I. Title.
   E445.V8R66 2008
   973.7'11—dc22   2007043513

Printed in the United States of America

Contents

Acknowledgments

I would like to take this opportunity to thank several who deserve recognition in the production of this book. This book is the outgrowth of my dissertation. I undertook research for this project while I was at the Claremont Graduate School (now Claremont Graduate University). I owe much to my dissertation committee members, who were very helpful. Special thanks are reserved for Joseph Bessette, Harry V. Jaffa, Harry Neumann, and Jean Schroedel.

Harry Jaffa encouraged me to pursue this topic after I became interested in how the "sons of the Fathers" carried, or did not carry, the idea "all men are created equal" to their generation and beyond. Both Harry Neumann and Jean Schroedel offered invaluable advice, and Joseph Bessette offered a critical eye to the project. If there are any mistakes, infelicitous comments, or awful prose, the responsibility is solely mine.

This book would not have been possible without the helpful assistance of Brent Tarter at the Library of Virginia. He encouraged me early on in the research of this project. His help was unselfish and invaluable. He also made several helpful suggestions and read a few early chapters of the dissertation. I would also like to thank the helpful staff of the College of William and Mary Swem Library, and in particular the great staff at the special collections annex at Toano. I would also like to note the valuable help I received from the Perkins Library at Duke, the D.H. Hill Library at North Carolina State (and especially the digital media lab at the same library), the Library of Congress, and the Virginia Historical Society.

I would be remiss if I did not thank my wife, Stephanie, for her help in the preparation of this manuscript and the countless hours she spent reading and rereading drafts. She was more than patient with me and always generous with her time. Any thanks I relate here could not be conveyed adequately, such was her support, love, and dedication. I owe her beyond words.

I should also recognize my parents, who always encouraged me in my education. They more than anyone were my inspiration and oracles. Without them I would never have finished my degree. From them I learned to pursue my dreams and not to squander talent.

Finally, I want to thank the fine folks at Lexington, including the anonymous reader, for support and guidance. Joe Parry provided fine commentary and Patricia Stevenson was very patient with me in getting the manuscript ready for print. She endured many questions and was always helpful and understanding.

Chapter 1

Introduction

> The United States of America may be said to be the only country in the world
> which was founded in explicit opposition to Machiavellian principles.
>
> Leo Strauss[1]

Virginia's statesmen had a profound influence on the American Founding. Of the first five presidents, four of them were Virginians. Three of those four were sent to the presidential mansion in succession. By 1800 Virginia sent more representatives to Congress than any other state. Old Dominion thus held an influential position in the Union.[2] The most prominent Founders held a reluctant tolerance of slavery. However, they expressed their distaste of the peculiar institution in different ways. All wrote privately about their aversion of the institution, and some took unmistakable public positions. Several also found ways to demonstrate implicitly their opinion about slavery.

In 1824 the Marquis de Lafayette returned to the United States. At the prompting of President James Monroe, Congress proclaimed Lafayette an honorary citizen and invited him to tour the United States as an honorary guest.[3] During the Revolutionary period, the Continental Congress commissioned Lafayette a major general, and a portion of his service to the budding nation was spent under the command of General George Washington. The Marquis's support for the American Revolution was, hence, unquestioned. Upon hearing of Lafayette's return to America, Thomas Jefferson invited him to Monticello. The Marquis arrived at Jefferson's home with much fanfare. His carriage was decorated with revolutionary banners and he was escorted by "martial trumpets."[4]

Jefferson and Lafayette were both elderly men in 1824 and they had limited mobility resulting from their advanced age. Jefferson was eighty-one. Yet, when the Frenchman emerged from the carriage, both the men perambulated toward each other as fast as they could until they embraced, both in tears. Lafayette spent the next two weeks at Monticello where the two conversed on many subjects, including slavery. At a point thereafter, he was treated to a banquet where President Monroe, James Madison, and Jefferson drank toasts to the ardent anti-slavery Frenchman.

The grand gesture extended to Lafayette ought not go overlooked. While it might seem like an insignificant event in American history, the celebration of Lafayette's contribution to the Founding was significant. Along with many influential Virginians, he shared a commitment to the emancipationist cause. Though he returned to France after the war, he corresponded with many of the Founders, Washington and Jefferson in particular. The post-war letters frequently broached the issue of slavery. He solicited his American friends to live up to the principles of the revolution and chart a course to free the slaves. At one point, Lafayette proposed a plan for private manumissions that would have set up small estates where blacks could work as free tenants. In a letter to the Marquis, Washington wrote: "The scheme, my dear Marquis which you propose as a precedent, to encourage emancipation of the black people of this country from that state of Bondage in which they are held, is striking evidence of that benevolence of your Heart. I shall be happy to join you in so laudable a work."[5] Lafayette's visit to America lasted about a year in total. His warm reception by many prominent Virginians, three of whom were either currently serving, or did serve, as President, demonstrates their public support for a man who shared their commitment to liberty. While Lafayette holds no prominent place in this book, because he is not a Virginian, his reception and public embrace demonstrates, at least, that renowned Virginians did not shy away from the slave issue and quietly, yet openly and publicly, embraced a man who supported emancipation. They certainly supported his status as an honorary citizen and, we might argue, his commitment to the anti-slavery cause did not detract from that honor. His opinion about the institution may have contributed to the great tribute.

Lafayette's visit to the United States had a profound effect on him. He left the country convinced that emancipation was inevitable because Virginia's elite did not support the institution. After a lengthy conversation with Madison at Montpelier, Lafayette concluded: "It seems to me that slavery cannot subsist much longer in Virginia; for the principle is condemned by all enlightened men; and when public opinion condemns a principle, its consequences cannot long continue."[6] While this book will pay particular attention to the public debate over slavery, it will not ignore other ways, symbolic or otherwise, in which Virginia's most prominent statesmen expressed their opposition to the institution. If we are to believe Lafayette, Virginia's most significant statesmen were united in their distaste of slavery and expressed such sentiments to him.

The purpose of this book is to elucidate the moral controversy over slavery between the Founding and the Civil War, focusing in particular on the Virginia slavery debates that occurred between 1829-1832. It will examine the historical events that led up to the debates as well as the ideological development of one of the earliest public articulations of the "positive good" thesis. This book will address four questions: (1) What was the importance of the slavery issue in the United States at about the midway point between the Founding and Civil War? (2) How did the participants in the Virginia slavery debates understand the principles of the Founding and how did they seek to apply those principles practically? (3) How should we understand the principles of the Declaration in light of the arguments raised during the debates? (4) How did the advance of the "positive good" thesis change the understanding of the Founding? The 1829-1832 slave debates in Virginia are important because of the influence the state had on the rest of the country. The political direction of Old Dominion was a bellwether for the Union. Virginians had an opportunity to reaffirm the principles of liberty, but ultimately that argument lost. The forces of self-interest defeated those who articulated the principles of the Declaration of Independence. Therefore, this book will detail the advance of the pro-slavery argument and the "positive good" thesis in Virginia. In the process, we will be able to understand how the participants in the Virginia slavery debate understood the principles of the Founding and sought to apply those principles practically.

In order to develop some understanding of the Founding principles, and to gauge just how far Virginians strayed from the dispensation of the Founding by the 1830s, this book will examine the early anti-slavery development in the state as well as the opinions of some of Virginia's most prominent statesmen. The Founders may have indeed tolerated the peculiar institution, but that is not the same thing as condoning it.

Every leading Founder believed, or acknowledged, that slavery was wrong. They based this argument on the natural rights all men, all humans, possessed. The Founding was not, then, an articulation of mere English rights. With a natural rights understanding of the American Founding, it is an inescapable conclusion that slavery is a violation of those rights: it takes the property of one and gives it to another without the consent on the part of the former.[7] Many modern scholars and historians have expressed much anxiety over slavery because the Founding seemed to secure it. However, according to Herbert Storing: "Some concessions to slavery were thought to be necessary in order to secure Union, with its promise of a broad and long lasting foundation for freedom; the problem was to make the minimum concessions consistent with that end, to express them in language that would not sanction slavery, and so far as possible to avoid blotting a free Constitution with the stain of slavery."[8] The Founders fashioned the republic on eternal principles and hence did not intend to secure the institution indefinitely in the Union. They planned for just the opposite:

> Slavery was an evil to be tolerated, allowed to enter the Constitution only by the back door, grudgingly, unacknowledged, on the presumption that the house would be truly fit to live in only when it was gone, and that it would ultimately be gone.
>
> In their accommodation to slavery, the founders limited and confined it and carefully withheld any indication of moral approval, while they built a union that they thought was the greatest instrument of human liberty ever made, that they thought would lead and that did in fact lead to the extinction of Negro slavery.[9]

Storing represents one side of the dispute over the American Founding. His point is difficult to refute: we are hard pressed to find any *positive* gesture toward the peculiar institution. Jefferson, for example, never equivocated as to the injustice of slavery.[10] As alluded above, however, there is little scholarly consensus on this issue. There are many who dispute the natural rights understanding of the American Founding. They contend that it produced no real benefits for many groups including blacks, Indians, and females.[11] In other words, the Founding only profited a few wealthy, white men. The critique of the Founders' intentions is legion. It is almost impossible to write about the Founders without at least acknowledging and answering their critics. Since this book takes the unorthodox position that the Founders were anti-slavery, let us meet the criticizers head-on and grapple with the most serious charges.

Criticizing the Criticizers

On the issue of slavery, the Founders have come under intense scrutiny. However, most of this criticism is of fairly recent origin. Many biographies on Thomas Jefferson after World War Two painted the Sage from Monticello in a positive light. These historians portrayed Jefferson as a symbol of freedom, equality, and universal rights. He was someone who was "disturbed by slavery."[12] There were, however, certain scholars, like Carl Becker, who held that natural rights were not worthy of serious consideration. He denied there was an unchanging reality and hence thought it was a "delusion" to believe in natural rights: "to ask whether the natural rights philosophy of the Declaration of Independence is true or false is essentially a meaningless question."[13] Despite this early criticism, the modern attack on the Founding generation began in earnest in the 1960s. This critique eventually extended to Jefferson's biographers: Dumas Malone, Merrill Peterson, and Julian Boyd, to name a few. According to historian Sean Wilentz, Jefferson "infuriates" both the "religious right" and the "post-modern left" because he embraced enlightenment principles.[14] Of course, this criticism does not only apply to Jefferson because he is not the sole expositor of the enlightenment. The modern scholarship of the American Founding has become so acrimonious that anyone defending Jefferson is believed to be, somehow, a defender of slavery. It should be no surprise, then, that the detractors have also extended their critique to include others in the American pantheon like Washington, Madison, and Monroe.[15]

   Historian Henry Wiencek contends that the general problem vexing us in the present springs from the Founding itself: "how is it that the nation—conceived in liberty and dedicated to the proposition that all men are created equal—preserved slavery?"[16] It is the inability of many scholars to understand this albeit fair question that is the basis of so many other attacks on the Founders. One of the most obvious oversights from modern scholars is that while they criticize the Founders for not freeing the slaves, they seem to diminish the fact that it was slaveholders who declared such overarching principles as a foundation for the government.

   One of the most often heard arguments against Jefferson is that he believed in "negro inferiority" and, as a result, his "public actions frequently favored the slave system."[17] John Hope Franklin cast a wider net in the mid 1970s to accuse all of the Founders with betraying their ideals by failing to take a stand against slavery.[18] They spoke about their objection to the institution, but did not act to eliminate it because they were economically self-interested. For example, by 1787 Jefferson was deeply in debt and sold some of his slaves to try to ameliorate his financial troubles. A portion of a letter to his plantation manger suffices as evidence:

> The torment of mind I endure till the moment shall arrive when I shall not owe a shilling on earth is such really as to render life of little value. I cannot decide to sell my lands. I have sold too much of them already, and they are the only sure provision for my children, nor would I willingly sell the slaves as long as there remains any prospect of paying my debts with their labor. In this I am governed solely by views to their happiness which will render it worth their while to use extraordinary exertions for some time to enable me to put them ultimately on an easier footing, which I will do the moment they have paid the debts due from the estate, two thirds of which have been contracted by purchasing them.[19]

Author William Cohen remarks that at first glance the letter gives the impression that Jefferson is concerned for the welfare of his slaves, but just the opposite is true. He asserts that Jefferson believes his slaves owe him a living, and if they do not provide him with such, then his slaves will be sold. If Jefferson had any concern for the welfare of his slaves, Cohen continues, that ceased when financial hardship fell upon him. While we could engage in a lengthy critique of this argument, suffice to say that at this juncture Jefferson does not appear to contend that the slaves owe him a debt. It is the debt he owes that precludes the freeing of his slaves. Further, their happiness does not depend on mere emancipation, but on something else.

It is a legitimate criticism of Jefferson's character that he did not find some way to free his slaves. While some contend that Jefferson's hatred of free blacks and his own slaves prevented him from freeing but only a few, historian Joseph Ellis notes that it was more likely that the Sage's onerous debts prevented him from freeing his slaves. The contributions to his debt were twofold: his personal extravagance and the failure of his plantation system to provide the necessary income. Jefferson owned about eleven thousand acres of land total, but only about one thousand of that was under cultivation. To increase his income, he would have to convert his mostly forested lands into land suitable for cultivation. In addition to the lack of cultivated land, especially in the case of Monticello, his land sat atop a hill. Most of the fertile soil was in the valley below. Monticello lacked the basic nutrients needed for crops to succeed consistently.

The other source of Jefferson's debt was his extravagant lifestyle. His personal debt was great, but this had "no discernable effect on his indulgent habits of consumption."[20] During his first presidential term, his wine bill approached ten thousand dollars. Furthermore, he engaged in extensive renovations of Monticello that proceeded for many years. Between 1784-1794 he sold one hundred sixty-one of his two hundred slaves in an attempt to alleviate the debt, but, due to natural increase, by 1796 the number of slaves owned was at one hundred sixty-seven. Despite these valid criticisms, Jefferson believed he, as well as all slaveholders, had a moral responsibility, to prepare the slaves for freedom. Simple emancipation under any circumstance was considered immoral. Critics of Jefferson and the Founders do not confront this argument.

Cohen also asserts that Jefferson solidified the slave's subordinate position. For example, President Jefferson did not secure the freedom of the slaves in the Louisiana territory when the land was purchased. Instead, the treaty allowed Spanish and French inhabitants to keep their slaves. He even fell silent during the increased public calls within the Indiana Territory to allow slaves throughout that area and throughout the Northwest Territory.[21] In these instances and many others, President Jefferson did not utter words publicly that he favored emancipation even though he had numerous opportunities.

Another opportunity to state publicly his opposition to slavery occurred in 1805 when Thomas Brannagan wrote an emancipationist tract and forwarded a copy to Jefferson in hopes that he might endorse it. Jefferson denied his request and wrote to another person (seemingly to relay his message to Brannagan) for fear that to acknowledge that he received the paper would cause political alarm. Jefferson wrote to Dr. George Logan that

> the cause in which he embarks is so holy, the sentiments he expresses in his letter so friendly that it is highly painful to me to hesitate on a compliance which appears so small. But that is not its true character, and it would be injurious even to his views, for me to commit myself on paper by answering his letter. I have most carefully avoided every public act or manifestation on that subject. Should an occasion occur which I can interpose with decisive effect, I shall certainly know and do my duty with promptitude and zeal.[22]

Jefferson thus chose to stand by in silence rather than publicly secure a goal he supposedly supported in the abstract. Jefferson, and the rest of the Founders, have thus opened themselves up to the criticism that they did not do all they could to eradicate slavery—especially as elder statesmen.

We previously considered that debt kept Jefferson from personally acting on his belief to emancipate his slaves. Modern constitutional law professor Paul Finkleman adds that Jefferson remained energetic on such issues as religious freedom and public education while he was not so regarding slavery. However, at least one moderate critic has argued that Jefferson's withdrawal from the public debate over slavery was not because he hated blacks, but because of his own personal proclivities. Jefferson even worried about public censure as a result of the publication of his *Notes on the State of Virginia* (hereafter *Notes*). He was apprehensive about the consequences of exposing his thoughts to the public. From the time after the publication of his *Notes*, Jefferson became a more cautious diplomat. According to Ellis, it was a part of Jefferson's character to avoid conflict over explosive issues—he preferred "courtesy" to "candor."[23] He therefore tried to avoid unpleasant confrontations: "what his critics took to be hypocrisy was not really that at all. In some cases it was the desire to please different constituencies, to avoid conflict with colleagues."[24] The *Notes* made him a controversial figure, and he was not emotionally equipped, Ellis contends, to remain steadfast on the issue.

Despite the apparent flaws in his character, silence on slavery does not necessarily imply moral assent. Contra Finkleman, perhaps there was more widespread positive political will for religious freedom and public education than there was for the end of slavery. As a policy goal, the consequences of emancipation seemed great. Still, while it is true that Jefferson did not act in many instances, and remained silent in many others, there is something obvious in his private correspondence that critics either have rejected or have not taken seriously. If Jefferson only feigned belief in natural rights, would he not in his private correspondence reveal himself? However, as we shall see, he does not change his position on the moral turpitude of slavery in either his private writings or his public utterances. The letter to Logan is but one of many letters in which the Sage of Monticello reaffirms his desire to effect emancipation—a goal that for him is a duty to fulfill should the opportunity arise. Modern critics of Jefferson and the Founders limit their focus to the slave issue and hence suffer from considering other political realities that might cause those statesmen to be prudential in their decision-making. For example, Cohen believes that Jefferson's opinions on the Missouri crisis further lend evidence that he encouraged the spread of the institution rather than place it on the road to extinction.

The controversy over whether to add Missouri as a slave or free state caused Jefferson to endorse the "southern position" that slavery should be extended.[25] This policy position leads Cohen to conclude that Jefferson was not a strict constructionist on constitutional matters nor was he a strict believer in rights. While Cohen does not develop the constitutional aspect of his argument in detail, he seems to be stating that the Congress could require a state to enter the Union as a free state. However, the Missouri question is the first such attempt where Congress tried to impose such a result. Most of the Founders believed that the Constitution forbade such stipulations on new states, Madison included. Nevertheless, all of Jefferson's transgressions in terms of slavery, Cohen continues, emanate from one thing—his inability to admit that slaves had rights. Critics thus believe that if Jefferson and the other Founders truly believed in rights, they would have pressed for slavery's extinction in Missouri.

To that end, Cohen believes that "from an intellectual point of view, his strong 'suspicion' that the Negroes were innately inferior is probably of great significance in explaining his ability to ignore his own strictures about their rights."[26] Because he thought they were an inferior class of being, he "more often than not" only served to "strengthen the institution."[27] The author faults the former president on the fact that the Virginian never "actively" pursued or proposed a plan that "jeopardized" the status of slavery.[28] This theme has been furthered by Finkleman, who contends that "it is hard to imagine how someone as intelligent, wealthy, and well connected as Jefferson could 'hate' an institution and be unable to do anything about it or at least take some risks to try to do something about it."[29] Compared to what he did for religious freedom, Finkle-man continues, he did relatively little for slavery:

> If the test of greatness for a politician is the willingness to lead a nation or state to what is right, even when it is unpopular, then Jefferson as a Virginia legisla-tor and wartime governor fails the test on slavery. His occasional mumbling about evils of slavery pale in comparison to the eloquent attacks on the institu-tion by chancellor George Wythe, who in addition to his role as a leading Vir-ginia jurist, had been Jefferson's mentor at William and Mary. In *Hudgins v. Wrights*, Wythe single-handedly tried to abolish slavery through judicial inter-pretation.[30]

Wythe did indeed seek to overturn slavery by seizing on the free and equal clause in the Declaration of Rights—what Wythe terms the "first article of our 'political catechism'"—to contend that since all men were equally free the *onus probandi* lies with the claimant.[31] In other words, the slave no longer had to prove his freedom. The burden was on the master. In contrast, Finkleman con-tinues to assert that the Sage was so lackadaisical on the topic that he only of-fered an occasional private thought on the matter. However, Finkleman's attack on Jefferson is selective. For example, Jefferson tried to free a slave client in court on the grounds that slavery violated the law of nature. Furthermore, the law professor neglects the significance of Jefferson's public anti-slavery account in the *Notes*, even though he accounts for the document. He also omits Jeffer-son's public service on behalf of the state legislature to revise the laws. Among his revisions was a gradual emancipation plan.

Finkleman broadens Cohen's arguments and asserts that Jefferson only hated slavery because of the ill effects it produced on the white race, not because of what it did to the slaves. Jefferson could not look at the slaves as individuals for he "hated slavery because he hated the slave and the Negro because he hated what slavery did to white people."[32] Jefferson hated slavery because it turned the masters into tyrants not because of the harm it caused the slaves. Therefore, Jef-ferson's self-interest in his own race demonstrates he was no champion of hu-man rights. Historian Robert McColley contends that early Virginia as a whole has more in common with Roger Taney's Dred Scot decision than with such reformers as Abraham Lincoln and the post Civil War Republicans. He asserts that the Northwest Ordinance was crafted with "the best interest of white peo-ple" in mind because the "best republics" had "no Negroes" in them.[33] There-fore, racism, miscegenation, and economic interests conspired to prevent eman-cipation in Virginia. Finkleman and Wiencek concur and assert that the former president was a racist at heart because he coupled emancipation with removal, or colonization, and thought that they were a lower species, inferior to whites by nature. If Jefferson truly believed in the natural rights of the slaves, then he would have merely argued for their freedom.

Revisionist scholars have articulated many of the arguments noted above. More recently, Ellis laid a more philosophical charge against the Founders' ideas in a review of Thomas G. West's *Vindicating the Founders*. Ellis accuses

West of being "presentist" because West believed that the ideas of the eighteenth century could "land intact" in "our time."[34] He claimed that West's arguments on behalf of the Founders were "stunningly bold," "bizarre," that he "abuses the past," and that he "remains trapped in the moralistic and melodramatic framework of heroic or villainous stereotypes."[35] Ellis believes that men are incapable of understanding anything outside of their own time, but if we cannot understand anything outside our own time, and if history somehow makes the past irrelevant, it fails to explain why scholars are consumed with Jefferson and the American Founders when time has supposedly passed them by.

Finkleman, however, invokes Jefferson biographer Merrill D. Peterson to explain the reason the Sage remains controversial. According to Peterson, the former president personifies an image or a vision of America. Jefferson is the author of the Declaration of Independence and that document represents what America ought to be. Peterson concludes: "tamper with Jefferson and you tamper with that image."[36] In other words, the attacks on Jefferson are really an attack on the American Founding, and natural rights in particular, because these rights were "allegedly" supposed to be shared by all men.[37] In this instance, Ellis is persuaded by John Hope Franklin's criticisms. Because the Founders did not impose equality in fact in 1787, they are guilty of not believing in their own words. For example, they secured their lofty position by degrading the slave's humanity through the 3/5 clause in the Constitution. The Founding is essentially racist because the slaves were not included in the rights stated in the Declaration and because the Constitution codified that racial prejudice and this made the Founders "vulnerable" to the charges of "moral blindness."[38]

Though Jefferson will be featured prominently, he will not be the sole focus of the next few chapters. Virginia produced other influential statesmen, among who are James Madison, James Monroe, George Washington, George Wythe, George Mason, St. George Tucker, Patrick Henry, and Richard Henry Lee. Of all the inhabitants of Old Dominion, these men had the highest public profile and were influential members in their community and state. They served their state and their country in various capacities, but all of them were in basic agreement on one thing: slavery must come to an end sooner rather than later, and all believed the institution an evil. However, some have great difficulty in properly understanding the political opinions of the Founders. The result of criticisms since the 1960s has left Virginians like Jefferson so elusive as to make capture of the real Jefferson problematic.[39] In an attempt to try to capture him again, this book will approach the Founders genuinely, and hence try to understand them as they understood themselves.

The Founders may have held apparently contradictory opinions about slavery and/or emancipation. However, modern scholars seem to have a central flaw in their critique: some fail to recognize the role of statesmanship (or prudence), and this leads them to search into the heart and mind of the founding generation, where they believe they find an abundance of hypocrisy. They confound the assertion of rights with the practice of slavery. Somehow, the latter nullifies the former. Some actually do not take natural rights for granted and perhaps legitimately criticize the Founders for the contradictions existent between their actions and beliefs. Yet, many of these arguments are in a sense simplistic because the Founders did in fact claim that all humans possess rights found in nature: "[it] was hardly wonderful that a nation of slave holders, on becoming independent, did not abolish slavery. What was wonderful—nay, miraculous—was that a nation of slave holders, on becoming independent, declared that all men are created equal, and thereby made it a moral and political necessity, that slavery be abolished."[40] It is a difficult argument to sustain that the Founders, in general, would have been careless in their thoughts and actions as to say one thing yet do another consciously, and leave a public and private record behind to condemn them. Modern scholars have, in the mind of some academics, articulated a position that oversimplifies the age.[41] Therefore, it behooves us to delve into the complexities of the thoughts of Virginia's statesmen in order to decipher if, indeed, they believed in the emancipationsist cause.

Notes

1. Leo Strauss, *Thoughts on Machiavelli* (Chicago: University of Chicago Press, 1958), 13.

2. In January 1659, Virginia recognized Charles II as king before England did. It was Charles that called the colony "Old Dominion." K.R. Constantine Gutzman, "Old Dominion, New Republic: Making Virginia Republican, 1776-1840" (Ph.D. diss., University of Virginia, 1999), 45.

3. Though noted in private journals and public papers, there is no official record that a vote ever took place. There is evidence that only the states of Maryland and Virginia voted on his citizenry status, but such an honor only pertained to those states. This was remedied in 2002 when the United States Congress took an official vote confirming Lafayette as an honorary citizen.

4. Saul K. Padover, *Jefferson: A Great American's Life and Ideas* (New York: Mentor, 1952), 180. Another account of Lafayette's visit may be found in Dumas Malone, *Jefferson and His Time: The Sage of Monticello*, vol. 6 (Boston: Little, Brown, & Company, 1981), 402-408.

5. Washington to Lafayette, Head Quarters, Newburgh, 5 April 1783, *George Washington: Writings*, ed. John Rhodehamel (New York: Library of America, 1997), 510.

6. Auguste Levasseur, *Lafayette in America in 1824 and 1825: or Journals of Travels in the United States*, vol. 1 (New York: White, Galaher & White, 1829), 222. The Marquis loved America. He named his son after George Washington and on his visit brought back to France American soil to have scattered around his casket upon his death.

7. Thomas G. West, *Vindicating the Founders: Race, Sex, Class, and Justice in the Origins of America* (Lanham, Md.: Rowman & Littlefield Publishers, 1997), xiii, 6-7. Gordon Wood believes that the Revolution was one in which the colonists secured their British rights and acted "on behalf of it." See Gordon S. Wood, *The Creation of the American Republic, 1776-1787* (New York: W.W. Norton & Company, 1969), 10.

8. Herbert J. Storing, *Toward a More Perfect Union: Writings of Herbert J. Storing*, ed. Joseph M. Bessette (Washington, D.C.: The AEI Press, 1995), 138. I should note that there are two recent works that approach this topic in a similar manner: William Lee Miller, *Arguing about Slavery: The Great Battle in the United States Congress* (New

York: Alfred A. Knopf, 1996), and Gary V. Wood, *Heir to the Fathers: John Quincy Adams and the Spirit of Constitutional Government* (Lanham, Md.: Lexington Books, 2004). However, these works cover a period different from the time under consideration here.

9. Storing, 142.

10. Jaffa, *A New Birth of Freedom* (Lanham, Md.: Rowman and Littlefield, 2000), 21.

11. West, *Vindicating the Founders*, xii.

12. Robert G. Parkinson, "First from the Right," *Virginia Magazine of History and Biography* 112 (2004) : 3.

13. Carl L. Becker, *The Declaration of Independence: A Study in the History of Political Ideas* (New York: Vintage Books, 1942), 277; Thomas G. West, "Jaffa's Lincolnian Defense of the Founding," *Interpretation* 28, no. 3 (Spring 2001) : 286.

14. Sean Wilentz, "The Details of Greatness," *The New Republic*, 29 March 2004, 29. For a particularly engaging defense of Jefferson and his commitment to natural rights and equality, see Julian Boyd, "Thomas Jefferson's 'Empire of Liberty,'" *The Virginia Quarterly Review* 24, no. 4 (Autumn 1948) : 545. Consider this from one of Jefferson's earliest compilers of his correspondence: "But however that might be, he never failed to utter his opinion where freedom and justice were concerned whoever might be hurt or whoever might be angered. In the midst of slaveholding Virginia he was wont to speak of the cause of the abolition of slavery as 'the sacred side' and to say that he looked to the young for its accomplishment." Albert Ellery Bergh, ed., *The Writings of Thomas Jefferson* (Washington, D.C.: The Thomas Jefferson Memorial Association, 1907), xi.

15. Many scholars have cataloged the critique beginning in the 60s including, ibid.; Douglass Adair, *Fame and the Founding Fathers*, ed. Trevor Colbourn (New York: W.W. Norton & Company, 1974), 235-236; J.G.A. Pocock, "Virtue and Commerce in the Eighteenth Century," *Journal of Interdisciplinary History* 3 (Summer 1972) : 119.

16. Henry Wiencek, *An Imperfect God: George Washington, His Slaves, and the Creation of America* (New York: Farrar, Strauss, and Giroux, 2003), 5.

17. William Cohen, "Thomas Jefferson and the Problem of Slavery," *The Journal of American History* 56, no. 3 (December 1969) : 505.

18. Storing, 131.

19. Quoted in Cohen, 517. Cohen is somewhat of a moderate as far as critics go. He at least recognizes Jefferson was steadfastly opposed the slave trade throughout his life.

20. Joseph J. Ellis, *American Sphinx: The Character of Thomas Jefferson* (New York: Alfred A. Knopf, 1997), 196.

21. Ibid., 522.

22. Ibid.; Jefferson to George Logan, 11 May 1805, *The Writings of Thomas Jefferson*, vol. 8, ed. Paul Leicester Ford, (New York: G.P. Putnam's Sons, 1898), 352-353.

23. Ellis, *American Sphinx*, 89.

24. Ibid.

25. Cohen, 523.

26. Ibid., 525.

27. Ibid.

28. Ibid.

29. Paul Finkleman, "Thomas Jefferson and Antislavery: The Myth Goes On," *The Virginia Magazine of History and Biography* 102 (April 1994) : 202.

30. Ibid., 211.

31. Phillip Hamilton, "Revolutionary Principles and Family Loyalties: Slavery's Transformation in the St. George Tucker Household of Early National Virginia," *The*

William and Mary Quarterly, 3rd Ser., 55, no. 4 (October 1998) : 543. St. George Tucker disagreed with his friend, believing that the judiciary ought not be used to overturn the ownership of such "property." Jefferson held a high opinion of Wythe and admired his "unequivocal" position on slavery as one of his most "virtuous" qualities. He praised the College of William and Mary for having such sentiments as well. See in particular, Jefferson to Dr. Price, 7 August 1785, in "Education in Colonial Virginia: Part IV, The Higher Education," *William and Mary College Quarterly Historical Magazine* 6, no. 3 (January 1898) : 185.

32. Finklemen, 208, and also 206, 222, and 225; Robert McColley, *Slavery and Jeffersonian Virginia* (Urbana: University of Illinois Press, 1964), 128-129. Cohen also asserts that Jefferson believed the slaves were so inferior they did not really deserve to enjoy their rights. This demonstrates a "profound racism" in the heart of Jefferson. A portion of the evidentiary proof comes from the fact that the Sage did not free his slaves, even in death. He actually did free five, however.

33. McColley, 171, and 137-138.

34. Joseph J. Ellis, "Who Owns the Eighteenth Century?" *The William and Mary Quarterly* 57, no. 2 (April 2000) : 418.

35. Ibid.

36. Quoted in Finkleman, 198.

37. Joseph J. Ellis, *Founding Brothers* (New York: Vintage Books, 2000), 10. See also Storing, 131-132.

38. Wiencek, 270.

39. Andrew Burnstein, "The Problem of Jefferson Biography," *The Virginia Quarterly Review* 70 (Summer 1994) : 403.

40. Harry V. Jaffa, "The False Prophets of American Conservatism" (paper delivered at the Claremont Institute's Lincoln Day Conference, Washington, D.C. February 12, 1998), 16. A variation of this quote appears in Jaffa, *A New Birth of Freedom*, 211.

41. Hamilton, 532. Hamilton singles out Finkleman and Ellis as leading the way in these unjustified critiques.

Chapter 2

Early Anti-Slavery Efforts

> Under the law of nature, all are born free, everyone comes into the world with a
> right to his own person, which includes the liberty of moving and using it at his
> will. This is what is called personal liberty, and it is given him by the author of
> nature, because necessary for his own sustenance.
>
> Thomas Jefferson[1]

Before we embark on an explication of Virginia's most prominent statesmen, we should make note of the early anti-slavery efforts in the colony in order to address the charge by historian Robert McColley that "the anti-slavery pronouncements of Virginia's statesmen were so rarely accompanied by any positive efforts against slavery as to cast doubt on the sincerity" of Virginia's statesmen.[2] Despite this contention, both legislatively and privately, in colonial Virginia, there is much evidence that Old Dominion, generally, strove toward emancipation and believed that the elimination of the slave trade was a political necessity. There were both official legislative attempts and efforts by private associations to express displeasure of the peculiar institution. Some of the early anti-slavery efforts of prominent Virginians on both the state and the national level are quite remarkable.

After a period of time in the early to mid 1600s, when slave importations in Virginia were either nil or very low, there was little legislative action directed at impeding the institution. Between 1650-1680 the importation of slaves grew more rapidly. By 1671, there were 6,000 servants and 2,000 slaves in the colony. Beginning in 1668 the first traces of encouraging of emancipation became evident in the form of a tithable. Throughout the late 1600s to 1700s, even though there were at times some setbacks, the colony sought to lay taxes and duties on the trade so as to discourage it. Nevertheless, the crown attempted to solidify the slave trade beginning in 1698. The trade was seen as beneficial and advantageous to the kingdom of England. The economic influence encouraged increased involvement, and acceleration, of the trade.[3] However, in 1699, the Virginia colony laid a duty on the importation of slaves. The act was renewed in 1701, 1704, and 1705. The act was not meant to raise revenue purely because a rebate of three-fourths of the tax took effect when the slave was transported out of Dominion within six weeks. Despite the rebate, there was a strong reaction to these duties: "When large and successive increases were made, the slave traders readily saw that the intent was to lay prohibitive duties. They consequently protested vigorously, and secured the withholding of the king's assent to as many as thirty-three different acts passed by the Virginia Assembly prior to 1772 to discourage the slave trade."[4] What is remarkable about the duties laid in the early to mid 1700s was that they seemed intended to attack the slave institution itself. Although many of the legislative acts were blocked by England, the colony continued to press for legislation to at least retard the trade. According to historian James Ballagh,

> no colony made a more strenuous and prolonged effort to prevent the imposition of negro slavery upon it, and no State a more earnest attempt to alleviate or rid itself of that burden than Virginia...by skillful wording of preambles and brief limitations to the acts imposing duties, and by judicious expenditure upon public works of the revenue raised, the colonists had partially concealed the true intent of the acts.[5]

In order to avoid political scrutiny from the mother country, the assembly explained that some of the duties were to be used to pay for some public work, not to prohibit the importation of slaves. Yet, despite their attempts to levy such taxes, the royal crown and colonial governor believed that the duties were meant to prohibit the trade. This was the case in 1710 when colonial Governor Alexander Spotswood vetoed a £5 duty on importations because he perceived that the duty was high and meant to discourage the trade. Between 1710 and 1718, the assembly became more aggressive in the application and amount of duty laid.[6] The desire of the assembly to pass importation acts was so vigilant that Spotswood soon relented to the representatives, saying that the public will desired the taxes.

The duty was continued in 1712 and 1714. Spotswood concluded to the crown that these acts were necessary for the public treasury. Even if the colony needed tax revenue, his opinion of the intent of the assembly—to retard or eliminate the trade—appears unchanged. Spotswood noted in his personal journal that the purpose of the legislation was to discourage the importation and the trade. Yet, to assuage the potential conflict with England, the colonial governor explained that the duty resulted from economic necessity. After this aggressive period, inexplicably the assembly retreated. Between 1718 and 1723 the tax was not collected because England reasserted political pressure. The frustration with the crown reached a boiling point in 1723 when the assembly tried to pass a duty but did not insert a clause suspending the operation of the act until the royal will was known. The omission offended the crown to such an extent that the mother country instructed the colonial governor to quash any duty pertaining to the importation of slaves. The assembly nevertheless tried for nine years (until 1732) to renew the tax, and even included the flattering phrase, to no avail. Beginning in 1723, several acts to check the trade were passed in an almost unbroken series of acts that continued through the Revolution.

In 1732, the colony laid a 5 percent duty on the buyers of slaves. This duty continued in various forms until 1769. The colony intended to check the slave trade and the tax reached a high of 35 percent. The English crown finally had enough of the independence of the colonial assembly and commanded the Virginia governor "upon the pain of the highest displeasure to assent to no laws by which the importation of slaves should be in any respect prohibited or obstructed."[7] Old Dominion's representatives remained defiant and increasingly challenged the king. As anti-slavery feeling matured in the colony, the assembly petitioned the king in 1772:

> We implore your Majesty's paternal assistance in averting a calamity of a most alarming nature. The importation of slaves into the colonies from the coast of Africa hath long been considered as a trade of great inhumanity, and under its present encouragement we have too much reason to fear it will endanger the very existence of your Majesty's American dominions. We are sensible that some of your Majesty's subjects may reap emoluments from this sort of traffic, but when we consider that it greatly retards the settlement of the colonies with more useful inhabitants and may in time have the most destructive influence, we presume to hope that the interest of a few will be disregarded when placed in competition with the security and happiness of such numbers of your majesty's dutiful and loyal subjects. We therefore beseech your Majesty to remove all those restraints on your Majesty's governors in this colony which inhibit their assenting to such laws as might check so pernicious a commerce.[8]

The candid prayer suggests that Old Dominion was increasingly becoming more independent from England, and demonstrates in a clear manner the intention of the colonial assembly—to effect prohibitive legislation on the slave trade. The crown met the appeal with silence and the House of Burgesses was notified that no reply from the king would come. Thus, Virginia's plea to end slave importations, and the prophetic assessment that slavery would cause political unrest in the future, passed without affirmative action. There were no further official efforts to abolish slavery after the war. From 1772 to 1778, the duty on the trade ranged from 20 to 40 percent. However, we should not think that these were the only efforts to bring the trade to heel. There were several private and public attempts to affect the trade as well.

In addition to the efforts from the assembly and with the royal negative employed often, the colonists resorted to other means to express their opinion on the nefarious traffic. Before the 1772 prayer to the king, the House of Burgesses drew up a resolution on May 11, 1769, recommending to the colonial traders and merchants that they not import any slaves, or purchase any slaves imported. A more expansive non-importation association that included the members of the House of Burgesses and over one hundred seventy signatures total, was conferred in June 1770 stating that they would not purchase slaves. The aim was to weaken England and her merchants economically by not participating in, and encouraging, such traffic. These non-intercourse resolutions became more frequent as the war approached. George Mason participated several times in associations that aimed at the economic boycott of the slave trade. On December 23, 1765, Mason authored a "Scheme for Replevying Goods and Distress for Rent." Though it was seen as a way to articulate dissent of the Stamp Act, the lengthy tract expressed an opinion on the slave trade and slavery in general:

> The Policy of encouraging the Importation of free People & discouraging that of Slaves has never been duly considered in this Colony, or we shou'd not at this Day see one Half of our best Lands in most Parts of the Country remain unsettled, & the other cultivated with slaves; not to mention the ill Effect such a Practice has upon the Morals and Manners of our People: one of the first Signs of the Decay, & perhaps the primary Cause of the Destruction of the most flourishing Government that ever existed was the Introduction of great numbers of Slaves—an Evil very pathetically described by Roman Historians—but 'tis not the present Intention to expose our Weakness by examining this Subject too freely.[9]

On the slavery issue, Mason took an early, public stand, against the "chronic disease" caused by the institution.[10] Mason authored another non-importation agreement on April 23, 1769, which encouraged businessmen, traders, and merchants to boycott the importing and purchasing of slaves. Of these more independent agreements, we find among the signers not only Mason, but also Richard Henry Lee, George Washington, Carter Braxton, Thomas Jefferson, and Patrick Henry, among others.

Mason followed up the 1769 agreement with a May 11 newspaper piece under the pseudonym "Letter of Atticus" in which he encouraged all Virginians not to purchase slaves. These efforts did not end in the 1760s, but as late as 1774, Mason authored the "Fairfax County Resolves," which declared the "most earnest Wishes to see an entire Stop for ever put to such a wicked cruel and unnatural Trade."[11] The Resolves were adopted at a general meeting of freeholders and inhabitants of Fairfax County. The meeting took place at the county court house and George Washington served as chairman. Those in attendance, including George Wythe, took an oath not to support the trade. Soon after the Fairfax meeting Washington wrote:

> For my own part, I shall not undertake to say where the Line between Great Britain and the Colonies should be drawn, but I am clearly of the opinion that one ought to be drawn; and our Rights clearly ascertained. I could wish, I own, that the dispute had been left to Posterity to determine, but the Crisis is arrived when we must assert our Rights, or Submit to every Imposition that can be heaped upon us; till custom and use, will make us as tame and abject Slaves, as the Blacks we Rule over with such arbitrary Sway.[12]

What is perhaps most notable about these agreements is that Old Dominion's prominent statesmen believed that slavery was an evil that had an ill effect on the colony. Furthermore, Washington believed that the slaves were entitled to the same rights and liberties as the colonists. The law of nature extended to whites and blacks equally. Why Mason and the other Virginians could have believed such will be vetted in the next chapter. However, suffice to say that the opinion of the Founders, and early colonialists before the war, was one of hostility to the institution. Indeed, soon after the Resolves were made public, the Virginia Colonial Convention resolved in August 1774 that the colony would neither import nor purchase slaves.[13]

One of Virginia's signers of the Declaration of Independence, Richard Henry Lee, entered the Virginia House of Burgesses in 1758. He proposed in 1759 "to lay so heavy a duty on the importation of slaves as effectually to put an end to that iniquitous and disgraceful traffic within the colony of Virginia."[14] In his first speech before that body, he argued that the slave-trade was dangerous and harmful of the colony's moral interests. He further contended:

> Nor, sir, are these the only reasons to be urged against the importation. In my opinion, not the cruelties practiced in the conquest of Spanish America, not the savage barbarity of a Saracen, can be more big with atrocity, than our cruel trade to Africa. There we encourage those poor, ignorant people, to wage eternal war against each other; not nation against nation, but father against son, children against parents, and brothers against brothers, whereby parental, filial, and fraternal duty is terribly violated; that by war, stealth, or surprise, we Christians may be furnished with our fellow creatures, who are no longer to be considered as created in the image of God as well as ourselves, and equally entitled to liberty and freedom by the great law of nature, but they are to be deprived, for ever deprived, of all the comforts of life, and to be made the most wretched of the human kind. I have seen it observed by a great writer that Christianity, by introducing into Europe the truest principle of humanity, universal benevolence, and brotherly love, had happily abolished civil slavery. Let us, who profess the same religion, practice its precepts; and by agreeing to this duty, convince the world that we know and practice our true interests, and that we pay a proper regard to the dictates of justice and humanity.[15]

Lee's speech amounted to an open challenge to his fellow citizens. It was clearly a denunciation of slavery and an argument for equal liberty. The colonists, along with the crown, shared some responsibility in maintaining an unjust practice. Lee's speech appealed above the positive law to the dual sources of law mentioned in the Declaration of Independence: reason and revelation. Since God created all humans in his image, it does violence on God to attack that image or in any way treat human beings unjustly. It at once draws together the creation in Genesis with the Golden Rule of the New Testament. The law of nature recognizes that "all men are created equal" and therefore proscribes that a man not enslave another. On a practical level, his speech noted the real danger that slavery put the slaves in enmity with their masters. This antagonism presented a security risk. The downfall of many great political entities in Greece and Rome were spurred by slave revolts or servile wars. On several levels, Lee's speech foreshadowed the reasoning of the Declaration. Lee was prescient in his conviction that the colonies would inevitably find themselves in conflict with Great Britain. Perhaps he foresaw something like a civil war as well given that slavery is inherently at war with the rights of mankind. Nevertheless, while he was in the Burgesses, he was appointed as a member of the committee that drafted the legislation imposing a duty on slaves imported into Virginia. While there were some who voted against this measure, colonial Governor Francis Faquier believed that those who opposed the act did so out of selfishness (self-interest) rather than humanitarian concerns.[16]

Lee's position on the slaves did not change as he grew older, nor did he waiver from his position in later years or in his private correspondence: "In time to come, it may be known and sensibly felt I hope, that America can find Arms as well as Arts, to remove Demon Slavery far from its borders. If I should live to see that day, I shall be happy; and pleased to say with Sydney, 'Lord now lettest thou thy servant depart in peace.'"[17]

In the aforementioned 1772 petition to the king (imploring "your Majesty's paternal assistance in averting a calamity of a most alarming nature"), Lee's brother Arthur wrote that he was astonished by the petition because of its direct language. Arthur believed that the style of the petition reflected his brother's influence. That was not the case in the petition. He was not the author, but it was clear that Lee's position was one that condemned the whole institution, not just the trade merely. Perhaps what is most astonishing about Lee's opinion about the peculiar institution is that he and his family owned slaves. It would appear not in his self-interest to condemn the institution. Nevertheless, slavery was a complicated institution to unravel. Writing to his brother Arthur, he expressed his dismay that the trade would continue despite the taxes levied, yet he did not see how he could not take advantage of the selling of his slaves if he needed to do so. In January of 1778 he wrote another brother, William, asserting that the selling of slaves would be a desirous end if not for the "humanitarian concerns."[18] These seemingly contradictory opinions might confirm the criticisms scholars have leveled on the Founders. We should consider that the Founders chose the lesser of two evils: to be both for some sort of abolition and for continuing in the ownership of slaves. The "humanitarian" concern for the slaves may partly explain why the Founders continued their participation in slavery.

The laws regarding slavery, and importation of the same, also regulated the manner in which manumissions could take place. In the early years of the colony, Virginia prohibited the manumission of slaves at will. If owners did emancipate, they faced fines and possibly jail. Of course, this does not mean that manumission was impossible under the law, just that it was a difficult and cumbersome process. Dating as far back as 1619, there is evidence that some manumissions were approved.[19] Laws prohibiting the manumission of sick or old slaves were in place for obvious reasons: freeing a sick or elderly slave was seen as inhumane because the freedom would most certainly cause the human being a premature death, if not accelerate such an end.[20] Furthermore, as a matter of practicality, slaves who could not demonstrate to the government their ability to support themselves were not allowed their freedom. A former slave who could not provide for himself or herself would become a burden to the state or community. Therefore, the government would have to manage the problem under considerable taxpayer expense.

Virginia's early manumission law was in effect from 1691-1723. It required any slave that was freed to be removed from the colony. The owner was responsible for paying the former slave's passage out of the area. If a freed slave was found in the state six months after the date of manumission, the owner faced a fine. Old Dominion restricted the law drastically in 1723 and prohibited manumissions except for "some meritorious service."[21] However, the relative merit of the good deed(s) was left up to the governor and his council to decide. Needless to say, this law severely restricted manumissions and left the owner who wanted to free his slaves either inexorably tied to his slaves, or with the daunting task of relocation to free them. This law would remain in effect until 1782. As the revolutionary spirit took hold, these legal obstacles would undergo much reform.

At the height of revolutionary agitation, Virginia passed the Declaration of Rights unanimously. One of the first acts of Virginia as a state was the prohibition of the slave trade. In 1778, Virginia prohibited importation of slaves by sea or land.[22] The prohibition intended to stop the legal slave trade and it slapped a heavy fine upon the importer of the slave. The Negro was freed if illegally smuggled into the state. Virginia was the first state to ban slave trafficking. Both during and following the Revolution a substantial number of slaves gained their freedom. In addition, the assembly freed many slaves for their participation in the war. They participated in the quest for liberty and so they thought those slaves should enjoy the benefits of freedom. In 1782, Virginia repealed its prohibition against private manumissions on slaveholders by authorizing them to free slaves under the age of forty-five. In other words, the act authorized the emancipation of some slaves: "That act was passed at the close of the revolutionary war, when our councils were guided by some of our best and wisest men, men who looked upon the existence of slavery among us not as a blessing, but as a national misfortune, and whose benevolence taught them to consider the slave not as property only, but as man."[23] The following year slaves who served in the Revolutionary War were freed. Over the next eight years over 12,000 Virginia slaves were freed. The 1783 act proclaimed that they "should enjoy the blessings of freedom as a reward for their toils and labours."[24] Virginians responded with the state's most widespread emancipation of slaves in the state's antebellum period. Sensing that an emancipation plan might succeed, Jefferson prepared a draft of a new constitution for Virginia in anticipation of a constitutional convention. It forbade "the introduction of any more slaves to reside in this State, or the continuance of slavery beyond the generation which shall be living on the thirty-first day of December, one thousand eight hundred; all persons born after that day being hereby declared free."[25] Whereas before 1782 manumissions were regulated by the government and had to have approval by a council, under the influence of the revolutionary spirit, the Virginia legislature granted unrestricted private manumissions by deed or will. Several supportive measures to encourage manumissions followed.[26]

Three years later, in 1785, the Assembly passed a law providing that slaves brought into the state and remaining for twelve months, would thereafter be freed. In 1787, the legislature passed the "Validating Acts" which covered attempts of manumission via will prior to 1782.[27] By 1788, they had passed an act making it a crime punishable by death to enslave a child of free blacks. Finally, in 1795, the slaves were given the right to sue in court on the question of their right to freedom. The acts passed in 1778, which were reaffirmed in 1792 though the duties were decreased, were set to confront a "growing evil" and "to crush for ever so pernicious and infamous a commerce."[28]

We should note that contrary to the public opinion of Virginia's statesmen, there were many petitions delivered to the General Assembly in Richmond pleading that the manumission laws not be liberalized. These so called "pro-slavery" petitions did not contend that slaves were chattel as much as they expressed a fear of free slaves causing an increase in crime.[29] These petitions were, in part, also a response to the anti-slavery missionary work of the Quakers, Methodists, and Baptists who spent much time in the state advocating the abolition of slavery. In a Christmas Eve 1785 vote to repeal the 1782 manumission law, the pro-slavery petitioners lost by a vote of 52-35. James Madison was among those voting for defeat, but a gradual emancipation proposal failed during this session. Madison thought that if the repeal had passed that it would not speak well for the state. The burgeoning free black population in Virginia caused some alarm, however, and legislative efforts on behalf of emancipation slowed.

Between 1800 and 1832, there was little action on behalf of the state to further limit the slave trade or encourage emancipation. Certain prominent Virginians did, however, make efforts on a national level to eliminate the trade. President Madison delivered a message to Congress on December 5, 1810, and asked Congress to devise more stringent measures to suppress the illegal import of slaves into the country:

> Among the commercial abuses still committed under the American flag, . . . it appears that American citizens are instrumental in carrying on a traffic in enslaved Africans, equally in violation of the laws of humanity, and in defiance of those of their own country. The same just and benevolent motives which produced the interdiction in force against this criminal conduct, will doubtless be felt by Congress, in devising further means of suppressing the evil.

And again in 1816:

> The Unites States having been the first to abolish, within the extent of their authority, the transportation of the natives of Africa into slavery, by prohibiting the introduction of slaves, and by punishing their citizens participating in the traffick, cannot but be gratified at the progress, made by concurrent efforts of other nations, towards a general suppression of so great an evil.[30]

Likewise, President James Monroe supported the suppression of the trade by condoning the seizure of vessels engaging in the traffic so as to "terminate a commerce so disgraceful."[31] Between 1818 and 1822, Monroe confirmed his assent to these measures and encouraged a vigorous prosecution of those engaging in the practice. Monroe, at the insistence of many Virginians, allowed armed cruisers to suppress the trade and immediately return to Africa any slave found on such smuggling vessels.

In Virginia itself, even though there were few efforts after 1800, the state passed a few important and revealing anti-slave acts. In 1806, Virginia amended several acts and passed a law imposing a penalty of four-hundred dollars on the slave trafficker per slave imported.[32] In one sense, the 1806 law could be viewed as a restriction on the 1782 law in that the slaves freed had to leave the state within the year they were emancipated or forfeit their freedom. It seems that Virginia, which grew markedly over the other states, was concerned about the burgeoning free black population. This restriction was not made in haste. The foiled slave conspiracy of 1800 played into the decision.[33] Virginians, though concerned for the overall emancipation of the slaves, were also worried about acts of revenge. Nevertheless, by the 1810 census, Virginia had over 30,000 free blacks within its borders. In 1812, slaveholders moving to Virginia from elsewhere in the United States were permitted to bring slaves with them, but they could not sell them and they had to export a female slave for every slave they brought with them. Still, the increase of free blacks in the state rose steadily until 1830.[34] On the early period of Virginia's efforts to influence the trade the colonists tried to persuade, cajole, and resort to political and economic pressure. Failing those avenues, the colonists increasingly became more belligerent and eventually threatened rebellion. On a national level, some Virginians made their opinion known about slavery and requested national action to prevent the spread of the peculiar institution. Virginia's statesmen may have disagreed on the particular practical ways to deal with slavery, but they were united on the fact that slavery was an evil, as we shall see in the next chapter. When Jefferson became President of the United States, his public pronouncements were certainly not as oft heard as before. As already noted, Jefferson admitted that he was deliberately careful in causing agitation over the issue. He saw a schism developing in the Union that would "produce great public evil," and contended that his duty was not to exacerbate such sectional tension, but to chart a path, which kept the Union and "good government" from "despotism."[35] Should the Union fail, the government that would replace the United States would be more unjust; slavery would be more secure, not on the road to extinction, outside of the Union.

The early history of discouraging slavery in Old Dominion is generally coherent. The practical politicking between England and the colonies might seem to indicate a lack of consistency, but Virginia's early statesmen passed what legislation they could to keep the peculiar institution from becoming permanently rooted. While the legislation passed might seem to demonstrate variation, Virginia's most prominent statesmen steadily promoted the cause of liberty in their public and private writings. Of all of Virginia's leading figures, Thomas Jefferson's opinions are the most extant. For those reasons, and because he authored the Declaration of Independence, that makes him the focus of much criticism related to the American Founding.

Notes

1. Quoted in Henry Wiencek, *An Imperfect God: George Washington, His Slaves and the Creation of America* (New York: Farrar, Strauss and Giroux, 2003), 161.

2. Robert McColley, *Slavery and Jeffersonian Virginia* (Urbana: University of Illinois Press, 1964), 124.

3. W.E.B. Dubois, *The Suppression of the African Slave-Trade to the United States of America: 1638-1870*, with an Introduction by Herbert Aptheker (Millwood, New York: Kraus-Thomson, 1973), 3-4.

4. James Curtis Ballagh, *A History of Slavery in Virginia* (Baltimore: Johns Hopkins Press, 1902), 11.

5. Ibid., 14.

6. Ibid., 14-15, and DuBois, 13. DuBois is somewhat ambivalent on Virginia's dedication, at this time, to banning the slave trade. He asserts that they were certainly alarmed at the great amount being imported. There is also some discrepancy between Ballagh and DuBois in that Ballagh uncovers two instances where the assembly continued to lay a duty on the trade (1712 and 1714). For whatever reason, DuBois misses these.

7. Oliver Perry Chitwood, *Richard Henry Lee: Statesman of the Revolution* (Morgantown: West Virginia University, 1967), 20.

8. Ballagh, *A History of Slavery*, 22. DuBois states that in 1772, the colonists' antislavery opinion of slavery was quite developed.

9. Robert A. Rutland, ed., *The Papers of George Mason*, vol. 1 (Chapel Hill: The University of North Carolina Press, 1970), 61-62.

10. Ibid., cxi and cxv.

11. Ibid., 207. Concerning his Atticus letter: Mason could be taking the name Titus Pomponius Atticus (110-32 BC), who was a friend of Cicero and hence of republican government. Some of Cicero's letters to Atticus are extant. The letters of Atticus to Cicero have not survived. For the Atticus letter see ibid, 108.

12. Washington to Bryan Fairfax, Mount Vernon, 24 August 1774, *George Washington: Writings*, ed. John Rhodehamel (New York: Library of America, 1997), 158.

13. DuBois, 43. To be fair these were primarily war measures used as economic weapons against England, but they also had "strong moral backing" according to DuBois.

14. Quoted in Frank Gaylord Cook, "Richard Henry Lee," *The Atlantic Monthly* 66 (July 1890) : 25.

15. Quoted in Chitwood, 18-19.

16. Ibid., 18.

17. Lee to Landon Carter, Chantilly, 15 August 1765, *The Letters of Richard Henry Lee*, vol. 1, ed. James Curtis Ballagh (New York: DeCapo Press, 1970), 11-12.

18. Chitwood, 19.

19. Luther P. Jackson, "Manumission in Certain Virginia Cities," *The Journal of Negro History* 15, no. 3 (July 1930) : 278.

20. Sumner Eliot Matison, "Manumission by Purchase," *The Journal of Negro History* 33, no. 2 (April 1948) : 146 and 148. Virginia, however, had far more lenient laws granting the release of infirm or ill slaves compared to the other southern states. On the recognition the laws limited emancipation, Jefferson to Edward Coles, Monticello, 25 August 1814, *Thomas Jefferson: Writings*, ed. Merrill Peterson (New York: Library of America, 1984), 1346.

21. Matison, 148; Benjamin Joseph Klebaner, "American Manumission Laws and the Responsibility for Supporting Slaves," *The Virginia Magazine of History and Biography* 63 (1955) : 443-453; William M. Wiecek, "The Statutory Law of Slavery and Race in the Thirteen Mainland Colonies of British America," *The William and Mary Quarterly* 34, no. 2 (April 1977) : 279.

22. DuBois, 14; Ballagh, *A History of Slavery in Virginia*, 23.

23. Quoted in Helen Tunnicliff Catterall, ed., *Judicial Cases Concerning American Slavery and the Negro*, vol. 1 (Washington, D.C.: Carnegie Institution of Washington, 1926), 72. Comment was made by Henry St. George Tucker in 1836. He was the son of St. George Tucker. McColley, 186, criticizes the Founders for this reasoning: since they considered slaves a species of property, they denied they had "rights."

24. Alison Goodyear Freehling, *Drift Toward Dissolution: The Virginia Slavery Debate of 1831-1832* (Baton Rouge: Louisiana State University Press, 1982), 88. Some did suggest the state should renege on the promise and the Virginia Assembly stepped in to chastise them for acting "contrary to principles of justice and their own solemn promise"; the assembly decreed these men free and ordered the attorney general to represent any black claimant. See Wiencek, 248.

25. Bergh, ed., *The Writings of Thomas Jefferson*, vol. 2, 288.

26. In 1723 manumission was prohibited except for some meritorious service to be judged by the governor and his council. As noted earlier, laws made it difficult to manumit. For example, as early as 1691 it was compulsory for slave owners to pay for their manumitted slave's travel out of the colony. A fine was levied if the slave was found in the state after a slave was given his freedom. This law was also in effect in 1735. For more information on this see Adele Hast, "The Legal Status of the Negro in Virginia 1705-1765," *The Journal of Negro History* 54, no. 3 (July 1969) : 217-239; and Matison, 146-167.

27. Alton B. Parker, "The Foundations in Virginia," *William and Mary College Quarterly Historical Magazine* 1, no. 1 (January 1921) : 13. There were several petitions in the 1785 session for gradual emancipation and for repealing the current emancipation laws in effect. Jefferson blamed the failure of enacting a gradual emancipation plan, in part, on the absence of great patriots like Wythe. See Albert Matthews, *Notes on the Proposed Abolition of Slavery in Virginia in 1785* (Cambridge: John Wilson and Son, 1903), 11-12.

28. St. George Tucker, *View of the Constitution of the United States*, with a Foreword by Clyde N. Wilson (Indianapolis: Liberty Fund, 1999), 418. Tucker is not oblivious to the fact that many did successfully evade the duties. That is partly why he pressed for emancipation.

29. Fredrika Teute Schmidt and Barbara Ripel Wilhelm, "Early Proslavery Petitions in Virginia," *William and Mary Quarterly* 30, no. 1 (January 1973) : 134; Cf. Anthony Alfred Iaccarino, "Virginia and the National Contest over Slavery in the Early Republic, 1780-1833" (Ph.D. diss., University of California, Los Angeles, 1999), 25-26; Hamilton, 535; Madison to George Washington, Richmond, 11 November 1785, *The Papers of James Madison*, vol. 8, ed. Robert A. Rutland (Chicago: University of Chicago Press, 1973), 403-405.

30. This quote and the one above from DuBois, 246 and 248 respectively.

31. Ibid., 251.

32. DuBois, 243.

33. A blacksmith named Gabriel planned to enter Richmond with force, capture the capitol and the Virginia State Armory, and hold Governor James Monroe hostage to demand freedom for Virginia's slaves. A few slaves told their masters of the plot. The arrests of the conspirators, including Gabriel, led to trials in Richmond, Petersburg, Norfolk, and several surrounding counties. The conspirators were tried under a 1692 statute in which testimony was heard by five justices, not a jury, with appeal only to the governor. Twenty-six slaves were hanged, and another committed suicide. Several convicted slaves were sold and transported out of Virginia. Two slaves, who had informed their masters about the intended rebellion, received their freedom.

34. Ballagh, *A History of Slavery in Virginia*, 26.

35. Jefferson to George Logan, 11 May 1805, *The Writings of Thomas Jefferson*, 352-353.

Chapter 3

Jefferson, Virginia, and the Founders

> We came equal into this world, and equal shall we go out of it. All men
> are by nature born equally free and independent.
>
> George Mason[1]

Several notable Virginians supported the cause of emancipation: Thomas Jefferson, George Wythe, George Mason, James Monroe, St. George Tucker, George Washington, Patrick Henry, and James Madison. The intellectual father of gradual, and compensated, emancipation was perhaps Virginia's greatest statesman, Thomas Jefferson. It was Jefferson who became the focal point of emancipation debates throughout the early years of the republic and into the late 1820s-1830s. It was his plan that influenced the more formal proposal presented by St. George Tucker. In 1796, Tucker, a William and Mary law professor, published *A Dissertation on Slavery: with a Proposal for the Gradual Abolition of it in the State of Virginia* (hereafter *Dissertation*), in which he encouraged the state legislature to adopt a gradual emancipation policy. Popularly known as the *post nati* plan, Jefferson wrote in his *Notes on the State of Virginia* (hereafter *Notes*) that emancipation could be practically achieved by freeing the children of female slaves after a certain date.[2]

Put simply, the state of Virginia could set a time in the future when the proposal would take effect, and children born after that date would be emancipated. The benefit of such a plan is that it would give the slave owner ample opportunity to prepare his estate for the change. There is considerable evidence that the intellectual forbears in Virginia desired the adoption of some sort of emancipation policy as soon as the state could summon the political will. This does not mean that the Founders were united as to the best way to realize that goal, but it does signify the commitment to the idea that "all men are created equal."

Jefferson's first direct foray into the slave debate came in 1769-1770. Two years after he entered private practice, he took the case of Samuel Howell pro bono. The client was suing for his freedom and he had, apparently, escaped from his master. Howell was a mulatto and his family had been held in servitude for three generations under a Virginia law that kept them, and their offspring, in bondage until the age of thirty-one. Jefferson argued that under the law of nature all men are born free and deserved personal liberty. Since the "author of nature" endowed all men with this freedom, he held the legislature of Virginia responsible for allowing this politically wicked law to continue.[3] Needless to say, his argument did not prevail.

Jefferson confronted the slavery issue again as a member of the House of Burgesses when he seconded the motion of Richard Bland that would provide for emancipation of the slaves at will of the owner. The particular details of the motion are unknown, but it would have granted owners wide latitude in the emancipation of their slaves. That Jefferson seconded the motion lends evidence that he not only held a philosophical opposition to slavery, but also acted on that belief when he thought it might be effective. Reflecting on the incident years later to Edward Coles, Jefferson explained his mind on the matter, and the debate that ensued:

> Mine on the subject of slavery of negroes have long since been in possession of the public, and time has only served to give them stronger root. The love of justice and the love of country plead equally the cause of these people, and it is a moral reproach to us that they should have pleaded it so long in vain, and should have produced not a single effort, nay I fear not much serious willingness to relieve them & ourselves from our present condition of moral & political reprobation.[4]

It is apparent that Jefferson believed that the slaves ought to be freed, and he confirms that the people were well aware of his position on the matter. Furthermore, he asserts in a most direct way that the foundation of the country was antislavery. If the Union sanctioned slavery, then there would be no reason to plead for their freedom. Those who love their country ought to plead for the liberty of the slaves. If the cause of justice is the liberty of the slaves, then those who are keeping them enslaved are committing an injustice. Jefferson continues:

> From those of the former generation who were in the fullness of age when I came into public life, which was while our controversy with England was on paper only, I soon saw that nothing was to be hoped. Nursed and educated in the daily habit of seeing the degraded condition, both bodily and mental, of those unfortunate beings, not reflecting that that degradation was very much the work of themselves & their fathers, few minds have yet doubted but that they were as legitimate subjects of property as their horses and cattle. The quiet and monotonous course of colonial life has been disturbed by no alarm, and little reflection on the value of liberty. And when alarm was taken at an enterprize on their own, it was not easy to carry them to the whole length of the principles which they invoked for themselves.[5]

Jefferson seems to lament the fact that the people are not ready for emancipation, but he perspicuously places blacks in the corpus of human rights. He was not unaware how difficult it was, and is, for men who proclaim principles for themselves to think through such claims to their logical conclusion. The former generation may not have been consistent in securing natural rights, but it is clear that Jefferson believed they needed to "carry them to the whole length." His frustration with such inconsistency was duly noted as far back as 1786: "What a stupendous, what an incomprehensible machine is man! Who can endure toil, famine, stripes, imprisonment & death itself in vindication of his own liberty, and the next moment be deaf to all those motives whose power supported him thro' his trial, and inflict on his fellow men a bondage, one hour of which is fraught with more misery than ages of that which he rose in rebellion to oppose."[6]

Jefferson recognizes that there was something left unfinished in the Founding, and that is the failure of Americans to extend rights they claimed for themselves. The perennial political question, or problem, facing a society is will the people choose good government? An appeal to such reflection and choice is acknowledged by Publius in *Federalist* One. The fact that the Constitution secured a "more perfect Union" in no way diminishes the fact that the people need to continually live up to those principles that lie at the foundation of the fundamental law.[7] It is difficult to apply the principles we claim for ourselves to others. Slavery, then, is an eminent expression of human selfishness. Self-interest may overcome principle, and overcoming selfishness is arduous, but just because narcissism exists in the world, it does not mean we are free from the moral law. Jefferson contends that slavery is dulling the senses, so to speak, to the fact that slaves are human beings. However, the Declaration states that it is not only a right, but also a duty, of the people to secure their own rights and the rights of others. Jefferson noted the difficulty of doing just that as he recounted the motion in the Burgesses:

> In the first or second session of the Legislature after I became a member, I drew to this subject the attention of Col. Bland, one of the oldest, ablest, & most respected members, and he undertook to move for certain moderate extensions of the protection of the laws to these people. I seconded his motion, and, as a younger member, was more spared in the debate; but he was denounced as an enemy of his country, & was treated with the grossest indecorum.[8]

In seconding Bland's motion Jefferson displayed a certain courage. While one of the aims of this book is to demonstrate the evolution of Virginia from acknowledging slavery an evil to the public promotion of it as a "positive good," there is evidence that in the late colonial era, there was an element of hostile opposition to emancipation. However, such hostility in no way means that a majority of Virginia's statesmen favored the institution or thought it a blessing.

Jefferson's Appeal to Natural Rights

In 1774, after Lord Dunmore dissolved the colonial assembly for its protest against the Coercive Acts, Jefferson was elected to the colony's revolutionary convention, which met in Williamsburg. This convention chose delegates to the first Continental Congress. Though Jefferson contracted dysentery on the way to Williamsburg, he forwarded what became known as the *Summary View of the*

Rights of British America (hereafter *Summary*) to that body. While there was no official action taken on the document, it was set for printing and became widely circulated. It is a foretaste of the Declaration and no less than that 1776 document it is written in the language of natural rights. The *Summary* does not mention natural rights specifically, but the entire argument flows from it:

> At no point is the authority of the British constitution derived from prescriptive or historic right, as distinct from, and opposed to, natural right. Right is prescriptive only insofar as the right that is inherited is itself natural in its genesis and its reason. It is also true that the stated (or prudent) objective of the address is reconciliation. But the tone and manner in which it speaks to the king is one of independence.[9]

We see this tone early on in the document:

> Our ancestors, before their emigration to America, were the free inhabitants of the British dominions in Europe, and possessed a right which nature has given to all men, of departing from the country in which chance, not choice, has placed them, of going in quest of new habitations, and of there establishing new societies, under such laws and regulations as to them shall seem most likely to promote public happiness. That their Saxon ancestors had, under this universal law, in like manner left their native wilds and woods in the north of Europe, had possessed themselves of the island of Britain, then less charged with inhabitants, and had established there that system of laws which has so long been the glory and protection of that country.[10]

The title itself does not overtly speak of universal law, but the content does refer to universal rights; the essay speaks to the rights all men possess—a "universal law"—and not mere British rights. The *Summary* asserts that the colonies have taken to pen in a "joint address" in order to defend "those rights which god [sic] and the laws have given equally and independently to all."[11] This idea transcends British rights. The rights he speaks of are not derived from any positive compact per se, but from nature. He thus contends that all men are by nature equal and that men have always been so—the English as well as the colonists, the black as well as the white. Jefferson states that the colonists are not approaching "his majesty" in a servile manner, so he will not be mistaken that the colonists are requesting "favors" when they are in fact asserting their "rights."[12] The *Summary* seems to speak of Union and Liberty (which is synonymous with equality) in the context of asserting those rights. Liberty and equality are inseparable. Equality in this sense is not equality of condition, but equality of natural rights: without liberty, there is no equality, and without equality, there can be no liberty. Humans are equal in their liberty and have liberty in their equality. A union would not long last if its citizens were not bound to respect the rights of man. Interestingly enough, the preamble of the Constitution states that the "more perfect Union" is to "secure the blessings of Liberty." The union of the states is somehow necessary to secure that liberty.

While we may find much language to explain the nature of the Union, Jefferson goes on to expound on the rights of the colonists and that they are as equally justified as the Saxons in securing their liberty. To underscore this point, he writes that "America was conquered, and her settlements made and firmly established, at the expence of individuals, and not of the British public. Their own blood was spilt in acquiring lands for their settlement, their own fortunes expended in making that settlement effectual; for themselves they fought, for themselves they conquered, and for themselves alone they have right to hold."[13] Historian Robert Middlekauff explains that the colonies' departure from the mother country was an exercise in natural rights. Derived from natural right is the claim, most famously uttered by Abraham Lincoln: a person may keep that which he has earned by the sweat of his brow.[14] It is just for the colonists, who have labored for themselves, to keep that with which they have acquired. However, rights are not merely reducible to self-interest, or simple economic calculations. People form societies to promote public happiness: "happiness is the objective good, and therefore the rational good, at which all laws and institutions aim."[15] Colonial Virginia tried to pass laws and regulations to promote such happiness by attempting to secure the termination of slavery, to no avail.

Under the universal law, people may, of right, choose where and how to live as will most likely foster their happiness. Therefore, the colonists lived under a set of English laws not because they were English laws, but because they judged those laws to be good. In other words, Jefferson is building an argument in which the people have the right to rule themselves. However, in order for a people to have a chance to rule themselves rightly, government must be based on equality. If all individuals are equal, then it follows that enslavement of another person regardless of race or ethnic origin would be immoral. Everyone's liberty is in jeopardy if slavery is just. Based on the doctrine of equal rights, Jefferson launches into a condemnation of slavery. The passage is so remarkable in its candor it bears a lengthy quote:

It is now, therefore, the great office of his majesty, to resume the exercise of his negative power, and to prevent the passage of laws by any one legislature of the empire, which might bear injuriously on the rights and interests of another. Yet this will not excuse the wanton exercise of this power which we have seen his majesty practise on the laws of the American legislatures. For the most trifling reasons, and sometimes for no conceivable reason at all, his majesty has rejected laws of the most salutary tendency. The abolition of domestic slavery is the great object of desire in those colonies, where it was unhappily introduced in their infant state. But previous to the enfranchisement of the slaves we have, it is necessary to exclude all further importations from Africa; yet our repeated attempts to effect this by prohibitions, and by imposing duties which might amount to a prohibition, have been hitherto defeated by his majesty's negative: thus preferring the immediate advantages of a few African corsairs to the lasting interests of the American states, and to the rights of human nature, deeply wounded by this infamous practice. Nay, the single interposition of an interested individual against a law was scarcely ever known to fail of success, though in the opposite scale were placed the interests of a whole country. That this is so shameful an abuse of a power trusted with his majesty for other purposes, as if not reformed, would call for some legal restrictions.[16]

Earlier in the *Summary*, Jefferson concluded that the interest the crown took in the colonies was commercial. Slavery, we might add, was a part of that interest. Yet, just because the colonies received aid from Great Britain, it did not mean they abrogated their natural rights and submitted to her majesty's wanton will. Regardless, the king's unruly actions are ultimately lawless. In the forgoing passage, Jefferson wrote that "abolition" of slavery was a "great object of desire" in the colonies. What is significant in the passage is that he states the slaves might well receive their "enfranchisement."

There is some evidence to suggest that many colonists believed that blacks, in time, could stand equally with whites in the exercise of political rights. Jefferson spoke of the "equality of political rights as well as personal freedom"; he even remarked in his *Notes*, the slaves were one-half the citizens of the state.[17] Therefore, full citizenship could be open to anyone regardless of color. Historian Edmund S. Morgan wrote that "while racial feelings undoubtedly affected the position of Negroes, there is more than a little evidence that Virginians . . . were ready to think of [them] as members or potential members of the community on the same terms as other men and to demand of them the same standards of behavior."[18] Once the slaves were free, at some point their "enfranchisement" should follow. In principle, Jefferson believed that blacks ought to inherit the political rights that whites had available to them. Despite the very forward-looking passage, it is clear that his public opinion on the matter was, first, emancipation. The conclusion of the trade was the first step to ending slavery altogether. The argument against the king's actions, and for the slaves' freedom present in the *Summary*, is also evident in the original draft of the Declaration:

> He has waged cruel war against human nature itself, violating its most sacred rights of life and liberty in the persons of a distant people who never offended him, captivating and carrying them into slavery in another hemisphere, or to incure miserable death in their transportation hither. This piratical warfare, the opprobrium of INFIDEL powers, is the warfare of the CHRISTIAN king of Great Britain. Determined to keep open a market where MEN should be bought and sold, he has prostituted his negative for suppressing every legislative attempt to prohibit or to restrain this execrable commerce. And that this assemblage of horrors might want no fact of distinguished die, he is now exciting those very people to rise in arms among us, and to purchase that liberty of which he had deprived them, by murdering the people upon whom he also obtruded them: thus paying off former crimes committed against the LIBERTIES of one people, with crimes which he urges them to commit against the LIVES of another.[19]

Though struck out of the engrossed copy, a semblance of this charge was kept:

> He has refused his Assent to Laws, the most wholesome and necessary for the public good.

> He has forbidden his Governors to pass laws of immediate and pressing
> importance, unless suspended in their operation till his Assent should be ob-
> tained; and when so suspended, he has utterly neglected to attend them.

As will be discussed later, the passage was amended at the insistence of South
Carolina and Georgia. There is symmetry between the *Summary* and the Declaration in that both contend that there was "no conceivable reason" (*Summary*)
why the king kept "an open market where men should be bought and sold"
(Declaration). That Jefferson linked the slaves to a "distant people" in the original draft of the Declaration is evidence he believed they possessed the same inalienable rights as anybody else.[20] The word "people" connotes a commonality
all men, all human beings, share—it is not a word that presages color, or asserts
that blacks are fit for servitude. Similarly, in the original draft, the appeal to the
King's Christian morals reflects the belief that those who took the revealed will
of God seriously, believed that Christianity and slavery were incompatible. Slavery is at war with a particular part of our religious persuasion, which is derived
from the Golden Rule of the Old and New Testaments: "Therefore, however you
want people to treat you, so treat them, for this is the Law and the Prophets."[21]
Jefferson not only believed that slavery was condemned in revelation, but
thought God would take an active part in the emancipation of the slaves.[22] We
could conclude that the orthodox position at the time of the Founding was that
reason and revelation renounced slavery.

Patrick Henry, who served on the committee that drafted the Virginia Declaration of Rights, noted as much to Robert Pleasants in 1773:

> I take this oppo. to acknowledge the receipt of A. Benezets Book against the
> Slave Trade. I thank you for it. It is not a little surprising that Christianity,
> whose chief excellence consists in softening the human heart, in cherishing &
> improving its finer Feelings, should encourage a Practice so totally repugnant
> to the first Impression of right & wrong. What adds to the wonder is that this
> Abominable Practice has been introduced in ye. most enlightened Ages, Times
> that seem to have pretensions to boast of high Improvements in the Arts,
> Sciences, & refined Morality, h[ave] brought into general use, & guarded by
> many Laws, a Species of Violence & Tyranny, which our more rude & barbar-
> ous, but more honest Ancestors detested. Is it not amazing, that at a time, when
> ye. Rights of Humanity are defined & understood with precision, in a Country
> above all others fond of Liberty, that in such an Age, & such a Country we find
> Men, professing a Religion ye. most humane, mild, meek, gentle & generous;
> adopting a Principle as repugnant to humanity as it is inconsistent with the Bi-
> ble and destructive to Liberty.[23]

Henry brings together reason (the enlightenment of the age) with revelation (religion, and more specifically Christianity). The law of liberty is found in both
sources and all "humanity" deserves liberty. Reason, no less than revelation,
informs us that this is the truth of the matter. However, as noted earlier, he, like
Jefferson, understands that men do not act consistently with what they know.
We might say that Henry realizes that history does not automatically tend to-

ward freedom. In the letter to Pleasants, Henry continues to praise the Quakers in Virginia for their dedication to the "noble Effort" of abolishing slavery, which he believes would produce a "moral and political good." It is in this context that Henry writes a very revealing paragraph: "Would any one believe that I am Master of Slaves of my own purchase! I am drawn along by ye. general inconvenience of living without them, I will not, I cannot justify it. However culpable my Conduct, I will so far pay my devoir to Virtue, as to own the excellence & rectitude of her Precepts, & to lament my want of conforming to them."[24] The enlightened person, the faithful person, cannot reasonably justify slavery. The implication of Henry's opinions on emancipation seems to make it obligatory for the master to find a way to free his slaves. Emancipation is a personal duty to virtuous conduct. Recall, though, that in the 1770s the slave-owner could not emancipate slaves effortlessly. This roadblock, however, did not free the slave owner of a certain responsibility:

> A time will come when an oppo. will be offered to abolish this lamentable Evil.—Every thing we can do is to improve it, if it happens in our day, if not, let us transmit to our descendants together with our Slaves, a pity for their unhappy Lot, & an abhorrence for Slavery. If we cannot reduce this wished for Reformation to practice, let us treat the unhappy victims with lenity, it is ye. furthest advance we can make toward Justice [We owe to the] purity of our Religion to shew that it is at variance with that Law which warrants Slavery.[25]

Henry emphasizes four things regarding the slave situation. If slavery cannot be abolished immediately the people must (1) not lose feelings of pity for the slaves, (2) believe the slaves are victims of a gross injustice, (3) be lenient in the treatment of the slaves, and (4) pass onto descendents these beliefs and feelings. All four of these recommendations would create the right conditions for just sentiments necessary to rid the institution at the earliest opportunity. Indeed, Jefferson was also aware that, given the situation, the people must "endeavor" to feed, "clothe," and "protect" the slave from "ill-usage."[26] Of course, none of the sentiments should be inculcated if slavery were not an evil.

Others were no less aware that owning slaves contradicted the central precepts of the Declaration. For example, in 1788-1789, David Humphreys visited Washington and recorded a conversation in which Washington thought that

> the unfortunate condition of the persons whose labour in part I employed, has been the only unavoidable subject of regret. To make the Adults among them as easy & as comfortable in their circumstance as their actual state of ignorance & improvidence would admit; & to lay a foundation to prepare the rising generation for a destiny different from that in which they were born; afforded some satisfaction to my mind, & could not I hoped be displeasing to the justice of the Creator.[27]

Washington's quandary was the same as any slave owner who believed in the principles of the revolution: the "slaves were bequeathed to us by Europeans, and time alone can change them; an event . . . no man desires more heartily than

I do. Not only do I pray for it, on the score of human dignity, but I can clearly foresee that nothing but the rooting out of slavery can perpetuate our union, by consolidating it on a common bond of principle."[28] This "rooting out" must come state by state. In the case of Virginia, it was the duty of the state government to secure that end.[29] Even though many of the Founders owned slaves, they continued to speak in terms of liberty for all men and they expressed moral regret that the institution existed on American soil.

Modern critics of the Founders have overlooked the real moral angst the Founders exhibited. They have sought to "historicize" their thoughts and actions in order to criticize the Founders' apparent denial of the rights of the slaves. Those critics proceed from certain historicist assumptions. They attend to the belief that abstract principles must give way to the unfolding of "history," and/or emphasize the "priority of the right over the good."[30] The historical assumption about rights emphasizes freedom over moral restraints. Yet, Jefferson, for example, never made judgments about individuals on the basis of uninhibited right. While the slaves were quite obviously members of the human race, they were not above the consideration of virtue or moral behavior. These considerations moderate the impulse of mere abolition, but historicists are primarily concerned with mere freedom, which tends to free them from considering other political realities.

Despite the theoretical assumptions of many critics, we should limit ourselves, at the moment, to the anti-slavery thought of Jefferson and the other Founders in Virginia, which seems to challenge certain historicist notions. The fact that a nation of slaveholders declared that all men are equal is remarkable in itself. Against their own self-interest, they did not assert that slaves deserved their enslavement. If slavery is natural, then the master who owns the slave has no possible reasonable argument that could be offered to resist his own enslavement, unless slavery is racially justified. However, Lincoln countered in his fragment on slavery that slavery based on color would mean that the first person of lighter skin would be the ruler of the other, more darkly complected, person. Such arguments, Lincoln believed, could be turned on those justifying slavery. Furthermore, if the master claims he owns the property of the slave, he falls into the same quandary: "But, say you, it is a question of *interest*; and, if you can make it your *interest*, you have the right to enslave another. Very well. And if he can make his interest, he has the right to enslave you."[31] The right to own property is grounded in the right to self-ownership and both flow from the law of nature. If a person does not own his body, he does not own his labor and vice-versa. The right to property (and oneself) is just as inalienable as the right to "life and liberty"; slavery "is nothing but taxation without representation carried to its ultimate extreme."[32] Jefferson claims near the conclusion of the *Summary* that a free people derive their freedom from the rights found in nature and those rights are not a gift of any magistrate. These rights limit the power of the government and most particularly that of the crown. The *Summary* is thus a prelude to the Declaration. What it states implicitly, the Declaration makes explicit. We find in the *Summary* many of the ideas and phrases repeated in that 1776 docu-

ment. It no less than the Declaration affirms a timeless truth that God, and Nature's God, gave us life and liberty and these gifts ought not be torn asunder by
man.[33] Its plain meaning was understood by the Founders to denote man's independence. One of Washington's friends, Landon Carter, understood the implications of the Declaration and believed that it demanded the slaves' freedom.[34]

As noted above, the draft of the Declaration used the most condemnatory
language toward the king for using his negative on petitions to end the slave-
trade, if not slavery itself. It was fellow Virginian, Richard Henry Lee, who
moved in the Continental Congress the resolution, which declared the right of
the colonies to be free. The Declaration of Independence emanated from that
parliamentary act, and it formally completed what the *Summary* began—the
"laws of Nature and of Nature's God" ordain "Safety and Happiness" as the
great objects at which political institutions aim.[35] Equality is the foundation of
civil society and is hence no respecter of persons. All men are equal in the sense
that all species are equally of the same species. John Locke asserted as much in
The Second Treatise:

> Nothing is more evident, than that Creatures of the same species and rank pro-
> miscuously born to all the same advantages of Nature, and the use of the same
> faculties, should also be equal one amongst another without Subordination or
> Subjection, unless the Lord and Master of them all, should by any manifest
> Declaration of his Will set one above another, and confer on him by an evident
> and clear appointment an undoubted Right to Dominion and Sovereignty.[36]

Locke goes on to contend that such equality is self-evident. Horses are born with
saddles on their back in ways humans can never be—a horse is incapable of
consent because it is unable to reason. Jefferson believed that both Locke and
Algernon Sydney were among the most able political philosophers of the principles of liberty. Sydney asserted that God gave us our rights and only He could
take such a gift away; He has not "caused some to be born with crowns upon
their heads, and all others with saddles upon their backs."[37] Any reasonable person understands that a man is not a hog, and ruling men as if they are a part of
the irrational order is arbitrary and despotic. Since the sub-rational animal lacks
the capacity of reason, it cannot enter into a contract. Yet, equality does not extend to other characteristics like talent or skill. Men differ in various talents—
one man may have a greater skill at something while another has little to no
skill—but that does not make the man who has the lesser skill any less equal to
the man who has great skill. Men are not naturally born better than others. When
we understand what a man is, we understand the self-evident truth of equality.

The Declaration of Independence establishes a theoretical foundation for the
nation in the same way the Virginia Declaration of Rights is the foundation for
Old Dominion. Like the Declaration of Independence, the Virginia Declaration
provides a philosophical justification for the ground of legitimate government. It
begins with the definitive statement that it is "a declaration of rights made by the
representatives of the good people of Virginia . . . which rights do pertain to
them and their posterity, as the basis and foundation of government." Indeed, the

same document asserts: "That all men are by nature equally free and independent, and have certain inherent rights, of which, when they enter into a state of society, they cannot, by any compact, deprive or divest their posterity; namely, the enjoyment of life and liberty, with the means of acquiring and possessing property, and pursuing and obtaining happiness and safety." The Virginia Declaration, whose author is Mason, precedes the Declaration of Independence by less than one month. Lee, the prime mover of Independence in the Continental Congress, also moved a resolution in the Virginia Congress that the colony should draw up a Declaration of Rights. The basic teaching of the Virginia Declaration is that rights are the ground of government—and certainly of republican government—and the compact cannot deprive men of their rights. Though the Union did degrade the slave to a low position, that was the work of positive law. There was nothing inherently just about such degradation. The significance of the Virginia Declaration is that it initiates a process whereby the Founders begin to consitutionalize individual rights in the civil law. The Virginia Declaration had such an impact that it became the model for other states. Clinton Rossiter asserted its importance by writing that it was "among the world's most memorable triumphs in applied political theory."[38] In any regard, the language employed in both Declarations implicitly holds up the eradication of slavery as a goal. If it were true that "all men are by nature equally free and independent," then it would mean that slavery was the result of arbitrary positive law.

Some in the assembly worried that such an appeal to universal rights in the Virginia Declaration would cause slave insurrections. Robert Carter Nicholas, in particular, criticized the document for the practical effects of declaring the equality of men. The first few lines in Mason's original draft caused the trepidation: "all men are *born* equally free and independent." Nicholas did not necessarily disagree with the principle, but was worried that such a strong statement would be an "open invitation to a slave insurrection."[39] Therefore, he was concerned about the safety of the community. Despite the concerns, Virginians changed the text little, replacing "born" with "by nature." Eventually, the document was adopted unanimously.

Mason thought that the Declaration of Rights and the notion of equality was a proper design for a just commonwealth, which means that it provides the foundation and validity for a just politics. Mason's document is similar to Jefferson's in that it is wholly forward looking; both documents do not seek to accommodate existing governmental institutions but are written to establish a political framework on a general truth.[40] They both make abolition a moral and political necessity. Because men are equal, legitimate political authority arises through consent; the only way human beings may justly be governed is through the recognition that men are non-rulers of one another. Since there is no natural ruler, consent is the only legitimate ground for political rule. However, men ought not to exercise their consent for any end. For example, the Declaration of Independence avows that only the "just powers" arise from the "consent of the governed." Similarly, the Declaration of Rights states, "all power is vested in" and "derived from, the people" in order to produce the "greatest degree of happiness and safety." Not just any consent will secure the proper ends of government. Mere consent is insufficient. Consent must be enlightened for the powers of government to be just: "Men who understand their natural equality or natural rights do not agree or consent to governments which do not secure their rights."[41] The Declaration of Rights delineates more on this front: "no free government, or the blessings of liberty, can be preserved to any people, but by a firm adherence to justice, moderation, temperance, frugality, and virtue, and by frequent recurrence to fundamental principles." It is a political truth that mere consent may be the avenue within which an unjust government is formed. The Founders were no doubt aware of many examples in history where that was the case. We only have to remember that Plutarch's biography of Lycurgus portrays an obedient people who consent to the Spartan leader's illiberal policies.[42] Sparta eventually became a communal society where there were no property rights, no personal property, and families were governed commonly by the city. The citizens of Sparta were unenlightened because even though they consented to a form of government, they surrendered all of their rights in the process; they may have been democratic, but they were illiberal.

Both Mason's Declaration and Jefferson's Declaration state that safety and happiness are the beginning and end of politics. While liberty, equality, and property are the ground of legitimate politics, they are not the end of politics. We notice that once safety is secured, the aim of politics is happiness. Happiness, or the possibility of the good life, is achievable only when life, liberty, and property are protected. Therefore, liberty is ultimately in service of the good life. Some may object by pointing out that the Declaration of Independence states that government is instituted among men to secure rights. While this is the initial reason for government, it is not the end of government. The Virginia Declaration perhaps makes it more evident. In section three, it states that the purpose of government is ultimately to secure the common good, yet neither Virginia nor the Union secured equality for all. Jefferson wrote in his "Autobiography" that the clause condemning the slavery trade in the original draft of the Declaration was struck out to assuage objections from Georgia and South Carolina. There are particular self-interested reasons that both the North (traffickers in slaves) and the South (importers of slaves) capitulated to this demand.[43] However, there is a more persuasive reason why the Founders bargained with the slave states: prudence.

If the first act of government is to secure the safety of the people, then we might argue that the deal with South Carolina and Georgia in 1776 to strike out the severe condemnation of slavery and the slave trade, but to secure better the Union, was a prudent one. If they had not moderated the language condemning the king for waging a "cruel war against human nature itself" then it would have been more difficult for the colonies to win the impending Revolutionary War; the colonies would have been less united, making victory less sure. A similar dilemma faced the Founders in the ratification of the Constitution. In the Constitutional Convention of 1787, North Carolina, South Carolina, and Georgia claimed that they would not support the proposed constitution unless their slaves were somehow protected. The fugitive slave clause was the result of these demands. Further, concerning the slave trade, the three southern states asserted that the traffic be left untouched. Even though they reached a compromise (the federal government could not close the trade for twenty years), John Rutledge of South Carolina made it clear that the slave trade (and slavery) would not be an interest the South would part with easily. Faced with such opposition from the southern states—the insistence that the status of slavery be left up to the states—the Founders reluctantly accepted their demands. We ought not conclude, though, that the Constitution sanctioned slavery. The Founders took care to avoid the word slaves in the compact; they called the slaves "persons." Madison argued that the Constitution itself did not sanction the right to property in men. Therefore, in the creation of the Declaration of Independence, and in the Constitutional Convention of 1787, if the South was turned aside, it would have made military defeat for the colonies more likely, if not certain. The impediments to slavery in the Declaration and the Constitution would not have existed if the newly constructed United States had been conquered. Slavery would have been more secure in defeat than grudgingly acknowledged in the Union. Benjamin Franklin is purported to have commented upon signing the Declaration that if the colonies did not hang together, they would definitely hang separately.

Perhaps we should turn to the foremost expositor of prudence, Aristotle. The ancient philosopher addressed the role of prudence, or practical wisdom, in politics in the *Nicomachean Ethics*. In the Greek, prudence (φρόνησις) is a skill, or rather an excellence or virtue, that the statesman acquires. φρόνησις requires the statesman have the ability to deliberate and have the capacity to know what is good for himself and for the community in general.[44] He must be able to act with the aim of what is good for man. Virtue and happiness is found in immutable human nature: "it is up to man to discover what the good of nature is, and how to acquire it; but man is not free to determine that human good on the basis of his subjective preferences," and yet, prudence modifies the application of right.[45] A prudential decision is not a morally relative decision; it is not situation ethics, so to speak. For example, if we choose a lesser evil over a greater evil we have acted in a prudential manner. Such a decision in no way denies a standard of right and wrong, or good and evil. Therefore, there are a variety of forms of legitimate, but imperfect, governments. What is acceptable in a "given set of circumstances" is not the same as what is "desirable in itself."[46] Therefore, the decision to bargain with the slave South in order to construct the Union, especially in terms of the Constitution, was a prudential decision because there was a greater evil awaiting had they not entered into the compact. Abraham Lincoln provided an example of φρόνησις in his 1854 Peoria speech: "Much as I hate slavery, I would consent to the extension of it rather than see the Union dissolved, just as I would consent to any GREAT evil, to avoid a GREATER one."[47] Similarly, Jefferson was concerned about his "strictures on slavery" in his *Notes on the State of Virginia* only because he did not "know whether their publication would do most harm or good."[48] Jefferson did not want to cause the people of Virginia to retreat in their, albeit deliberate, progress toward emancipation and a more republican state constitution.

Anything that might retard the progress of emancipation was harmful; acts that hastened a reasonable scheme were beneficial. Madison also demonstrated prudence when, in 1790, several emancipation memorials reached the Congress and representatives from South Carolina and Georgia expressed intemperance and used "the most virulent language" in reaction to such petitions.[49] The hostility the emancipation question generated in the halls of Congress from the members of the deep South caused Madison to fear for the Union. The Founders were well aware that it was difficult to form a national, or governing, party out of free and slave states. Madison contended that anti-slavery petitions caused "a public wound" and urged those petitioning the Congress to proceed with delicacy on the subject.[50] He did not try to discourage the submission of these petitions, but encouraged prudence. Therefore, Madison encouraged those that submitted anti-slavery petitions to include some reference to colonization because such a clause might build a larger coalition and increase the chances of passage. If outright emancipation was not practically attainable, something that moved the nation closer to that end, or avoided retrenchment, was preferable.

Both the Declaration of Independence and the Declaration of Rights represent a serious turn in the foundation of politics. The United States is the first to claim independence based on the rights all men share everywhere at all times. As previously noted, the slaveholders proclaimed rights all men shared while at the same time they practiced and participated in the institution. This contradiction could only be resolved by the abolition of legalized slavery. The principles espoused by both declarations provide a common framework, or goal, within which prudence works. Although something like gradual emancipation might not attain abolition immediately, such a policy may determine whether such an end will ever be attainable in fact. The desire to pass an emancipation plan in his state was foremost on Jefferson's mind. While he was dealing with matters of national importance soon after independence, he preferred to get back to Old Dominion to have some effect on the new state government, especially in the area of slavery.[51]

In June of 1776, Jefferson authored a draft of a constitution for the new state of Virginia and he gave it to George Wythe to deliver. However, the copy arrived late and was not considered by the assembly. In his draft, though, he leveled many of the same charges at the king that appeared in his original draft of the Declaration, but he also provided a clause meant to retard the growth of slaves in the state: "No person hereafter coming into this country shall be held within the same in slavery under any pretext whatever."[52] The proposed Constitution was liberal for the time and encouraged broad suffrage with the equal distribution of representation. Any male who owned ¼ acre of land or who paid "scot and lot" taxes for two years was eligible to vote.[53] We ought to observe here that his proposed enfranchisement made no distinction of the color of one's skin.

Though his initial foray into crafting a state constitution was not successful, Jefferson, along with Edmund Pendleton, Thomas Lee, Wythe, and Mason, were appointed to a "Committee of Revisors" by the Virginia legislature at a later date in order to modify the laws. Jefferson rejected an offer to represent the United States in France in order to serve on the committee. It was Jefferson's intent to make Old Dominion more republican. According to one of his biographers, "Jefferson was, as author or chief advocate, responsible for the introduction and adoption of more bills than any single member of the General Assembly in the years 1776 to 1779."[54] The committee submitted an extensive list of revisions on June 18, 1779.

The list of the laws was really a modified digest of existing laws. Bill Fifty-One of the revised laws, however, sought to strengthen the law concerning the slave-trade and proposed

> that no persons shall, henceforth, be slaves within this commonwealth, except such as were so on the first day of this present session of Assembly, and the descendants of the females of them.
> Negroes and mullattoes which shall hereafter be brought into this commonwealth and kept therein one whole year, together, or so long at different times as shall amount to one year, shall be free.[55]

In 1778, Virginia ended the slave-trade, but the Sage had more than mere passage of that law in mind. The law above limits slavery by freeing any brought into the state. It also protects free blacks by prohibiting their re-enslavement. Jefferson wrote in his "Autobiography" that an amendment gradually to free the slaves was also prepared to be attached to the bill and introduced should circumstances permit, and the assembly seemed willing. The amendment would have instituted a *post nati* plan, freed the slaves after a certain age (females at age eighteen and males at age twenty-one), and came coupled with deportation. The proposed bill also provided for more liberal manumissions (by deed). Jefferson noted that the amendment did not pass because public opinion appeared unable to accept it and seemed ill prepared for it.[56] In 1785, Madison tried to get Jefferson's version of the bill moved, to no avail. However, the Virginia Assembly finally passed a similar version of Bill Fifty-One, but did not provide for gradual emancipation. In a sense, they did provide for some emancipation. The slaves brought into the state illegally were freed.[57]

The private and public persona of Jefferson to this point in his career was one that strongly favored emancipation. He was active in trying to secure some sort of emancipation plan both for his state and for the new republic. In 1784, the delegates from Virginia informed the Continental Congress that they wanted to cede their territory beyond the Ohio. Jefferson prepared a plan and drew up what became known as the Ordinance of 1784. This plan formed a basis for the Northwest Ordinance of 1787. The 1784 plan is significant on many levels. It included a statement on the illegality of secession, but also contained a remarkable statement concerning the slave institution. The Ordinance of 1784 would have prevented the spread of slavery in the territories by banning it across the

entire North and South (from Lake Erie to Florida) after the year 1800. It would
have banned it from what are now Kentucky, Tennessee, Alabama, and Mississippi. There was nothing in the Articles of Confederation that spoke to the abolition of slavery until this Ordinance. In the original proposal, Jefferson noted that
its passage would promote the harmony of the Union, and it would prevent slavery from becoming a sectional issue. It provided for the regulations of all future
states and hence banned the slavery in all future territories as well, whereas the
1787 Ordinance limited the slave ban to the area northwest of the Ohio. Nevertheless, the 1784 section of the bill dealing with the "abominable crime" of slavery almost passed the Congress, losing by only one vote.[58]

Some argue that this was Jefferson's last public act on behalf of freedom,
but that is not necessarily so. It may have been his last formal public policy proposal, but it was not his last public statement on the issue. In 1781, Jefferson
began writing his *Notes*. He enlarged the work in 1784 and published two hundred copies while representing the U.S. in Paris. It is true that he sent his draft to
his friends and did not intend the book for publication, but eventually, he assented to its circulation. Reverend James Madison, of the College of William
and Mary, believed that while the entries on slavery might offend, the work was
too valuable not to be made public. By 1787 portions of the book appeared in
several newspapers. The first edition appeared in 1788. Jefferson knew before
its printing that several of his friends had their anti-slavery tracts attacked.[59] We
could confidently assert that he expected the entries of the *Notes* addressing the
issue of slavery to be received coolly. Nevertheless, the book was published
under his name and he did not attempt to modify, or edit, the relevant passages
for publication.

The most relevant entries on the slavery issue appear in Query XIV and
XVIII respectively. Query XIV addresses the laws of Virginia and the role of the
Committee of Revisors. In it, he publicly reveals that the initial aforementioned
bill was to be followed by an amendment, which amounted to the *post-nati* plan.
The amendment also provided for the public education of the slaves and an al-
lowance of property (seed, animals, arms, and other household instruments).
Colonization after the education accompanied this plan as it did in most emanci-
pation plans of the early republic:

> It will probably be asked, Why not retain and incorporate the blacks into the
> State, and thus save the expense of supplying by importation of white settlers,
> the vacancies they will leave? Deep-rooted prejudices entertained by the
> whites; ten thousand recollections, by the blacks, of the injuries they have sus-
> tained; new provocations; the real distinctions which nature has made; and
> many other circumstances, will divide us into parties, and produce convulsions,
> which will probably never end but in the extermination of the one or the other
> race.[60]

The admission that prejudice existed in the young republic does not limit, or
deny, the slave's claim to rights. Emancipation absent a concern for preparing
the slaves for freedom we might conclude is irresponsible. Jefferson desired

abolition, but in a way that the slaves received the necessary moral preparation. His opinion on this matter was not limited to slaves, but all souls.[61] The colonization of the slaves represents a practical solution to a political problem. Colonization, in this sense, is in no way a rejection of right, but a reflection of it. To turn the slaves out into the world without some education would probably ensure their failure. Washington affirmed the necessity of education in a 1798 speech: "When we profess, as our fundamental principle, that liberty is the inalienable right of every man, we do not include madmen or idiots; liberty in their hands would be a scourge. Till the mind of the slave has been educated to perceive what are the obligations of a state of freedom, and not confound a man's with a brute's, the gift would insure its abuse."[62]

While this may sound like a harsh judgment, he meant to convey that freedom placed in the hands of those who are either unenlightened or literally dangerous to the lives of others, have no claim to political liberty. While the former (unenlightened) may remedy their deficiency, the latter (dangerous) are best removed from society in order to protect the liberty of others. There was hope, however, that the slaves might be enlightened. Washington fully expected them to be. In his will, he stipulated that the slaves he freed were to be held in servitude until age of twenty-five so that they could be taught to read, write, and thus better adapt to freedom. Furthermore, that animosity might exist on the part of the slaves is understandable. After the Santo Domingo upheaval, Jefferson expressed the horror that if something was done about slavery in the states "we shall be the murderers of our own children."[63] Jefferson thus recognized the great injustice done to them. Their anger resulting from generations of bondage is explicable in that sense. Jefferson reflects in Query XIV that the master not only has a self-interest in survival, but blacks deserve the equal opportunity of freedom as anyone else.

Their talents, or lack of them, are no barrier to their deserving freedom:

> The opinion that they are inferior in the faculties of reason and imagination, must be hazarded with great diffidence. To justify a general conclusion, requires many observations, even where the subject may be submitted to the anatomical knife, to optical glasses, to analysis by fire or by solvents. How much more then where it is a faculty, not a substance, we are examining; where it eludes the research of all the senses; where the conditions of its existence are various and variously combined; where the effects of those which are present or absent bid defiance to calculation; let me add too, as a circumstance of great tenderness, where our conclusion would degrade a whole race of men from the rank in the scale of beings which their Creator may perhaps have given them.[64]

That the slaves are said to be inferior in mental capacity, or in talent, should be viewed with great suspicion or distrust. To draw a conclusion that they are inferior would, scientifically speaking, require much observation. However, such a general study, if it could be conducted in the 1780s, would still fail in its conclusiveness:

To our reproach it must be said, that though for a century and a half we have
had under our eyes the races of black and of red men, they have never yet been
viewed by us as subjects of natural history. I advance it, therefore, as a suspicion only, that the blacks, whether originally a distinct race, or made distinct by
time and circumstances, are inferior to the whites in the endowments both of
body and mind. It is not against experience to suppose that different species of
the same genus, or varieties of the same species, may possess different qualifi-
cations. Will not a lover of natural history then, one who views the gradations
in all the races of animals with the eye of philosophy, excuse an effort to keep
those in the department of man as distinct as nature has formed them?

The so called inferior characteristics that blacks might possess are caused by
historical accident, a result of their bondage, or a combination of the two. The
other possibility is that nature has fitted them with most to all the endowments
of their faculties with no hope for improvement. Practically speaking, the unde-
veloped "faculty, is a powerful obstacle to the emancipation of these people."
Still, that the slaves are inferior is only a "suspicion" to Jefferson. His mind had
not yet congealed on the question. He notes that men—any animal in the same
species—regardless of color vary in talents. The obstacle to emancipation is not
the lack of natural rights—indeed the passage above speaks to their possession
of rights—but practical obstacles.

The natural differences that Jefferson observed in blacks are only "perhaps"
true. Both prejudice and lack of talent present a barrier to emancipation. Nevertheless, he desired to see a "complete refutation of the doubts . . . on the grade of
understanding allotted to them by nature, and to find that . . . they are on a par
with ourselves."[65] Even if the slaves were naturally inferior, the consideration of
talent is no measure of their rights. The smartest man is not the *natural* ruler of
those inferior. While the Sage writes that blacks are gaining recognition in the
ability to meet whites on equal footing and this development would have a positive effect on their freedom, the quickest solution to that end still appeared to be
some form of colonization so that white prejudices, and the understandable animosity on the part of the slaves for being held in chains, do not cause disorder.

In Query XVIII, Jefferson addressed a different aspect of slavery. In this
section of the *Notes*, he devoted his attention to the public detriment caused by
slavery. He focuses on private detriments, or rather, the problems slavery foists
on the manners of people:

There must doubtless be an unhappy influence on the manners of our people
produced by the existence of slavery among us. The whole commerce between
master and slave is a perpetual exercise of the most boisterous passions, the
most unremitting despotism on the one part, and degrading submissions on the
other. Our children see this, and learn to imitate it; for man is an imitative animal. This quality is the germ of all education in him. From his cradle to his
grave he is learning to do what he sees others do. If a parent could find no motive either in his philanthropy or his self-love, for restraining the intemperance
of passion towards his slave, it should always be a sufficient one that his child
is present. But generally it is not sufficient. The parent storms, the child looks,

on catches the lineaments of wrath, puts on the same airs in the circle of smaller slaves, gives a loose to the worst of passions, and thus nursed, educated, and daily exercised in tyranny, cannot but be stamped by it with odious peculiarities. The man must be a prodigy who can retain his manners and morals undepraved by such circumstances.[66]

We should observe that, contrary to many of the revisionist historians noted in chapter one, Jefferson believes slavery has ill effects on *both* whites and blacks. On the one hand, the master feeds his passions the longer he subsists in domination over another human being, and he also passes on an unreasonable education to his children. On the other hand, slavery unnaturally debases the slave because it degrades his humanity and habituates him to that lifestyle. The peculiar institution has a reciprocal influence on both parties, not just whites. In some sense, Jefferson is saying that neither are free and at liberty. A master might be able to rise above the ill effects of slavery but, he would have to be someone extraordinary, almost god-like. In other words, it is impossible for mortals to escape the institution's destructive influence:

And with what execration should the statesman be loaded, who, permitting one half the citizens thus to trample on the rights of the other, transforms those into despots, and these into enemies, destroys the morals of the one part, and the amor patriæ of the other. For if a slave can have a country in this world, it must be any other in preference to that in which he is born to live and labour for another; in which he must lock up the faculties of his nature, contribute as far as depends on his individual endeavors to the evanishment of the human race, or entail his own miserable condition on the endless generations proceeding from him.[67]

The political effect of slavery on the master is for those "boisterous passions" to encourage their despotism. The consequence of slavery is that it corrupts private morals of the master, but it also makes it difficult, if not impossible, for the slaves to love the country they reside. Virginia's Founders did not expect an enslaved people to love the country that enslaved them after emancipation.

Whereas in Query XIV he entertains the idea that there might be a natural explanation to the slaves' inferiority, he now appears to contend that slavery has kept the slaves from developing their faculties or talents. Could it be that natural history has not fitted them as an inferior species after all? In his aforementioned letter to Edward Coles in 1814, Jefferson states that the degradation of body and mind was the consequence of slavery and years of bondage, while about thirty years earlier, in the *Notes*, he expressed much doubt in the veracity of the claim because his observations were limited to number and geography. It appears that over time he came to a definitive conclusion that nature did not inherently deny blacks the ability to be enlightened. In order for the slaves to unlock their faculties, they should have a political system of their own that secures their liberty. It is difficult to conclude anything other than that the slaves have had a grave injustice forced upon them. Jefferson recognizes that fact and speculates that sla-

very tends to destroy the moral foundations that are necessary for a lasting republic:

> And can the liberties of a nation be thought secure when we have removed their
> only firm basis, a conviction in the minds of the people that these liberties are
> of the gift of God? That they are not to be violated but with His wrath? Indeed I
> tremble for my country when I reflect that God is just; that his justice cannot
> sleep forever; that considering numbers, nature and natural means only, a revo-
> lution of the wheel of fortune, an exchange of situation is among possible
> events; that it may become probable by supernatural interference![68]

Jefferson concludes this query with a trembling optimism: slavery is coming to
an end. Though he understood that God's wrath would judge the new nation for
its misdeeds, he fully expected the institution to disappear. He hoped that it
would end peaceably for the sake of both sides. Yet it was in the realm of possibility that blacks could reverse their fortunes and enslave whites and that God
might favor such a reversal of fortune.

In order to encourage a peaceable end to slavery and preserve the Union, he
thought that the "mind of the master" must be prepared "against the obstacles of
self-interest to an acquiescence in the rights of others" while the slave must be
"prepared by instruction and habit for self government."[69] He believed that the
preparation of the mind of the master must precede the preparation of the slave
for freedom. The master no less than the slave needs enlightenment. Consent by
the slave-holder provides a peaceful way to effect the end of slavery. As late as
1815, he believed that the only practicable emancipation plan was noted in
Query XIV.[70]

Slavery and the Federal Constitution

During the constitutional convention of 1787, Virginia took the initiative to persuade her fellow state delegations that the slave trade ought to be abolished immediately. However, with Jefferson serving his country in Paris, other Virginians served Old Dominion at the Convention. James Madison recognized that
the differences between the states was not rooted in their sizes as much as their
interests. The Union was divided North and South "principally from <the effects
of> their having or not having slaves."[71] Slavery was a foul stain and yet seemed
to persist in the age of enlightenment: "We have seen the mere distinction of
colour made in the most enlightened period of time, a ground of the most oppressive dominion ever exercised by man over man."[72] Despite Madison's seem-
ing condemnation of slavery, the real debate over the institution did not come
until nearly one month later, when George Mason objected to counting the
slaves in full proportion even though, he admitted, it would be beneficial to Old
Dominion.

Mason believed that it would be "unjust" to count the slaves fully and instead supported the three-fifths clause.[73] He contended that they ought not be
counted as "freemen" because they were not properly such. They were partly

considered property, but only in the conventional sense. This argument does not support the contention that the slaves are fitted for slavery. On the contrary, he ends his address by reaffirming their humanity and notes that even the southern states believe this form of "peculiar species of property" is "over and above other species of property." The context of the debate centered on the slaves as taxable property. The conventioneers agreed to place a tax on such importations, not because they were property, but to discourage their importation until such a time as they could abolish it altogether. Treating the slaves as property in law prevented their being treated as mere property in practice.[74] Yet, James Madison thought that continuing the trade twenty years post 1787 would be "dishonorable" to the nation.[75] Ultimately, it was "wrong to admit in the Constitution the idea that there could be property in men" because they are not like other "merchandise."[76]

Mason was most vocal in condemning the slave trade: "This infernal traffic originates in the avarice of British Merchants. The British Government constantly checked the attempts of Virginia to put a stop to it."[77] His speech essentially repeated the charge against the king formerly noted in the original draft of the Declaration and other documents. He did not hesitate to call the institution an "evil" that affected the "whole Union." While some of his criticisms of the trade were not moral, but practical—slavery hinders the economy and "discourages arts and manufacturers"—he emphasized moral and religious themes: "every master of slaves is born a petty tyrant. They bring the judgment of heaven on a Country. As nations cannot be rewarded or punished in the next world they must be in this. By an inevitable chain of causes & effects providence punishes national sins, by national calamities."[78] The similarities between Mason and Jefferson are striking. Neither the Sage nor Mason believed that the judgment of God would be on the side of those who kept the unfortunate race in bondage.

During the Virginia state ratifying convention, Mason and Madison continued their criticism of the peculiar institution as it pertained to the trade. Mason considered it a "nefarious traffic" and "detestable trade" that weakened the state.[79] However, he also believed the proposed Constitution was faulty because it did not protect the South from Northern interest in that property. In other words, Mason feared that states in the North might try to seize that property. This prompted a serious rebuke by Richard Henry Lee: "The Honorable gentleman abominates it because it does not prohibit the importation of slaves, and because it does not secure the continuance of the existing slavery! Is it not obviously inconsistent to criminate it for two contradictory reasons? I submit it to the consideration of the gentlemen, whether, it be reprehensible in one case, it can be censurable in the other."[80] Lee believed that both the trade and the ownership of human beings were unjust. Mason's conflicting opinion on this matter was not a support of the institution per se, but a realistic acknowledgment of a serious division in the Union. His complaint centered on the fact that if the property could be seized it would cause difficulty and infelicity. The fact that he was concerned that slave property may be seized suggests that anti-slavery feeling was great in the Union. Regardless, Mason appeared to be trying to balance the principle of liberty with the practical question of securing that end without causing financial hardship on the owners. He feared that the government might confiscate all forms of property, not just slave property. Still, Lee's critique might have been the cause of Mason returning to the issue a few days later in a more lengthy explication of his position. He begins with a brief history of the motives for revolution:

> The first clause allows the importation of slaves for twenty years. Under the royal government, this evil was looked upon as a great oppression, and many attempts were made to prevent it; but the interest of the African merchants prevented its prohibition. No sooner did the revolution take place, than it was thought of. It was one of the great causes of our separation from Great Britain. Its exclusion has been a principal object of this state, and most of the states in the Union.[81]

If we are to believe Mason, the slave trade was a "great cause" of the Revolution. In light of that evidence, perhaps we could consider the Revolution, in part, the first war over slavery, and the Civil War its omnipotent conclusion. Nevertheless, his opinion on the matter was that the Union was not perfect because the institution was allowed to exist:

> Such a trade is diabolical in itself, and disgraceful to mankind; yet by this Constitution, it is continued for twenty years. As much as I value a union of all the states, I would not admit the Southern State into the Union unless they agree to the discontinuance of this disgraceful trade, because it would bring weakness, not strength, to the Union. And though this infamous traffic be continued, we have no security for the property of that kind we have already. There is no clause in this Constitution to secure it; for they may lay such a tax as will amount to manumission. I cannot express my detestation of it. Yet they have not secured us the property of the slaves we have already. So that they have done what they ought not to have done, and have left undone what they ought to have done.

Mason disagreed with the Constitution in that it secured the slave trade. Slavery threatened the consensus of the Union geographically. According to Mason, the Constitution did not guarantee the security the master had in his slaves. On the one hand, Mason objected to the Constitution because it did not ban the trade. On the other hand, it did not secure slave property. As a result, it seems that he would have challenged the South and forced them to join or reject the compact. Mason's exposition did not settle the matter. Whereas he drew the criticism of Lee the first time, in this instance Madison prudentially responded.

According to Madison the "southern states would not have entered the Union . . . without the temporary permission of that trade." He contended that without Union "the consequences might be dreadful to them and to us." Insisting that slavery be left out of the Union would have been a disaster, a "greater [evil]." Disunion, under the circumstances, would be worse than compromise on slavery. The defeat at the hands of the British would, in all likelihood, be assured because the splintered states might "solicit and obtain aid from foreign powers." Therefore, he concluded that the Union was in a better situation considering the state of affairs. The slaves were also better off because under the Articles of Confederation the trade might be continued perpetually. The Constitution at least allowed for its discontinuance after twenty years and Madison fully expected the trade to end in 1808. In contrast, whether by the Articles or by military defeat at the hands of the British, slavery would not be on the road to extinction. Under either of those scenarios, slavery would be more secure.

During the debate, no one publicly called slavery a good, and/or that the slaves deserved their enslavement. Aside from the lengthy oratory from Lee, Mason, and Madison, fellow Virginian John Tyler also called it a "disgraceful and wicked traffic"; Patrick Henry, also concerned with the status of property under the Constitution, "detested" slavery and thought its effects "fatal."[82] Perhaps Henry more eloquently than Mason explained the practical problem:

> I repeat again, that it would rejoice my very soul that every one of my fellow-beings was emancipated. As we ought with gratitude to admire that decree of Heaven which has numbered us among the free, we ought to lament and deplore the necessity of holding our fellow men in bondage. But is it practicable, by any human means to liberate them without producing the most dreadful and ruinous consequences? We ought to possess them in the manner we inherited them from our ancestors.

It might seem that Henry argued for the perpetual enslavement of his fellow humans, but that is not so. Henry calls the slaves his "fellow men" and we ought to conclude that there is nothing philosophically speaking in his rhetoric that precludes their emancipation. In that the slaves are his fellow men, Henry declares their equality. As beings, they are no different from Henry. According to the fiery orator, their condition ought to be meliorated and the question of emancipation should be left to the state legislatures. Indeed, he admitted a "variety of particular instances, the legislature, listening to complaints, have admitted their emancipation." The question of slavery as it pertained to emancipation was a "local matter" and not subject to the authority of the central government. Like Mason, Henry concerned himself with the ability of the federal government to usurp property owners of their possessions. However, while he was concerned with the protection of property, he did not believe the peculiar institution was a blessing bestowed upon the white race. With the compact assented to in the form of the Constitution, if slavery was to be extinguished it would have to occur state by state. Virginia, compared to other slave states in the Union, represents one of the most active states, as her elite statesmen attempted to effect some sort of emancipation plan.

In the few times Virginia's leading figures debated slavery in the constitutional convention and in the ratifying convention, they regarded slavery a curse. Some have charged that nobody in the Virginia convention appealed to either Declaration because slavery was central to the state's identity. Those who purport the importance of those documents are perpetrating a myth.[83] However, nothing could be further from the truth. Similar to the *Summary*, which invoked "natural rights" without ever mentioning the phrase directly, the debates in Virginia were nothing but a discussion of how to codify, or secure, those rights. Politics is always concerned with right and wrong, good and evil, just and unjust. The conventioneers considered slavery an evil and they could have only been informed of that conclusion if they were enlightened as to the rights of man. Before the eighteenth century drew to a close, St. George Tucker drafted an emancipation plan for the state of Virginia, largely based on Jefferson's *post nati* proposal.

St. George Tucker and the Virginia Emancipation Plan

William and Mary law professor St. George Tucker, like Jefferson, studied law under George Wythe. Tucker desired to put into practice what was only speculated by the major theoretical writers of public right. Tucker was committed to the natural rights idea of the American Revolution. This prompted him to challenge the slave institution. The principles of the Revolution could not support chattel slavery.[84] While initially encouraged in the beginning of the Revolutionary period, Tucker became disenchanted with the inability of Virginia to liberalize her laws. In 1795, he still believed that the majority of slave-holders would "cheerfully concur in any feasible plan" for the institution's abolition.[85] Confident that something could, and would, be done to end slavery, he wrote the *Dissertation* (1796). The proposal argued for a plan that would keep the slaves in their current condition for life. However, females born after the plan's adoption would be freed when they reached the age of twenty-eight. These females would then transmit their free status to all of their subsequent offspring.

When he finished drafting the *Dissertation*, Tucker confidently submitted it to the Virginia House of Delegates and included a note to the Speaker of that body: "The Representatives of a free people . . . have declared that all Men are by nature equally free and independent, can not disapprove a moral Truth into practical effect."[86] In the opening sentences of the essay, he attacked the immorality of the slave institution:

> Whilst we were offering up vows at the shrine of Liberty, and sacrificing hecatombs upon her altars; whilst we swore irreconcilable hostility to her enemies, and hurled defiance in their faces; whilst we adjured the God of Hosts to witness our resolution to live free, or die, and imprecated curses on their heads who refused to unite with us in establishing the empire of freedom; we were imposing upon our fellow men, who differ in complexion from us, a *slavery*, ten thousand times more cruel than the utmost extremity of those grievances and oppressions, of which we complained. Such are the inconsistencies of human nature; such the blindness of those who pluck not the beam out of their own eyes, whilst they can espy a moat in the eyes of their brother; such that partial system of morality which confines rights and injuries, to particular complexions; such the effect that self-love which justifies, or condemns, not according to principle, but to the agent.[87]

The early themes of the writing ought to sound familiar. Tucker believes that something was left undone in the American Founding. The reason slavery was not eradicated stemmed from self-interest, or more correctly self-love, which overcame principle. He blamed the "forefathers" for sowing the "seeds of evil" which "like leprosy" infected the Union and projected their "sins" on the "succeeding generations."[88] His invoking the scriptures regarding the beam and moat in our eyes is a religious teaching on hypocrisy. Tucker is contending that men are being hypocrites who claim for themselves rights they deny to others. Slaves are fellow men not only in eyes of reason, but also in the eyes of the Lord. Like other Virginia statesmen, then, Tucker believed that reason and revelation condemn the practice of slavery. Reflecting on the religious teaching, Tucker, a bit later in the essay, mentions that slaves have souls. Aristotle noted as much in *The Politics*. People are often moved by what they see than by what they do not see. Aristotle's teaching is that we cannot tell what a person is by what that person looks like: "It is evident . . . that if they were to be born as different only in body as the images of the gods, everyone would assert that those not so favored merited being their slaves. But if this is true in the case of the body, it is much more justifiable to make this distinction on the case of the soul; yet it is not as easy to see the beauty of the soul as it is that of the body."[89] Aristotle's political teaching here is that all men are equal because all men have souls. The inconsistency in the application of principle is derivative of economic self-interest. The evil of slavery became rooted in the colonies and hence the states, because of its economic appeal.

The profit motive on both sides of the Atlantic kept Old Dominion from effecting change. For example, the slave owner regarded female slaves highly because their offspring could potentially be worth more than if the master had no increase. However, the institution has caused much unrest throughout history and though it might appeal to man's baser interests, it does not contribute to the happiness of the citizens. The nefarious slave trade traffic in particular has been one of the most "atrocious aggravations of cruelty, perfidy, and intrigues the objects of which have been the perpetual fomentation of predatory and intestine wars."[90] Tucker also accused Europe for causing warfare among Africans themselves, making those unhappy people the sellers as well as the sold. Before embarking on a discussion of the history of slavery in other countries, Tucker criticized the "insidious" and "infernal" practice:

> That such horrid practices have been sanctioned by a civilized nation; that a nation ardent in the cause of liberty, and enjoying its blessing in the fullest extent, can continue to vindicate a right established upon such a foundation; that a people who have declared, "That *all men* are by nature *equally free* and *independent*" and have made this declaration the first article in the foundation of their government, should in defiance of so sacred a truth, recognized by themselves in so solemn a manner, and on so important an occasion, tolerate a practice incompatible therewith, is such an evidence of the weakness and inconsistency of human nature as every man who hath a spark of patriotic fire in his bosom must wish to see removed from his own country.[91]

Serious lovers of republicanism would wish to see the institution eradicated. While Tucker asserts that there have been some attempts to reduce slaves to mere property, they have usually been considered a distinct class of persons whose rights were reduced by positive law. According to Tucker, all men possess natural rights because they are equal. Natural rights are a guide to civil rights, which Tucker lists as the right of personal security, the right of personal liberty, and the right of private property. Slavery wholly abolishes the latter two:

> Hence it will appear perfectly irreconcilable a state of slavery is to the principles of a democracy, which form the *basis* and *foundation* of our government. For our bill of rights declares, "that all men are by nature *equally free* and independent, and have certain rights of which they cannot deprive or divest their posterity, namely, the enjoyment of life and *liberty*, with the means of *acquiring* and *possessing property*." This is indeed no more than a recognition of the first principles of the law of nature, which teaches us this equality, and enjoins every man, whatever advantages he may posses over another, as to the various qualities or endowments of body or mind, to practice the precepts of the law of nature to those who are in these respects his *inferior*, no less than it enjoins his *inferiors* to practice them towards *him*.[91]

Tucker unambiguously sets out the maxim that talent is no measure of our liberty. Again, the Virginia Declaration is so much a foundation of good government that he appeals to it twice.

It is clear that the foundation of a just government, not simply the government in Virginia, springs from natural rights. If the law of nature were the ground of government, "it would be hard to reconcile reducing the negroes to a state of slavery to these principles, unless we first degrade them below the rank of human beings, not only politically, but also physically and morally."[92] It is a moral imperative to recognize the rights of the slaves. To allow the institution to continue is inconsistent with Virginia's founding as expressed in the Declaration of Rights. Hence, Tucker follows with an exhortation: "but surely it is time we should admit the evidence of moral truth, and learn to regard them as our fellow men, and equals, except in those particulars where accident, or perhaps nature, may have given us some advantage; a recompense for which they perhaps enjoy in other respects."[93] Thus, if talent is the measurement of rights, then even the master must submit to the first person that has more talent than he does; Tucker believes that blacks may have talents that whites do not. Yet, the language we have become familiar with—"fellow men," "fellow beings," and "fellow creatures"—might be considered a synonym for the recognition of the law of nature and the equality of all men, and hence represents an admission that they are included in the corpus of natural rights that all men are bound to respect.

While early in the essay he asserts that liberty and property are abolished under slavery, the legal restrictions on the slaves have also threatened their security. For example, a slave could not prepare and administer any medicine with felonious act. Even unlawful assemblies might be punishable by the lash. They are also unequally punished for some crimes; whites receive a lesser punishment for the same except in the case of interracial marriage, where the white person and the clergy performing the ceremony are both subject to fine and imprisonment. In this instance, Tucker asserts the laws are more harsh on the white. Despite some of these unjust laws, he believed that the "progress of emancipation" was steady and continual "but not rapid" enough.[95] The laws implicitly recognize the humanity of the slaves by subjecting them to the laws in ways that hogs and cows are not.

The emancipation of slaves, then, is desired, but the task is not an easy one to effect. It is a cause, however, that God would find favor:

> The extirpation of slavery from the United States is a task equally arduous and momentous. To restore the blessings of liberty to near a million of oppressed individuals, who have groaned under the yoke of bondage, and to their descendents, is an object, which those who trust in Providence, will be convinced would not be unaided by the divine Author of our being, should we invoke his blessing upon our endeavours.[96]

The state had more free blacks than any other state, and more than all the northeastern states combined. The task of emancipation, and what to do with the former slaves after emancipation, was no easy legislative matter. While Tucker would like to see more progress in terms of emancipation, he did not believe that such policy could be instituted haphazardly:

> Yet human prudence forbids that we should precipitately engage in a work of such hazard as a general and simultaneous emancipation. The mind of man must in some measure be formed for his future condition. The early impressions of obedience and submission, which slaves have received among us, and the no less habitual arrogance and assumption of superiority, among the whites, contribute, equally, to unfit the former for *freedom*, and the latter for *equality*.

Despite his overall optimism that slavery would end, Tucker was not unrealistic. Simple emancipation would be imprudent and harm the status of the slaves in two ways: (1) The arrogance of the masters who have succumbed to the unreasonable conclusion that the slaves are inferior to whites; and (2) that the slaves have suffered at the hands of whites who have kept them in bondage. They have been denied, generally, the most basic forms of education and prepared skills necessary for freedom. The first buttresses Jefferson's conclusion that the peculiar institution cultivates "boisterous passions" in the master, and the second affirms that mere abolition without some assistance to prepare the slaves for liberty is an immoral act. It was a widely held opinion that emancipation would force the slaves to engage in criminal activity to provide for their support.[97] Tucker believed that mere abolition could be a death sentence on many of them. It is prudential that a gradual plan be found to solve the problem of slavery. The arrogance on the part of the master has the effect of making those emancipated miserable, and the fact that slaves have suffered in bondage more than likely would fuel their desire to revenge that injustice.

The practical dilemma before Virginians, then, was how to end slavery and address these two problems. Both problems must be overcome to end slavery. One major obstacle was the fact that masters had property in slaves; the positive law had sanctioned such property and therefore compensation seemed the only viable instrument to secure emancipation. An additional problem might be that people who are not slave-owners would object to paying slave-owners tax monies for emancipation of the slaves. In other words, the non-slave owners might oppose a tax that is not in their direct interest. Therefore, Tucker proposed a gradual emancipation plan that was exceedingly moderate; it would have taken a century to complete. Nevertheless, he contends "that the abolition of slavery may be effected without the *emancipation* of a single slave; without depriving any man of the *property* which he *possesses*, and without defrauding a creditor who has trusted him on the faith of that property."[98] Washington had an analogous idea when he wrote that slavery ought to be "abolished by slow, sure, & imperceptible degrees."[99]

The political reality is that prejudices against blacks are firmly rooted in public opinion. The same prejudice that has prevented emancipation also desires colonization. Therefore, colonization seemed like the best available remedy to a pernicious problem because "Negro inferiority hindered emancipation . . . not because it justified slavery, but because it increased the difficulty of knowing how to deal with Negroes once freed."[100]

To persuade successfully, the Founders had to account for the various prejudices of the day. We cannot expect the Founders simply to demand their constituents listen to them and follow their advice. The Founders had to make concessions to the conventional wisdom of the time. This practice is, of course, different from arguments independent of time, but the Founders could not change the public opinion of their audience. Therefore, they proceeded not from what was most desirable, they wrote and spoke in a "civil" manner.[101] Tucker understands that if the slaves are freed, at some point, they ought to enjoy full participation in civil and social rights. The enjoyment of political rights would better secure their pursuit of happiness. Therefore, Tucker and Jefferson are politically wise to make use of existing prejudices, because they cannot change them significantly. It is easier to free the slaves by utilizing the prejudice that existed than by waiting for wholesale eradication of that prejudice. However, freeing the slaves into a state that would make them miserable does them no good and causes much harm. Prudence dictates that some course must be found:

> We must therefore endeavor to find some middle course, between the tyrannical and iniquitous policy which holds so many human creatures in a state of grievous bondage, and that which would turn loose a numerous, starving, and enraged banditti, upon the innocent descendants of their former oppressors. *Nature, time,* and *sound policy* must co-operate with each other to produce such a change: if either be neglected, the work will be incomplete, dangerous, and not improbably destructive.[102]

Gradual emancipation takes into account these concerns. It allows the slave owner to advert the bankruptcy that would result from the slaves' immediate uncompensated freedom. This design, given its lengthy and plodding progression, would also give the citizens time to develop a more enlightened view of the slaves.[103]

It is on the issue of colonization that Tucker seems to depart most from Jefferson. He acknowledges the fact that prejudice exists and that such feelings are probably unjust and ill founded. Still, these feelings must be accommodated in order to increase their chances of survival and their ability to secure political liberty for themselves. Instead of colonization to a far away, distant land, like Africa or Haiti, Tucker believes that the freed slaves should move into unsettled territory like Louisiana. In time, Tucker believes that those prejudices against the former slaves would moderate. He appears to believe that incorporation, or intermixing of the races peaceably, might occur in the future.

If there is an objection to incorporation, he believes it will come from a minority:

> Those slaveholders (whose numbers I trust are few) who have been in the habit of considering their fellow creatures as no more than cattle, and the rest of the brute creation, will exclaim that they are to be deprived of their *property*, without compensation. Men who will shut their ears against this moral truth, that all men are by nature *free*, and *equal*, will not even be convinced that they do not possess a *property* in an *unborn* child: they will not distinguish between allowing to *unborn* generations the absolute and unalienable rights of human nature, and taking away that which they *now possess*; they will shut their ears against the truth, should you tell them the loss of the mother's labour for nine months, and the maintenance of a child for a dozen or fourteen years, is amply compensated by the services of that child for as many years more, as he has been an expence to them.[104]

Tucker, by bringing this up, must have feared the unreasonable position that masters would claim the right to property yet be created. By pointing out some slaveholders believed such already, he reveals the absurdity of their position. The claim to the increase of the slaves could only be made if the voice of reason is stifled:

> But if the voice of reason, justice and humanity be not stifled by sordid avarice, or unfeeling tyranny, it would be easy to convince even those who have entertained such erroneous notions, that the right of one man over another is neither founded in nature, nor sound in policy. That it cannot extend to those not in being; that no man can in reality be deprived of what he doth not possess . . . that a state of slavery is not only perfectly incompatible with the principles of government, but with the safety and security of their masters.[105]

Tucker was right in one aspect. Masters would claim ownership of the yet to be born. They believed that compensated emancipation would not work because of the infinite increase in offspring, and hence lost revenues, would cause the slaveholder. This opinion only caught on as the belief in the abstract truth that "all men are created equal" abated. Given the historical evidence that seemed to support the notion that Virginia would have rid herself of slavery if given the chance, Tucker's eagerness in drafting the *Dissertation* appears well placed. However, the Virginia Assembly did not receive Tucker's proposition enthusiastically. Most delegates refused to consider it. Tucker was dismayed by the negative reaction and never again pursued the issue with the legislature.

By 1803, he held out little hope that any *post nati* plan would be adopted by the state in his lifetime. Could it be that slavery was having the ill-effect both Jefferson and Tucker asserted it would? Washington also anticipated its conclusion: "I wish from my soul that the Legislature of this State could see the policy of a gradual Abolition of Slavery; It would prevent much future mischief."[106] Though slavery was considered an evil, perhaps avarice and despotic feelings were permeating the southern half of the Union.

Conclusion

Given the similar themes between Tucker's *Dissertation* and Jefferson's *Notes*, while we might criticize the Sage for his apparent lethargic efforts in his later years, his public and private record influenced the likes of Tucker to fashion a broad gradual emancipation plan. Whatever the charges against the Founders, one cannot conclude they were indifferent or obtuse to the moral implications of the peculiar institution. As the war approached, Washington articulated what many of the Founders believed and noted the parallel between British arbitrary rule over the colonies and the arbitrary control Virginians had over slaves.[107]

The Founders, then, were not hypocrites in the literal meaning of the word. It is difficult to convict them from the primary source material that they did not believe in their heart things they wrote and spoke. Until the end of his life, Jefferson maintained that he would gladly bear financial loss from emancipation if a practicable plan could be adopted, and encouraged others to take up the cause. Near his death, Jefferson wrote in 1826 that his opinions on slavery had been public for forty years.[108] Therefore, his opinions on how much he deplored the institution were well known—further elaboration was unnecessary because his record was public and he had not changed his mind.

Jefferson was one of the first Americans to propose a specific plan of emancipation and throughout his life he spoke publicly and privately of his desire to effect a plan. In 1815, he stated that had he been in the service of his state of Virginia, he would endeavor to make emancipation a policy goal. Even his private correspondence, however, was made public from time to time.[109] Responding to Jared Sparks, Jefferson thanked him for a copy of the January 1824 issue of the *North American Review* that included the sixth annual report of the American Colonization Society. In that document, the society mentions Jefferson's letter to Monroe in the first annual report of 1818. The letter was read into the record at that first meeting and it delineated Jefferson's active role in trying to secure a land for colonization for his state.[110] His opinion on the matter was, therefore, unquestioned and public.

Since Jefferson's main concern centered on the perpetuation of the Union— after all, the success of it was not guaranteed—he was prudently cautious in disturbing public tranquility. However, he acted when the opportunity of success was great. Jefferson may not have prohibited slavery in the Louisiana Territory, but he wanted to limit the slave population as much as possible. Even though the inhabitants wanted to open the trade, the government prohibited it. In his "Sixth Annual Message," delivered in his second term, Jefferson publicly lent his support to the ending of the slave-trade well before 1808:

> I congratulate you, fellow-citizens, on the approach of the period at which you may interpose your authority constitutionally, to withdraw the citizens of the United States from all further participation in the violation of human rights which have been so long continued on the unoffending inhabitants of Africa, and which the morality, the reputation, and the best interest of our country, have long been eager to proscribe. Although no law you may pass can take prohibitory effect till the first day of the year one thousand eight hundred and eight, yet the intervening period is not too long to prevent, by timely notice, expeditions which cannot be completed before that day.[111]

The national legislature arrested the trade before January 1, 1808 (the act was passed on March 2, 1807), and that part of a "great moral and political error" was a thing of history.[112] His critics are thus incorrect to assert that he did nothing as president to affect slavery. The abolition of the trade was one step of many needed to end the institution in total. The prohibition of the slave trade was believed to be a first step in the abolition of slavery. He therefore acted when his intervention would create more good than harm. Even though his public pronouncements against slavery were fewer than before he became president, judging from his private correspondence, it was widely recognized he was a supporter of emancipation.[113] In those private letters, he never denied the natural right of the slaves.

The problem confronting the Virginia Founders was that self-interest was at the root of the slavery problem. They understood that justice could be reduced to mere self-preservation. From preservation, we might reduce it to self-interest, and finally, what is in one's interest could be defined as what is "convenient and achievable."[114] What worried the Founders was that slavery would so corrupt the master, he would cease believing emancipation was a worthy goal. The master might just come to believe that slaves must be kept indefinitely in bondage. The demoralization of the master as a result would have detrimental effects to free government and undermine the ground of legitimate government: the natural equality of all men. However, there was hope that the advancement, or enlightenment, of the "human mind" might overcome "the obstacles of self-interest"— though they understood that where the institution was most "deeply seated" it would "be slowest in eradication."[115] Jefferson in particular recognized that, in the south, it would take time, patience, and perseverance.

Happiness of mankind is found in Union than outside it; slavery was more secure outside the Union than in it. The Founders articulated the argument that the ideas of the republic would better create an enduring, happy, people. A nation based on the unchanging idea of the rights of men is the very foundation of self-government. The Revolution and the ratification of the Constitution demonstrated that the American people could transcend local concerns by reflection and choice. In the 1780s-1790s, slavery was considered a dying institution. Justice required emancipation, but in a gradual manner. With the commencement of the Missouri crisis, the Founders still believed that slavery would end, but perhaps not as quickly as originally believed.

Notes

1. Kate Mason Rowland, *The Life of George Mason, 1725-1792*, vol. 1 (New York: Russell & Russell, 1964), 196-197.
2. Thomas Jefferson, *Notes on the State of Virginia* in *The Portable Thomas Jefferson*, ed. Merrill D. Peterson, (New York: Penguin Books, 1975), 185-186. See also Jefferson to Jared Sparks, Monticello, 4 February 1824, *Thomas Jefferson: Writings*, ed. Merrill Peterson (New York: Library of America, 1984), 1484-1487.
3. Dumas Malone, *Jefferson and His Time: The Virginian*, vol. 1 (Boston: Little, Brown, and Co., 1948), 121-122. See also Henry Wiencek, *An Imperfect God: George Washington, his Slaves, and the Creation of America* (New York: Farrar, Straus, and Giroux, 2003), 161.
4. Jefferson to Edward Coles, Monticello, 25 August 1814, *Thomas Jefferson: Writings*, ed., Merrill D. Peterson (New York: Library of America, 1984), 1344. See also Dumas Malone, *Jefferson and His Time: The Virginian*, vol. 1, 141.
5. Jefferson to Edward Coles, Monticello, 25 August 1814, *Thomas Jefferson: Writings*, 1344.
6. Jefferson to Jean Nicolas DéMeunier, 26 June 1786, *Thomas Jefferson: Writings*, 592.
7. Jaffa, *How to Think about the American Revolution*, 115: "That men are originally—or by nature—equal, and that the natural ground of civil society is this equality, is easily forgotten in civil society. Moreover, it is easy for rulers to deceive both themselves and their subjects into thinking that they are inherently different and superior. It is easy to confuse the Prince's clothes—with his nature. That 'frequent recurrence to fundamental principles,' of which the Virginia Bill of Rights (June 12 1776) so eloquently speaks, is needed precisely to remind the citizens, both governors and governed, of natures which the instituted laws are meant to serve."
8. Jefferson to Edward Coles, Monticello, 25 August 1814, *Thomas Jefferson: Writings*, 1344.
9. Harry V. Jaffa, *A New Birth of Freedom* (Lanham, Md.: Rowman & Littlefield, 2000), 7.
10. Jefferson, *Summary View of the Rights of British America*, in *The Portable Thomas Jefferson*, ed. Peterson, 4. On equality and liberty, and Union see Jaffa, *A New Birth of Freedom*, 7, 334-335; Jaffa, *Equality and Liberty* (Claremont: The Claremont Institute, 1999), xvi-xvii, xix, 176-177; Jaffa, "Equality, Liberty, Wisdom, Morality and Consent in the Idea of Political Freedom," *Interpretation* 15, no. 1 (1987) : 5, 8.
11. Jefferson, *Summary View of the Rights of British America*, 3.

12. Ibid., 4; See Jaffa, *A New Birth of Freedom*, 7, on the language of Union and Liberty in the *Summary*.

13. Jefferson, *A Summary View of the Rights of British America*, 4-5.

14. Abraham Lincoln, "Speech at Cincinnati, Ohio," 17 September 1859, in *Abraham Lincoln: Speeches and Writings, 1859-1865*, ed. Don E. Fehrenbacher (New York: Library of America, 1989), 85; Robert Middlekauff, *The Glorious Cause* (New York: Oxford University Press, 1982), 236.

15. Jaffa, *A New Birth of Freedom*, 9. Aristotle asserts that all politics aims at some good and that the city exists for living well and for happiness: Aristotle, *The Politics*, trans. Carnes Lord (Chicago: University of Chicago Press, 1984), 35, 37, and 217. Interestingly Robert Middlekauff makes the connection between the exercise of natural rights and happiness in Jefferson's *Summary*. See Middlekauff, 236.

16. Jefferson, *A Summary View of the Rights of British America*, 14-15. For much of the analysis of the *Summary*, I have profited greatly from Jaffa, *A New Birth of Freedom*, 22-23.

17. Jaffa, *A New Birth of Freedom*, 22.

18. Edmund S. Morgan, *American Slavery, American Freedom: The Ordeal of Colonial Virginia* (New York: W.W. Norton and Company, 1975), 155. There is some evidence to back up this claim. In 1712 Virginia only required a person to hold one-half acre of land to be eligible to vote. The right applied to any free man, including blacks. See Julian A.C. Chandler, *The History of Suffrage in Virginia* (Baltimore: Johns Hopkins Press, 1901), 12.

19. Peterson, ed., *Thomas Jefferson: Writings*, 22.

20. William Cohen, "Thomas Jefferson and the Problem of Slavery," *The Journal of American History* 56 (December 1969) : 507.

21. Matthew 7:12; Jefferson to Edward Coles, Monticello, 25 August 1814, *Thomas Jefferson: Writings*, 1346; Morgan, 331. In the early colonial period, *anyone* who could prove their baptism could sue for their freedom.

22. Jefferson to Jean Nicolas DéMeunier, 26 June 1786, *Thomas Jefferson: Writings*, 592: "But we must await with patience the workings of an overruling providence, and hope that that is preparing the deliverance of these, our suffering brethren. When the measure of their tears shall be full, when the groans shall have involved heaven itself in darkness, doubtless a god of justice will awaken to their distress, and by diffusing light & liberality among their oppressors, or at length by his exterminating thunder manifest his attention to the things of this world, and that they are not left to the guidance of a blind fatality."

23. Henry to Robert Pleasants, 18 January 1773, *The Founders' Constitution*, vol. 1. ed. Philip B. Kurland and Ralph Lerner (Indianapolis: Liberty Fund, 1987), 517.

24. Ibid.

25. Ibid. See also Henry Mayer, *A Son of Thunder: Patrick Henry and the American Republic* (New York: Franklin Watts, 1986), 168 & 299. It should not be lost on the reader the dual meaning of Henry's use of the word Reformation. Emancipation would not only complete the religious reformation that began in the 1500s, but the political one that began with the Founding.

26. Jefferson to Edward Coles, Monticello, 25 August 1814, *Thomas Jefferson: Writings*, 479.

27. "Reflection on Slavery," in *George Washington: Writings*, 701-702; Wiencek, *An Imperfect God*, 272. Many of the Founders expressed anxiety over the disconnect between the principles of the Revolution and the practice of slavery: Washington to Alexander Spotswood, Philadelphia, 23 November 1794, *George Washington: Writings*,

58   Chapter 3

900; Edmund Randolph noted his "anxiety about the injustice of holding [slaves]," Randolph to James Madison, 19 May 1789, *The Founders' Constitution*, vol. 1, 551-552. On Lee and the slaves as fellow men see Frank Gaylord Cook, "Richard Henry Lee," *Atlantic Monthly* 66, no. 33 (July 1890) : 25-26.

28. Wiencek, *An Imperfect God*, 352. The author generally praises Washington over all other Founders because he freed his slaves in his will. Most others, like Jefferson, freed few, if any, slaves upon death.

29. Washington to Marquis de Lafayette, Mount Vernon, 10 May 1786, *George Washington: A Collection*, ed., W.B. Allen (Indianapolis: Liberty Classics, 1988), 322.

30. Ari Helo and Peter Onuf, "Jefferson, Morality, and the Problem of Slavery," *William and Mary Quarterly* 60 (July 2003) : 583; and see in particular on the Kantian development of the right over the good: John Rawls, *A Theory of Justice* (Cambridge: The Belknap Press, 1971), 31, 446-452; Leo Strauss, *What is Political Philosophy?* (Glencoe, Ill.: The Free Press, 1959; reprint, Chicago: University of Chicago Press, 1988), 61.

31. Abraham Lincoln, "Fragment on Slavery," in *Abraham Lincoln: Speeches and Writings, 1859-1865*, 303.

32. Jaffa, *A New Birth of Freedom*, 26.

33. Jaffa, *How to Think About the American Revolution*, 118; Jaffa, "The Decline and Fall of the American Idea: Reflections on the Failure of American Conservatism" (paper presented for the 25th Anniversary Symposium of the Henry Salvatori Center for the Study of Individual Freedom, Claremont, Ca., April 18-20, 1996), 16.

34. Wiencek, *An Imperfect God*, 192.

35. James Madison, "Federalist #43" in Clinton Rossiter, ed., *The Federalist Papers*, with an Introduction and Notes by Charles R. Kesler (New York: Mentor, 1999), 247; Jaffa, *How to Think about the American Revolution*, 110.

36. Peter Laslett, ed., *Two Treatises of Government* (Cambridge: Cambridge University Press, 1988), 269 & 270.

37. Algernon Sydney, *Discourses Concerning Government*, ed. Thomas West (Indianapolis: Liberty Classics, 1990), xv, 510-511; See also Jefferson to Henry Lee, 8 May 1825, *Thomas Jefferson: Writings*, 1500-1501; Jaffa, *A New Birth of Freedom*, 44-45, 81, and 106.

38. Quoted in Robert A. Rutland, ed., *The Papers of George Mason*, vol. 1 (Chapel Hill: University of North Carolina Press, 1970), 276. Mason, like Jefferson, was well versed in the authors of political right including Locke and Sydney.

39. Ibid., 275. Mason also contended that all men were not equal in all respects, but this was a clarification in language really—as noted elsewhere concerning the Declaration of Independence, Mason is speaking of equality of rights, not talents.

40. Helen Hill, *George Mason: Constitutionalist* (Cambridge, Mass.: Harvard University Press, 1938), xix-xxi; Rutland, ed., *The Papers of George Mason*, vol. 3, 966.

41. Jaffa, *How to Think about the American Revolution*, 115-116.

42. A.H. Clough, ed., *Plutarch's Lives* (Boston: Little, Brown, and Company, 1876), 28-43.

43. Jefferson, "Autobiography," in *Thomas Jefferson: Writings*, 18.

44. Aristotle, *Nicomachean Ethics*, Translated with an Introduction by Martin Ostwald (New York: Macmillan, 1986), 152-153. Or rather see 1140a25-1140b10.

45. Jaffa, "The Decline and Fall of the American Idea," 12; *How to Think about the American Revolution*, 119 & 121.

46. Strauss, *What is Political Philosophy?*, 61.

47. Don E. Fehrenbacher, ed., *Abraham Lincoln: Speeches and Writings*, vol. 1 (New York: Library of America, 1989), 333; cf. James Madison, "Federalist #41," in Rossiter, ed., 223: "[A] cool and candid people will at once reflect that the purest human blessings must have a portion of alloy in them; that the choice must always be made, if not the lesser evil, at least of the GREATER, not the PERFECT, good."

48. Jefferson to Chastellux, Paris, 7 June 1785, *Thomas Jefferson: Writings*, 799-800; Jefferson repeated this sentiment to Madison, Paris, 17 June 1785, ibid., 804-805. When speaking of slavery as a necessary evil, the Founders mean prudence. It would not be prudent to emancipate the slaves simply. Part of the reason for this was the training and education that the slaves needed to prepare them for freedom. The other reason stemmed from the fact that they feared for their own safety; the slaves would understand they were held in bondage unjustly. Patrick Henry noted as much in the Virginia ratifying convention: "As much as I deplore slavery, I see that prudence forbids its abolition," Jonathan Elliot, ed., *The Debates in the Several State Conventions, on the Adoption of the Federal Constitution as Recommended by the General Convention at Philadelphia in 1787*, vol. 3 (Philadelphia: J.B. Lippincott and Co., 1861), 590; West, *Vindicating the Founders*, 23.

49. Madison to Benjamin Rush, 20 March 1790, *The Founders' Constitution*, vol. 1, 555.

50. Madison to Robert Pleasants, Philadelphia, 30 October 1791, *Letters and Other Writings*, vol. 1 (New York: R. Worthington, 1884), 542-543.

51. Middlekauff, *The Glorious Cause*, 609. On anti-slavery feeling in early Virginia see Gutzman, 37 and 136.

52. Ford, ed., *The Writings of Thomas Jefferson*, vol. 2, 180.

53. Ibid., 166.

54. Boyd, ed., *The Papers of Thomas Jefferson*, vol. 2, 306.

55. Ibid., 470.

56. Ibid., 472; Jefferson, "Autobiography," *Thomas Jefferson: Writings*, 43-44; Cohen, 510.

57. DuBois, 72 and 235. DuBois does not mention the 1785 act, but Gutzman, 140, references *Hening's Statutes* as evidence the assembly passed a bill similar to what the revisors recommended. The act amounted to a ban in intra-state trade. Slaves were prohibited from entering by sea or land.

58. Jefferson to James Madison, Annapolis, 25 April 1784, *The Works of Thomas Jefferson*, vol. 4, ed. Paul Leicester Ford (New York: G.P. Putnam's Sons, 1904), 329-330; Hill, 288; Boyd, ed., *The Papers of Thomas Jefferson*, vol. 6, 581-617; Malone, *Jefferson and His Time: Jefferson the Virginian*, vol. 1, 411-414; and Cohen, 503, 508-509, 511. Cohen contends that the 1784 Ordinance represents Jefferson's last public act.

59. Malone, *Jefferson and His Time: Jefferson and the Rights of Man*, vol. 2, 95-98. We should also note that George Wythe supported distribution of the *Notes* in Virginia, especially to the students of the College of William and Mary; Madison to Thomas Jefferson, Richmond, 22 January 1786, *Letters and Other Writings*, vol. 1, 211. Rev. Madison thought that the work should see the "light of the sun." See Malone, *Jefferson and His Time: The Rights of Man*, vol. 2, 97; Rev. Madison to Thomas Jefferson, 28 December 1787, "Letters of Rev. James Madison, President of the College of William and Mary, to Thomas Jefferson," *William and Mary Quarterly Historical Magazine*, 5 (April 1925): 87.

60. Jefferson, *Notes on the State of Virginia*, in *The Portable Thomas Jefferson*, 186.

61. Jefferson to Monsieur A. Coray, Monticello, 31 October 1823, *The Writings of Thomas Jefferson*, 481; Jefferson to Edward Coles, Monticello, 25 August 1814, *Thomas Jefferson: Writings*, 1345.

62. Quoted in Wiencek, *An Imperfect God*, 352.

63. Cohen, 520-521.

64. Unless otherwise noted, quotes may be found in Peterson, ed., *The Portable Thomas Jefferson*, 192-193.

65. Jefferson to Henri Gregorie, Washington, 25 February 1809, *Thomas Jefferson: Writings*, 1202; West, 9.

66. Jefferson, *Notes on the State of Virginia*, in *The Portable Thomas Jefferson*, 214.

67. Ibid., 214-215.

68. Ibid., 215.

69. Jefferson to David Barrow, Monticello, 1 May 1815, *The Works of Thomas Jefferson*, vol. 9, 516.

70. Ibid., 515; Jefferson to Edward Coles, Monticello, 25 August 1814, *Thomas Jefferson: Writings*, 478.

71. Max Farrand, ed., *The Records of the Federal Convention of 1787*, vol. 1 (New Haven: Yale University Press, 1966), 486. See also ibid., 476.

72. Ibid., 135. Madison utters this statement in the context of societies being divided into sects and factions. See also Paul Rahe, *Republics Ancient and Modern: Inventions of Prudence Constituting the American Regime* (Chapel Hill: The University of North Carolina Press, 1994), 76-77; DuBois, 43.

73. Farrand, ed., vol. 1, 581. Unless otherwise noted, all quotes from this edition and page. See also Mason to Thomas Jefferson, 1788, *George Mason: Constitutionalist*, 216.

74. Ibid., vol. 3, 355-356. Madison asserted this argument on the floor of the House of Representatives, May 13, 1789. See also James Madison "Import Duty on Slaves," *The Founders' Constitution*, vol. 3, 295-296; W.B. Allen, "A New Birth of Freedom: Fulfillment or Derailment?" in *Slavery and Its Consequences: The Constitution, Equality, and Race*, ed. Robert A. Goldwin and Art Kaufman (Washington, D.C.: AEI, 1988), 69.

75. Farrand, vol. 2, 415.

76. Ibid., 417. The Constitution states that slaves are "Persons."

77. Farrand, vol. 2, 370. Unless otherwise noted, all quotes from this edition and page.

78. Ibid.

79. Elliot, vol. 3, 269-270. Mason's speech delivered on June 11, 1788.

80. Ibid., 273.

81. Ibid., 452-453. Unless otherwise noted, all quotes below are from this citation.

82. Ibid., 454 and 590-591. Hereafter, Henry quotes are from 590-591.

83. Gutzman, 261. Gutzman criticizes Harry V. Jaffa in particular for perpetuating this "myth." Cf., Edward J. Erler, "Philosophy, History, and Jaffa's Universe," *Interpretation* 28, no. 3 (Spring 2001) : 245.

84. Phillip Hamilton, "Revolutionary Principles and Family Loyalties: Slaver's Transformation in the St. George Tucker Household of Early National Virginia," *The William and Mary Quarterly* 55 (October 1998) : 533-534.

85. Tucker to Jeremy Belknap, 29 June 1795, *The Founders' Constitution*, vol. 1, 559-560, 535.

86. Ibid., 536.

87. St. George Tucker, *View of the Constitution of the United States with Selected Writings*, with a Foreword by Clyde N. Wilson (Indianapolis: Liberty Fund, 1999), 403. Cf. Matthew 7:3-5 and Luke 6:41-42.

88. Ibid., 405.
89. Aristotle, *The Politics*, 41.
90. Tucker, 405-406.
91. Ibid., 411-412. Italics in the original.
92. Ibid., 419-420.
93. Ibid., 420.
94. Ibid.
95. Ibid., 431.
96. Unless otherwise noted, quotes are from ibid., 433. We should note here that Tucker footnotes Query XVIII of Jefferson's *Notes* in this section of his *Dissertation*.
97. Morgan, *American Slavery, American Freedom*, 385 and 376.
98. Tucker, 436.
99. Washington to John Francis Mercer, Mount Vernon, 9 September 1786, *George Washington: Writings*, 607. Like other Virginia statesmen, Washington believed that with education, the slaves had a better chance of prospering as a free people.
100. Herbert J. Storing, *Toward a More Perfect Union: The Writings of Herbert J. Storing*, ed. Joseph M. Bessette (Washington, D.C.: AEI Press, 1995), 137.
101. Strauss, *What is Political Philosophy?*, 65.
102. Tucker, 440. James Madison believed in colonization as the best remedy for possible destructive consequences after emancipation see "Memorandum on an African Colony for Freed Slaves," 20 October 1789, *The Papers of James Madison*, vol. 12, ed., Charles F. Hobson and Robert A. Rutland (Charlottesville: University Press of Virginia, 1979), 438.
103. Tucker also thought that colonization was wholly impracticable, as it would take a vast maritime force to ship the slaves to any distant land. He thought they should move to another area on the continent, ibid., 442. See Tucker to Jeremy Belknap, 29 June 1795, *The Founders' Constitution*, vol. 1, 559-560. The Founders were generally split on the colonization issue. Washington, for instance, believed that the slaves should live on American soil, Wiencek, 356.
104. Tucker, 443.
105. Ibid.
106. Washington to Lawrence Lewis, Mount Vernon, 4 August 1797, and to John Francis Mercer, Mount Vernon, 9 September 1786, ed. Rhodehamel, 607-608 and 1002 respectively; Wiencek, *An Imperfect God*, 274.
107. Matthew Spalding and Patrick J. Garrity, *A Sacred Union of Citizens*, with an Introduction by Daniel Boorstin (Lanham, Md.: Rowman and Littlefield, 1996), xiv.
108. Malone, *Jefferson and His Time: Sage of Monticello*, 312 and 316; Jefferson to Edward Coles, Monticello, 25 August 1814, *Thomas Jefferson: Writings*, 479.
109. Jefferson to David Barrow, Monticello, 1 May 1815, *The Writings of Thomas Jefferson*, 515; Malone, *Jefferson and His Time: The Sage of Monticello*, 325. Furthermore, the original draft of the Declaration of Independence and proposed Virginia Constitution were widely publicized in 1806. The public thus knew of Jefferson's opinions on slavery and other matters of government.
110. Jefferson to Jared Sparks, 4 February 1824, *Thomas Jefferson: Writings*, 1484; "The Sixth Annual Report of the American Society for Colonizing the Free People of Color of the United States," *North American Review* 18 (January 1824), 41; For the 21 January 1818 letter to then Governor Monroe see *The First Annual Report of the American Society for Colonizing the Free People of Color of the United States* (Washington City: D. Rapine, January 1818), 13-14.

111. Jefferson, "Sixth Annual Message, 2 December 1806," *Thomas Jefferson: Writings*, 528.

112. Jefferson to Messrs Thomas, Elliot, and Others, 13 November 1807, *Jefferson and His Time: Jefferson the President*, vol. 5, ed. Dumas Malone (Boston: Little, Brown, and Company, 1974), 546.

113. Malone, *Jefferson and His Time: The Sage from Monticello*, 323 and 325. Slave traders who were apprehended in violation of the trade ban faced heavy fines, and the confiscation of their ships and human contraband.

114. Storing, 143-144; Jefferson to Edward Coles, Monticello, 25 August 1814, *Thomas Jefferson: Writings*, 1344-1346, and see Malone, *Sage of Monticello*, 318.

115. Jefferson to David Barrow, Monticello, 1 May 1815, *The Writings of Thomas Jefferson*, vol. 9, 516.

Chapter 4

The Tide Begins to Turn: The Virginia Constitutional Convention of 1829-1830 and the Attack on Natural Rights

> The time to guard against corruption and tyranny, is before they shall have gotten hold on us. It is better to keep the wolf out of the fold, than to trust to drawing his teeth and talons after he shall have entered.
>
> Thomas Jefferson
>
> We are preparing for war—Sharpening our swords and lances.
>
> Alexander Campbell[1]

By 1800, the effort to emancipate the slaves in Virginia received a setback. Despite St. George Tucker's pessimism after the legislature rejected his gradual emancipation plan put forth in *A Dissertation on Slavery: with a Proposal for the Gradual Abolition of it in the State of Virginia*, it did not dampen his desire to end slavery. Virginia's most prominent statesman, like Tucker, hoped that the state assembly might one day find a way to place slavery on the road to extinction. If they could not have an effect on the institution, they looked to a future generation of Virginians to take up the cause. Many attempted to do just that. In addition to sending legislative petitions to the assembly seeking to eradicate the peculiar institution, some Virginians increasingly called for a state constitutional convention. Virginia's Founders considered the original state constitution a flawed document. Both James Madison and Thomas Jefferson desired constitutional reform. Jefferson, for example, was critical of it and spent a large part of Query XIII in the *Notes on the State of Virginia* (hereafter *Notes*) criticizing it. Madison spent the 1784 session of the Virginia assembly pushing for a state constitutional convention.[2]

By the early nineteenth century, most of the emancipationist sentiment came from the western part of the state, where they also supported reapportionment (an increase in western representation in the state legislature), and more liberal suffrage. To effect changes in apportionment and suffrage, the state constitution needed modification. However, it was not just those two issues that Virginians thought needed modification. Slavery also needed to be dealt with. Eventually, a convention was called in 1829. Though the 1829-1830 constitutional convention held national interest, the Missouri question colored the slavery debate. In order to address the evolution of the slave debate, we should note the impact of the Missouri question and the response of Virginia's most prominent statesmen to that crisis.

In 1790, a majority of the nation's free blacks lived south of the Mason-Dixon Line and such was still the case in 1819. As late as 1827, there were more anti-slavery societies in the South than in the North. Even though many states in the Union were allowing manumission only through court action or special legislative enactment by the 1830s, there was evidence that, in Virginia, there was a sense that slavery would be eradicated eventually.[3] That outlook became strained, however, with the Missouri question.

The Missouri Crisis

On February 13, 1819, the House of Representatives took up bills of Missouri and Alabama to form state governments. Representative James Tallmadge, Jr., (N.Y.) moved concerning the Missouri bill that, "the further introduction of slavery or involuntary servitude be prohibited, except for the punishment of crimes, whereof the party shall be duly convicted; and that all children of slaves, born within the said state, after admission thereof into the Union, shall be free, but may be held to service until the age of twenty-five years."[4] Thus began the great controversy. The galleries filled with blacks outnumbering whites during many parts of the debate. The Tallmadge amendment proposed a version of the *post nati* plan that the state of New York had instituted in 1799: all persons born after passage of the act remained in servitude until twenty-five for women and twenty-eight for men.

The significance of his amendment shifted the authority of Congress from regulating territories to a more expansive oversight, controlling the statehood process itself. Representative Philip P. Barbour (Va) argued that Congress had the authority to prohibit slavery in the territories, but that it did not in the states. It would violate the understanding of federalism. Barbour believed that a slave Missouri would allow the slaves to be diffused over a larger expanse, and that would decrease their density, which would in part diminish the likelihood of revolt. Still, "most Southern members of Congress conceded that slavery in itself was wrong" and Representative John Tyler (Va) called it a "dark cloud."[5] Not surprisingly, Jefferson's thoughts became a focal point of the debate, as anti-slave proponents frequently quoted from his *Notes*. Those who objected to the Tallmadge amendments stated Jefferson repudiated his youthful anti-slavery opinions. A similar contention was extended to other Virginians such as George Washington and Patrick Henry. It should probably be no surprise that Jefferson became a feature of the debates since Virginia was an important and influential state and historically Jefferson was considered an ardent defender of liberty.[6]

The amendments passed the House along sectional lines. The amendments failed in the Senate as a united South voted against it. The government was therefore deadlocked over Missouri. Through the efforts of Henry Clay, Congress reached a compromise on March 3, 1820, after Maine petitioned Congress for statehood. Both states were admitted: a free Maine and a slave Missouri. The compromise was interesting in that it demonstrated a favorable opinion against slave expansion. It forever excluded slavery from the part of the Louisiana Purchase lying north of the 36° 30′.

In Virginia, there was much anti-slavery sentiment, but it was politically drowned out by the eastern section of the state, which held most of the political power. Some Virginians opposed the compromise because it did not restrict slavery enough. For example, Thomas Ritchie, editor of the *Richmond Enquirer*, wrote that slavery was an evil "we know not how to get ride of" and went on to contend that "we do not vindicate servitude; we wish no slave had touched our soil; we wish it could be exterminated."[7] The majority of the state delegation, however, supported the compromise. It left internal matters to the states and stemmed the perceived growing centralization of the federal government at the expense of state sovereignty. Jefferson and Madison were also concerned over the Missouri question. Jefferson saw the controversy not in light of protecting, or advancing, slavery, but in terms of its threat to Union. At root, both sides in the Missouri debate were using the incident as a quest for power. While Jefferson and Madison seemed to believe that Federalist opportunists were motivated by their desire for power—using the slave issue in Missouri in an attempt to divide the Republican party—John Quincy Adams blamed both sides.[8]

Jefferson had made a point to extricate himself from the burning issues of the day while he was in retirement—because he needed to attend to personal business and because of his health—but the Missouri debate brought him out of seclusion.[9] Jefferson believed that the interference in Missouri's statehood was more than just a constitutional violation and supposed that the controversy was "more ominous" than any during the time of the revolution because it would dismantle the Union.[10] Jefferson believed that such sectional antagonism would make disunion inevitable. His letter to John Holmes—one of the few Northern Representatives who did not support the Tallmadge amendments—underscores this fear:

> But this momentous question, like a fire bell in the night, awakened and filled me with terror. I considered it at once as the knell of the Union. It is husked, indeed, for the moment. But this is a reprieve only, not a final sentence. A geographical line, coinciding with a marked principle, moral and political, once conceived and held up to the angry passions of men, will never be obliterated; and every new irritation will mark it deeper and deeper.[11]

With such a friendly member of the South in Holmes, we might surmise that Jefferson would be candid. Divisions existed even on the local, state, level. The old political divisions between the powers of federal and state were not as threatening as the slave issue. In this way, such commonality united the people and the states together in a common, shared experience. However, slavery was more divisive. Similar to Washington's warning in his "Farewell Address," Jefferson lamented that sectional division could lead to disunion. Yet, his fear of disunion did not mean he abandoned his position on slavery:

> I can say, with conscious truth, that there is not a man on earth who would sacrifice more than I would to relieve us from this heavy reproach, in any *practicable* way. The cession of that kind of property, for so it is misnamed, is a bagatelle which would not cost me a second thought, if, in that way a general emancipation and *expatriation* could be effected, and gradually, and with due sacrifices I think it might be. But as it is, we have the wolf by the ears, and can neither hold him, nor safely let him go. Justice is on one scale, and self-preservation on the other.[12]

Jefferson does not view the slaves as mere property, and finds such arguments a trifle compared to the justice due to the slaves. Justice here means the slaves should be free. We should also note that the sacrifices he speaks to here are not limited to one section or another. Both the North and South presumably share the responsibility of emancipation. Still, the practicable remedy is not an easy one to effect. Any remedy ought to be prudential. Many critics suggest that at this point of the letter, Jefferson abandons his anti-slavery stance for a pro-slavery remedy: "Of one thing I am certain, that as the passage of slaves from one State to another, would not make a slave of a single human being who would not be so without it, so their diffusion over a greater surface would make them individually happier, and proportionally facilitate the accomplishment of their emancipation, by dividing the burthen on a greater number of coadjutors."[13]

According to Jefferson and Madison, diffusion would benefit the slaves and the country by encouraging emancipation.[14] Madison contended that with the trade banned, diffusion would assist in alleviating the ill-effects of slaves packed into a small geographic area. Diffusion would dilute racial anxieties. Jefferson contended that the "removal of slaves from one state to another adds no more to their numbers than their removal from one country to another, the spreading them over a larger surface adds to their happiness and renders their future emancipation more practicable."[15] In other words, diffusion would encourage abolition (this is somewhat different from Lincoln's view of the Missouri question).[16] The Missouri debate did not cause Jefferson to defend slavery, but it did cause him to change tactics in regard to ending slavery. We might argue whether his remedy given the present circumstances was prudent, but it would be incorrect, and a misrepresentation of Jefferson, to charge him with Calhounism:

> I regret that I am now to die in the belief, that the useless sacrifice of themselves by the generation of 1776, to acquire self-government and happiness to their country is to be thrown away by the unwise and the unworthy passions of their sons, and that my only consolation is to be, that I live not to weep over it. If they would but dispassionately weigh the blessings they will throw away against an abstract principle more likely to be effected by union than by scis-

sion, they would pause before they would perpetuate this act of suicide on themselves, and of treason against the hopes of the world.[17]

The Missouri question demonstrates how Jefferson became pessimistic; it awakened him as only a "fire bell" would. The rancor over the Missouri question might discourage anyone living at the time. Both sides seemed rigid in their position. Yet, both are responsible for the predicament, a problem which passions of varying degrees had blinded both sides like "quarrelling lovers": to the North for thinking that the "hideous evil" of slavery was easy to abolish, and the South for understanding the difficulty, but not aware enough of the importance of emancipation.[18] It is important to note that Jefferson thought the fulfillment of the "abstract principle" that "all men are created equal" is "more likely to be realized" in the Union. Emancipation of the slaves is more assured with the Union intact. America was founded in direct opposition to "accident and force" and there was not only the hope that self-government would be successful, but that slavery would end.[19] The Founding under the laws of nature and nature's God challenged the politics of chance and war, thus bringing together a people in a common bond which despised distinctions based on ethnicity and race. If slavery were to end in the modern world, the Union—founded on the natural rights of man—was the best hope where that would be accomplished.

As a legal matter, Jefferson and Madison believed that the Tallmadge amendments were unconstitutional. Congress attempted to extend its power too broadly; they placed on Missouri requirements they did not when she was a territory. In this way, the national government was doing something it had not done with the Ordinances. Missouri was a part of the Louisiana Purchase territory and under the treaty of 1803 slavery was allowed to exist. Constitutionally speaking, "if Congress has a power to regulate the conditions of the inhabitants of the states, within the states, it will be but another exercise of that power to declare that all shall be free."[20] Madison's problem with the Talamadge amendments is that, if passed, it fomented lawlessness in general. The people had not consented that slavery might be regulated in the states. If such regulation were allowed, it would represent an usurpation of powers, and, in principle, would have "defeated the end of human freedom" and perhaps enslaved free men.[21] This lawlessness would terminate the Union. If the Congress could take the slave property of another, then they could take *any* property in theory. This is why Jefferson would write to Albert Gallatin, and others, that the issue was really one of power, and that for many in the South it was "a question of existence."[22] It is not the mere emancipation that Jefferson feared, but the ability of the federal government to regulate every internal matter of the states. This the Constitution forbids: to act against slavery in the states where it existed would have been to act unconstitutionally. If the Congress succeeded, they could reach into the states to regulate anything. A sectional war would result. Furthermore, if they freed the slaves, Jefferson feared slave violence. This fear was real and the reason why most of the Founders supported colonization.

Similarly, Madison, the father of the Constitution, contended that "the great object of the convention seemed to prohibit the increase by the *importation* of slaves. A power to emancipate the slaves was disclaimed."[23] Madison was not speaking in terms of the justice of slavery, but the legal construction of the Union. As it pertains to Article Five of the Constitution, Congress could only abolish the importation of slaves. There is no authority for Congress to prohibit the migration of slaves already in the U.S. He also seemed to question the authority of Congress to ban slavery in the territories.[24] Nevertheless, the territorial ban was necessary, for when it was passed the importation of slaves continued. The only way to limit the effect of slavery was to prohibit it in the territories. Still, Congress had no constitutional authority to regulate slavery in the states.

The Constitution, or rule of law, was being undermined by a "state of parties" founded on "geographical boundaries."[25] Perhaps in an effort to influence the executive decision in these matters, he wrote fellow Virginian, and then President, Monroe, that Congress did not have the constitutional authority and in the same letter made the case for diffusion in its facilitation of emancipation.[26] Madison essentially conveyed to Monroe that if the Congress could meddle in the state of Missouri, it could meddle in the affairs of Virginia. Despite the constitutional argument, Madison in no way supported the expansion of slavery in order to solidify its existence. He wanted to end it. Like Jefferson, he worried about disunion. Allowing Missouri to enter a slave state made practical sense.

It was not just enough to ban slavery. That was a shortsighted goal. Madison supported colonization—he was a lifelong member of the American Colonization Society—because of the racial prejudices that existed. Madison believed that colonization could be secured with the sale of public lands. Like Jefferson, Madison did not believe that blacks were inferior, but he worried that they would become a "permanent underclass" if they remained.[27] Whilst the Missouri debate raged, in a letter to Robert Evans, he outlined his thoughts on how "a general emancipation ought to be (1) gradual. (2) equitable and satisfactory to the individuals immediately concerned. (3) consistent with the existing and durable prejudices of the nation."[28] Gradual emancipation was considered the best practical means because of the sheer magnitude of endeavor: the slaves needed to be enlightened for freedom and the South needed to change its economic practices. Masters also needed compensation for the emancipation of the slaves. Compensated emancipation would entice or provide incentive for the master to forego the institution. Such a large social goal would take millions of dollars, and much time, to effect. Emancipation also needed to be gradual, not immediate, because of the great prejudices harbored by both masters and slaves. Because of the recollections of the former slaves, there would be "reciprocal antipathies" and "double the danger" of violence. Therefore, colonization was needed and it "merits encouragement from all who regard slavery as an evil, who wish to see it diminished and abolished by peaceable & just means; and who have themselves no better mode to propose. Those who have most doubted the success of the experiment must at least have wished to find themselves in an error." Again, the remedy is a difficult and burdensome one:

The magnitude of this evil among us is so deeply felt, and so universally acknowledged, that no merit could be greater than that of devising a satisfactory
remedy for it. Unfortunately the task, not easy under any other circumstances,
is vastly augmented by the physical peculiarities of those held in bondage,
which preclude their incorporation with the white population; and by the blank
in the general field of labour to be occasioned by their exile; a blank into which
there would not be an influx of white labourers, successively taking the place of
the exiles, and which, without such an influx, would have an effect distressing
in prospect to the proprietors of the soil.[29]

According to Madison, since the nation would reap benefit of abolition, the nation would have to "bear the burden" or the cost, of emancipation. Indeed, he
believed that abolishing slavery would benefit all of humanity and therefore
needed to be shared equally. Madison did not believe this process would be
easy. Just how we might achieve the consent of the master and slaves for emancipation, would be the fruit of "mature deliberations of the National Councils."[30]
    The question was never if, but when and how, emancipation might be
brought to fruition. Slaves were, like all men, human beings and the institution
was an embarrassment: "Negro slavery is, as you justly complain, a sad blot on
our free country, though a very ungracious subject of reproaches from the quarter which has been most lavish of them. No satisfactory plan has yet been de-
vised for taking out the stain."[31] Near the conclusion of the Missouri crisis, Jefferson recovered some of his optimism and predicted that liberty would succeed
in the Union as in Europe: "The boisterous sea of liberty indeed is never without
a wave, and that from Missouri is now rolling towards us, but we shall ride over
it as we have all others."[32] Diffusion would thus be a boon to liberty because it
would facilitate emancipation. Despite the Federalist Party trying to use slavery
as a wedge issue to divide the Republican party in hopes of reclaiming their majority status, Jefferson believed that the passions would subside and that they
would "return to the embraces of their natural and best friends."[33]
    Ultimately, the Missouri controversy did not move the South toward a Cal-
hounian position. Historian William Freehling believes that it is a "myth" that
Virginians "repudiated old apologetics" of their past and moved toward perpetuation of slavery; Calhoun wanted to expand slavery to expand it, Jefferson
wanted to diffuse it to end it.[34] Speaking of Jefferson, historian Peter Onuf concluded the "response to the Missouri crisis did not mean he had abandoned his
lifelong opposition to slavery. The central issue . . . was the nature of the union
itself, and the equal rights of member states—Virginia as well as Missouri—to
draft their own constitutions and then govern themselves without outside interference."[35] The Union was becoming more sectional, to be sure, but the public
rhetoric over slavery was not one of overarching acceptance of the institution.
Between 1784 and 1821, the Southern position was fairly consistent: they admitted the evil of slavery but feared slave retaliation if they were freed. Until such a
time that colonization could be enacted, diffusion would dilute the concentration
on the seaboard states ameliorating the slaves' condition while reducing the
danger of rebellion. We must recall that after Missouri, Jefferson wrote to *North*

American Review owner and editor, Jared Sparks, after the Missouri Crisis that "nothing is more certainly written in the book of fate than that these people are to be free."[36] In the same letter, he reiterated a colonization scheme where the slaves would be bought from their "owners" and shipped to Santo Domingo, which had offered to bear the cost of passage. In addition to the compensated emancipation scheme, Jefferson also supported a federally financed colonization plan.

While in retrospect Madison and Jefferson may not have furthered the cause of emancipation by siding with the so called pro-slave Missourians, the decision to support diffusion was a matter of prudence in light of principle. However, it was not that Jefferson and Madison believed that Missouri *must* enter as a slave state. They thought that Missouri should determine for herself whether it enter as a free or slave state.[37] Though they may have supported diffusion, the ultimate decision, constitutionally speaking, was up to Missourians.

Despite the obstacles to emancipation presented by the concerns over Missouri, it did not preclude Virginians from trying to effect some plan. In the shadow of Missouri, in December of 1820, Governor Thomas Mann Randolph (Jefferson's son-in-law) proposed an emancipation plan to the legislature of his state. His proposal included a clause that would have deported all freed slaves to Santo Domingo. Randolph condemned the institution in strong terms, disapproving of "the new morality which tolerates perpetuity of slavery, and the new doctrine of civil benefits supposed to be derived from that system."[38] Despite his failure to secure passage of the proposal, he was re-elected governor of Virginia two years later. The Missouri crisis revealed a national geographic division, North and South; the Virginia constitutional convention would reveal a state geographic division, east and west.

After Missouri and Toward the Convention

Between 1824-1825 nine Northern states followed the lead of Ohio and passed resolutions endorsing federal emancipation and colonization. Copies of the resolution were distributed to every state legislature and the representatives in Congress. The resolution did not condemn the South, but claimed that slavery was an evil. It encouraged the people of the Union to band together and mutually participate in the burdens to remove it. While some southern states (Georgia) crafted a counter resolution claiming that the anti-slavery resolution was an attack on the constitutional rights of the southern states, Virginia refused to participate. Old Dominion opposed *mandated* abolition and removal, yet looked forward to emancipation. According to historian Glover Moore, the southern position from 1784-1821 could be summarized:

> We admit that slavery is an evil of great magnitude, but the slaves might cut our throats if set at liberty. We dare not free them now, though we hope that eventually emancipation and colonization will be possible. In the meantime, slaves are property, and it would be unfair to the owners to exclude them from the west. If they remain concentrated in a few seaboard states, it will be

necessary to keep them under tight police control to prevent rebellion. Scattering them over the western country will ameliorate their condition and reduce the danger to the whites in the older states.[39]

The general hostility to the slave institution would begin to undergo a change in the Virginia Constitutional Convention of 1829-1830. The reason that slavery was considered an evil was because there was a belief in the natural equality of men. In the convention, this belief would come under attack in a most peculiar way.

In the *Notes*, Jefferson expressed his dissatisfaction with the 1776 Virginia Constitution. He thought that the constitution carried too much over from the colonial period and, in essence, was not genuinely republican. Of the several reforms he proposed, the issue of unequal representation in the state legislature was particularly bothersome to Virginians in the western portion of the state. They had long believed that the eastern, slave-holding plantation interest, controlled too much of Old Dominion's politics. Jefferson noted this problem in an 1816 letter to Samuel Kercheval: "But inequality of representation in both Houses of our legislature, is not the only republican heresy in this first essay of our Revolutionary patriots at forming a Constitution. For let it be agreed that a government is republican in proportion as every member composing it has equal voice in the direction of its concerns . . . "[40] Jefferson went on to lament that in the state of Virginia, less than half of the people were allowed to vote and that the unequal representation could cause Old Dominion to suffer from bad, or despotic, government. A portion of that potential despotism would be the unwavering attachment to slavery. Jefferson referred to his gradual emancipation proposal many times in his personal correspondence. He defended this proposal, which originally appeared in his *Notes*, as the best possible means to end the peculiar institution.[41] In his letter to Samuel Kercheval, he also supported two issues that would become a point of contention in the convention: equal representation in the legislature, and the enfranchisement of all who paid taxes or served in the military.

Jefferson was an authority for many who wished a constitutional convention. In Query XIII, he urged a convention be called to remedy a "perilous" situation and to "bind up the several branches of government by certain laws" in order to better secure the "rights" of the people.[42] Coupled with the poor representation, Jefferson thought that the constitution paid too little attention to the separation of powers: "173 despots would surely be as oppressive as one . . . An elective despotism was not the government we fought for."[43] The powers should be so divided as to not only represent, but balance the varied interests in the state. This way, each interest would be able to check and restrain the other while coincidentally not tyrannizing over each other. Part of the problem in Virginia was that wealth dominated the legislature and, assembly was too homogenous. According to Jefferson, the "true foundation of Republican Government is the equal right of every citizen, in his person and property, and in their management."[44] His understanding of who should have the right to vote for the lower house was broad indeed: "Whoever tends to live in a country must wish that country well, and has a natural right of assisting in the preservation of it."[45] Homogeneity coupled with the fact that the wealthy controlled state politics made Jefferson doubt the common good could be secured in the state. Madison generally concurred and urged the general assembly to call a constitutional convention. In his personal notes, as he prepared for a series of essays in the *National Gazette*, he wrote: "The Southern States of America, are on the same principle aristocracies. In Virginia, the aristocratic character is increased by the rule of suffrage, which requiring a freehold in land excludes nearly half the free inhabitants, and must exclude a greater proportion, as the population increases." And this problem is linked to the slave problem: "In proportion as slavery prevails in a State, the Government, however, democratic in name, must be aristocratic in fact. The power lies in a part instead of the whole; in the hands of property, not of numbers. All antient popular governments, were for this reason aristocracies. The majority were slaves."[46] For Madison, the suffrage/representation issue and the slavery issue were related. No less than a constitutional convention could take care of all of them.

Several attempts were made to revise the Virginia constitution. As it relates to the convention of 1829-1830, two events stand out. In 1816, the people of the western half of Virginia held a convention in the city of Staunton to inform the general assembly of their desire for a statewide constitutional convention. Their aim was to eliminate the freehold requirement as well as equalize representation. In 1824, Jefferson wrote a letter to the *Richmond Enquirer* in which he publicly announced his support for a constitutional convention: "The basis of our constitution is in opposition to the principle of equal political rights, refusing to all but freeholders any participation on the rights of self-government. The exclusion of the majority of free men from the right of representation is merely arbitrary and an assumption of the minority over the majority."[47] His support for a convention inspired many. In order to pressure the assembly to call a convention, a second, larger, convention in Staunton was held in 1825. Thirty-five counties were represented at this meeting. This convention also called for apportionment based on the white population and for white manhood suffrage. Petitions flowed into Richmond and twenty-eight counties passed referenda instructing their representatives to support a call for a convention. However, some believed that the Staunton conventions really had the object of inducing the gradual abolition of slavery in the state and they accused those efforts as "preaching anarchy and disunion."[48] Though both the 1816 and 1825 conventions failed immediately to achieve their objective, they went a long way to garnering public support for a convention.

Some believe that the constitutional convention was not really about slavery, but merely about suffrage and representation.[49] There is some merit to that argument. The suffrage requirement was fifty acres, and by 1830 that disenfranchised about one-half of the adult white male population. Furthermore, the House had a disproportionate balance favoring the east.[50] The Tidewater and Piedmont region had almost no population growth in the nineteenth century while the area west of the Blue Ridge Mountains increased by 500 percent between 1790 and 1830. The 1815-1816 House had seventy-five Tidewater, fifty-eight Piedmont, twenty-four Valley, and forty-two Trans-Allegheny delegates (for a total of one hundred thirty-three delegates east of the Blue Ridge Mountains). If the same House had been apportioned based on the 1810 census, the apportionment would have been much different: fifty-six Tidewater, sixty-eight Piedmont, thirty-eight Valley, and thirty-seven Trans-Allegheny delegates (for a total of one hundred twenty-four delegates east of the Blue Ridge Mountains). In the meantime, the western portion of the state attracted more whites than the east. In the Trans-Allegheny, the percentage of the white population in the state grew from 7 percent in 1790 to 26 in 1830. By 1830, the land east of the Blue Ridge had a white population of 375,657, and west of the Blue Ridge the white population was 318,645. Between 1820-1829 the east population grew by 2 percent while the west grew by over 36 percent. The eastern part of the state thus represented less people but had greater numbers of the assembly. In the west, the reverse was true. In the Senate, four senators represented 212,036 people in the west, and thirteen senators represented 162,717 people in the east or Tidewater region. Absent reapportionment (or the creation of more counties west of the Blue Ridge), the eastern section of the state would continue to dominate state politics.[51] We should note, however, that the Tidewater and Piedmont had the greatest slave population and hence the most slave plantations.

Some scholars have noticed that the convention represented more than just a political power struggle over representation and suffrage: "beneath the conflicts over representation, and suffrage, lay the contention over the future of slavery" which was the motivation for an ever widening breach.[52] Slavery was an underlying issue because slave owners feared that if the constitution were ratified under a new representation and suffrage scheme, westerners would use their newfound power to emancipate the slaves at the expense of the slaveholders. This is probably why the first stages of the debate were almost exclusively a discussion about natural rights. Historian Charles Ambler contended that, "all realized that slavery was at the bottom of the difference between eastern and western Virginia and that inaction on the subject meant dismemberment of the commonwealth, if not immediately, certainly in the future."[53]

The political pressure was so great on the state assembly in Richmond that the House of Delegates and Senate eventually conceded to a popular referendum on the convention for the April 1828 elections. Only those qualified to vote under the existing laws were eligible. The referendum passed with 21,896 in favor and 16,646 opposed. Delegates were chosen from the twenty-four senatorial districts. Each district was able to elect four representatives. The record of these debates is unmatched in quality. Of all the state conventions on record Merrill D. Peterson claims, "that of the Virginia convention is unquestionably the fullest and the best. Thomas Ritchie, editor of the *Richmond Enquirer*, employed Arthur Stansbury to report the debates. Because Stansbury was both skilled in shorthand and experienced in legislative proceedings, as a recorder of Congressional debates, he was able to offer a superb stenographic transcription of everything said and done in the convention."[54] Many of the speeches were published in Ritchie's paper. Longer speeches were printed in a book, which exceeded nine hundred pages, shortly thereafter.

The convention had many notable men elected to serve in it. There were two ex-presidents (James Madison and James Monroe), a future president (John Tyler), Chief Justice John Marshall, several who were, or had been, U.S. Senators, and many who were members of Congress. The men in attendance commanded national attention in part because Virginia influenced the Union. There was never another time when a state constitutional convention sported such august talent, making it the "last of the great constituent assemblies in American history."[55] Spectators of the debates included Vice-president John C. Calhoun, and Secretary of State Martin van Buren. The importance of the convention prompted *Richmond Enquirer* editor Thomas Ritchie to write, "the eyes of the world are upon us."[56] In addition to these more prominent spectators, citizens packed the halls and galleries of the convention's meeting place to listen to America's prominent orators deliberate. It attracted visitors from many other states as well, hoping to catch a glimpse of the many luminaries and illustrious Virginians present in the hall below. Put simply, there was much interest in the debate. For approximately three months, the state capital that Jefferson designed was the scene of a deliberation on the nature of man and the theory and practice of government.

The Constitutional Convention of 1829-1830

The convention's ninety-six members assembled on October 5, 1829. Monroe presided as chair of the convention and cautioned those in attendance of the task before them: "All other republics have failed. Those of Rome and Greece exist only in History. In the territories which they ruled, we see the ruins of ancient buildings only; the Governments have perished, and the inhabitants exhibit a state of decrepitude and wretchedness, which is frightful to those who visit them."[57] Republics do not have a glorious history. We might surmise that Monroe understood that if the Union would persevere, it would depend on whether the conventioneers adhered to the principles of republicanism. One of the first acts of the convention was the motion by William H. Brodnax (Dinwiddie) to have the Declaration of Rights and the Constitution printed for all members so it could be readily consulted. While the first few days were occupied with these internal matters and minor sparring, the impetus leading to a full debate of the rights of man came on October 13.

Chief Justice John Marshall (Richmond) read into the record a memorial from non-freeholders of Richmond seeking an extension of suffrage. The petitioners appealed to the Virginia Declaration's claim that the basis, or foundation, of government is "that all men are by nature equally free and independent."[58] Invoking Jefferson, the memorialists asserted that "the venerated author of the Declaration of Independence, and the Act of Religious Freedom" articulate the best guide to the practical application of the equal rights all men possess. Not only Jefferson's "great name," but "reason and justice equally condemn" the exclusion of some members of the community simply because they do not own a certain amount of land or wealth. The petitioners appealed to certain passages in the Declaration of Rights to support their position:

> That all power is vested in, and consequently derived from, the people.
> That a majority of the community hath an indubitable, unalienable, and indefeasible right to reform, alter or abolish the Government
> That no man nor set of men, are entitled to exclusive or separate emoluments or privileges, but in consideration of public services.
> That all men, having sufficient evidence of permanent common interest with, and attachment to, the community, have a right of suffrage, and cannot be taxed, or deprived of their property without their consent, or that of their representative, nor bound by any law, to which they have not, in like manner assented, for the public good.

If it is true that all power is vested in the people, the petitioners claimed they ought not to be denied the civil right to vote. They appealed to the "venerated author of the Declaration of Independence" whereby "if we are sincerely republican, we must give our confidence to the principles we profess." They thus asserted that the civil voting right is based on something higher than mere law: "to give all power, or an undue share, to one, is obviously not to remedy but to ensure the evil. Its safest check, its best corrective, is found in a general admission of all upon a footing of equality." If suffrage did not come from some idea of the natural equality of man, for example, then the vote some enjoy is based on either power of the stronger, or "a favored class." They believed that distinction is "odious."

Near the conclusion, the memorialists closed their petition with an appeal to the Founding. The Revolution was justified by the assertion of an abstract right condemning taxation without representation. The basis of the Revolution was the affirmation of those rights found in nature. It was not, according to the memorialists, the simple taxation of property that caused the war. They asserted that since all men are created equal, it did not forbid the extension of suffrage. Broadening suffrage would ensure a greater protection of those rights. If suffrage was not extended to other members of the community, then those without the vote would be less secure in their rights (their property) because they did not have the means to defend themselves politically—to vote for or elect representatives who shared their sentiments. Those who had the right of suffrage possessed a great power over those who did not.

While the particular debate over suffrage and its extension is not the purpose of this chapter, the memorial was a loadstar for a deeper debate over the meaning of natural rights and if those rights ought to be a guide for practical politics. More importantly, the memorial plunged the body into an acrimonious debate over whether such rights in fact did exist. Marshall thought the petition ought to be considered because "the subject was one of the deepest interest" and demanded the "serious attention of this body." The petition from Richmond led Charles F. Mercer (Loudoun), William Anderson (Shenandoah), and Peachy Harrison (Rockingham) to introduce similar petitions. There was no formal floor debate over the subject matter of the petitions until much later, when, on October 19, the committee on the Declaration of Rights reported that the august document needed no amendment, and several resolutions followed stating that the body should extend suffrage and reapportion representation. The great debate over the broadening of suffrage and representation based on the natural rights of men thus commenced.

This debate generally split the convention into two camps. The first are the reformers (most of whom were representatives west of the Blue Ridge Mountains), and they looked first to the Declaration of Rights (and Declaration of Independence) to justify their positions. They believed that suffrage ought to be extended as an application of the Declaration of Rights' assertion that all men are by nature free and independent. At one point in the debate, one such reformer, Alexander Campbell (Brooke) resolved that all free white males twenty-three years of age and born within the Commonwealth had sufficient common interest, and attachment to, the community to have the vote extended to them. Additionally, reformers desired to see representation, at least for the House, based on the white population. That position was called the "white basis."[59] Reformers objected to the current apportionment of the general assembly because it was a holdover from the colonial days when the Tidewater region was virtually the only settled area of the state.

The other camp in the convention may be called conservative (representing the Piedmont and Tidewater regions east of the Blue Ridge Mountains). They objected to any change in the suffrage or freehold requirements for voting and they baulked at reapportionment. Those conservatives who accepted reapportionment wanted it linked to the federal numbers, or three-fifths clause of the Constitution, because counting the slaves would have politically favored the eastern slaveholding part of the state. Furthermore, they believed that the Declaration of Rights was not as instrumental as the remainder of the state constitution. In particular, they thought that adherence to natural rights would upset the tranquility of the state and adversely affect their ability to keep hold of their slaves. Because some reform members supported the federal numbers and some conservatives accepted reapportionment and/or broader suffrage, perhaps more correct division would look like this: on the one side, were those who believed in the rights of man and thought that they ought to be a guide to the conventioneers, and on the other side, were those who rejected those rights and thought they were not of any tangible use. Generally speaking, reformers fall into the former, while conservatives fall into the latter.

Robert B. Taylor (Norfolk) defended his own resolutions of October 23 in which he resolved that the elective franchise should be uniform, and that there should be universal white suffrage. He asserted that the imbalance in representation and suffrage embodied a violation of the principles of equality:

> There are some truths so simple and self-evident that their most perfect demonstration is furnished by the terms of the proposition itself. Axioms, or self-evident truths, carry conviction to the human mind, the moment they are announced. And it may be safely affirmed of all propositions which the wit of man can suggest, that the probability of their truth, is in an inverse ratio, to the reasoning and proof required to sustain them. Just in proportion as any affirmation approaches the axiomatic character, in that same degree is the range of argument in its support, limited and restrained. If the resolutions I have submitted have any merit, it lies in this solely: the principles they contain are so evident and obvious, that they neither require nor admit of argument to sustain them.[60]

That all men are created equal is a self-evident truth. The justification for extending suffrage on that ground might need explanation, but the equality of man does not. Whoever understands what a human is understands all men are created equal. Free representative governments reside in the recognition of that political truth. Republican government, or a representative republic, reposes sovereignty in the people. Therefore, the participation of the people in the elective franchise is "essential." If men are equal, and by their consent political liberty is more secure, then the elective franchise should be as liberal as circumstances will permit. It would follow that representation should be apportioned to reflect the population movements in the state—as in where there is more population so should there be more representation than in less populated areas. Broader suffrage and equal representation is but a practical application of "all men are created equal." Taylor's appeal to the Declaration of Independence and the Declaration of Rights drew several criticisms.

Philip N. Nicholas (Richmond) replied that the abstract principles could not be applied without regard to actual circumstances. Though he contended that there were some principles he might agree, ultimately there was no such thing as an abstract truth in politics. Nicholas believed that experience, or political realities, outweigh an adherence to abstract principles. Taylor believed that Nicholas's speech amounted to a devaluing of the self-evident truths stated in the Declaration of Rights:

> What was the Bill of Rights? It was to settle the very abstractions, to which the gentleman seemed so averse; to settle principles; to set up certain landmarks for the framing of a Constitution. It prescribed the general rules which it was the purpose of the Constitution to develop and expand. Its use was to familiarize the people to a consideration of these great principles of free Government, and thereby to control the action of the Legislature.[61]

Virginia's Declaration, then, provided the basis for setting up good government and for judging the actions of government. For the conventioneers, it supplied a set of guidelines, which statesmen could use to craft a more just constitution:

If the principles he had brought forward were right in themselves, and worthy
of adoption in any form, it should be in the Bill of Rights. Let them stand there
as touch-stones, to try with what fidelity the Constitution should be drawn, and
the legislation of the State carried on under it. Gentlemen object to abstractions:
the Bill of Rights declares all men to be born by nature, free and equal. Does
the gentleman call that an abstraction?[62]

Taylor further argued that the equality of man did not remain in the state of
nature, but man carried that inherent equality with him into society. In other
words, if there was a degradation of man's status in society, it was not because
he somehow became unequal, but because of positive law. Conservatives
objected to this understanding. Benjamin Watkins Leigh (Chesterfield), for
example, attacked Nicholas's argument and the idea of abstract rights by
emphasizing political realities.

Leigh assailed broader suffrage and reapportionment because it would
commit the balance of power into different hands. This new division of power
would have an unsettling effect on state politics; it would make society unstable
and the source of that instability was the attachment to universals. He declared
that the attachment to natural rights was a novel idea: "such principles were
unknown to our English ancestors, from whom we have derived our institutions;
better than the rights of man as held in the French school."[63] The concept of
rights, he explained, is a French idea. In other words, history demonstrated that
government based on natural rights leads to "rapine, anarchy and bloodshed, and
in the end, to military despotism." Leigh is the first conventioneer to articulate a
comprehensive argument that the American Founding had little to do with
natural rights. He asserted that the Revolution was a culmination of experience,
an organic evolution: "the free spirit of the Saxon laws, mingling with the
sterner spirit of the feudal system, had decreed that property was sacred."[64]
Government's most important job is to secure property. The revolution occurred
because the British failed to abide by the lamp of experience, that which
worked, or history. They tried to assert their control over property that was not
theirs and to which the owner had not, and could not, consent. The revolution
was not an assertion of right, but came about because Britain tried to seize
property via taxation and without the consent of the owners of that property.
Toward that end, the American Constitution and the Virginia Constitution are an
organic expression because they grew out of experience.

The American system of government is really an imitation of the practical
British system—it is not really a new system of government.[65] According to
Leigh, despite the conflict with Britain, the mother country invented and
perfected representative government. Despite the war, England was, until that
time, more free than any other government in history. Though not perfect,
England secured property through the rule of law and was the foundation of
American rights. Leigh thus exclaimed, "give me liberty in the English sense—
liberty founded on law, and protected by law . . . no liberty for me to prey on
others—no liberty for others to prey on me. I want no French liberty—none."
Certainly, Jefferson, and the reformers, did not characterize the war that way.

Jefferson thought that slavery was a greater evil than, say, the slavery presented by the tax on tea, and the Founding was anything but an organic evolution:

> But with respect to our rights, and the acts of the British government contravening those rights, there was but one opinion on this side of the water. All American whigs thought alike on these subjects. When forced, therefore, to resort to arms for redress, an appeal to the tribunal of the world was deemed proper for our justification. This was the object of the Declaration of Independence. Not to find out any new principles, or new arguments, never before thought of . . . but to place before mankind the common sense of the subject in terms so plain and firm as to command their assent . . . All its authority rests then on the harmonizing sentiments of the day, whether expressed in conversation, in letters, printed essays, or in the elementary books of public right, as Aristotle, Cicero, Locke, Sidney, &c.[66]

It seems that, in Jefferson's mind at the least, the American Founding—as represented in the Declaration of Independence—was based on man's inalienable natural rights. The Founding was thus not an organic development, but rested on "harmonizing sentiments" that assented to "convictions that were profoundly American, while peculiarly and profoundly representative of a natural law tradition."[67] Tidewater conservatives like Leigh had forgotten that Britain also had a rich heritage of natural rights philosophy. Part of the ancestral inheritance from the United Kingdom was an attachment to natural rights, of which Locke and Sydney are representative. They criticized the "slavish doctrine of *jus divinium* of kings."[68] It is not mere heritage, then, but a heritage that is good which is worth preserving.

Leigh then made a most serious attack on natural rights: "Give us something which we may at least call reasons for it: not arithmetical and mathematical reasons; no mere abstractions; but referring to the actual state of things as they are; to the circumstances and condition of this Commonwealth."[69] He asserted that the platitudes in the Declaration of Independence were "mere abstractions." These abstractions are not worthy of consideration because they cannot be verified. We might say that Leigh wanted Taylor to justify his opinions on facts, not values. Leigh's apparent contempt for natural rights did much to draw the reformers into the debate; for without the laws of nature and nature's God, nobody would be secure. Politics would become the will of the stronger. According to the reformers, a government based on will is arbitrary.

John R. Cooke (Frederick) was astonished by Leigh's speech. The gentleman from Chesterfield asserted the Declaration of Rights was "wild and visionary" and Cooke thought that represented a direct attack on Virginia's Founding and the American Founding. The founding documents iterated "sacred truths" that were received by the "genius of Locke and Sydney."[70] The "deliberate sanction of the most enlightened friends of liberty" were "fathers of the Revolution" who risked their lives and their fortunes for those sacred principles: "And for what did they make these mighty sacrifices! For Wild 'abstractions, and metaphysical subtleties!' No, Sir. For principles of eternal truth; as practical, in character, as they are vital, in importance; for principles deep-seated in the nature of man, by whose development, alone, he can attain the happiness which is the great object of his being."[71] Cooke asserted that far from the wild and visionary speculations, the equality of man was "a compendium of the whole law of rational and practical liberty." It was a "primary postulate of the science of government" and means that "no *one* man is born with a natural right to control any *other* man; that no one comes into the world with a mark on him, to designate him as possessing superior rights to any other man." Nature had not marked some men for slavery and others for rule. Any rule or law that subjects one man to another is an "artificial distinction" and is the result of "fraud or violence." In this way, Cooke implicitly condemned the entire slavocracy. The language of the Declaration of Rights pointed to the fact that the slaves were not inherently inferior to anyone else and that their subjugation was artificial. In tones harking back to Jefferson's *Summary*, Cooke contended that in principle, the universal sense of the equality of men in practical application is that those of "mature reason" and who are "free agents . . . [are] *equally* entitled to the exercise of political power."

Drawing from Query XIII of Jefferson's *Notes*, Cooke contended that the Virginia constitution needed reform. The author of great abstract principles thought that the Constitution was unsuitable. The circumstance in which the Constitution was crafted was not conducive to mild deliberation: "True it is, this is no time for deliberating on forms of government. While an enemy is within our bowles, the first object is to expel him. But when this shall be done, when peace shall be established, and leisure given us for intrenching good forms, the rights for which we have bled, let no man be found indolent enough to decline a little more trouble for placing them beyond the reach of question."[72] Because of the impending war, Virginia's statesmen could not have crafted a constitution as perfectly as they might have wished. It was impossible under the circumstances to erect a new government under such duress. That is why Jefferson often appealed to the rights of man as a guide to the reformation of the Virginia Constitution, and why he believed the initial constitution did not go far enough in the protection of "rights" for which the colonists had "bled." Still, even though Virginia's Founders did not establish the republican constitution they wanted, they were able to articulate the principles upon which the initial constitution, and all subsequent reforms to that document, should be derived. Therefore, the Virginia constitution is not sufficiently republican because it gives "to the few who are rich, a control over the many who are poor."[73] In other words, Virginia has features of an oligarchy. A majority of the populace is excluded from participating in any level of state politics because of their lack of wealth and that jeopardizes not only the property and safety of the many, but also their happiness.

The conservatives rejected that. Far from speculative theories is man as he *is*. Philip P. Barbour (Orange) iterated that to proceed on how men ought to be is fantasy: "we must discard mere theory, adopt nothing on the ground of mere speculation, but proceed to men and things as they are."[74] Indeed, Governor

William B. Giles (Amelia) stated that, "slaves are born slaves before us every day" that "disproves" the assertion that "all men are *born* free and equal."[75] The Declaration of Independence, then, was a diplomatic document more than a statement of non-arbitrary truth applicable to all men at all times. Giles would go on to state that slavery was acknowledged by the law of God and hence supersedes the law of nature. Another grand orator, John Randolph (Charlotte), cleverly agreed with every word of the Declaration of Rights, but that "the Bill of Rights contains unmodified principles" that need modification in reality.[76] Randolph asserted that the argument in the convention seemed similar to the one during the Missouri debate. The claims of those who began from a natural rights basis were making "monstrous claims to power" in the name of majority rule, or as he liked to say, "king numbers."

The conservatives feared a majority in numbers in part because of their impression of the nature of man. Conservatives viewed human nature very dimly. John Scott (Fauquier) voiced the conservative fear most bluntly. He stated that man is a passionate being and derives this passion from his "self-love."[77] He is jealous and filled with "ambition and avarice." If left to himself, man would be a thief. Without a government to moderate, or check, those passions the consequences to freedom would be dire as the "dark shades of the human character" would be rendered more "visible." To give the many the authority to participate in state politics would ravage the wealthy as the poor follow their passions to seek higher taxes on the rich. In other words, the west had numbers, or a majority, and the east had property that the west valued. Summoning Edmund Burke, Randolph contended that the strict application of natural right must be modified: "But I hold with one of the greatest masters of political philosophy, that 'no rational man ever did govern himself by abstractions and universals.'"[78] Reality must govern the view of man more, and government is necessary to provide restraints on man's passionate nature. A politics based on numbers would thus spell the ruin of the wealthy property-owning minority. If men were indeed selfish, passionate beings, then that could be harnessed by directing that interest into one's own property. If the selfish interest of an individual could be focused on their own property—the most sure foundation of society—then self-interest could be converted into the interests of the whole community. Hence, people will not harm the community because they are rooted to their property. They would be more frugal in terms of taxation than if they did not own property. Ownership of property demonstrates a community interest.

Leigh linked the debate over slavery between the east and west of the state with the same that afflicts the Union, North and South. The motivating factor is self-love. The reason that the west will take the property of the east is because all men are selfish. Self-love prompted the French to assist the Revolutionaries in the war, self-love divides the North from the South, and self-love divides the convention in Richmond. Therefore, nobody is objective enough to be trusted with the control over another's property. At best, those who articulate their position from the standpoint of natural rights have deluded themselves into believing that society writ large is virtuous. Men cannot ever be virtuous since all men are easily corrupted. Since, in reality, all men are contending for power out of their self-love, it means that the only way the slaves may be emancipated, would come from the private actions of the various slaveholders. If all men are truly self-interested, the individual person is the best judge of the means of his property.

In contrast, Cooke held that the slaveholder's view represented an incomplete view of man. Man is a "compound creature" who is not only capable of much evil, but much good.[79] Man may be passionate, but he is not *only* passionate; he also has the capability to reason. Nevertheless, if the conservatives are correct—that man is greedy and that the majority would violate the property rights of the minority—then they are caught by their own argument:

> Does it follow that the aspirants after the enjoyments that property confers, will seek to attain their object in the manner which the argument in question supposes? If it be contended that man is [a] greedy and avaricious, it will, still, not be denied, that he is a reasoning and calculating animal. When he desires to *attain* property it is in order that he may *possess and enjoy it*. But if he join in establishing the rule that the right of the strongest is the best right, what security has he, in his turn, will not soon be deprived of his property by some one stronger than himself?[80]

The conservative position is that there is no such thing as abstract rights, or if there is such a thing, it is not prudent to base a government on it. Cooke continued, if the pro-slave advocates reject a law of nature, they make an appeal to power and must submit, to be consistent, to the power of the majority, which is truly the stronger. It is also fathomable, in theory, that an individual who is stronger could dispossess an original owner of his land. Nevertheless, even though man is affected by his passions, he is equally a reasonable being and that reason may be cultivated or enlightened.

Taking a page from Aristotle's *Politics* and *Nicomachean Ethics*, Cooke asserts that all men are political animals and that his reason may moderate his passions. The political nature of man is implanted in *all* human beings. All men govern themselves by some belief in universals about what they think is good. The slave-owner, then, is also influenced by his own ideas or abstract notions.[81] The most important thing is to reason rightly. It establishes habits in him that are more virtuous. He concludes from this that man's political nature makes him "an *affectionate*, a *social*, a *patriotic*, a *conscientious*, and a *religious* creature." It is "nature" that has "implanted" in man an "affection" for others like him. Man as a "religious creature" looks to something higher than himself. The greatest, or foremost, law that man has learned is the golden rule: "do unto others as we would have them do unto us." Cooke thus makes an unmistakable connection between the immorality of slavery and Biblical revelation. What slaveholder truly desires to be a slave? No man wishes to enslave himself, so why would he wish that on others? According to Cooke, if the conservatives are correct that man is so consumed with his own interests so that it "swallows up all other passions, and feelings, and principles" and not just "in particular cases," but in all cases, then such a doctrine is "monstrous" and "hateful." The poor would be in perpetual war against the rich, and the master could be passionately attached to slavery. Cooke seemed to chastise the slaveholder for his greedy concern for property. Their concern has affected their passions to such an extent, that they have subverted the greatest rule of revelation and enslaved their fellow man. This appears to be what he means by the concern with property in all cases, not just "particular cases."

Ultimately, the argument emanating from the pro-slave wing of the state desired to "destroy the great landmarks of natural right, established in the era of the revolution—to repudiate all the principles of Government, which have been, until now, held sacred and inviolable." Campbell agreed. Though his major speech in the convention was yet to come, he urged the members to consider carefully how they were grounding their arguments. The rejection of abstract principles would set a course of "confusion and darkness;" he concluded, "either adopt the principles in the Bill of Rights as canonical, and base all your subsequent proceedings on them," or amend the document.[82]

Abel P. Upshur (Northampton) responded and rose to the defense of Leigh. He was one of the most articulate speakers representing the Tidewater and Piedmont and was long active in Virginia politics, eventually becoming secretary of state in the John Tyler administration. In a speech that lasted a day and a half, Upshur built on the assertion that the government could not be based on principles, but must be based on experience and practicality. In particular, he attacked majority rule because there were two different kinds of majorities: a "majority of interests," and a "majority of numbers." Upshur believed the former was worth preserving, while the latter would lead the state to ruin:

Those who have the greatest stake in the government, shall have the greatest share of power in the administration of it . . . If there be, as our opponents assume, an original, *a priori*, inherent and indestructible right in a majority to control a minority, from what source permit me to inquire, is that right derived? If it exist at all, it must I apprehend, be found either in some positive compact or agreement conferring it, or else in some order of our nature, independent of all compact, and consequently prior to all Government.[83]

The notion that the majority ought to rule is not found in the law of nature. The natural law is really a law of force. From force comes right. It is from the law of nature, we find the power of the stronger:

The law of nature will be found to confer no other right than this: the right in every creature to use the powers derived from nature, in such mode as will best promote his own happiness . . . Throughout her boundless domain, the law of force gives the only rule of right. The lion devours the ox; the ox drives the lamb from the green pasture; the lamb exerts the same law of power over the animal that is weaker and more timid than itself; and thus the rule runs, throughout all the gradations of life, until at last, the worm devours us all.[84]

The law of nature is a highly individualistic place. Therefore, in the law of nature there is no principle that dictates majority rule. Nevertheless, there is one aspect of majority rule that resembles the state of nature. The right of the majority is akin to force—it places restraints on minority members of the community. If the state of nature were a reality, when forming a social compact, each person would bring with him all the rights he derived in that state, "and among these rights, would be found the right to say *whether a majority should rule him or not.*" It is not that Upshur believes that force is the ground to social compact, but his assertion that all men are created equal translates into a politics based on the stronger. If in fact Virginia is founded on state of nature theory, Upshur asserts that the propertied, when forming the compact, never consented to majority rule. Far from those who contend that natural rights are not the basis of power politics, the argument for a majority in numbers is the very definition of physical power.

Eventually, Upshur shakes off any consideration of the state of nature, because it possibly never existed. The state of nature is conjecture. Virginians ought not base a government on some imagined abstract principle. Rather, real principles, at least the ones that should guide the conventioneers, are not found in the state of nature, but come from the compact:

> In truth . . . *there are no original principles of Government at all.* Novel and strange as the idea may appear, it is nevertheless, strictly true, in the sense which I announce it. There are no original principles, existing in the nature of things and independent of agreement, to which Government must of necessity conform, on order to be either legitimate or philosophical. The principles of Government, are those principles only, which the people who form the Government choose to *adopt and apply themselves.* Principles do not *precede,* but spring out of Government.[85]

Since principles "spring out of government," politics is organic in nature. There is nothing fixed. In such instances, history (or tradition?) is the only guide. In history, there are several examples of government in one, a few, or the many. Given that there is no one form of government that has existed in history, there is no definite science of government that makes a republic based on broad suffrage and equal representation a better form of government than, say, a monarchy. Experience is the only guide as to choosing what government should look like. Does that mean that the reformers may have a just claim to change the constitution? Upshur contends that even though there are no first principles to government, that there is no mandatory requirement to acknowledge the claim of those who want broader suffrage and equal representation.

He seems to conduct an about-face, however, later in his speech. After dispatching the majority in numbers principle, he finally explains his idea of majority of interests: "The question before us, is prior to actual Government: it is not whether a majority shall rule in the Legislature, but *of what elements that majority shall be composed.* If the interests of the several parts of the

Commonwealth were identical, it would be, we admit, safe and proper that a majority of *persons only* should give the rule of political power."[86] Majority rule is preferable only if all men are of the same mind or have the same interests. Appealing to the historical record, he notes that almost every government since time began has been created with a view to protecting persons and property:

> We do not propose to represent money, but the *rights and interests which spring from the possession of money* . . . If men enter into the social compact upon unequal terms; if one man brings into the partnership his rights of person alone, and another brings into it, equal rights of person and all the rights of property beside, can they be said to have an equal interest in the common stock? Shall not he who has most at stake; who has not only a *greater* interest, but a *peculiar* interest in society, possess an authority proportioned to that interest, and adequate interest in society, possess an authority proportioned to that interest, and adequate to its protection?[87]

The Virginia compact granted to the propertied a greater share of the government. To tamper with that would upset the stability of the government. Government's aim is security and security comes through the protection of property. In the words of Randolph: "I go for solid security, and I never will knowingly, take any other."[88] To Upshur, depart from that maxim and the consequences are dire: "Take away all protection from property, and our next business is to cut each other's throats. All experience proves this. The safety of men depends on the safety of property . . . shall not he who has the most at stake; who has not only a *greater* interest, but a *peculiar* interest in society, possess an authority proportioned to that interest, and adequate to its protection?"[89] Though he rejects the state of nature theory in fact, somehow no longer protecting property would lead to something like a state of war. Nevertheless, since the interests of the state of Virginia are not identical, and the most important division is over property, he believes that the protection of it should be the first and foremost object of the government. Upshur stated as much when he asserted that whatever the position of man before a government is formed, "nature and all her principles are swept away" when entering social compact.[90] Upshur, Randolph, Leigh, and many others like them, seem to prefer one thing above all others: security.

If the convention changed suffrage and representation, those without property would be able to tax the property of the propertied. Property of the east cannot be safe if the west has a say in the disposal of such property. Since society "cannot exist without property"—the minority interest—and since the "safety of men depends on the safety of property," those who own property should continue to have the most influence in the government.[91] To broaden suffrage and to equalize representation, then, would be to upset the coincidence of interests and thus upset the tranquil operations of government, whose chief object is the protection of property. This argument is beside the point, for Upshur believes that the people of Virginia, when setting up the Constitution, gave the propertied more authority than the non-propertied. Though he dismissed the existence of a real state of nature, he contends that "if we stood in the nakedness of nature" all could come together on equal terms; since that is impossible, and since property has been acquired by some people, the people have a moral obligation to protect those who have amassed such possessions: "*our* property imperiously demands *that kind of protection* which flows from the possession of power."[92] Should anything change, it leaves property less secure. Those who own much would lose everything. Those who would gain would be committing "*violence* and *fraud.*"

Upshur fears that should the western part of the state (the largest population of those with either less property, or no property, and certainly little in slave property) receive more representation in the assembly, and/or should more people be granted the right to vote, they would use that political power to tax the slaves so as to make the ownership of them impossible. It is clear he resents the fact that slave property is taxed; his desire is to protect slavery:

> No such tax is laid on the white labourer of the West . . . [but] property should possess an influence in Government, it is certainly right as to us. It is right, because *our* property, so far as slaves are concerned, is *peculiar*; because it is of imposing magnitude; because it affords almost a half of the productive labour of the State; because it is exposed to peculiar impositions, and therefore peculiar hazards; and because it is the interest of the whole Commonwealth, that this power should not be taken away.

If there was any statement demonstrating what the debate was about, it was that which came from Upshur. It is quite interesting that Upshur referenced a "peculiar interest" in his defense of who should have the most say in government operations. It seems that he believed the natural rights argument would have devastating implications to the slaveholder should that argument prevail. At least we can conclude that Upshur's primary goal was the protection of that "peculiar property" and that everyone knew that the only property called peculiar was that of slaves. The majority interest that ought to be protected is the slave interest. The permanent common interest in the community is not, then, mere property, but *slave* property. If the west were to demonstrate to the east that they had the same interest, they would need more than the possession of land, they would need slaves as well. This would be almost impossible, since Upshur stated in his speech that the preponderate majority of the state is against slavery. Therefore, slavery was at the heart of the debate and he stated such at the conclusion of his speech on the second day: "there exists in a great portion of the west, a rooted antipathy to this species of population; the habits of the people are strongly opposed to it." To view property this way, the slave-owner has a specific and permanent attachment to the community that the non-slaveholder does not.

Upshur's fears are not completely unfounded. If the slaves were emancipated, what would be done with those freed would be a concern of the state. However, in Upshur, we do not seem to find a politics based on the principles articulated by Jefferson, but a politics based on something else. It is true that if the reformers won the debate, slavery would be more insecure, thus setting up emancipation as a political and moral necessity. Upshur found such ideas "mere theoretical principles, or speculative doctrines" that would produce "new and hazardous" problems for the government. Not speculative ideas from philosophers like Plato, but "experience" is the "best guide in Government." Power in the wrong hands, and driven by abstract principles, will be abused.

At the beginning of business on October 31, Campbell gave one of the most important speeches of the convention. It was one of the few times he spoke, but it impressed many of the elder Virginia statesmen. James Madison noted that "the greatest man [of the convention] was Alexander Campbell . . . His mastery of the great questions which came before us, his skill in debate, was a constant surprise."[93] Campbell is most widely known as a religious figure who founded what is now known as the Church of Christ. It is perhaps because of his theological interests, and because he is not as major a figure as Madison, that his few speeches before the convention are overlooked by modern scholars.

At the beginning of the speech, Campbell appealed to the common nature all men possessed: "I am a *man*, Sir, and as such I cannot but feel interested in every thing which concerns the prosperity and happiness of man . . . I cannot but feel a deep interest in everything connected with the happiness of my species."[94] He continued to assert that he would have this same interest or idea no matter what part of the state he resided. Campbell asserted that as a matter of reason, all men have the same interest, especially when they recall that they are of the same species. Campbell is no respecter of persons, yet, he was dismayed that the convention was trying to make decisions on matters without regard to the Declaration of Rights:

> It was *principles*, Mr. Chairman which brought me here. *Principles*, Sir, which reason, observation, and experience convinced me are inseparably connected with the temporal prosperity of men; and our State of Virginia: And principles, Sir, which are not to be sacrificed . . . But, Mr. Chairman, we are entirely out to sea in this debate. We set sail without compass, rudder, or pilot. So anxious were some gentlemen here to put to sea, that when we called for the compass and the pilot, they exclaimed: Never mind we will get the compass and pilot when we get to port. We are now a thousand miles from land.
>
> I am sorry, Sir, that we did not first establish the principles, or at least agree upon all the principles on which the frame of Government should be based, before we attempted to form the Constitution...Call me orthodox, or call me heterodox, I confess that I believe, that in the science of politics, there are as in all other sciences, certain fundamental principles, as true and unchangeable as any of the fundamental principles of physics or morals.
>
> It is just as true, that Government ought to be instituted for the benefit of the governed, as that a whole is greater than a part; or that a straight line is the shortest possible distance between any two given points.[95]

Campbell's speech is important because it explains more fully Taylor's earlier speech on self-evident truths and represents a fundamental disagreement between those who believed in the truths stated in the Declaration of

Independence and the Virginia Declaration of Rights and those who did not. Part of the improvement in the science of politics is the recognition that there are ultimate truths. Even if those truths are not literally imported, or even approximated, they provide a guide to political action. Campbell does not understand the discontinuity in the mind of those who oppose natural rights: on the one hand, they claim to support the Declaration of Rights; on the other hand, they are "continually oppugning it." If there is no agreement as to the ground of politics, then there is no guide for the conventioneers. There would be no reason, for example, to preserve the republic. His colleague William Naylor (Hampshire) concurred: "I would as soon believe that there was no truth, no justice, no rule of right or wrong, as to believe this. If there is no undeniable truth here, such as are called first principles, we have no premises and can never come to any conclusion."[96] Without some agreed principles, Campbell continued, the resulting constitution would be an arbitrary work:

> *All men are born free and independent.* This is a position much older than these United States, and flowed from a gentleman, to whom, more than any other, these American States are indebted for all their civil and religious liberties . . . but there is no man more worthy of American admiration, than the statesman, the philosopher, and the Christian who is the legitimate father of the first article of the Bill of Rights. I need not tell you . . . that I allude to the Author of the Essay on Toleration, the Author of the Essay upon Human Understanding.[97]

The similarity between the first article of the Declaration of Rights and Locke's section on the beginning of political societies in the "Second Treatise" is striking.[98] Campbell asserts that a self-evident truth is eternal, and such truths had been recognized long before the U.S. articulated a politics based on those truths. There is a truth outside of human experience, outside the will, and certainly positive law. These truths are not only true in the present, but will be in the future, and have been in the past.[99] These ideas are far from novel truths. However, does the equality of man turn into a requirement that everyone should have equal political rights?

Campbell seems to think that is the case: "but logic is yet wanting to show why A, in entering society, should surrender more of his natural rights than B."[100] If all men have equal natural rights, they ought to have equal political rights. Natural rights not only protect the non-slaveholder, but also the slaveholder. Natural rights belong to all men. Campbell is not saying that everyone ought to immediately have, for example, the right to vote, but he is stating that there is no reason why one ought to be excluded over another just because he has less. There is nothing in the natural equality of man, for instance, that makes a man the slave of another:

> Man is a social animal, and in obedience to this law of his nature, he seeks society, and desires the countenance of man. But as all men are not born on the same day, and do not all place their eyes upon the same object, at the same time, nor receive the same education, they cannot all be of the same opinion.

Some arrangement, founded on the nature of man, for men's living together, must then be adopted. And the impossibility of gratifying their social desires, but in yielding to differences of opinion, presents itself among the very first reflections.[101]

In other words, in order to account for the different opinions of man, majorities must somehow be counted in order to define the interest of the community. For Campbell, rights belong to individual men, not to land or other property. Part of the contention against the reformers was that they had different interests from those of the eastern slave-holding part of the state, but Campbell took that to its logical conclusion. If there are differing majorities, as Upshur believed—a majority in numbers and a majority in interests—why not also carve out a place for "majorities of talent, physical strength, scientific skill" or anything else? A majority in talent, one could claim, is just as, if not more, valuable to the community than a majority of wealth or property.

The concept of majority rule as he understands it is that "every man surrenders himself to the community, and the whole community to him." Man does not receive the right of suffrage from the society. The community does not merely confer such a right to a person. The right to vote emanates from man's equal nature. The justification for suffrage is anterior to man coming into society. While society might divest someone of the vote, the right does not come merely from the community. Naylor expanded on this idea:

We cannot, indeed, divest ourselves of the idea of the state which man must have been in previous to the formation of the social compact. This was a treaty to which every member of the community became a party, by which they unanimously agreed to form a body, and so became incorporated as such.
This was formed not only by the consent of the majority, but by the consent of the whole.[102]

Indeed, Campbell argued that in any social compact, the first act is an act of suffrage—all who agree to enter into a compact are basically casting their vote in agreement to enter into a community with others. The form of rule thereafter is based on majority rule. Even the convention proceedings function in that rule. A motion carries if the majority votes for it.

Naylor appealed to Locke's *Second Treatise* to justify this position: "For when any number of men have, by the consent of every individual, made a community, they have thereby made that community one body, with a power to act as a body, which is by the will and determination of the majority."[103] The equality of man, not positive law, provides the basis for the initial coming together. The first act to form a compact is consent. Everyone who enters the compact is bound by the compact and bound by majority will. However, according to Campbell, many conventioneers reject majority rule, and ergo natural rights, because they are more concerned with their peculiar property. This concern emanates from the self-interested desire to keep human beings enslaved.

If allowed to be the basis of government, Campbell thought, Virginia would be less a republic and more an aristocracy or oligarchy. According to Campbell, if the convention rejects the law of nature, "a new principle will be sanctioned; the very principle on which the aristocracies and monarchies of the old world would have been founded. Give men political power according to their wealth, and soon we shall have a legalized *oligarchy*."[104]

On November 2, James Monroe (Loudoun) rose to address the convention, exposing the root of the division. Monroe thought the divisions were so acute, reminiscent of the Missouri debacle, that he feared the dismemberment of the Union. The issue dividing the state is the same that threatens to divide the Union—slavery:

> It is contended by those who reside in the western part of the State, that representation in the Legislature, shall be based on white population alone: It is contended on the other hand, by those who live in the east, that it shall be based on the principle of population and taxation combined. These are the two grounds of difference. I am satisfied, that the claim of those in the west, is rational under particular circumstances. It has often been suggested here, and I accord with that view, that putting the citizens in an equal condition, and the basis which they claim is just: It is founded on the natural rights of man, . . . But look at the Atlantic country, what is their claim? . . . they have a species of property, in a much greater amount than the people of the west, and this they wish to protect. It consists of slaves. I am satisfied, if no such thing as slavery existed, that the people of the Atlantic border, would meet their brethren of the west, upon the basis of a majority of the free white population.[105]

The seriousness of the divide is revealed in his oration. Slavery is at the heart of the division. Monroe identified himself with the western portion of the state and more specifically those who believed in the natural rights of man. He further placed the blame on the eastern intransigence regarding slaves; for if the slaves did not exist in the eastern part of the state, they would be more apt to agree with the west. Additionally, Monroe delivers a subtle message that slavery is corrupting the slaveholder—on the one side was natural rights, on the other side was personal interest. If the selfish interest in slaves did not exist, majority rule based on the rights of man would find greater acceptance among the slaveholders. It is interesting that Monroe notes the west also held slaves, albeit it is a tiny fraction of the numbers in the west. Still, the west was more dedicated than the east to equality despite that influence. The venerable president of the convention went on to explain the foundation of the state, and of the Union, was, and is, based on the natural rights of man. Even though the state had slaves, the Founders proclaimed all men had equal rights:

> What was the origin of our slave population? The evil commenced when we were in our Colonial state, but acts were passed by our Colonial Legislature, prohibiting the importation, of more slaves, into the Colony. These were rejected by the Crown. We declared our independence, and the prohibition of a further importation, was among the first acts of State sovereignty . . . [Virginia]

did all that was in her power to do, to prevent the extension of slavery, and to mitigate its evils.[106]

Monroe articulated the documentary record we examined in chapter two, that Old Dominion tried unsuccessfully many times to thwart the slave trade and hence slavery in general. He confirms that the emancipation of the slaves is a political, if not a moral, necessity. However, Monroe is not blind to the effect such emancipation would have on the slaves if they are not prepared for it. Some free states have driven, or tried to drive, the freed slaves from their boundaries because the population inside those states, though loathing the peculiar institution, have certain prejudices. Furthermore, Monroe asserts that freed blacks are discouraged from settling in the free states because they have no perceived skills with which to contribute to society. If slavery is to end, it must take the entire Union's aid to effect that end.

After nearly one month of debate, the convention was no closer to a conclusion or resolution. There were, as Monroe articulately pointed out, two sides to the debate: those who supported the natural rights foundation of politics, and those who rejected that foundation for something else whether it is wealth, property, or the rights of the minority (majority interest). His attempt to split the difference by urging the convention to adopt the white basis for representation in the House and the compound basis (roughly something like the three-fifths clause in the Constitution) for the Senate was not accepted by the east. Indeed, after Monroe spoke, the arguments against natural rights became more lengthy and oration for and against the same became more repetitive. Of those reacting against Monroe's speech, some chose to not only attack the concept of natural rights and the theories of Locke, but they also attacked the Founders, and Jefferson in particular.

Monroe's speech, then, did not end the debate, but briefly inspired additional deliberation. Leigh launched into a lengthy critique of Monroe. He approached a defense of slavery by remarking that every civilized country has an economic relationship where all labor in subjection to others, or for themselves. While he does not state that the slaves deserve their enslavement, he comes awfully close to that argument:

> Slaves . . . are not and never will be comparable with the hardy peasantry of the mountains, in intellectual power, in moral worth, in all that determines man's degree in the moral scale, and raises him above the brute . . . above the savage—above that wretched state, of which the only comfort is the natural rights of man. I have as sincere feelings of regard for that people, as any man who lives among them. But I ask gentlemen to say, whether they believe, that those who are obliged to depend on their daily labour for daily subsistence, can, or do ever enter into political affairs? They never do—never will—never can.[107]

It is remarkable that Leigh lifts the European peasant above the American slave. Despite that oddity, he seems to degrade the slave to the level of a beast. Is the slave the same as a hog? Is the slave naturally a slave? Regardless, he unequivocally asserts that slaves can never be a part of the body politic. They should never exercise political rights on the same level as others. Leigh also seems to reject their intellectual capacity of participating in politics. In that way, Leigh took an important step toward the positive good thesis.

The objection to the reformers seems based on a fear of what might happen. The fear that the west would seize the property of the east, then, is really based on the fear that the west would attempt to free the slaves without the consent of the owners, either by outright emancipation or by onerous taxation. The pro-slaveholder faction believed that the federal government should not ever be involved in such a decision. Monroe, who desired the assistance of the federal government, rebutted that he would never argue that the slaves could be emancipated without first receiving the invitation of the state(s) for such assistance. Furthermore, Monroe asserted that he did not believe emancipation could occur without it coinciding with their exportation because they would never be able to exercise equal political rights with blacks because that would cause an "interminable war."[108] While the Union may not have an interest in the decision for emancipation, both North and South had an interest in what happens after emancipation because the effects are not just visited on the southern states but all states. Therefore, the entire Union has an interest in the peaceful conclusion of slavery, and colonization would take the monetary assistance from all the states, not just the South.

Despite his objection to federal assistance, and the belief in the brute nature of the slave, Leigh did perceive slavery as an evil:

> I wish, indeed, that I had been born in a land where domestic and negro slavery is unknown . . . I shall never wish that I had been born out of Virginia—but I wish, that Providence had spared my country this moral and political evil . . . the evil of slavery is greatest to the master, than the slave: He is interested in all their wants, all their distresses . . . The relation between the master and slave, imposes on the master a heavy and painful responsibility.[109]

Leigh considers slavery an evil, but the reason it is evil is because of the pecuniary imposition it places on the master. It does not appear to affect the master morally. What harm it does the slave he does not address. This is a self-interested evil, not an evil violating the inherent rights of man. Even though this is probably not a strong denunciation of the peculiar institution, it is yet an evil and not a good.

On November 19, the philosophical debate more or less ended after the defeat of four resolutions put forth by Alexander Campbell. In a nutshell, the resolutions would have opened up the vote to all white males at the age of twenty-two. Anyone who had resided in the state for one year would be considered to have demonstrated attachment to the community. Virginia was the only state other than North Carolina that required a freehold in addition to age and residency.[110] Campbell thought that the "reason and nature of things" should be directed toward the foundation of republican government; the "whole system of government" depended whether it was in "accordance with *reason*."[111] Campbell was optimistic that after thousands of years, Virginia created a constitution far better, or more perfect, than any other government had before it. Nevertheless, after coming out of ages of darkness and superstition, we could not expect the Founders to rid the earth of all such errors immediately:

> Those illustrious fathers of the American Revolution, and founders of these Republics, are entitled to the admiration and gratitude of all friends of the rights of man. But it was not to be expected that these sages, great and wise, and good, as they were, could have perfectly emerged out of the political darkness and errors, consecrated by the prescriptions of the monarchies of the old world for thousands of years.[112]

As far as Virginia is concerned, the Founders could only progress as far as immediacy allowed and only insofar as the public would accept. This meant that the compact could, and ought to, be perfected:

> They declared the principles, the just and righteous principles of the social compact; and progressed so far in the application as they supposed the then existing state of society required and permitted. But foreseeing that changes would take place, and that the human mind was progressing and would progress, they revised, and most prudently advised, a frequent recurrence to fundamental principles: Not to change those principles as one gentle man, (Mr. Giles) asked, but to purge and reform our institutions by bringing them up near to the unchangeable principles; by a continual approximation to the cardinal principles which they propounded.[113]

Conclusion

If Virginia would continue to prosper, if the Union would survive, a dedication to, and recognition of, those principles is necessary: "this instrument has been our palladium, and the only bulwark against the demolition of our republican citadel, and the destruction of the Republican character of our Government." Campbell's oration and the defeat of his resolutions seem to mark the end of the real debate over the Declaration of Rights and republican government. After one month and fourteen days of debate, the convention was deadlocked. The eastern portion of the state generally rejected the natural rights basis of government, while the west insisted upon them. Perhaps Doddridge summed it up best when he stated that the doctrines espoused by the slaveholding east would make him a slave. The tone of his speech, and the language he employed, got to the center of the debate: the slaves are just as equal as whites in the west and if the chains of the west were broken, then *all* chains should be broken. On the principles of the Founding, the natural rights coalition proceeded to nail their flag and go no further.[114]

Sensing deadlock, on December 2, Madison finally rose to address the convention to call for compromise. It was his first address to the convention and upon his rising, members leapt from their seats to be nearer to him. They did not want to miss a spoken word. Madison asserted that persons and property are the two "great subjects" of government action.[115] People have a natural right to acquire property and that right manifests itself as a social right. The great danger is that in republics, the majority may tyrannize over the minority. Experience has taught men that goodwill, generosity, or the best intentions, do not safeguard the minority. Therefore, the protection of the rights of the minority, as well as the majority relies in part on the structure of the government itself. Like Monroe, Madison admits that the "peculiar division in the basis of our Government, I mean the coloured part of our population" is the primary cause of the failure of consensus. If the slave population were of a different color—white, not black—the probability that compromise would be reached would increase dramatically. However, he asserts they are "human beings" and as such not "mere property." Their complexion cannot deprive them of their status as men. In order to secure better the rights of all interests involved, then, Madison proposed the general assembly be reapportioned and that the House be based on white basis while the Senate determine its representation on the federal ratio of the three-fifths clause in the Constitution. He asserted that "such an arrangement might prove favourable to the slaves themselves," as the west being sympathetic with the slaves will have incentive to make sure they are protected by the law whilst they remain in bondage.

   Just after the acrimonious Missouri debate over whether the federal government could, or should, monetarily assist in the eradication of slavery, the question of federal assistance in emancipating the slaves was still on the minds of the pro-slave southerners in Virginia. When Monroe raised the issue, those not in favor recoiled and denounced this idea. However, Monroe stipulated that only after a state's invitation should the federal government assist. Even Madison's compromise, offered on December 2, was couched in a way that emphasized the rights of all men; to this the pro-slave owner could not assent because it meant that as a matter of moral fulfillment the slaves ought to be emancipated.

   On one level, it is a bit surprising that the convention debated the Declaration of Rights because it was adopted unanimously, without amendment. The conservatives knew the meaning of both declarations. One eastern delegate understood the implications: "if you give to the language, all the force which the words literally import, (as they are, I believe, but an echo of those in the Declaration of Independence,) what will they amount to, but a declaration of universal emancipation."[116] Barbour would make an early historicist argument in the convention by asserting that we could not take the words in the Declaration of Rights literally, but must read them as the Founders read them—take into account the historical situation of things. Ten years after Missouri, it would seem that the window of opportunity to ending slavery was closing.

   Many scholars have overlooked the ideological change in the understanding among pro-slave thinkers who believed that political morality and, hence, constitutional government is not derived from standards found in nature, but from historical evolution and practical experience. It would seem that not only were the pro-slave southerners departing from that maxim, but they were also departing, ever so slowly from the Union and the belief in the laws of nature and nature's God. Prominent southerners were rejecting the Founding for a new dispensation—the primacy of the practical over theoretical reason.[117] Less were they members of the same political society, than individuals creeping toward something else.[118]

Notes

1. Thomas Jefferson, *Notes on the State of Virginia*, *The Portable Thomas Jefferson*, ed. Merrill Peterson (New York: Penguin Books, 1975), 166; Campbell to Selina Campbell, Richmond, 12 October 1829, [Online] Available http://www.bible.acu.edu/crs/doc/ac/acl01.htm. [February 21, 2001].

2. Julian A.C. Chandler, *Representation in Virginia* (Baltimore: The Johns Hopkins University Press, 1961), 22.

3. Don E. Fehrenbacher, *Constitutions and Constitutionalism in the Slaveholding South* (Athens: The University of Georgia Press, 1989), 27 and 28; Theodore M. Whitfield, *Slavery Agitation in Virginia 1829-1832* (New York: Negro Universities Press, 1930), vii.

4. Glover Moore, *The Missouri Controversy 1819-1821* (Lexington: University of Kentucky Press, 1953), 35.

5. Ibid., 124. Some Virginians believed that Missouri, as a state, should take action against slavery. Tyler did question the applicability of the Declaration, however, during the Missouri debate: William Sumner Jenkins, *Proslavery Thought in the Old South* (Gloucester, Mass.: University of North Carolina Press, 1935), 60.

6. Moore, 240-243.

7. Ibid., 233. See also William W. Freehling, *Road to Disunion: Secessionists at Bay, 1776-1854* (New York: Oxford University Press, 1990), 150. The *Richmond Enquirer* was the only paper Jefferson subscribed to at the time; Peter Onuf, *Jefferson's Empire: The Language of American Nationhood* (Charlottesville: University Press of Virginia, 2000), 109.

8. Moore, 254, 256, and 127. See also Dumas Malone, *Jefferson and His Time: The Sage from Monticello*, vol. 6 (Boston: Little, Brown, and Company, 1981), 330-331, 329; Jefferson to Marquis de Lafayette, Monticello, 26 December 1820, *The Writings of Thomas Jefferson* (Washington, D.C.: The Thomas Jefferson Memorial Association, 1907, vol. 15, ed. Ellery Albert Bergh, 301; Marvin Meyers, ed. *The Mind of the Founder* (Hanover: Brandeis University Press, 1981), 320; Jefferson to David Bailey Warden, Monticello, 26 December 1820, vol. 15, in Bergh, 180.

9. Jefferson to William Short, Monticello, 13 April 1820, in Bergh, vol. 15, 247-248; Jefferson to Hugh Nelson, Monticello, 12 March 1820, ibid., 238; Onuf, 109-110.

10. Jefferson to John Adams, 10 December 1819, *The Adams-Jefferson Letters*, ed. Lester J. Cappon (New York: Simon and Schuster, 1959), 328. Though not commenting on the Missouri debate (for he was deceased), Washington too warned of such sectional partisanship and believed that disunion was a great "evil"; Washington to James McHenry, Mount Vernon, 22 August 1785, *George Washington: Writings*, ed. John Rhodehamel (New York: Library of America, 1997), 588. He also warned of a sectional divide causing disunion in his "Farewell Address."

11. Jefferson to John Holmes, Monticello, 22 April 1820, *Thomas Jefferson: Writings*, ed. Merrill D. Peterson (New York: Library of America, 1984), 1434. Italics in

the original.

12. Ibid.

13. Ibid.

14. For Madison's assent to diffusion similar to Jefferson's see Madison to General La Fayette, Montpelier, 25 November 1820, in Madison, vol. 3, 190, and Madison to Tench Coxe, Montpelier, 20 March 1820, in ibid., 170. On some of the scholarship critical of Jefferson, Madison and Missouri, see Robert E. Shalhope, "Thomas Jefferson's Republicanism and Antebellum Southern Thought," *The Journal of Southern History* 42 (November 1976) : 531; Freehling, *The Road to Disunion*, 144 and 155.

15. Jefferson to David Bailey Warden, Monticello, 26 December 1820, in Bergh, ed. vol. 12, 180. Jefferson lauds the "courage" of Thomas Mann Randolph, his son-in-law and governor of Virginia, for his gradual emancipation plan. See also Jefferson to Marquis de Lafayette, Monticello, 26 December 1820, ibid., 300-301.

16. Abraham Lincoln, "Speech on the Kansas-Nebraska Act at Peoria, Illinois," 16 October 1854, *Abraham Lincoln: Speeches and Writings*, ed., Don Fehrenbacher, vol. 1 (New York: Library of America, 1989), 308-309.

17. Jefferson to John Holmes, Monticello, 22 April 1820, *Thomas Jefferson: Writings*, 1434-1435. Some claim that this letter represents Jefferson's acceptance of a more Calhounian position on slavery. See note 11 above.

18. Jefferson to Richard Rush, Monticello, 20 October 1820, in Bergh, ed., vol. 15, 283-284.

19. Federalist no. 1, Clinton Rossiter, ed., *The Federalist Papers*, with an Introduction by Charles Kesler (New York: Mentor, 1999), 1; Harry V. Jaffa, *The American Founding as the Best Regime: The Bonding of Civil and Religious Liberty* (Claremont: The Claremont Institute, 1987), 13.

20. Jefferson to John Adams, Monticello, 22 January 1821, *The Adams-Jefferson Letters*, 570. See also Meyers, 319. On the Louisiana Purchase see Moore, 31-32.

21. Jaffa, *A New Birth of Freedom*, 79-80.

22. Jefferson to Albert Gallatin, Monticello, 26 December 1820, *Thomas Jefferson: Writings*, 1448-1449. Unless otherwise noted, subsequent quotes from this work. Cf. Jefferson to David Bailey Warden, Monticello, 26 December 1820, *The Works of Thomas Jefferson*, vol. 12, 179-180.

23. Madison to Robert Walsh, Montpelier, 27 November 1819, in Meyers, 324-325. Italics in the original. Jefferson to John Holmes, Monticello, 22 April 1820, *Thomas Jefferson: Writings*, 1434; Shalhope, "Thomas Jefferson's Republicanism and Antebellum Southern Thought," 548.

24. Madison to Robert Walsh, Montpelier, 27 November 1819, in Meyers, 324-325. Meyers asserts that Madison questioned the entire prohibitory scheme of the Northwest Ordinance. Madison certainly questioned the authority of the Congress under the Articles, but he did not contend the Congress under the Constitution lacked the authority. He did question whether the ban was necessary in light of the importation ban however. Drew R. McCoy, *The Last of the Fathers: James Madison and the Republican Legacy* (Cambridge: Cambridge University Press, 1989), 107-114, contends that Madison opposed using Article 1, §9 as a justification for banning slavery in the territories. He thought a better Constitutional argument could be found in Article 4, §3 and that it left much room for legislative discretion.

We should note that in Lincoln's Cooper Union speech, he stated that Madison was among those voting for the Ordinance. Harold Holzer, *Lincoln at Cooper Union* (New York: Simon and Schuster, 2004), 256-257, tracked the progression of the bill. Both houses of Congress voted in the affirmative unanimously.

25. Meyers, ed., 324-325; McCoy, 262.

26. Madison to President Monroe, Montpelier, 23 February 1820, *Letters and Other Writings*, vol. 3 (New York: R. Worthington, 1884), 168-169. Lincoln stated that Madison was among the original Founders who opposed the extension of slavery. How might we explain his apparent acquiescence in this case? According to McCoy, 267-268, Madison came to support the Ordinance because slavery was yet expanding via importation. With imports banned, diffusion would be the most expedient way to decrease their suffering. Nevertheless, Madison supported the Compromise. Cf. Lincoln, "Speech at Cooper Union," 27 February 1860, *Lincoln at Cooper Union*, Holzer, 257-258.

27. McCoy, 265, 270, and 277-279.

28. Madison to Robert Evans, Montpelier, 15 June 1819, in Meyer, 314-316. Quotes hereafter from this source and letter unless otherwise noted.

29. Madison to Frances Wright, Montpelier, 1 September 1825, ibid., 328-329.

30. Madison to Robert Evans, Montpelier, 15 June 1819, ibid., 318.

31. Madison to General La Fayette, 1821, in Madison, vol. 3, 239.

32. Jefferson to Marquis de Lafayette, Monticello, 26 December 1820, in Bergh, vol. 15, 300-301.

33. Jefferson to Charles Pinckney, Monticello, 30 September 1820, in ibid., 280-281.

34. Freehling, *Road to Disunion*, 162 & 156.

35. Onuf, 185.

36. Jefferson to Jared Sparks, Monticello, 4 February 1824, *Thomas Jefferson: Writings*, 1484-1487; Moore, 30; Cohen, 524; Malone, *Jefferson and His Time: The Sage of Monticello*, vol. 6, 341.

37. Jefferson to James Madison, Monticello, 21 January 1821, *The Works of Thomas Jefferson*, vol. 12, 193-194.

38. Malone, *Jefferson and His Time: The Sage of Monticello*, vol. 6, 341. Jefferson lauded his son-in-law for the "courage" of proposing the plan, Jefferson to David Bailey Warden, Monticello, 26 December 1820, in Ford, 181.

39. Moore, 30, 126, and 14.

40. Jefferson to Samuel Kercheval, Monticello, 12 July 1816, *The Portable Thomas Jefferson*, 553. Kercheval solicited Jefferson's opinion because he desired to call a state convention. As far as the suffrage issue is concerned, there was substantial agreement between Jefferson, Madison, Wythe, and Mason.

41. Jefferson to Jared Sparks, Monticello, 4 February 1824, *Thomas Jefferson: Writings*, 1484-1487.

42. Thomas Jefferson, *Notes on the State of Virginia*, 175-176.

43. Ibid., 164; William G. Shade, *Democratizing Old Dominion: Virginia and the Second Party System 1824-1861* (Charlottesville: University Press of Virginia, 1996), 51.

44. Jefferson to Samuel Kercheval, Monticello, July 12, 1816, *The Portable Thomas Jefferson*, 555. After the 1816 convention, Jefferson asserted that if a constitutional convention was called, it ought not be limited, but the entire document should be fully examined; Jefferson to Samuel Kercheval, Monticello, 5 September 1816, *The Writings of Thomas Jefferson*, vol. 15, 70.

45. Jefferson to Edmund Pendleton, Philadelphia, 26 August 1776, *Thomas Jefferson: Writings*, 756. Jefferson thought that property, family, or residing in a place for a certain time might demonstrate a certain attachment to community and an interest in the state. We should note that for Jefferson this proceeds from natural right. This fact is important as we consider the pro-slave argument in the constitutional convention.

46. James Madison, "Notes for the *National Gazette*," *The Papers of James Madison*, vol. 14, eds. Robert A. Rutland and Thomas A. Mason (Charlottesville: University Press of Virginia, 1983), 163. Madison also encouraged Kentucky to liberalize her laws on the basis of "equal political rights," Julius F. Prufer, "The Franchise in Virginia from Jefferson Through the Convention of 1829," *William and Mary College Quarterly Historical Magazine* 8, no. 1 (January 1928) : 25; Shade, 53.

47. Quoted in Julian A.C. Chandler, *The History of Suffrage in Virginia* (Baltimore: The Johns Hopkins University Press, 1901), 29. There were ten other times between 1801-1813 that convention resolutions were introduced in the House of Delegates. Twice they passed the House only to die in the Senate, see Shade, 57. Jefferson also wrote Madison in 1824 that the constitution denied the principle of equal political rights, Prufer, 25.

48. Such a claim was made by Littleton Waller Tazewell and Benjamin Watkins Leigh. Leigh would be a prominent figure in the convention, while Tazewell would be influential in the slave debates of 1831-32. See Shade, 61. Leigh took to pen to defend his position that the old constitution served Virginia well and to declare that those who wanted reform desired to expand the "right of suffrage to free negroes." See Shade, 62. Abel P. Upshur thought that those calling for a convention were the "childish fripperies of natural rights." See Claude H. Hall, *Abel Parker Upshur: Conservative Virginian 1790-1844* (Madison, Wisconsin: The State Historical Society of Wisconsin, 1964), 40.

49. Charles Ambler, *Sectionalism in Virginia from 1776-1861* (New York: Russell and Russell, Inc., 1964), 137; Dickson D. Bruce, *The Rhetoric of Conservatism: The Virginia Convention of 1829-30 and the Conservative Tradition of the South* (San Marino, Ca.: Huntington Library, 1982), 90. Bruce asserts that slavery was only a small part of the convention debates and much more time was spent on other topics. William M. Moorhouse, "Alexander Campbell and the Virginia Constitutional Convention of 1829-1830," *Virginia Cavalcade* 20 (Spring 1975): 185, disagrees.

50. Chandler, *Representation in Virginia*, 18-19, notes that Virginia's representation was based on districts, not population. According to the 1776 constitution, the House of Delegates representation was based on counties (two per county, for sixty-two counties and two boroughs), while the Senate was based on districts (for a total of 24). Apportionment was arbitrary and the state constitution had no provision for future apportionments.

51. Freehling, *Road to Disunion*, 170; Alison Goodyear Freehling, *Drift Toward Dissolution: The Virginia Slavery Debate of 1831-1832* (Baton Rouge: Louisiana State University Press, 1982, 40-44, 270; Bruce, 2-3. Whitfield, 14 notes that there were 134 delegates and 15 senators for 348,873 whites east of the Allegheny, while there were 80 delegates and 9 senators for 249,196 west of the same mountain range.

52. Moorhouse, 188; Prufer, 31, notes that it was during this period that the land of what is now West Virginia began to form secessionist (from Virginia) sentiments.

53. Charles H. Ambler, *A History of West Virginia* (New York: Prentice-Hall Inc., 1933), 230 and 219. Certainly, it was the Sage's hope that, in 1778, and after bringing a bill to halt the importation of slaves, there would be future efforts to bring about the "final eradication" of the peculiar institution; Thomas Jefferson, "Autobiography," *The Portable Thomas Jefferson*, 34. James Madison contended that the conventioneers "tenaciously" debated slavery, see Meyers, ed., *The Mind of the Founder*, 413.

54. Merrill D. Peterson, *Democracy, Liberty, and Property: The State Constitutional Conventions of the 1820s* (Indianapolis: The Bobbs-Merrill Company, 1966), xxiii.

55. Ibid., 271; Chandler, *The History of Suffrage in Virginia*, 31; Laura J. Scalia, *America's Jeffersonian Experiment: Remaking State Constitutions* (Dekalb: Northern

Illinois University Press, 1999), 12 and 33.

56. Ambler, *Sectionalism in Virginia*, 146; Virginia, Virginia Constitutional Convention (1829-30), *Proceedings and Debates of the Virginia State Convention of 1829-1830*, vol. 1 (Richmond: Samuel Shepherd and Co., 1830), iii. Hereafter references to this work noted as *Proceedings and Debates*.

57. James Monroe, Speech before the Convention, 5 October 1829, *Proceedings and Debates*, 2-3.

58. John Marshall, Speech before the Convention, 13 October 1829, *Proceedings and Debates*, 26. Unless otherwise noted, quotes from Marshall reflect this citation, 27 and 31.

59. Alexander Campbell, Speech before the Convention, 24 October 1829, *Proceedings and Debates*, 42-43. See also Bruce, 19 and 23; Whitefield, 34-42; Ambler, *Sectionalism in Virginia from 1776-1861*, 137, 148-149.

60. Robert B. Taylor, Speech before the Convention, October 26, 1829, *Proceedings and Debates*, 46; Cf. the second article of question 94 of the *Summa Theologica* in St. Thomas Aquinas, *Treatise on Law* (Chicago: Henry Regnery, 1967), 58-59; and Federalist no. 31 in Rossiter, ed., 161.

61. Ibid., 52.

62. Ibid.

63. Benjamin Watkins Leigh, Speech before the Convention, 26 October 1829, *Proceedings and Debates*, 53. He also claimed that adherence to natural rights would lead to a bloody politics of "fever, frenzy, madness, and death," 3 November 1829, 151; Philip Barbour, Speech before the Convention, 2 November 1829, ibid., 138, and 29 October 1829, 91. We should note that Jefferson condemned the terror; Onuf, 55.

64. Benjamin Watkins Leigh, Speech before the Convention, 3 November 1829, *Proceedings and Debates*, 157; Philip Barbour, Speech before the Convention, 2 November 1829, ibid., 137, and 29 October 1829, 98; Richard Morris (Hanover), Speech before the Convention, 30 October 1829, ibid, 114, asserted that the reason for the war was because British rights were violated, not natural rights. Cf. Jefferson's *A Summary View of the Rights of British America*, in *The Portable Thomas Jefferson*, 4, where the Sage employs the language of natural rights.

65. William Giles, Speech before the Convention, 9 November 1829, *Proceedings and Debates*, 238.

66. Jefferson to Henry Lee, Monticello, 8 May 1825, *Thomas Jefferson: Writings*, 1501.

67. Ibid., and Harry V. Jaffa, *Original Intent and the Framers of the Constitution: A Disputed Question* (Washington, D.C.: Regnery Gateway, 1994), 76.

68. John R. Cooke, Speech before the Convention, 27 October 1829, *Proceedings and Debates*, 55.

69. Benjamin Watkins Leigh, Speech before the Convention, 26 October 1829, *Proceedings and Debates*, 53. It seemed that Leigh's politics was that the powerful had always and should always rule; Freehling, *The Road to Disunion*, 173.

70. John R. Cooke, Speech before the Convention, 27 October 1829, *Proceedings and Debates*, 54 and 55. Unless otherwise noted, quotes from Cooke's speech, 54-56. Italics in the original. Cf. Jaffa, *A New Birth of Freedom*, 67.

71. Ibid., 54.

72. Jefferson, *Notes on the State of Virginia*, in *The Portable Thomas Jefferson*, 170-171. Cf. Cooke's speech, 29 October 1829, *Proceedings and Debates*, 57.

73. John R. Cooke, Speech before the Convention, 27 October 1829, *Proceedings and Debates*, 58.

74. Philip P. Barbour (Orange), Speech before the Convention, 29 October 1829, ibid., 94 and 97. Some agreed that abstract principles were best left out of the convention, but did not agree there were no principles to politics, Briscoe Baldwin (Augusta), Speech before the Convention, 29 October 1829, ibid., 99-100.

75. William B. Giles, Speech before the Convention, 7 November 1829, ibid, 244, italics in the original; K. R. Constantine Gutzman, "Old Dominion, New Republic: Making Virginia Republican, 1776-1840" (Ph.D. diss. University of Virginia, 1999), 438. Giles also represented Virginia in the Senate. Some thought his position and those similar smacked of a complete rejection of the natural rights doctrines articulated by Locke and Algernon Sydney; Charles F. Mercer, Speech before the Convention, 4 November 1829, *Proceedings and Debates*, 193.

76. John Randolph, Speech before the Convention, 14 November 1829, ibid., 317. Randolph served in the House and in the Senate. He was serving in the U.S. Senate during the Missouri debate. He would have a dramatic impact on the sons of St. George Tucker. All quotes hereafter from Randolph, 316.

77. John Scott, Speech before the Convention, 31 October 1829, ibid., 125. All Scott quotes from this source and page. Cf. Bruce, 74-76.

78. John Randolph, Speech before the Convention, 14 November 1829, *Proceedings and Debates*, 317; Bruce, 74-75, 82. Leigh claimed that all ancient republics died because they divorced power from property; Leigh, 3 November 1829, *Proceedings and Debates*, 157. The Burke speech Randolph referred was the "Speech on the Petition of the Unitarians, 1792," *The Speeches of the Right Honorable Edmund Burke,* ed. James Burke (Dublin: James Duffy, 1874), 414-424.

79. John R. Cooke, Speech before the Convention, 27 October 1829, ibid, 59. Unless otherwise noted, quotes from this source, 59-60. Italics in the original.

80. Ibid., 60.

81. Aristotle speaks of the connection between the good and proper moral conduct in the *Nicomachean Ethics* 1094a-1095b, Cf. Cooke's speech, 27 October 1829, *Proceedings and Debates*, 60. Further quotes from ibid, 60-62.

82. Alexander Campbell, Speech before the Convention, October 27, 1829, *Proceedings and Debates*, 64.

83. Abel P. Upshur, Speech before the Convention, 27 October 1829, ibid, 66. Italics in the original. John W. Green (Culpepper) introduced the argument, 27 October 1829, ibid., 62, but Upshur was by far the most articulate member on the issue.

84. Abel P. Upshur, Speech before the Convention, 27 October 1829, ibid, 66-67. Unless noted, quotes are from this source.

85. Ibid., 69, italics in original; Robert Stanard (Spotsylvania), 13 November 1829, ibid, 297, remarked something similar, "Let me tell that gentleman, that for the construction of political and moral theorems, there are no postula, which give him a straight line."

86. Abel P. Upshur, Speech before the Convention, 27 October 1829, ibid, 70.

87. Ibid., 71. Italics in original. As to the acknowledgement of the peculiar property, Upshur makes a direct connection to that and slaves later, 74-75. Cf. the speech of Doddridge, 28 October 1829, ibid, 79.

88. John Randolph, Speech before the Convention, 14 November 1829, ibid, 319.

89. Abel P. Upshur, Speech before the Convention, 28 October 1829, ibid., 70 and 71.

90. Quoting Upshur is Philip Doddridge, Speech before the Convention, 28 October 1829, ibid., 85.

91. Abel P. Upshur, Speech before the Convention, 27 October 1829, ibid., 70; and

28 October 1829, 72-73.

92. Ibid., 71 and 76 respectively. Italics in the original. Leigh contended that power and property ought not be separated; see his comments on 3 November 1829, ibid., 156. Unless otherwise noted, quotes taken from Upshur's speech 27-28 October 1829, 75-79; Fehrenbacher, *Constitutions and Constitutionalism*, 14.

93. Quoted in Moorhouse, 190.

94. Alexander Campbell, Speech before the Convention, 31 October 1829, in *Proceedings and Debates*, 117.

95. Ibid.

96. William Naylor, Speech before the Convention, 31 October 1829, *Proceedings and Debates*, 129.

97. Alexander Campbell, Speech before the Convention, 31 October 1829, ibid, 120.

98. Cf. §95 of Locke, *Two Treatises of Government*, 330: "Men being, as has been said, by Nature, all free, equal and independent . . . " and the Declaration of Rights "That all men are by nature equally free and independent . . . "

99. Alexander Campbell, Speech before the Convention, 31 October 1829, ibid, 120.

100. Ibid., 117.

101. Ibid., 121. Unless otherwise noted, quotes from Campbell, 121-122.

102. William Naylor, Speech before the Convention, 31 October 1829, in *Proceedings and Debates*, 129.

103. Ibid., 130; see §95-99 of the *Second Treatise* in John Locke, *Two Treatises of Government*, ed., Peter Laslett (Cambridge: Cambridge University Press, 1988), 330-333.

104. Alexander Campbell, Speech before the Convention, October 31, 1829, *Proceedings and Debates*, 122.

105. James Monroe, Speech before the Convention, November 2, 1829, ibid., 149.

106. Ibid.

107. Benjamin Watkins Leigh, Speech before the Convention, November 3, 1829, ibid, 158.

108. Monroe, ibid., 174. Monroe was for a very cautious approach regarding this issue because the pro-slave supporters were frank in their assessment that interference by the north would mean violence between the two sections.

109. Ibid., 173.

110. Morgan (Monongalia), 19 November 1829, ibid., 380.

111. Alexander Campbell, Speech before the Convention, 19 November 1829, ibid., 383. Italics in the original.

112. Ibid., 384.

113. Ibid., 385.

114. Doddridge, 28 October 1829, ibid., 83-89; 3 December 1829, 555; Freehling, *The Road to Disunion*, 171; Peterson, *Democracy, Liberty, and Property*, 279.

115. James Madison, Speech before the Convention, 2 December 1829, *Proceedings and Debates*, 537. Unless otherwise noted, all quotes from Madison, 537-539.

116. Speech of Philip P. Barbour, Speech before the Convention, 29 October 1829, *Proceedings and Debates*, 91.

117. Philip Doddridge, Speech before the Convention, 28 October 1829, *Proceedings and Debates*, 89, asserted "that while gentlemen are demanding representation for this species of property, they are demanding a new thing, and are proceeding on a principle never before recognized in the Colony or State."

118. Chapman Johnson, 12 November 1829, ibid., 274-275.

Chapter 5

Firebell in the Night: Natural Rights Abandoned

Yet the hour of emancipation is advancing, in the march of time. It will come; and whether the bloody process of St. Domingo, excited and conducted by the power of our present enemy, if once stationed permanently within our Country, and offering asylum and arms to the oppressed, is a leaf of our history not yet turned over.

Thomas Jefferson

The sailors are quarreling with one another about the piloting, each supposing he ought to pilot, although he has never learned the art and can't produce his teacher or prove there was a time when he was learning it. Besides this, they claim it isn't even teachable and are ready to cut to pieces the man who says it is teachable.

Plato

But the city stands or falls by violence, compulsion, or coercion. There is, then, no essential difference between political rule and the rule of a master over his slaves. But the unnatural character of slavery seems to be obvious: it goes against any man's grain to be made a slave or to be treated as a slave.

Leo Strauss[1]

The convention of 1829-1830 modified the 1776 Virginia Constitution only slightly. William Gordon (Albemarle) proposed the basics of the plan that was eventually accepted. The new document was silent on the white basis of representation for the House and sought to try to distribute somewhat arbitrarily, yet more equally, representation across the state. Principle, as the west understood it, was abandoned and the apportionment was arbitrary—based on what the east would accept. Therefore, the convention came to an agreement whereby the east still controlled state politics.[2] The agreement gave the west about one-half the expected increase under the white basis plan. The east rejected the white basis for the House because they believed the west would eventually acquire too much power—even though the east still would have retained superiority in the Senate.[3] Concerning apportionment, the general assembly was allowed to reapportion after 1841 at intervals of ten years, which could only be called by two-thirds majority of each house. In essence, the apportionment proposal stymied hope for meaningful equal representation in the near future.

With regard to suffrage, even though twenty-two of the twenty-four states had universal white suffrage, and even though the reformers noted that New York and North Carolina permitted free negroes to vote, Virginia lowered the voting requirements only slightly. Indeed, even in the state of Virginia, there were accounts of free men of color voting and participating in Independence Day celebrations featuring speeches from those men. Nevertheless, broader suffrage was rejected, despite another argument proffered by Eugenius M. Wilson (Monongolia): white male suffrage had secured slavery in states like Alabama and Mississippi and would do the same for Virginia. He believed that extending suffrage to white males was necessary because of the coming war with the Northern states. Poorer whites would be needed to fight in that conflict. The best way to secure white participation in the defense of the state would be to grant them the vote.[4] He believed that it would unite the propertied and non-propertied in a common interest. By excluding the poorer whites from the vote, it divided the allegiance of whites on the slavery issue. However, conservatives Benjamin Watkins Leigh (Chesterfield), Abel P. Upshur (Northampton), John Randolph (Charlotte), and William Giles (Amelia) opposed it. In the end, suffrage was only extended to leaseholders and housekeepers. This excluded approximately 30,000 white men.

When the proposed constitution came to a vote in the convention, almost every western delegate voted against it because it did not recognize, or settle, the white basis question. The outcome of the convention was a complete defeat for the reformers.[5] There was talk even before the convention concluded of the western delegation either walking out to retire into a body of their own. This all too pleased Randolph, who moved in vain for *sine die* adjournment. When the convention did adjourn, January 14, 1830, the new constitution was sent to the counties for approval or rejection. In April of 1830, the constitution was ratified with 26,055 approving and 15,563 rejecting. Voters in the west overwhelmingly rejected it 13,282 to 5,985. The opposite resulted in the east: 20,070 to 2,281.

As it pertains to slavery, between 1790-1820 there was really not much in the way of pro-slavery rhetoric—which stands in stark contrast to the aggressive and belligerent defenses of the peculiar institution later. Natural rights philosophy had influenced the revolutionary period, leading to a growth in emancipationist sentiment and actual emancipations. Much of that sentiment continued at the midpoint between 1776 and 1860. Between 1825-1830 manumissions were on the rise in Virginia. Some consider this the high point of anti-slavery feeling. Yet, trouble loomed on the horizon. By 1820 whites only made up 56 percent of the Virginia population. The state was headed for a black majority. This meant that the majority of the population in the state—whether free or slave—would be something other than white. Given the prejudice that the likes of Jefferson and Madison thought existed, many believed that something must be done about the problem before anti-slavery sentiment dissipated. The hope that slavery would recede was overly optimistic, given the fact that even though manumissions were up between 1825-1830, it would never keep up with the natural increase. Virginians were faced with a problem difficult to resolve. This was complicated further by the interest the slaveholder had in the peculiar institution. According to historian Merrill Peterson, every delegate at the convention recognized the truth of Monroe's statement that if slavery did not exist, the conventioneers would be able to meet each other in friendship and trust. Considering that Jefferson and Madison called for a new convention beginning in the early 1780s, the Virginia experience provides a glimpse into the tenacity of those who did not want change.[6]

The convention of 1829-1830 was the "best opportunity" for two generations (The Founders and the subsequent generation) to come together to debate the future of slavery in Virginia.[7] Yet, what came out of the convention was largely unacceptable to everyone. It created an "irredentist problem threatening future war."[8] The new constitution only lasted twenty-one years. The western delegates largely viewed the convention as a defeat. They came to the convention waving the banner of principle and on that score they did not achieve their objective. They were only successful in a modest modification of the property requirement and less successful in equitable apportionment. By 1851, a new convention was called and it finally approved universal white manhood suffrage. The convention, then, was really a victory for pro-slave easterners, who retained their geographic power in the state government and staved off emancipation plans of the west. It is difficult to say whether the east succeeded in convincing Virginians of the superiority of property over liberty and equality, but the fact that they openly attacked the primacy of natural rights is alarming. The conventioneers could not come to an agreement as to the basic principles of free government.

The importance of the debate and the volatility of some of the rhetoric might lead one to the conclusion that the time between 1829-1832 marked a "critical period" in the politics of slavery.[9] During the convention, one side of the debate attacked, or diluted the importance of, natural rights for a politics based on something else. The ultimate question is whether the debate uncovered anything new in the public/political rhetoric and ideas of the time, or since the Founding. One is hard pressed to find similar widespread public speech in a legislative body proclaiming that natural rights are a chimera until that time. Though there are isolated instances when such public rhetoric was uttered, it does not appear as pervasive as when the conventioneers gathered in Richmond in 1829.[10] There is considerable evidence that the slave-owners were becoming more attached to their peculiar property.

There is significance in paying more attention to the public utterances of Old Dominion's statesmen rather than to their private opinions. Some claim that southern orators started the Civil War. It is one thing to write or speak privately, but it is quite another thing to speak publicly. Rhetorical ability is crucial in a republic that is designed in a way that free men cannot be coerced, but must be persuaded. Persuasion, then, is only possible through oratory or public writing.

What one speaks privately might not find favor with the public, yet it does not have the political effect of public speech. However, what a representative speaks publicly, even if it is unaccepted among many, is more ready to be accepted. It also has the capability of influencing public opinion.[11] Abraham Lincoln asserted that,

> our Government rests in public opinion. Whoever can change public opinion can change the government, practically just so much. Public opinion, on any subject, always has a "*central idea*," from which all minor thoughts radiate. That "*central idea*" in our political public opinion, at the beginning was, and until recently has continued to be, "the equality of men." And although it was always submitted patiently to whatever of inequality there seemed to be as matter of actual necessity, its constant working has been a steady progress towards the practical equality of all men.[12]

In republics, public opinion is paramount. Those that seek to change it may "practically" do so "just so much." Usually, they will not have a dramatic effect on public opinion. Perhaps more importantly, in every opinion, there is an idea, which is the motivator of expression. As we have seen in the Founding Virginia generation, that central idea was the equality of men. Statesmen like Madison, Monroe, and Jefferson did their best to approximate that idea in political reality. We might be able to claim as an extension of Lincoln's statement that, generally, those elected by their constituents reflect in some way the opinions of the public. Reflexively, the representative's speech also has an effect on the voter. Therefore, we are able to gauge the progression of the slave interest in Virginia by examining the public orations of her most prominent statesmen and determine just how far Virginia strayed, or was wandering, from the Founders by 1829-1830.

The Framers designed the national government for deliberative democracy. As noted in chapter three, Madison, Monroe, and Jefferson supported the western view that a new constitution was desirable. As a part of that reform, they supported universal white manhood suffrage and equal representation. They thought that a revised constitution would better secure the safety, welfare, and rights of the people, while also fostering deliberative democracy.[13] The expansion of the franchise and reapportionment would better serve the common interest of Virginia by thwarting narrow or parochial interests—in this case the eastern pro-slave faction. Their goal was, in part, to revise the constitution in order to moderate the attachment to slavery.

The legislature of Virginia was famous for subsuming much of the state politics in its "impetuous vortex."[14] Even though the state constitution required the branches to be distinct and separate, in reality the general assembly had the most power, and served a peculiar interest:

> Yet we find not only this express exception with respect to the members of the inferior courts, but that the chief magistrate, with his executive council, are appointable by the legislature; that two members of the latter are triennially displaced at the pleasure of the legislative; and that all the

principal offices, both executive and judiciary, are filled by the same department.[15]

In Query XIII of his *Notes on the State of Virginia* (hereafter *Notes*), Jefferson considered the legislative domination in the state an example of despotic government.[16] While Jefferson and Madison preferred reworking the constitution in order to better separate the powers, another important step in taming the legislature was the broadening of suffrage and reapportionment. If we may apply some of the reasoning of Publius in regard to parochial interests to the function of the state, then the aim was clear.

The spirit of party and faction threatened the "sound deliberation" of the assembly, or the state governing bodies. An excessive attachment to local interests poisoned deliberation and contaminated proceedings:

> Everyone knows that a great proportion of the errors committed by the State legislatures proceeds from the disposition of the members to sacrifice the comprehensive and permanent interest of the State to the particular and separate views of the counties or districts in which they reside . . . the great interests of the nation have suffered . . . from an undue attention to the local prejudices, interests and views of the particular States.[17]

This problem no less affected politics in Virginia. If there was an "undue attention to the local prejudices, interests, and views" of the particular counties and districts in the state, then the common good would suffer. Such representatives would not sacrifice the local interests to the interest of justice and the common good. Yet, there is, in all republics, or representative governments, the tendency for the "spirit of faction" to "poison" the "deliberations of all bodies of men."[18] The slaveholders in the convention were affected by just that. They were too concerned with their narrow interest—their possession of slaves—and less concerned with justice; they allowed their selfish interest to enslave their opinions.

The fact that pro-slave Virginians veered toward a defense of slavery raises the possibility that self-interest overcame principle. Thomas G. West noted this inconsistency in *Vindicating the Founders*. According to West, "there will always be a gap between moral principles and actions."[19] West points out that it is easy to confuse principles with interest:

> Selfish interest sometimes led men to misunderstand their own principles. In 1785 six Virginia counties petitioned the state legislature, objecting to any emancipation of slaves "on the ground that the Revolution had been fought to preserve liberty and property." These Virginians, and other slaveholders who shared their view, forgot that the right to property flows from—is part of—the natural right to liberty. If there is no natural right to liberty, there can be no natural right to property. If men are rightfully free, they all may keep the bread they earn with their own hands. Therefore, there can be no right to property *in slaves*.[20]

We have seen that this interest in 1785 was just as rooted, or perhaps became more rooted, in 1829-1830. Abraham Lincoln also articulated the gap between principle and interest. During the "house divided" speech, he argued that only one side in the debate would win because that division cannot exist interminably. The house was divided against itself because self-interest clouded reason. In his second inaugural address, Lincoln stated that slavery "constituted a peculiar and powerful interest. All knew that this interest was, somehow, the cause of the war."[21] According to Lincoln, there was no way to keep together liberty and slavery. Those who wanted slavery had to develop a new philosophy to justify holding men in bondage. In Virginia, Monroe noted much the same thing. In the 1829 convention, he explained that if slavery did not exist, Virginia would not be divided over that interest.[22] The Virginia convention, then, is an act in a play that led to the Civil War, and where we see the division of the house of Old Dominion.

Conservatives at the convention acknowledged the role self-interest played in politics, however they did not think it was something to overcome. They saw it realistically. John Scott (Faquier) admitted as much when he announced: "If we look around us into the ordinary affairs of men, we shall find that interest is the great spring of action. What is it that makes agriculture flourish? What is it that builds your cities, and makes commerce spread her wings? . . . It is love of wealth, fame, and distinction. In a word, it is self-love."[23] This self-love turns into personal self-interest which overtakes all other feelings: "[M]y experience teaches me, that I am never so sure of the good offices of another, as when I make it his interest to serve me." According to Scott, while there are examples of men acting in unselfish ways, all men are basically selfish and interested in what is theirs, what they own, and what they desire to acquire from someone else. Therefore, the proper role of government is to protect, yet confine, that interest lest selfishness overpower the body politic, leaving nothing safe from the avarice of others. Reformer Philip Doddridge (Brooke) also noted the influence of interest. It sought to protect a part of the society at the expense of all others. The selfishness of the slaveholder so consumed him that it became a "tyrant passion" and led him to declare that there are "no principles in Government at all."[24]

Not only did their passion overcome principle, but also their economic concerns countermanded the importance for the common good. Because the slaveholders feared that they would lose their property to excessive taxation, or outright immediate emancipation, they abandoned the principles of the Revolution: "And to avert imminent peril and flagrant injustice, you are asked to invest the 409,758 [slaves] with *factitious Constitutional power*—to destroy the great landmarks of natural right, established at the æra of the revolution—to repudiate all the principles of Government, which have been, until now, held sacred and inviolable."[25] The belief that self-interest is the primary motivator of man led Upshur to assert that there are two kinds of majorities: those of numbers and those of interests.[26] He simply contended that the interest in slave property should be secured against the majority who in numbers desired to see the peculiar institution put on the road to extinction. Since the protection of property is paramount to a secure society, the interest in property (slaves) should be protected. The argument on behalf of majority/minority interests ought to sound familiar. John C. Calhoun most popularized this idea in terms of the concurrent majority in *A Disquisition of Government* (hereafter *Disquisition*). Perhaps he got the idea from the convention? Recall, he spent time in Richmond during the debates and listened to the orations.

If the Virginia Constitutional Convention of 1829-1830 is any indication, the essential elements of Calhoun's *Disquisition* were worked out long before he published his work. We find arguments in the convention that Calhoun popularizes in the *Disquisition*. Therefore, the argument on behalf of the pro-slave eastern delegation provided Calhoun with more than enough material with which to base his political thought. By the 1829-1830 Constitutional Convention, the representatives of the slaveholding interest openly challenged compact theory. They attacked the Declaration of Independence and Declaration of Rights by rejecting compact theory. In its place, they formed an organic theory of society, which placed emphasis on the positive law, history, and experience as a more reliable principle. This organic theory left the reconciliation of slavery and liberty to the state, local community, or, ultimately the individual who owned the property. Indeed, in the *Disquisition*, Calhoun spoke often of the constitution as an "organism."[27] Whatever rights one had in a community emanated from the positive law. Therefore, Calhoun's political theory "is not related to any particular end or good."[28] In many ways, his concurrent majority resembles Jean-Jacques Rousseau's general will: the competing majorities mete out their differences until they have reached a consensus until everyone's particular will matches will of the whole. It is as if Calhoun goes to great lengths to avoid making value judgments. He cares not what is willed as long as the process under which interests express themselves is protected. There is no intrinsic rightness or wrongness of what is willed, and hence no enlightened consent of what are the just powers of government. Just how much of a departure this is from the Founders, and Virginia's Founders in particular, we will turn to next.

The Basis of Government and the Attack on Jefferson

The pro-slave belief that all action sprang from selfishness was the basis of the departure from the Founders and natural rights. If man's nature is nasty and lustful—only concerned for its own material well-being—then happiness would be viewed differently. The Virginia Declaration of Rights contends that happiness comes from the enjoyment of life and liberty (equality), and acquiring property. Happiness was not the result of merely feeling safe, but came about through entrepreneurial pursuits, which did not deprive others of life and liberty. Leigh also asserted that happiness was the end of man. However, he seemed to view happiness quite lowly. What makes man happy is security.[29] Lucas Thompson (Amherst) disputed this view of government and thought that the pro-slave representatives repudiated Jefferson and the intellectual fathers of public right: "Then, the authority of the sage of Monticello would have stood against the world; now there are 'none so poor as to do him reverence.' Then, was Burke regarded as the enemy of human rights and the firmest defender of aristocracy and monarchy—but now Burke, Filmer, and Hobbes, judging from their argument, have become the text books of our statesmen."[30] The rejection of natural right also led to a rejection of Jefferson by the pro-slave faction. Indeed, the convention marks the first open disavowal of Jefferson's teachings. Jefferson, his opinions on slavery, and his role in the Founding as an author of the Declaration of Independence became a topic for political discussion because 1829 marked the publication of *The Memoirs, Correspondence and Private Papers of Thomas Jefferson*. The four volumes were edited by his grandson, Thomas Jefferson Randolph. Thus, in addition to his *Notes*, politicians had ample material with which to decipher Jefferson's political philosophy. The release of his papers helped to stir debate, and none were more critical than John Randolph: "I have not much deference for the opinion of Mr. Jefferson. We all know he was very confident in his theories—but I am a practical man and have no confidence a priori in the theories of Mr. Jefferson, or of any other man under the sun."[31] He concluded that the eastern delegate would not be "struck down by the authority of Mr. Jefferson" and Leigh added that "so important are a great man's errors."[32]

Not everyone criticized Jefferson. Alexander Campbell, for one, praised him as a learned "Sage."[33] The reformer claimed that every principle they supported could be found in Jefferson's opinions. Nevertheless, we can see the first rumblings of a transformation of southern attitudes toward slavery, and away from natural rights first in Virginia.

Pro-slave Virginians were thus apostatized from Jefferson and toward Burke.[34] The pro-slave conventioneers attacked the significance of the Virginia Declaration of Rights as a guide to action. To them human equality was a poor guide to political statesmanship. John Randolph was one of the chief offenders:

> But I hold with one of the greatest masters of political philosophy, that "no rational man ever did govern himself by abstractions and universals." I do not put abstract ideas wholly out of any question, because I know well that under that name I should dismiss principles; and that without the guide and light of sound, well understood principles, all reasonings in politics, as everything else, would be only a confused jumble of particular facts and details, without the means of drawing out any sort of theoretical or practical conclusion.[35]

The practical conclusion of which he speaks is not an admission that men govern themselves by abstract concepts, but that as a politician, he must take into account circumstances. While on the one hand he stated he subscribed to the "Bill of Rights," on the other hand he concluded that taken without modification, implementation of the principles in the document would end in political disaster. Actually, his circumstances must guide him in all his actions. In this way he moved away from a dedication to the rights of man. A person who follows principle without a view to reality, is "metaphysically mad."[36] There is much to examine in the political use of Burke as an authority, but such an examination is beyond our scope here. Suffice to say that the nineteenth-century politicians were (re)discovering Burke because a multivolume work of his was published over that century. Seven of the sixteen volumes were published in the 1830s. However, some have contended that various public figures at the time used Burke for their own ends. He appealed to both progressives, conservative Whigs, and even religious evangelicals.[37]

Leigh, Randolph, and Upshur rejected natural rights theory for a new, or older, dispensation of Machiavelli and Hobbes. Plato, Aristotle, Locke and Sydney were singled out as operating in a world of "visions." Theirs was a speculative philosophy that had no bearing on the real world. Presumably, the ancient and modern political philosophers had nothing to offer the practical development of founding.[38] In contrast, the Founders did not have a kind word for the political thought of Hobbes, or Machiavelli. The defense of the political philosophers fell to Chapman Johnson (Augusta). His lengthy defense of the Founding included affirmative appeals to not only Plato, Cicero, Sydney and Locke, but Publius, who contended in Federalist Thirty-One that there were first principles of government upon which all subsequent reasoning depends. The political wisdom of the ages has culminated in the first principles set down in the Virginia Declaration. Even Burke, who certainly did not like the French levelers, appealed to the British Declaration of Right as a non-arbitrary measurement of how the government should function. Indeed, Johnson claimed that the inspiration of the Virginia Declaration came right out of Locke's *Second Treatise*.

Pro-slave owners attacked the Declaration of Rights as too lofty a document to pay strict attention. They believed that the best model for government is how things are, and how man is, not how man ought to be. This, of course, sounds very much like Hobbes, who claimed that man is restless for power and has an intense desire to accumulate more power—he does not believe he can live well without the acquisition of more. Therefore, self-preservation and security is the chief end of government because fear of violence and death is the most powerful passion.[39]

With this understanding of the foundation of government and the nature of man, we ought not be surprised, then, that Leigh and his cohorts attacked the concept of liberty and equality. Leigh asserted that the Lockean state of nature is simply imaginary and hence that the concept of rights is something concocted in civil society: "I cannot conceive any natural right of man contra-distinguished from social Conventional right—the very word right is a word of relation and implies some society."[40] Indeed, Randolph exclaimed that, "I am an aristocrat. I Love Liberty. I hate equality."[41] To the east, the reformers not only overemphasize natural rights, but they disregard property. The Declaration of Rights asserts that no compact can divest or deprive anyone of life, liberty or the "means of acquiring and possessing property." According to Leigh, this means that along with life and liberty, property is necessary. However, he raises property to a level above liberty; there is more emphasis on property than on liberty. In a sense, conservatives would contend the reformers misread Locke or took him too seriously.

The east really held no regard for Locke though. They believed his theories were to blame for the reformer's position on matters like universal white manhood suffrage. Though Locke believed that property ought to be secure, his theories have influenced *"divine right democracy* . . . [but] it does not follow, that, because all men are born equal, and have equal rights to life, liberty, and the property they can acquire by honest industry, therefore, all men may rightly claim, in an established society, equal political powers."[42] It is not that Leigh believed nobody but the slaveholder should possess political power, but that equal representation in the west and broadened suffrage would threaten slave property:

> No Government can produce the greatest degree of happiness and safety, or fail to destroy them, which does not provide the most jealous security for property, which does not wed power to property, which disclaims, in the first principle of its organization, all regard to property. No Government can be just, or wise, or safe for Virginia, which shall place the property of the East in the Power and at the disposal of the West.[43]

The pro-slave east, in their challenge of compact theory, ended up rejecting majority rule.

James Madison on Majority Rule

Even Calhoun noted in the *Disquisition* that the minority in a concurrent majority political system could assert its negative on a given issue and used the terms "interposition" and "nullification" to describe that act. The doctrine of nullification became a popular theory for many of the southern states to thwart the federal government. In 1835, James Madison asserted in his essay "Sovereignty" that the Calhounian doctrine of nullification—concurrent majorities—was a faulty one. Calhoun argued that a state had the authority to interpose its authority between a federal law and the application of that law at the state level. In other words, a state could nullify, declare null and void, any law that it deemed in violation of the original compact. That extent of sovereign power the states did not retain in the compact. The constitution did not secure for a state the ability to nullify federal law. As far as the formation of a political community is concerned, Madison contended the first act is voluntary:

> [L]et us consult the Theory which contemplates a certain number of individuals as meeting and agreeing to form one political society, in order that the rights the safety & the interest of each may be under the safeguard of the whole.
>   The first supposition is, that each individual being previously independent of the others, the compact which is to make them one society must result from the free consent of *every* individual.[44]

The compact of society—the federal government as that of the state of Virginia—is entered into individually, but so as to safeguard the whole. The whole society is better able to safeguard the rights, safety, and interests of each individual than any individual may on his own. If someone argued that society exists to protect one's personal life, liberty, and property at the expense of others, this is tantamount to one part of the community risking their lives while the other part does not. We find similar perspective in Query XIII of the *Notes*. Those who fought to protect and defend the state of Virginia were being done an injustice because many of them were denied representation (a majority of those who fought were from the western portion of the state) and the right to vote.[45] Jefferson concluded near the end of his life that,

> the basis of our constitution is in opposition to the principle of equal, political rights, refusing to all but freeholders any participation in the natural right of self-government. It is believed, for example, that a very great majority of the militia, on whom the burden of military duty was imposed in the late war, were men unrepresented in the legislation which imposed this burden on them . . . The exclusion of a majority of our freemen from the right of representation is merely arbitrary, and an usurpation of the minority over the majority; for it is believed that the non-freeholders compose the majority of our free and adult male citizens.[46]

This issue was raised and debated in the convention as well. Non-freeholders complained that they had fought bravely for their state, but were denied participation in her politics.[47] When wars were fought all enjoyed protection; when peace was concluded the same occurred. The eastern representatives, then, were arguing exactly what they ought not have: they wanted protection of their property, but did not want to extend equal political rights to those who defended their property. They did not want the non-freeholder to have the same political protection the slaveholder enjoyed.

To claim that a part of the community deserves more political power and more protection because that part is somehow superior (the east), and the other part is inferior (the west), is fraudulent. It contradicts the initial voluntary act, which as Madison makes clear is unanimous consent:

> But as the objects in view could not be attained, if every measure conducive to them required the consent of every member of the society, the theory further supposes, either that it was a part of the original compact, that the will of the majority was to be deemed the will of the whole, or that this was a law of nature, resulting from the nature of political society itself, the offspring of the natural wants of man.
>
> Whatever be the hypothesis of the origin of the *lex majoris parties*, it is evident that it operates as a plenary substitute of the will of the majority of the society for the will of the whole society; and that the sovereignty of the society as vested in & exercisable by the majority, may do anything that could be *rightfully* done by the unanimous concurrence of the members; the reserved rights of individuals (of conscience for example) in becoming parties to the

original compact being beyond the legitimate reach of sovereignty, whenever vested or however viewed.[48]

Where the eastern slaveholder repudiates the natural equality of men, it is but a small step to abandon both universal consent and majority rule. Yet, according to Madison, when people agree to enter into a compact they unanimously consent to do so, and thereafter be governed by the will of the majority as if all unanimously agreed (however, if all people agreed on everything there would be no need for a compact in the first place). What the pro-slave representatives in the convention seemed to ignore was that the minority still retained their rights as they entered society. The first act is voluntary, and each individual must make a choice to either enter into the compact or not. Each individual has the same authority as every other person in making that choice. Madison notes that this is by nature. Once entered, they agree to be governed by the majority. Concerning the interest of the community, it is interesting that the pro-slave representatives did not consider the real minority interest, the slaves! If anybody was a true minority, it was those held in bondage, not those who "owned" those who were held in bondage. This inconsistency was noted by Samuel Moore (Rockridge) who asserted of the master: "what title has he, to count them on his side? Is it because their interests, and his are the same? Surely not; for every interest they have on earth is adverse to his, and if counted at all, they must be counted against him."[49]

Taking the Declaration of Rights seriously, nobody can rightfully demand the obedience of another. A free society depends on that recognition. Unanimous "consent in the establishment of a body politic follows necessarily from the recognition of the natural equality of mankind and is necessary if the society is to be free."[50] At the convention, William Naylor (Hampshire) expressed essentially the same Madisonian argument, yet more with a view to combat the contention by the slaveholding east that the will of the majority ought not rule:

> We cannot, indeed, divest ourselves of the idea of the state which man must have been in previous to the formation of the social compact. This was a treaty to which every member of the community became a party, by which they unanimously agreed to form one body, and so became incorporated as such.
>
> This was formed not only by the consent of the majority, but by the consent of the whole. And when the compact was formed, it resulted from the very nature of the case, without any formal stipulation, that it could only act, move or be guided by the consent of the majority. True, they might afterwards by the consent of that majority, agree that a minority should rule, or they could agree to create a monarchy; but still, the act that created the oligarchy or the monarchy, was the act of the majority.[51]

Virginia was thus founded on the principle of the equality of men and the rule of the majority even if it did not draft a constitution that was as republican as the Founders (Jefferson and Madison to name a few) would have liked. In other words, according to Naylor, there is no *right* for the slaveholders to have a disproportionate, or superior, position in society. They are just as equal as the non-freeholder in the west. In order for Virginia to be more republican, it needed to better ensconce majority rule.

The natural equality of man and majority rule does not mean that the majority could do anything it wanted to the east simply because they had the numbers. The minority has equal rights of the majority because they have the same natural rights. The majority ought not take away the minority's right to life, liberty, and property, for example, for it would violate the "necessary condition" of the compact.[52] Majority rule must be consistent with the law of nature and nature's God. Only a majority rule consistent with what is rightful is legitimate. Majority rule is not unlimited.[53] The majority must obey something higher than itself; it cannot be understood apart from the rights of the minority, which are also the rights the majority possesses. Therefore, some things are simply beyond the scope of majority rule. However, the pro-slave east in Virginia rejected this formulation, in part because they dismissed the equality of men, but also because they did not feel a friendship, a kinship with their fellow citizens in the west.[54] The doctrine of concurrent majorities, then, is a doctrine of antagonism. There is nothing in the doctrine of concurrent majorities that encourages the two sides to come together and discover what they have in common. It is difficult to believe that such a structure of government would have resolved the differences that exist in Virginia. It is just as possible that each side would remain intransigent in its opinions. The convention lends evidence to that phenomena when the west walked away unsatisfied and the east claimed it would never compromise to accept the rights of man. The slave-owner not only did not want the federal government meddling in slavery, but also they cast off members of their own community from such officiousness. Monroe urged that the whole state—the entire Union—should share in the burden of emancipation, but this the slaveholder rejected out of hand. Without friendship and common interest, then, there can be no community. Alexander Campbell demonstrated contra eastern arguments that "common interest" does not mean "equal interest."[55] As Madison also noted, not every interest is precisely equal:

> One Gentleman had spoken of the interest which one man might have in a ship which had valuable cargo aboard, and another who had only his person. They both had a common interest, it was true; but he might have given to the figure a greater extent, and supposed that many individuals might have had different stakes embarked on the same bottom. Besides their own persons, they might have a great diversity of interests, and though disproportioned in value, equally interesting them all in safety of the ship.[56]

Campbell was just one who contended that the west had in common with the east the interest of the state. The west did not have an equal interest in slavery to be sure, but they all had in common the safety and prosperity of the ship of state. The west was just as concerned with the safety of all in the state after emancipation as the east.

The slaveholder rejected a community of the whole, for a community of the part based on the interest they had in slavery. They based their claim on legal justice or we might say economic justice. The slaves became less a problem and more a possession; they became less human and more property. From the law came ownership and from that ownership came all the privileges of the possession of that property. Whatever was theirs was not for anybody to regulate but the owners of the slaves. Jefferson articulated, perhaps, another reason for the division. If the equality of man, and equal political rights, were rejected, "then no principles are important."[57] If there are no principles recognized, then perhaps Campbell was correct that the entire convention was set out to sea without rudder or pilot. Pro-slave supporters certainly asserted just that; there were no principles to government.[58] At the heart of the division was a disbelief in a non-arbitrary standard that served as a guide for actions of men.

Madison's essay on "Sovereignty" emphasized that the majority could only do what was rightful. Anything else was beyond the scope of their powers. The Declaration of Independence, no less than the Declaration of Rights, made a distinction that legitimate authority came from consent, and that legitimacy originated in the exercise of natural rights. We might practically say "so what?" Leaving aside the fact that the pro-slave representatives rejected the notion of natural equality, and that all forms of inequality were affected by political institutions, the problem remained as to what to do with the slaves should they be emancipated. The west did not articulate the immediate end of slavery. Rather, they emphasized their common interest with the east in dealing with the problem. Yet, as we have already noted, the slaveholders believed that man was intensely self-interested. While to Publius self-interest should be something counteracted, or controlled, the pro-slave faction celebrated it, and sought to protect it, not moderate it. They believed that a selfish majority would violate the rights of the minority if given a chance. Therefore, slave property needed to be protected and those who owned slaves needed to have a greater share in the operation of the government to ensure that security. Madison considered that argument unconvincing, for the east was being "merely arbitrary" in its "usurpation of the minority over the majority." An enlightened majority derives its opinions from the "laws of nature and of nature's God" and that provides necessary guidance under which that majority exercises their authority. Proceeding on that principle—recognizing that there is a natural law antecedent to the positive law—is what made the western arguments more legitimate than the east, whose arguments proceeded arbitrarily. Perhaps Madison's essay in Federalist Ten and his essay on "Parties" provides a necessary practical correction to the east's fear, and explains that fear.

In an essay featured in the *National Gazette*, Madison acknowledged that parties were inevitable. A difference of interests was the source of party. According to Madison there were ways to combat that evil:

1. By establishing a political equality among all. 2. By withholding *unnecessary* opportunities from a few, to increase the inequality of property, by an immoderate, and especially an unmerited, accumulation of riches. 3. By the silent operation of laws, which, without violating the rights of property, reduce

extreme wealth towards a state of mediocrity, and raise extreme indigence towards a state of comfort. 4. By abstaining from measures which operate differently on different interests, and particularly such as favor one interest at the expence of another. . . . If this is not the language of reason, it is that of republicanism.[59]

The slaveholding east in the convention contended for the opposite of each of the four points. They were being, if not unreasonable, unrepublican. They opposed political equality, encouraged the inequality of property and wealth, and finally, urged a politics that granted favor, or preference, to some interests and not others. In other words, if we follow Madison's advice, Virginia was not as republican (anti-republican?) as it should be. Indeed, the pro-slave argument amounted to this:

> In all political societies, different interests and parties arise out of the nature of things, and the great art of politicians lies in making them checks and balances to each other. Let us then increase these *natural distinctions* by favoring an inequality of property; and let us add to them *artificial distinctions,* by establishing *kings,* and *nobles,* and *plebeians.* We shall then have the more checks to oppose to each other: we shall then have the more scales and the more weights to perfect and maintain the equilibrium. This is as little the voice of reason, as it is that of republicanism.

The distinction the slave party desired was one that would defeat majority rule for a represented interested rule. Despite the claims that liberty would be secured with representation based on majority and minority interests, it is not reasonable nor republican. The argument, Madison asserts, is absurd: "From the expediency, in politics, of making natural parties, mutual checks on each other, to infer the propriety of creating artificial parties, in order to form them into mutual checks, is not less absurd than it would be in ethics, to say, that new vices ought to be promoted, where they would counteract each other, because this use may be made of existing vices." Madison thought that those who advanced the position that the majority and the minority should have a special place in the government were forwarding an heretical position: "The Patrons of this new heresy will attempt in vain to mask its anti-republicanism under a contrast between the extent and the discordant interests of the Union, and the limited dimensions and sameness of interests within its members."[60] Despite the fact that Madison is writing with a view to the Union, he nevertheless heard the similar arguments in the 1829-1830 Constitutional Convention. He continues to assert that "those who denounce majority Governments altogether because they may have an interest in abusing their power, denounce at the same time all Republican Government and must maintain that minority governments would feel less of the bias of interest or seductions of power."[61]

The remedy for this is the expansion of the sphere. Madison explained in his essay on "Parties" that to bolster republicanism, we must increase political equality and decrease the temptation to secure special privileges for the propertied and the wealthy. In Federalist Ten he asserts that giving everyone the same opinions is impossible. The opinions of man are varied and as long as the opinions of man are fallible, different opinions will be formed.[62] Though the pro-slave east and Calhoun seem to believe that interests can be generally identical in a given political community, Publius disagrees. Men will have an infinite variety of interests even in the same community. Similar interests may coalesce around a certain issue: most slaveholders in the east agreed that the slave property should be protected. In this sense, the self-interest of the slaveholder attached itself to perpetuating the peculiar institution. Publius calls this interest a faction because it is "actuated by some common impulse of passion, or of interest, adverse to the rights of other citizens, or to the permanent and aggregate interests of the community."[63] As Campbell asserted, the connection between the political power of the slave-owners and slavery provided a passionate incentive for them to maintain and retain that power. In Virginia, the slave owning landed interest possessed most of the political power in the state. It was that power that needed to be checked.[64] Therefore, taking in most all of the interests of the state, we would find that interests are generally varied.

Not only are people interested in their own property, but there are also those who are creditors, mercantilists, manufacturers, etc. Indeed, Madison asserted that Virginia had wide and varied interests: slavery, farming, and interests regarding whether to improve the interior of the state to better develop it for commerce and trade. Even among those who desired internal improvements in the western part of the state, there was no agreement as to the manner of the improvement, how it should be conducted, and when. We might say that even in a majority there are many minorities that make up the majority. The problem with Virginia's politics is that it did not take into account the vast interests residing in the state. There was no political equality of all interests to be taken into account. On a lesser scale, Federalist Ten explains a remedy to the diseases most afflicting republican government: "Extend the sphere and you take in a greater variety of parties and interests; you make it less probable that a majority of the whole will have a common motive to invade the rights of other citizens."[65] Even if a common motive existed, it would be difficult for the interest to act in unison. In the states, however, Publius asserts that factious leaders encouraged division and kindled party spirit. Similarly, Cooke stated that the Virginia Constitution was factitious. Factions are arbitrary and tended to divide the state by securing narrow interests and political power. The reformers in the convention thought that could be remedied by extending the sphere. In other words, even though Virginia is not as varied in interests as the compendium of interests that existed in the Union, the effects of majority faction in Virginia could be mitigated with equal representation and universal white suffrage. Both modifications to the Virginia Constitution would spread the interests of the state over a greater expanse, and hence, decrease the likelihood that a majority would invade the rights of the minority. The east thus fundamentally misunderstood majority rule.

A few of the Founders believed that property requirements for voting were wrong and akin to slavery. However, others thought that the limitation on voting rights was compatible with the equality of men. The point is that both believed in equality, but disagreed as how best to apply that principle. By 1792, only four states reduced or abolished property requirements as a qualification for voting.[66] The representatives in the eastern section of Virginia pointed to the Declaration of Rights, which stated that "all men, having sufficient evidence of permanent common interest with, and attachment to, the community, have the right of suffrage." According to this argument, those who were landed (held property) had demonstrated they had a permanent and common interest in the community. The two biggest requirements in Virginia were residency and property. However, the reformers asserted that if men are equal, then there should be no rule without consent. Voting for representatives is a way to demonstrate that consent and to exercise our right to liberty. Therefore, rule without consent is a species of slavery; the west was being enslaved by the east.

We have already addressed the argument that suffrage ought to be extended to those in the military, or militia, who had fought to protect the state. The reformers believed that they ought to be enfranchised because they put their life on the line. They had demonstrated their interest in the community of the state. Regarding this issue, Jefferson wrote to Edmund Pendleton to support a broad enfranchisement: "I was for extending the rights of suffrage . . . to all who had a permanent intention of living in the country. Take what circumstances you please as evidence for this, either the having resided a certain time, or having a family, or having property, any or all of them. Whoever intends to live in a country must wish the country well, and has a natural right of assisting in the preservation of it."[67] So important was the elective franchise to Jefferson, that he saw it as a direct extension of the equality principle. He objected to excluding those who had fought for Virginia because that would have left many without the means to defend those rights. Madison concurred. Property is exclusionary: "their exclusion would violate 'the vital principal of free government that those who are bound by the law ought to have a voice in making them.'"[68] Monroe also believed that the franchise should be extended. During the 1829 convention, he supported "equal and just principles" which would promote "equal liberty among our fellow citizens, inspire confidence, promote affection, and bind the state, in all its parts, more closely together."[69] Expanding, the elective franchise made practical sense then as well. It was not only to secure the rights of men, but also to bind a divided state together. It would make the east and west portions of the state more friendly to each other and lessen the antagonisms between them.

The objection to expanding the vote franchise was that it would be dangerous to property rights (slave property). The east feared the west would somehow seize their property. Such a move to "King Numbers" would lead to despotism. Randolph was one of the chief articulators of this position. However, in the case of the Virginia convention it was not to protect property per se, but chiefly to protect slave property. Madison would say that where slavery exists, a majority that has consented to hold a class of human beings in bondage, makes republicanism "fallacious."[70] The east, then, was occupying a seemingly hypocritical ground: they wanted their property rights protected at the same time they were denying the rights of the slaves. Indeed, they did not affirm the natural rights of anyone and rejected that idea. The slave-owner based his arguments on group rights. They thought that only those who were part of a certain group or class of individuals should be protected and granted the positive right to vote.

We should not make the mistake that the Founders viewed politics this lowly. Government did not exist for the mere management of the varied interests in politics. In Federalist Forty-Three Madison links the Declaration of Independence with the Constitution. If the law is to be properly read and interpreted, it should be done in light of the Declaration. The aim of government, then, is safety and happiness. The Declaration of Rights is virtually identical to the Declaration of Independence in this manner. The purpose of civil society is to secure inalienable rights. Therefore, whether in the Constitution or the Virginia Constitution, the foundation, or starting point, with which to judge the conduct of the government is the laws of nature. In the Constitutional Convention of 1829-1830, the east and west disputed the ends of government. Advocates for expanding the franchise and equalized apportionment argued for those reforms based on the immutable principles and abstract truths. For example, one of the leaders of the western reformers wrote as a reason for attending the convention that, "I was desirous of laying a foundation for the abolition of slavery."[71] While one side articulated the principles of the Declaration of Rights, the other side rejected it as a beginning point for politics. The Declaration of Rights claims that it articulated for all "posterity" the "basis and foundation of government." It is these disputes over the ends of government that make it more difficult, or even impossible, for the minority to accept the decisions of the majority. In Federalist Fifty-One, Publius contends that even though there are factions in society, justice ought to hold the balance between them. Therefore, not every interest is a faction—politics is not the mere balancing act between morally equal interest groups. Unjust interests are factions, while just interests are not. The government should be so constructed so as to allow the just, "nonfactious interests to predominate."[72] Even though governments do not arise by nature, nature remains the standard by which society is measured and judged.[73] The west spoke in similar terms.

Doddridge noted that human nature never changed. Equality is the distinguishing feature of human nature and human beings possess the same rights because they are equally possessed with the same nature. This is unlike other relationships we might think of. The relationship between man and man is not the same as between man and dog, or man and horse. The relationship between man and any other animal is inherently the relationship of master and servant: "all human beings are equally human beings in the same sense that all dogs are equally dogs, and all chairs are equally chairs."[74] This is why, between men, there are no natural rulers, nor are there any classes of individuals who are superior by nature to anyone else. There may be unequal talents, but none that make someone a natural ruler over another. Since every man is equally human, since human beings are neither gods, nor beasts, the Declaration of Rights condemns both divine right kings and slavery. This is why Campbell would proclaim in a July fourth speech after the convention concluded that the "genius of our Government is the genius of universal emancipation."[75] He derived this from that fact that "individuals have 'certain inherent rights of which when they enter into a state of society they cannot by any compact deprive or divest their posterity, namely the enjoyment of life and liberty, with the means of acquiring and possessing property.'"[76] This is precisely what concerned the slave-owner: if all men possessed rights inalienably, then the slaves too possessed these rights and slavery was unjust.

Campbell's aim was to not only emancipate the slaves, but also emancipate the masters. He believed the master was not truly free. They were enslaved to their interests. They were attached, sometimes passionately so, to the slaves and the economic value they placed on them. In addition, Campbell believed that the masters were enslaved because they were too afraid of the slaves. Of course, this fear would only increase after the Nat Turner insurrection. Nevertheless, he believed that even before that event, the master feared his slaves. Virginia had attempted after the convention to institute a law restricting the education of the slaves. It would have prohibited not only reading and writing, but also religious instruction. According to Campbell this demonstrated their fear, but it is also evident that the law would retard the speed of emancipation because the slaves need enlightenment before freedom. They needed enlightenment not only to survive on their own, but also to function peacefully in any society; education prepares the slaves for freedom and thus facilitates the end of slavery. The double standard is obvious: the slaves are prohibited from learning about citizenship, yet the master claims that the slaves are ignorant at best, and stupid at worst. The masters are obstructing an essential element for their emancipation, and they are abandoning arguments to protect the very rights they claim they want protected.[77]

Prudence and the Virginia Constitutional Convention

We have considered that Virginia's most prominent statesmen operated prudentially. The Missouri crisis represented one example of this: the Founders did not sanction the extension of slavery to expand slavery, but thought that slavery extending into Missouri would alleviate its high concentration and hence contribute to its eradication. They assented to an evil in order to avoid a greater evil. Abraham Lincoln also would have accepted extension of slavery if it meant to save the Union. His was no less a prudential position.[78] Patrick Henry specifically appealed to prudence during the Virginia ratifying convention: "As much as I deplore slavery, I see that prudence forbids its abolition."[79] He would go on to condemn the institution as a great evil and implore the slave owner to a just treatment of his slaves to preserve opportunity for emancipation in the future. Part of the reason Henry deemed emancipation imprudent, however, was because of the lack of good feelings the slaves would have toward the masters, and we might conclude other whites, for keeping them in bondage.

In the Virginia Constitutional Convention, Campbell specifically appealed to prudence and its application in politics:

> I have no new theory to offer; I only wish to see the principles already defined, understood, and canonized, carried out to their proper extent. I think we are prepared for nothing more; we can reasonably ask for no more at present. But I am very far from thinking that the social compact has yet been perfected, or that society is yet prepared for the best possible institutions. That Government is best for any people that is best adapted to their views, wants, wishes, and even prejudices: Not that which is best administered, but that which best suits itself to the great mass of society.[80]

Some easterners agreed that the conventioneers should not foist upon society what it is unprepared to accept. Campbell believed prudential decisions took first their cue from "principles already defined," but the slaveholding east asserted that plain practical sense ought to guide politics. They appealed to common sense, but took their understanding of common sense from history, or experience—in this way they went to the effectual truth of the matter. The easterners claimed that circumstances, or necessity, not only does not permit the extension of suffrage or the equalization of representation, but the law also forbids it. For eastern conventioneers, the Declaration of Rights is a practical document rather than a statement of a non-arbitrary standard. It is not a guide to future political action. Campbell disagreed, and explained:

> This seems not to have been overlooked by the framers of the Bill of Rights, and the founders of this Government. They declared the principles, the just and righteous principles of the social compact; and progressed so far in the application as they supposed the then existing state of society required and permitted. But foreseeing that changes would take place, and that the human mind was progressing and would progress, they revised, and most prudently advised, a frequent recurrence to fundamental principles: Not to change those principles as one gentleman, (Mr. Giles) asked, but to purge and reform our institutions by bringing them up near to the unchangeable principles; by a continual approximation to the cardinal principles which they propounded.

Prudence is enshrined in the Declaration of Rights no less than the Declaration of Independence—even though the Virginia document does not specifically mention the word. Campbell asserts that the portion of the Declaration of Rights that charges "no free government, or the blessing of liberty, can be preserved to any people, but by a firm adherence to justice, moderation, temperance, frugality, and virtue, and by frequent recurrence to fundamental principles" represents a statement of prudence in light of principle. Campbell might say that "prudence dictates" that Virginians frequently recur to "fundamental principles" in order to bolster, if not save, republican government.

If Campbell is any indication, the natural rights coalition at the convention believed they were operating on the same principles as the Founders. The conservatives conceived necessity as the most important, if not sole, ground of politics. However, the reformers recognized that "prudence is the virtue that selects the right means to the right end. Prudence in this sense requires a 'beginning behind or before politics,' against which all political choices are measured."[81] The natural equality of man was a truth applicable to everyone, everywhere, always. The pro-slave advocates were legal positivists in this way because they believed that everything that might be called principled spun out of the laws. Slavery was something that came out of the positive compact. Slavery depended on the positive law and was created by it—legalized by it. Without the emphasis on the positive law, there was no justification for the peculiar institution. However, the reformers believed there was a standard before or behind politics, which set a standard for political action and with which to judge the political. They understood that mere political right has no support outside itself and rests only on the authority of majority (and in this case minority) will.[82]

The conservatives were at least partly correct—the strict adherence to the doctrine of equality would seem to suggest that all people should vote regardless of circumstance. However, prudence, and natural right, does not omit circumstances from consideration. The western delegation were not categorical imperativists. Prudential morality is the antithesis of the categorical imperative and not only rejects the radical abolitionist appeal to let the South secede, but also rejects the perpetuity of slavery.[83] Prudence, then, is in service of justice— which is the aim of government.[84] The conservatives were correct for the wrong reasons that government, or the statesman, must adapt to circumstances. Campbell seemed to agree when he said that, "government is best for any people that is best adapted to their views, wants, wishes, and even prejudices: Not that which is best administered, but that which best suits itself to the great mass of society." Unlike the conservatives, however, he did not derive that from mere political right, but with a view to justice. We mentioned in chapter two that the statesman cannot demand the terms of political engagement with his constituents. Campbell recognized that political truth and sought to capitalize on what is good in public opinion in service of justice. He was seeking to reasonably accentuate what was most right and downplay what was not. He appealed to what was good in opinion—the belief in the equality of man—in order to move the state toward emancipation. Action guided by prudence is far more just than when it is not guided by it. To put it another way, natural right is a part of political right.

This means that natural right is changeable, or that, subject to prudence, natural right is changeable given specific situations, and yet, justice is independent of law:

> Aristotle observed that fire burns the same way both here and in Persia, but that the things regarded as just and unjust differ everywhere. The doubt of nature as a source of the principles of human conduct begins, not by doubting the existence of nature, but by doubting that human laws or morals can be other than conventional. It begins by doubting that law or morality can be called

good or bad with references to any unchanging principles outside human will or
human enactment.[85]

It is difficult to determine what is right in the here and now, but act in light of
what is just everywhere and always. The statesman is concerned with particular
circumstances or situations granted, but in every action, a general principle, or
standard, is presumed. The statesman proceeds from some non-arbitrary
standard and then if he must, deviates from it to secure justice or something
better for humanity: "there is a universally valid hierarchy of ends, but there are
no universally valid rules of action."[86] This is essentially what Campbell meant
when he said that he came to the convention to defend principles and what
Doddridge meant when he stated he would not abandon universal truths.
Prudence is thus the indispensable tool of the statesman because it is most able
to achieve "the closest approximation to perfect justice available" given the
circumstances.[87] Both men voted against the compromise constitution because,
for them, the convention proceeded on a complete rejection of something higher
than the will of man. A government that permits the violation of some rights is
far more preferable, or tolerable, to an alternative that will likely be worse.

The Nat Turner Insurrection

On August 23, 1831, Governor John Floyd wrote in his diary that it would be a
"noted day" for Virginia.[88] Nat Turner and a band of free blacks and slaves
proceeded to kill sixty to seventy whites on the evening of August 22, 1831. The
insurrection took everyone by surprise. Turner was not considered a threat.
Nobody would suspect him of organizing a slave revolt because he was a
faithful and highly trusted overseer on the plantation where he lived.[89] Slaves in
the neighboring counties did not know about the impending attack. There was
no coordination between slaves located on different plantations. Nevertheless,
Virginians, and people in neighboring southern states, feared the worst—that
Turner was only the beginning and more was to come.[90]
   The press reported the event with fear. Both the Richmond papers, the
Constitutional Whig and the Richmond Enquirer, reported that an insurrection
broke out in Southampton County and many families were murdered. This event
required a large military force to contain Turner's men and quell the violence.
There were calls in the papers for men to report for the formation of troops that
would be sent to Southampton to assist the efforts in county to round up the men
and bring them to justice. All told, the papers reported about one thousand
armed men of the militia assisted killing and/or catching Turner's men. There
were even letters from certain North Carolina border towns pledging their
support of arms and men.
   Early reports of the grisly murders in the press were that runaway slaves
had carried out the deed. The names of the murdered families and the number
put to death appeared in print by August 29. The Richmond Enquirer described
those who partook in the insurrection as a blood-thirsty pack of wolves. The

paper further stated that all black preachers (of which Turner was considered to be) should not be permitted in the future to speak in any public forum.

Turner, or General Nat as he became known, thought he was receiving messages from Heaven, in the form of the Holy Spirit, to take up arms and deliver the slaves from bondage. He had some influence over other slaves. Some believed him a prophet. Initially, he believed that July 4, 1831 would be a perfect day to secure freedom for him and his people, however, the "signs" were not there.[91] Turner waited until August 22 to carry out the deed. On Sunday evening of August 21, Turner and seven of his followers gathered in the woods to plot the attack. After midnight, armed with axes and other hand weapons, they proceeded to kill his master, Joseph Travis, and his entire family. Travis's wife was nearly decapitated. Her neck was severed. They killed the children in the house and then ransacked it. After they left to proceed to the next house, they remembered they forgot to kill the youngest child. Taking the child from his crib, they decapitated him and threw his body into a fire.

After killing Travis, they seized guns and powder from the residence. As the night wore on and into the next day, Turner picked up recruits. His force grew to about sixty slaves and free blacks. The killing proceeded from that Sunday night and did not end until noon the next day. In house after house the scene was the same. Many whites were beheaded. Some of the bodies were left for dead in the open air, others were burned. There were no rapes. When some militia happened upon the violence, those bodies that were not burned were being eaten by wolves. Turner spared several for whatever reasons. However, all told, there were about sixty men, women, and children who met their end at the hand of Turner's men. It was the intention of Turner to reach the county seat, Jerusalem, to seize more weapons and continue the insurrection. At one point, they were a mere three miles from the town. However, before they could proceed, they were met by the Southampton militia, which dispersed the gang for a time. As Turner's men approached the plantation home of Dr. Simon Blunt at daybreak on August 23, they were met with resistance by not only the master, but also the slaves. The attack was repulsed, leaving General Nat's forces in complete disarray.

By August 25, after three days of the uprising (it was really over by the afternoon of August 22 and was effective for only one evening) about 3,000 troops from Virginia and North Carolina were on the way to Southampton. Before they arrived, many who were thought to have participated in the massacre were shot indiscriminately, or decapitated by local whites. White militiamen and vigilantes killed black men, women and children. In the retaliation, over one hundred twenty blacks were killed. Many slaves were burned and tortured. By August 28, all the insurgents were apprehended and locked up in a small jail in Jerusalem. Only Tuner remained at large. He was finally caught on October 30 not far from the Travis farm. He had been living underground, in a hole he dug for himself, all of those weeks after August 22. Turner was tried and executed on November 11, 1831.

The Turner affair alarmed Thomas Jefferson Randolph and his wife.

Thomas Jefferson Randolph was the grandson of Thomas Jefferson and the son of Thomas Mann Randolph, who as governor proposed an emancipation plan during the Missouri crisis (see chapter 3). The Randolphs lived far away from the violence in Southampton, yet Jane Randolph urged her husband to sell their plantation and move to a free state. She favored Cincinnati, Ohio. Randolph wrote to his wife trying to assuage her fears: "The danger is our children's children forty or fifty years hence, not to us."[92] Nevertheless, it would be Thomas Jefferson Randolph, as a member of the House of Delegates, who would propose his grandfather's *post nati* plan as a way to emancipate the slaves. Unlike the convention of 1829-1830, General Nat's insurrection would launch the Old Dominion into a more forthright discussion of slavery and whether it can and should be abolished. Jefferson's grandson would lead the charge in the affirmative.

In a letter to the Governor of South Carolina, Floyd blamed the insurrection on northern religious preachers who taught the slaves that "God was no respecter of persons" and that "all men were born free and equal."[93] Surely, in spite of the uprising, and with Floyd's support, the incoming legislative session ought to be able to find a way to effect a gradual emancipation plan. Floyd wrote to the Governors of South Carolina and Georgia that his annual message would encourage emancipation of the slaves. He actually suggested that the state of Virginia would purchase slaves from their masters and then the state would put them to work on internal improvements. After a few years they would be transported out of the Union. He encouraged the two governors to join Virginia to devise a plan to rid the South of the black population. The timing seemed ripe. Turner's insurrection caused more cracks in the eastern slaveholder political alliance whereas they were more united in 1829-1830. Even well into the legislative debate, Governor Floyd wrote in his diary that he would "not rest until slavery is abolished in Virginia."[94] However, it seems that such optimism and resolve was misplaced. The General Assembly was slated to begin on December 5. Many of those in the legislature were elected in April, well before the insurrection. For the problems encountered in the constitutional convention, some one year earlier, the slave debates would come back in full force in the assembly. The Turner affair crystallized the slave situation in the state and brought out into the open strong emancipationist sentiment. The effect of the insurrection, and the debates that followed, extended far beyond the borders of Virginia.[95]

Conclusion

Looking at the state of the Virginia after the convention, we find a state very divided. The western representatives and those who appealed to natural rights thought that the eastern delegation believed that those in the west, and the poor unpropertied, were unfit for freedom. They were too poor, and too ignorant. Some of the pro-slave east appeared to have a philosopher-king complex. They basically asserted that they were wiser and more virtuous than the unpropertied and poorer citizen. This position is interesting in that the wise do not desire to rule.[96] To get an understanding of how far apart the two sections of the state had become, Monroe's initial support of the reformers led to intense and passionate denunciations. Upon hearing those criticisms, both Monroe and Madison thought that compromise was the only solution, for without some sort of agreement the state might opt for disunion. Indeed, the divide between east and west Virginia was but a microcosm of the future irrevocable division advancing in the Union. The older statesmen were against state dismemberment because they thought it would portend the breakup of the Union. Since both the east and west threatened disunion if they did not get their way, compromise seemed the best way to ameliorate that deplorable outcome. In other words, disunion was far worse than a Union not as republican as it should be.[97] Disunion would not solve the slave problem nor would it solve the suffrage or representation quandary in the state.

Those opposing change, the pro-slave easterners, portrayed themselves as defenders of property. However, they rejected the plea of the working man who assured them that they not only shared with them interest in the state, but also that they aspired to own property. As we have seen in the last two chapters, property was a euphemism for slavery. Some have claimed that the reformers made "no serious attack" on the institution of slavery.[98] However, it seems quite evident that the entire argument of the western delegation flowed from natural rights. In that light, their entire argument undermined the peculiar institution. The pro-slave delegation certainly understood that the arguments radiating from the likes of Campbell and Doddridge threatened the entire institution of slavery. While the Virginia convention represented that fiercest battle of all the states over representation and suffrage, it does not represent a complete picture.[99] Although the slave issue was not as openly debated as it would be during the slave debates in the House of Delegates in 1831-1832, it underlay everything else in the debate. With the constitutional convention concluded, the fiercest battle over slavery was yet to come, and after Turner, come it did. Yet, the same old impediments were in the way.

That debate was in many ways more important than the one conducted in the constitutional convention because it was solely about slavery, the status of slaves, and the practicality of emancipation. If Virginia was going to do something about the peculiar institution, the 1831-32 session was the perfect opportunity. The only question that remained was whether the old divisions between east and west would again prevent some sort of emancipation plan.

Notes

1. Jefferson to Edward Coles, Monticello, 25 August 1814, *Thomas Jefferson: Writings*, ed. Merrill D. Peterson (New York: Library of America, 1984), 1345; Plato, *The Republic of Plato*, ed. Allan Bloom (New York: Basic Books, 1991, 168, or 488b; Leo Strauss, *Natural Right and History* (Chicago: University of Chicago Press, 1965), 103.

2. The plan that was adopted made for a House of Delegates of 134 (a decrease from

214), 56 from the west and 78 from the east. The Senate would have 32: 13 from the west and 19 from the east: Julian A.C. Chandler, *Representation in Virginia* (Baltimore: The Johns Hopkins University Press, 1961), 40.

3. Since all money bills originated in the state House, the east balked at having the west control that body. The reformers also wanted to make the governor popularly elected, but the conservatives would have none of that. They kept the executive a product of the assembly elected by them for a period of three years. See Merrill D. Peterson, *Democracy, Liberty, and Property: The State Constitutional Conventions of the 1820s* (Indianapolis: The Bobbs-Merrill Company, 1966), 282.

4. Eugenius M. Wilson, Speech before the Convention, 18 November 1829, *Proceedings and Debates*, 356; 19 November 1829, ibid., 379, 382; Lucas P. Thompson, 21 November 1829, ibid., 417. Thompson in particular scolded the pro-slave, pro-freehold, delegation for proclaiming opposition to abstract rights in favor of reality and experience, when other states that had opted for universal white manhood suffrage were functioning just fine. The rich property owner was not losing his property by means of the poor voter. On free blacks, voting and the celebration of July 4, see John W. Cromwell, "The Aftermath of Nat Turner's Insurrection," *Journal of Negro History* 5, no. 2 (April 1920) : 226.

5. Charles H. Ambler, *Sectionalism in Virginia from 1776-1861* (New York: Russell and Russell Inc., 1964), 165; See various speeches, *Proceedings and Debates*, 479, 570-572.

6. William G. Shade, *Democratizing the Old Dominion: Virginia and the Second Party System 1824-1861* (Charlottesville: University Press of Virginia, 1996), 19; Theodore M. Whitfield, *Slavery Agitation in Virginia 1829-1832* (New York: Negro University Press, 1930), 47; William Sumner Jenkins, *Pro-Slavery Thought in the Old South* (Gloucester, Mass.: University of North Carolina Press, 1935), 48; Thomas G. West, *Vindicating the Founders: Race, Sex, Class, and Justice in the Origins of America* (Lanham, Md.: Rowman and Littlefield, 1997), 31; Edmund S. Morgan, *American Slavery, American Freedom: The Ordeal of Colonial Virginia* (New York: W.W. Norton and Company, 1975), 386-387; Peterson, *Democracy, Liberty, and Property: The State Constitutional Conventions of the 1820s*, 277; Drew R. McCoy, *The Last of the Fathers: James Madison and the Republican Legacy* (Cambridge: Cambridge University Press, 1989), 241; according to Shade, 19, many Virginians left the state for places west between 1790-1820 to set their slaves free.

7. K.R. Constantine Gutzman, "Old Dominion, New Republic: Making Virginia Republican, 1776-1840" (Ph.D. diss., University of Virginia, 1999), 432.

8. J.R. Pole, "Representation and Authority in Virginia from the Revolution to Reform," *The Journal of Southern History* 24, no. 1 (February 1958) : 47 and 38. John Randolph predicted near the end of the debate that the new constitution would not last but twenty years. He was correct: see his Speech before the Convention, 30 December 1829, *Proceedings and Debates*, 790.

9. Cf., Joseph M. Bessette, *The Mild Voice of Reason: Deliberative Democracy and American National Government* (Chicago: University of Chicago Press, 1994), 7. The critical period of 1787 concerned the failure of the Articles of Confederation. If the colonists were to preserve all they had fought for, a different constitution would have to be fashioned. Given the importance of Virginia to the Union, on the issue of slavery it was a critical time.

10. John Randolph said in the 1826 Congress that the Declaration of Independence was "a falsehood . . . a most pernicious falsehood," see Jenkins, 11; Alison Goodyear Freehling, *Drift Toward Dissolution: The Virginia Slavery Debate of 1831-1832* (Baton

Rouge: Louisiana State University Press, 1982), 63.

11. Dickson Bruce, *The Rhetoric of Conservatism: The Virginia Convention of 1829-1830 and the Conservative Tradition in the South* (SanMarino, Ca.: The Huntington Library, 1982), vii. The author believes that speech is important, but not to the exclusion of economics and other influences. Others place a higher value on public rhetoric, see Daniel Walker Howe, *The Political Culture of the American Whigs* (Chicago: University of Chicago Press, 1979), 27.

12. Abraham Lincoln, "Portion of Speech at Republican Banquet in Chicago, Illinois," 10 December 1856, *Abraham Lincoln: Speeches and Writings 1832-1858*, ed. Don E. Fehrenbacher (New York: Library of America, 1989), 385-386.

13. Federalist no. 1, Clinton Rossiter, ed., *The Federalist Papers*, with an Introduction by Charles Kesler (New York: Mentor, 1999), 1 and 3. All references to the Federalist are to this volume.

14. Federalist no. 48, 277.

15. Federalist no. 47, 274-275.

16. Thomas Jefferson, *Notes on the State of Virginia, The Portable Thomas Jefferson*, ed. Merrill D. Peterson (New York: Penguin Books, 1975), 164; Federalist no. 48, 278-279.

17. Federalist no. 46, 264; Bessette, *The Mild Voice of Reason*, 26-27.

18. Federalist no. 15, 79. See also Federalist no. 37, 199.

19. West, *Vindicating the Founders*, 21.

20. Ibid., 23.

21. Abraham Lincoln, "Second Inaugural Address," 4 March 1865, *Abraham Lincoln: Speeches and Writings 1832-1858*, 686; for the House Divided Speech see Lincoln, Speech of Abraham Lincoln, Springfield, 16 June 1858, *The Lincoln-Douglas Debates*, ed. Robert W. Johannsen (New York: Oxford University Press, 1965), 20.

22. James Monroe, Speech before the Convention, 2 November 1829, *Proceedings and Debates*, 149.

23. John Scott, Speech before the Convention, 31 October 1829, ibid, 125. Further quotes from Scott from this page and source.

24. Philip Doddridge, 28 October 1829, ibid, 86; see also ibid, 80; the evidence for the effect self-interest had on the representatives is great: see also John W. Green (Culpepper), 27 October 1829, ibid, 63; Benjamin Watkins Leigh, 4 November 1829, ibid, 167, agreed with Scott, stating that self-love was the spring of all action. Everyone acted out of self-love and nobody could escape that as a motivator.

25. John R. Cooke, 27 October 1829, ibid, 60-62. Italics in the original; Richard Morris (Hanover), Speech before the Convention, 30 October 1829, ibid, 116, explicitly stated that if the west rose to power, they would pass an emancipation law thus violating the right to property in slaves.

26. Abel P. Upshur, 27 October 1829, ibid, 66-67, 70-71; 28 October 1829, ibid., 88.

27. Calhoun, 12-13; Jenkins, 59. Those who most challenged both the compact and Declaration in the convention were Abel P. Upshur, Benjamin Watkins Leigh, and Chapman Johnson. Calhoun developed this idea somewhat publicly after the convention, e.g. John C. Calhoun, "South Carolina," *Constitutional Whig*, 31 August 1832, p. 1.

28. Jaffa, *A New Birth of Freedom*, 433.

29. Benjamin Watkins Leigh, Speech before the Convention, 3 November 1829, *Proceedings and Debates*, 161-162; 4 November 1829, ibid, 166-168; Bruce, 79; The Founders did not view happiness this way. Safety is but one pole of the complete field of politics. Happiness sets the highest aspiration of politics. This means that the good life is what all institutions should aim for: Aristotle, *The Politics*, Translated by Carnes Lord

(Chicago: University of Chicago Press, 1984), 35-37; Jaffa, *A New Birth of Freedom*, 383; West, "Jaffa versus Mansfield: Does America Have a Constitutional or a 'Declaration of Independence' Soul?," *Perspectives on Political Science* 31 (Fall 2002) : 239.

30. Lucas Thompson, Speech before the Convention, 21 November 1829, *Proceedings and Debates*, 411. Calhoun's understanding that the driving force of man toward security is the passions sounds very similar to Hobbes. But Calhoun rejects the central part of Hobbes's teaching, that all men have an equal right to life and liberty, Jaffa, *A New Birth of Freedom*, 448-449.

31. John Randolph, Speech before the Convention, 2 December 1829, ibid., 532; also 25 November 1829, ibid., 458; Philip Doddridge read into the record Jefferson's *Notes* and a 12 July 1816 letter to Samuel Kercheval in which the Sage criticized the constitution for the legislature holding too much power (he advocated for a more genuine separation of powers), Philip Doddridge, Speech before the Convention, 27 November 1829, ibid., 475-476. On the disavowal of Jefferson, see William E. Dodd, *The Cotton Kingdom: A Chronicle of the Old South* (Toronto: Glasgow, Brook and Co., 1919), 48-49.

32. John Randolph, Speech before the Convention, 2 December 1829, ibid., 533; Benjamin Watkins Leigh, Speech before the Convention, 3 November 1829, ibid., 160. Randolph stated that the only thing Jefferson did worthy of compliment was to build a better plow. For some of the controversy on Randolph's edition of Jefferson's writings, see Leonard C. Helderman, "A Social Scientist of the Old South," *The Journal of Southern History* 2 (May 1936) : 169-170.

33. Alexander Campbell, Speech before the Convention, 1 December 1829, *Proceedings and Debates*, 525; the first to invoke Jefferson's name (along with Locke and Sydney) was John Cooke, Speech before the Convention, 27 October 1829, ibid., 57; Peterson, *Democracy, Liberty, and Property: The State Constitutional Conventions of the 1820s*, 273. The primary critique is that the western delegates thought that the east had thrown over Jefferson as a heretic because they wanted to advocate southern right, minority rights, and/or group rights; see Charles Henry Ambler, "The Cleavage between Eastern and Western Virginia," *The American Historical Review* 15, no. 4 (July 1910) : 772.

34. Don E. Fehrenbacher, *Constitutions and Constitutionalism in the Slaveholding South* (Athens: The University of Georgia Press, 1989), 45; Gutzman, 452 and 456.

35. John Randolph, Speech before the Convention, 14 November 1829, *Proceedings and Debates*, 317. The document that Randolph is referring is Burke's "Speech on the Petition of the Unitarians (1792)."

36. Randolph, Speech before the Convention, 14 November 1829, *Proceedings and Debates*, 318.

37. Howe, 171, 235-237.

38. Littleton W. Tazewell (Norfolk Bourough), Speech before the Convention, 16 November 1829, *Proceedings and Debates*, 327.

39. Thomas Hobbes, *Leviathan*, ed. Michael Oakshott (New York: Collier Books, 1962), 80-81; Ambler, *Sectionalism in Virginia*, 151. John Coalter (Stafford) said that "the heart of man is deceitful," Speech before the Convention, 25 November 1829, *Proceedings and Debates*, 453; West, "Jaffa versus Mansfield," 239-240.

40. Benjamin Watkins Leigh, 3 November 1829, *Proceedings and Debates*, 160.

41. Quoted in Freehling, *Drift Toward Dissolution*, 63. When Randolph spoke, unprecedented crowds packed the meeting hall where the conventioneers met, see ibid.

42. Ibid., 161.

43. Ibid., 162. See also Chapman Johnson (Augusta) who contends that the whole debate is about power and no matter the argument is but the arms used for combat to cover up the real issue, ibid., 257.

44. Madison, "Sovereignty," 1835, *The Writings of James Madison*, vol. 9, ed. Gaillard Hunt (New York: G.P. Putnam's Sons, 1910), 570; on Madison's essay, I have profited greatly from Jaffa, *A New Birth of Freedom*, 44-48; Madison's criticism of nullification are well known, especially the misinterpretation of the Virginia and Kentucky Resolutions by Robert Hayne, see McCoy, 131-132, 140-142.

45. Jefferson, *Notes on the State of Virginia*, in *The Portable Thomas Jefferson*, 162-163; Jefferson to Samuel Kercheval, Monticello, 12 July 1816, *The Portable Thomas Jefferson*, 555; Chandler, *Representation in Virginia*, 21-22.

46. Jefferson to John Hambden Pleasants, Monticello, 19 April 1824, vol. 16, in Bergh, 28.

47. *Proceedings and Debates*, 26, 31, 32; Doddridge, Speech before the Convention, 28 October 1829, ibid., 80; Powell, 30 October 1829, ibid., 106; Chandler, *The History of Suffrage in Virginia*, 32.

48. Madison, "Sovereignty," 570-571; Cf. Federalist no. 39, 211-212.

49. Samuel Moore, Speech before the Convention, 6 November 1829, *Proceedings and Debates*, 230.

50. Jaffa, *A New Birth of Freedom*, 46.

51. William Naylor, Speech before the Convention, 31 October 1829, *Proceedings and Debates*, 129. Upshur stated that the law of nature does not require majority rule and likened majority rule to a the state of nature, Abel Upshur, Speech before the Convention, 27 October 1829, ibid., 66-67.

52. Jaffa, *A New Birth of Freedom*, 47.

53. Edward J. Erler, "Philosophy, History, and Jaffa's Universe," *Interpretation* 28, no. 3 (Spring 2001) : 250.

54. Both sides of the debate spoke of breaking the state into two separate entities. Easterners like Randolph seemed willing to let the west secede. Some members from the west, outside of the convention, also spoke of secession, Pole, 45.

55. Alexander Campbell, Speech before the Convention, 19 November 1829, *Proceedings and Debates*, 385 and 386; Jaffa, *A New Birth of Freedom*, 62-63. Jaffa argues, from Aristotle and Jefferson, that the friendly feeling dissipates when men conflict and their passions blind them to what they have in common. Even though the context is Union, we see a similar set of circumstances on the state level in Virginia.

56. Ibid., 386. Another topic covered in Campbell's speech, which will be addressed later and was a major rebuttal from the pro-slave east, is the connection between common interests and permanent interests.

57. Jefferson to John Hambden Pleasants, Monticello, 19 April 1824, vol. 16, in Bergh, 27-28.

58. Alexander Campbell, Speech before the Convention, 31 October 1829, *Proceedings and Debates*, 117; Abel P. Upshur, Speech before the Convention, 27 October 1829, ibid, 69.

59. James Madison, "Parties," *National Gazette*, 23 January 1792, in *The Founder's Constitution*, vol. 1, ed. Kurland and Lerner, 556. Unless otherwise noted, further quotes from this source.

60. James Madison, "Majority Governments," 1833, in *Mind of the Founder*, ed. Meyers, 411.

61. Ibid., 412-413.

62. Federalist no. 10, 46.

63. Federalist no. 10, 46.
64. Campbell, Speech in the Convention, *Proceedings and Debates*, 31 October 1829, 122; Bruce, 78.
65. Federalist no. 10, 51; Alfred H. Powell (Frederick), Speech before the Convention, 30 October 1829, *Proceedings and Debates*, 108: Powell rejected the claim that interests could be uniform, stating that in Virginia a diversity of interests existed; James Madison, "Majority Governments," 1833, ed. Myers, 413.
66. West, *Vindicating the Founders*, 113-114.
67. Jefferson to Edmund Pendleton, Philadelphia, 26 August 1776, *The Portable Thomas Jefferson*, 755; West, *Vindicating the Founders*, 120-121. On October 12, 1829 Doddridge proposed suffrage for all white males. On October 13, 1829, Cooke proposed at least a minimal residency and taxpaying requirement, Bruce, 64-65; J.N. Brenaman, *A History of Virginia Conventions* (Richmond, Va.: J.L. Hill Printing Co., 1902), 43 and 46.
68. Quoted in West, *Vindicating the Founders*, 127. Madison actually modified his views on the matter. At the 1787 convention he favored a property requirement in federal elections, but later he changed his mind, believing that even those without property should vote for at least one house of the legislature: Madison "Note on the Virginia Constitution," Meyers, 396-399, 406-407.
69. Monroe to S.M. Edwards, Oak Hill, 6 April 1829, *The Writings of James Monroe*, vol. 7, ed. Stanislaus Murray Hamilton (New York: G.P. Putnam's Sons, 1903), 195.
70. James Madison, Speech in Federal Convention, 19 June 1787, *The Records of the Federal Convention of 1787*, vol. 1, ed. Max Farrand (New Haven, Conn.: Yale University Press, 1966), 318; West, *Vindicating the Founders*, 125; Bruce, 80 and 65; Freehling, *The Road to Disunion*, 173-174.
71. Lunger, 77 and 67; Henry E. Webb, *In Search of Christian Unity: A History of the Restoration Movement* (Cincinnati: Standard Publishing, 1990), 123.
72. Kesler, ed., *Saving the Revolution* (New York: The Free Press, 1987), 32.
73. J. Jackson Barlow, Leonard W. Levy, and Ken Masugi, eds., *The American Founding* (New York: Greenwood Press, 1988), 124.
74. Jaffa, *A New Birth of Freedom*, 120. Common nouns are self-evident truths; Philip Doddridge asserted similar things in his Speech before the Convention, 27 November 1829, *Proceedings and Debates*, 478.
75. Alexander Campbell, *Popular Lectures and Addresses* (Philadelphia: James Challen and Son, 1863), 374. We should note that Campbell was no radical abolitionist, and also believed that compensated emancipation was the most practical option to secure their freedom: Webb, 187-188; Earl Eugene Eminhizer, "Alexander Campbell's Thoughts on Slavery and Abolition," *West Virginia History* 33 (1972) : 110 and 113; "Georgia Slaves," *Millennial Harbinger*, 4 January 1830, vol. 1, no. 1, 47.
76. Laura J. Scalia, *America's Jeffersonian Experiment: Remaking State Constitutions* (DeKalb: Northern Illinois University Press, 1999), 34; Alexander Campbell, Speech before the Convention, 31 October 1829, *Proceedings and Debates*, 119.
77. Campbell, "Emancipation of White Slaves," *Millennial Harbinger*, 129 and 132; Eminhizer, 111. The education law did not pass, but was negatived in the Senate. The pro-slave representative seemed not to understand Campbell's argument. For example, John Randolph claimed that he would not support equal representation or broader suffrage because he believed that there was no right to taxation without the consent of the person being taxed. In this sense, he seemed to confuse natural rights with positive rights.

Nevertheless, his language was not based on convention, but it was universal. It was *never* right to tax without consent: John Randolph, Speech before the Convention, 14 November 1829, *Proceedings and Debates*, 318.

78. Jaffa, *A New Birth of Freedom*, 168-169.

79. Patrick Henry, *The Debates in the Several State Conventions on the Adoption of the Federal Constitution as Recommended by the General Convention at Philadelphia in 1787*, vol. 3, ed. Jonathan Elliot (Philadelphia: J.B. Lippincott and Co., 1861), 590.

80. Alexander Campbell, Speech before the Convention, 19 November 1829, *Proceedings and Debates*, 385. Unless otherwise noted, quotes from this source and page.

81. West, "Jaffa versus Mansfield," 242.

82. Barlow, ed., 211.

83. We have already drawn attention to the fact that Campbell rejected both. Cf. Jaffa, *A New Birth of Freedom*, 297. Doddridge basically asserted that the east was proceeding from categorical moorings by stating they would not "sustain a principle which will not bear to be pushed to its practical results," Speech before the Convention, 28 October 1829, *Proceedings and Debates*, 84.

84. Federalist no. 51, 292; Plato, *Republic*, bk 1.

85. Jaffa, *A New Birth of Freedom*, 104; Strauss, *Natural Right and History*, 146.

86. Strauss, *Natural Right and History*, 162, 159.

87. West, "Jaffa's Lincolnian Defense of the Founding," *Interpretation* 28, no. 3 (Spring 2001) : 294.

88. Charles H. Ambler, ed., *The Life and Diary of John Floyd* (Richmond: Richmond Press, Inc., 1918), 155.

89. William Sidney Drewry, *The Southampton Insurrection* (Murfreesboro, N.C.: Johnson Publishing Company, 1968), 28.

90. Rumors fueled much of the speculation. The reports of the slaves involved in the insurrection approached 200 or more. This was not the case: *The Constitutional Whig*, 29 August 1831, p. 1.

91. Freehling, *The Road to Disunion*, 180.

92. Ibid., 182.

93. Ambler, ed., *The Life and Diary of John Floyd*, 89.

94. Floyd, 26 December 1831, ibid, 172.

95. Cromwell, 231.

96. Strauss, *Natural Right and History*, 151; Gutzman, 450, lends some evidence that the easterners saw themselves as the wiser counterparts over the οἱ πόλλοι; Freehling, *The Road to Disunion*, 173. Benjamin Watkins Leigh, John Randolph, and Abel Upshur were the most vigorous in contending that the few, virtuous, should rule. Those claiming to be wise and claiming to desire rule, are "charlatans." See Jaffa, *A New Birth of Freedom*, 338-339.

97. McCoy, 243; Ambler, *A History of West Virginia* (New York: Prentice-Hall, Inc., 1933), 225-226. John Randolph was one of the "most conspicuous disunionists," Moore, 93.

98. Bruce, 175.

99. Fehrenbacher, *Constitutions and Constitutionalism*, 13; Shade, 68-69.

Chapter 6

Toward Perpetual Slavery: The Virginia Slavery Debate of 1831-1832

No human being was ever born without the wish for liberty implanted in his breast. God never made a slave—for slavery is the work of man alone.

George I. Williams

In the Language of the wise and prophetic Jefferson, "you must approach it—you must bear it—YOU MUST ADOPT SOME PLAN OF EMANCIPATION, OR WORSE WILL FOLLOW."

Charles Faulkner

When the distant reader shall discover, that the Virginia Legislature, in the year 1832, is engaged in the solemn debate on the questions, whether "private property can be taken for public use without compensation," whether "slaves are property," and whether "the increase of slave is property;" he will be lost in amazement, and will be ready to exclaim of us "can these be the sons of their fathers?"

James H. Gholson[1]

There are many similarities between the Virginia Constitutional Convention of 1829-30 and the debates in the 1831-1832 House of Delegates, but the 1831-1832 version represented a more candid and unreserved debate over the institution of slavery. The delegates deliberated whether it was an evil and if it was practical to place it on the road to gradual extinction. Historian Joseph Clarke Robert argued that "the Virginia slavery debate of 1832, the final and most brilliant of the Southern attempts to abolish slavery, represents a line of demarcation between a public willing to hear the faults of slavery and one intolerant of criticism."[2] Robert believes that Virginians in 1832 left their Revolutionary heritage behind and that those involved in the debate were predominantly motivated by economic interests. Speaking of the new generation of statesmen, Charles Ambler concurred: the younger generation was not motivated by the ideas, but was more materially minded.[3] In other words, selfish interests motivated both sides.

While most historians accept Robert's thesis, Alison Goodyear Freehling, in the first lengthy scholarly study dedicated to the debate, disagreed. She thought that the debate was "not an isolated aberration, but rather part of an ongoing contest between a white community irrepressibly divided by slavery."[4] Even in 1776, there were many disputes over slavery, and that continued into the nineteenth century. While the 1831-1832 legislative session did not pass an emancipation plan, Freehling points out that they managed to reject perpetual slavery. Therefore, she disputes Robert's thesis and maintains that Old Dominion's irresolution of the matter of abolition left the state paralyzed politically—outsiders eventually resolved the slave issue for Virginians. However, Freehling has a limited view of the importance of the public rhetoric in the debate. Though it is true that the House adopted language rejecting perpetual slavery, a significant portion of the delegates justified their arguments on something other than the laws of nature and nature's God. This is quite different from Virginia's most prominent statesmen who believed that "all men are created equal." Far from drifting toward dissolution, a majority of Virginia's contemporary political elite initiated a new dispensation.

Virginia played an important role in the development of the positive good thesis and the debates in the House set the tone for the rest of the South: "almost every argument advanced by slavery advocates . . . from that time to the Civil War was anticipated in the debate of 1832."[5] Of course, without the Nat Turner affair, this debate would not have occurred. The magnitude of the deaths and the number of slaves involved prompted the first serious public debate about the institution in Old Dominion. Thomas Jefferson's *post nati* plan to rid the state of slavery became a focal point of the debates because his grandson formally proposed something very similar during the legislative session.

In the months following Turner's charge through the countryside, debate was carried out in the press leading up to the session in the General Assembly. Most of the newspapers of the day favored some sort of emancipation plan and welcomed an open discussion of it—*Richmond Enquirer* (hereafter *Enquirer*), and the *Constitutional Whig* (hereafter *Whig*), both located in Richmond, are the most notable. The *Whig* published several memorials in circulation before the session began in December. In November, a writer to the paper argued that the colonization of free Negroes was not enough. The state needed to "strike at the root of the evil."[6] The author recommended adopting some plan like Jefferson's *post nati* proposal. It sounded similar to the plan Randolph would eventually propose to the House. The *Enquirer* editorialized that "something must be done" about slavery and lamented "are we forever to suffer the greatest evil which can scourge our land?"[7]

As the debate carried in the House, the papers aided the anti-slavery cause and editorialized with increasing frequency, fueling the discussion. The *Whig* opined that the "pernicious effects of slavery" had "unshackled" the emancipation question and brought it into the public arena; that event ensured that "abolition was registered in the book of fate."[8] Alexander Campbell, a central figure in the Constitutional Convention of 1829-1830, wrote that "bitter root" of slavery "was the largest and blackest blot upon our national escutheon."[9] The *Enquirer* declared that, "the seals are broken, which have been put for fifty years upon the most delicate and difficult subject of state concernment."[10] It is worth noting that the seals were broken only when public deliberation (debate in the legislature) occurred, not just when the press was writing about it. Nevertheless, by the time the delegates assembled in Richmond, they had several petitions regarding slavery before them. The slave question generated so much interest that, similar to the Constitutional Convention of 1829-1830, people braved the cold weather and packed the gallery. The excitement exceeded that of the convention which bared "no comparison" to the question of abolition. States outside Virginia also monitored the debates carefully.[11] If Virginia, a state with the largest number of slaves in the Union, passed an emancipation plan, according to many of the pro-slave participants in the House, other Southern states would surely follow. For that reason, pro-emancipation delegate Thomas Marshall (Faquier) believed that Virginia would increase its stature in the Union by solving the slave issue.

Thomas Jefferson Randolph and the Legislative Maneuvers Leading to Debate

About one month before the legislative session convened, Governor John Floyd wrote in his diary that he desired to see an end to slavery in Virginia. However, his opening message to the Assembly did not reveal his emancipation sentiments. Instead, he blamed much of the unrest on "negro preachers" whom he thought should be "silenced."[12] He therefore requested that they revise the laws to ensure the subordination of the slave population. Yet, privately, he desired to see the Assembly engage in a debate over slavery—something many eastern delegates wanted to forestall. Those representing the area east of the Blue Ridge Mountains did their best to avoid a discussion on slavery, but Floyd, believed "it must come."[13] According to the Governor, the slave question was increasing daily and he held out specific praise for those who would become major figures of the pro-emancipation side of the debate.[14]

On December 13, William H. Roane (Hanover) presented a memorial for the gradual emancipation of slaves by the Society of Friends. They appealed to the Assembly to restore to that unfortunate race their inalienable rights. This prompted William O. Goode (Mecklenburg) to motion for rejecting the petition, which was overwhelmingly defeated. It was then referred to a subcommittee on the colored population. The conflict between Roane and Goode marked the beginning of the public confrontation over the slave question. Several more petitions followed and each memorial was referred to the committee on the colored population. By the end of December, there were so many petitions that the chairman of the committee reviewing the memorials requested his committee be increased from eight members to twenty-one.[15]

On January 10, William H. Brodnax (Dinwiddie) reported that the committee on the colored population was considering two actions: the removal of free blacks from the state, and the gradual extinction of slavery. Goode objected to the committee's consideration of emancipation, and he also tired hearing the seemingly endless petitions. Therefore, he moved on January 11 that the committee be discharged from further consideration of all petitions:

> Resolved, That the select committee raised on the subject of slaves, free negroes, and the melancholy occurrences growing out of the tragical massacre in Southampton, be discharged from the consideration of all petitions, memorials and resolutions, which have for their object the manumission of persons held in servitude under the existing laws of this commonwealth, and that it is not expedient to legislate on the subject.[16]

If Goode's motion was successful, the emancipation debate would end. There would be no legislative action on slavery and the supposed danger of taking up an emancipation bill would be averted. However, the pro-emancipation representatives seemed prepared for this move. Goode's motion prompted Thomas Jefferson Randolph (Albemarle) to offer an amendment, inserting after the word "Southampton:"

> [B]e instructed to enquire into the expediency of submitting to the vote of the qualified voters . . . the propriety of providing by law, that the children of all female slaves who may be born in this state on or after the fourth of July, 1840, shall become the property of the commonwealth, the males at the age of twenty-one years, and females at the age of eighteen, if detained by their owners within the limits of Virginia, until they shall respectively arrive at the ages aforesaid; to be hired out until the nett (sic) sum arising therefrom shall be sufficient to defray the expense of their removal beyond the limits of the United States.[17]

Randolph's speech in defense of his plan took two hours to deliver, and Governor Floyd thought he delivered one of the best speeches in the House. Goode's motion backfired on the anti-emancipationists. His effort to end discussion actually prompted a full public debate. Floyd commented that, "the slave party . . . have produced the very debate they wished to avoid, and too, have entered upon it with open doors."[18] Randolph, who thought that a majority of Virginians supported emancipation, believed that the silence was a bulwark to slavery and that public debate was necessary to rid the state of the institution.

Those who did not want a public debate on emancipation tried to gag the deliberations. On January 16, the Brodnax committee reported that "it is inexpedient for the present to make any legislative enactments for the abolition of slavery."[19] Undaunted, William B. Preston (Montgomery) resolved that instead of its inexpediency, the abolition of slavery was "expedient." The House was thus thrust into a debate over whether it was essential for Virginia to draft an emancipation plan in the current legislative session, and, if so, whether the *post nati* proposal was the most practical abolition proposition available. In the meantime, representatives continued to introduce petitions regarding emancipation and colonization. The House tried one more time to gag discussion of slavery on January 25 when a member unsuccessfully moved for an indefinite postponement of the debate.

Randolph's *post nati* gradual emancipation plan was simple: all children born to a slave after July 4, 1840 would become the property of the state of Virginia upon reaching the age twenty-one (for males) and eighteen (for females). The state would then hire them out, perhaps employing them in public works projects, until enough money was earned to colonize them. If the scheme were accepted, it would have freed the first male slave by 1861. It should be noted that Randolph's resolution did not prohibit the master from selling slaves before the age they were relinquished to the state. Regardless, Virginia would eventually be free of slavery. Randolph's proposal also required it be placed before the people in order to gauge their support for the plan. Legislative action in accordance with their will would follow in the next session. The reason he inserted such a clause was to garner political support for his resolution in the House. Many who personally favored abolition had no instruction from their constituents. The 1831-1832 House was elected before the Southampton insurrection and therefore, the campaign season did not address the question of emancipation. Many legislators, on both sides of the dispute, were concerned about passing an emancipation bill because they had been sent to the legislature before the Turner revolt and without any instruction on how to vote on such a topic.

In essence, Randolph proposed his grandfather's gradual emancipation scheme. Randolph was determined to follow the principles of the Revolutionary generation. However, he was doing so in an era when the application of those principles was waning. The pro-slave thinkers increasingly considered slaves property. They believed the government's primary function was to protect property holders. Randolph, however, asserted that the fundamental issue was the humanity of the slaves themselves:

> I cannot concur with the hopeless, ultra absolutism of the South. It has been the course of legislation here, to consider slaves as exclusively persons, as exclusively property, or as partaking jointly of both, as the exigencies of this commonwealth have required. Under the Constitution of the United States, slaves are deemed persons, degraded, it is true, . . . but nevertheless as persons . . . Under several of our laws, they are deemed exclusively as persons, inasmuch as the master cannot kill them as he would his oxen; nor can he maim or disfigure them—he cannot give them the ear-marks of his cattle or sheep.[20]

In his memoirs, Randolph explained that blacks were first and foremost persons not property. The inherent contradictions—confusing human beings as possessions—of the institution "gave me a disgust to the whole system and made me an abolitionist."[21] Yet, Randolph makes an important observation—the South is undergoing a transformation. Slaves are increasingly deemed property and less persons. The absolutism of the South was gaining enough respectability that Randolph thought to mention it. Some who objected to Randolph's plan asserted that even Jefferson considered the slaves as property even to the extent of supporting compensated emancipation. However, his grandson answered that they were not property as such, but that the Sage considered them partly as property for the purpose of compromise. Delaying their freedom as the *post nati* plan did was a compromise to mollify the slaveholder by allowing him to hold onto his property for a significant time. In other words, treating the slaves as property in some sense was a lesser evil than not treating them as property, which would most likely eliminate the legislative prospects for abolition. The *post nati* plan avoided a greater evil: the infinite continuation of human bondage.

Randolph defended his grandfather's plan on the grounds he consistently desired emancipation: "he still deemed abolition indispensable to the safety of the country. These dreams of his lasted a long time—some sixty years."[22] Randolph read into the record his grandfather's letter to Edward Coles to demonstrate that Jefferson's main concern was the liberty of the slaves: "The love of justice and the love of country plead equally the cause of these people, and it is a mortal reproach to us that they should have pleaded it so long in vain, and should have produced not a single effort, nay I fear not much serious willingness to relieve them and ourselves from our present condition of moral and political reprobation."[23] Perhaps providentially, Coles wrote Randolph before the session to encourage him to propose legislation for emancipation in the House. He was pleased that Randolph held the same principles as his grandfather. In his speech, Randolph claimed that Jefferson "deeply imbued in my mind" the substance of his position on slavery. Randolph explained that his plan would take eighty years before the entire slave population was freed. This would make the process sufficiently gradual and allow for a measured introduction of free labor. However, he asserted that, "if by 1860, the evil is found irremediable, a repeal of the law will place us where we now stand." Yet he clearly wanted to avoid that possibility. Randolph asserted that a civil war would occur over the issue of slavery if the institution was not arrested. Like Jefferson, he thought that it would come mainly at the hands of the slaves rising up to secure their own liberty—it would be a servile war.

Given the division caused by the peculiar institution, Randolph thought that the slave question was as important as those before the Revolutionaries: "On all occasions of vital interest, where the prosperity of the commonwealth is endangered, it is the duty of the legislature to take the lead, it is their duty to call public attention to the evil; such was the practice of our ancestors during the war which tore them from the parent stem, and gentlemen have urged, and I agree with them, that this revolution is not less important in its consequence."[24] He was not alone in this belief. John A. Chandler (Norfolk) and others believed that if Virginia rid herself of slavery, "it would be the most glorious since the Fourth of July 1776."[25] Natural rights were the central feature of the Revolution and whether the slaves have rights was a central feature of the debate over slavery in Virginia. The one attribute that suggests the 1831-1832 debate was more critical, is that some no longer abided by that central idea of the Declaration of Independence. For example, Randolph was surprised that some justified slavery for the simple fact that it existed in other countries. This argument was faulty, according to Randolph, because it perverted the central tenets of reason and revelation. In no Christian country except the United States did slavery exist. However, Christianity in the South was undergoing a change and was being invoked to justify slavery: "The gentleman has appealed to the Christian religion in justification of slavery—I would ask him what part of these pure doctrines does he rely; to which of those sublime precepts does he avert to sustain his position? Is it that which teaches charity, justice and good will to all, or is it that which teaches 'that ye do unto others as ye would they should do unto you?'"[26] The proposition all men are created equal is basically a restatement of the Golden Rule. Philip A. Bolling (Buckingham) expressed something similar, stating that the slaves "read in their Bibles 'do unto all men as you would have them do unto you'—and this golden rule and slavery are hard to reconcile."[27] According to the emancipationists, those who are Christians, and those who reasonably believe in the transcendent authority of nature and nature's God could not rationally come to any other conclusion.

Randolph asserted that selfish interest influenced the slaveholder's opinion and caused his aversion to emancipation. To the pro-slave east, the non-slaveholder had no genuine interest in slavery and should be prohibited from deciding if the slaves should be freed. However, Randolph emphasized that the non-slave holder had a compelling interest: "If you deny to the non-slaveholder the right to vote upon this question, in which his property and the lives of his family are interested, is it not just that he should have some sufficient guarantee from his wealthy neighbor, the slaveholder, that his wife and children should not be butchered by his slaves?"[28] The non-slaveholder had an interest in the property of the slaveholder because he was affected by the presence of that property, as the Turner affair demonstrated. Randolph capitalized on an inconsistency in the slaveholder's position—do they believe that the non-owner of a dog that presents a danger to the community should have no say in the management of that property? The slaveholder was not legally held responsible for the actions of his slaves in the same manner that he was responsible for other kinds of property. If in fact the slaves were property, Randolph contested, then why cannot the non-owner of that property have a say in how that property is managed especially considering that the property harmed the community in the past? According to Randolph, *salus populi suprema lex* (the health, or safety, of the people is the supreme law) trumped the strict protection of property. What would be the benefit of government if it did not secure their safety?

Part of the problem emanating from the pro-slave interest was not just a selfish interest in the peculiar institution, and a disregard for the rights of man, but also prejudice:

But, sir, how different is it with the African: nature has stamped upon him the indelible mark of his species; no lapse of time or generations, no clime or culture can weaken or obliteration her impression from his countenance . . . No matter what the grandeur of his soul, the elevation of his thought, the extent of his knowledge, or the purity of his character; he may be a Newton, or a Des

Cartes, a Tell or a Washington, he is chained down by adamantine fetters.[29]

Randolph feared that blacks and whites could not live together. In describing the reason that slavery was different from ancient slavery, Randolph noted that the slaves in America are black and they were not necessarily so in the ancient world. In Virginia, a prejudice existed based on the color of one's skin, yet Randolph also believed that the slaves had the ability to be virtuous and intelligent as any other man. Slavery kept them in a position that prohibited them from developing their talents. Slavery discouraged the talents of the slave from coming into view. The reason ancient slaves could assimilate was because they had no distinct mark on them. This was not the case with American slaves.

Emancipationists and the Case for Equality and Liberty

Randolph and the emancipationists appealed to more than just the abstract natural rights of the slave. Their aim was to convince, or persuade, a majority of those in the House that emancipation was necessary on many levels, including economic and moral. Since great prejudice existed, the emancipation delegation did not dwell solely on the natural right of the slaves. However, our project here is not to catalog their argument regarding the economic evils of slavery, but to understand the moral argument of those who supported emancipation. Contrary to the scholarship of modern historians, the pro-emancipation delegates publicly contended that the slaves deserved their freedom for reasons of justice. They primarily derived their argument from the belief in natural rights.

The pro-emancipationists asserted that those who opposed abolition based their ideas on nothing universal, solid, or stable. George I. Williams (Harrison) stated it most starkly:

> Unsatisfied—as they may be—of the strength of the argument that man possesses the natural right to hold his fellow in bondage, the gentleman . . . go for that right to the laws—they tell us that slaves are property under the statute. They are forced to abandon any pretensions to constitutional right, and settle down upon their sole defiance—the right under the statute. Reduced to this point, the argument presents no difficulty—for, if statutory provisions alone give the right, then, *eo nomine*, it may be taken away, by the power existing in the legislature to repeal the statutes.[30]

The right to property in slaves is a creation of positive law. Since statutes are created by the legislature, they had the authority to change it. According to the pro-slave delegation, the Assembly did not have the authority to pass an emancipation bill. William B. Preston (Montgomery) also rejected that argument: "They were made property here by the statutes, they are property under the statute, & they must—remain property until that statute is repealed— that statute was the result of a necessity, imposed upon us by the British Throne—but it is such a statute as can be repealed by this Legislature possessed of declaring what *shall be* property, also enables it to declare what *shall not* be property."[31] The emancipationists pointed out that the slaveholder had no right to his slaves, and held that species of property based on the force of the law. The legislature had the particular jurisdiction over slavery because it was by the mere act of law, or statute, that blacks were enslaved. There was thus no *right* to property in other human beings. Emancipation would not be the invasion of private property that the slaveholder claims it would be, but a prop to the liberty of all men. Liberty could not flourish in a land that supports slavery.

Like other emancipationists, Bolling claimed that individuals in society had a natural right to regulate dangerous property.[32] He claimed it was "monstrous" to maintain the inviolability of property, as the pro-slave faction did, without reference to uses or effects of that property: "If a man builds a valuable mill on his own land, and has a pond annexed to it which happens to infect the whole neighborhood with disease . . . what is the consequence? The mill-pond must come down, even though all the owner may be worth may be vested in the mill, and *he* gets not a cent of compensation."[33] A person ought not be rewarded for something that causes harm to the community. The owner of a property that harms the community does not receive compensation in such cases. Furthermore, the property owner would not receive any recompense for the loss of future profits should that property be taken from him. Regardless of the misconception of slaves for property, the emancipationists believed that securing natural rights was the most important task of government. The revival of an understanding of natural right was the most effective means to combat the confounding of humans for property.

According to Chandler the peculiar institution "interfered with our means of enjoying LIFE, LIBERTY, PROPERTY, HAPPINESS, and SAFETY."[34] The purpose of government was not merely to protect possessions, but encouraged loftier ends for man like happiness. Chandler drew from the Virginia Declaration to support his contention that aside from the accumulation of property, and from the immediate protection of life, happiness was the end of man. Property was a means to that higher end. The protection of property was not an end in itself. It held no teleological value by itself. Chandler wondered whether "as a man, as a moral man, as a christian (sic) man, whether [the master] has not SOME DOUBT of his claim to his slaves . . . " Slavery, then, violated the rights of the slave who is a human being, and was deleterious to his happiness. The simple protection of property without any understanding of the ends of man destroyed the possibility happiness could be achieved. Furthermore, the law of nature, which dictates certain obligations for man—that we not enslave others and pursue happiness— also grants him certain inalienable rights by which man is able to pursue happiness. Man held certain inalienable rights which ought not to be deprived by compact. Chandler thought that the General Assembly had a mandate to act in order to guarantee every man had the opportunity to enjoy those rights. Chandler continued: "if, then, liberty RIGHTFULLY cannot be converted into slavery, may I not question whether the title of the master to the slave is absolute and unqualified, and beyond the disposal of the government?"[35]

The reason that owning slaves is not rightful is because of the equality of

man. The Declaration of Rights spoke in general terms so as to include all men.
Preston thus spoke that, "the Bill of Rights . . . [asserts] that 'all men, by nature,
are equally free and independent.' What, Mr. Speaker is meant by this
declaration? Unquestionably as *human beings* . . . they are embraced within the
bounds of this broad, extensive, and eternal truth—one that is laid down as the
corner stone of all free governments."[36] The Declaration of Independence
represents the cornerstone of the Union in the same way that the Declaration of
Rights is the cornerstone for Virginia. According to Preston, Jefferson's
Declaration emphasized that the slaves were meant to be included in the corpus
of human rights. Indeed, the entire Revolution was based on rights shared by all
men, it was not simply for a few white men. The anti-emancipationists
maintained that the law and statutes had set an unapproachable redoubt against
abolition. However, according to Preston, who did not mince words, "the slave
has a *natural* right to regain his liberty." Compact could not divest the slave of
his rights and the slave understood that something was being denied to him.
Therefore, future violence was a surety: "The love of liberty is the ruling passion
of man; it has been implanted in his bosom by the voice of God, and he cannot
be happy if deprived of it." Therefore, another reason why the legislature must
act was because man's natural desires would not, and could not, be subsumed.
The slave would rise again in defense of his rights.

In every man, in every slave, there is a natural desire for freedom and the
slave may rightfully secure his own liberty. George W. Summers (Kanawha)
explained:

> There is a continual and abiding danger of insubordination from the natural
> love of liberty, which the great Author of our being has imparted, to all his
> creatures. It belongs to every thing which breathes the breath of life . . . It is a
> portion of the divine essence, which can never be wholly destroyed. Oppression
> cannot eradicate it. Amid the profoundest mental darkness, its feeble
> scintillation struck from the eternal rock of being, which can only be
> extinguished in the tomb.[37]

Since it is a part of man's nature to desire happiness, and since liberty is the best
means of achieving that happiness, man will not rest until he has attained a
measure of liberty. James McDowell (Rockbridge) maintained that there was a
natural connection between human nature and the desire for freedom:

> The truth is, sir, that although there are special instances of slaves who are
> willing to forego the benefits of *complete* freedom for certain other benefits
> which they enjoy under a *nominal* slavery, yet the instances, from their very
> nature, must be limited—they can extend only to a favored few and they
> furnish no authority for a decision upon conduct of others. Take the slave in his
> general relation to ourselves, and you cannot regard him otherwise than as a
> man,—having the capacities and resentments of man, both indeed repressed but
> both existing.[38]

The pro-slave representatives contended that the slaves were happy with their position. However, according to McDowell, that missed the point. The emancipation delegation seemed to grasp something about human nature that their opposition did not. No matter how happy a man might be with slavery, men will not be as happy and safe as they otherwise would, or should, be without securing the liberty of all men. Even if some slaves are happy with their position, it is not representative of a majority of those in bondage. Yet, Summers did not hesitate to point out that there were many educated blacks in the country who understood this and they had not resorted (as was feared) to the sword to exact revenge for their enslavement. Still, even if the anti-abolitionists tried to prohibit the slave's education, they would not be able to extinguish completely the natural spark for freedom. Since there was a natural desire for freedom, the slaves needed to be educated properly in order to not only understand the meaning of their rights, but also respect the rights of others. The slave who learns that man is the measure of all things will, if given the chance, rule others in like manner. The slaves might just overthrow the masters and enslave them in turn.[39]

Since Virginians expected more violence, in words shading Jefferson, Preston added that he "trembled" for Virginia because a point in time will come when the slaves will outnumber whites and, hence, be able to take revenge for the injustice forced upon them. This fear was especially important to those living west of the Blue Ridge Mountains: "we attack that property, because it is dangerous—we attack it, because it is subversive of the well being of society— we attack it on principles of necessity and policy—we wish to remove the danger from the East, and to prevent its existence in the West."[40] Summers explicated on the western desire to remain unaffected by slavery:

> We see, that ours must necessarily become a slave-holding community, not from choice, but from inability to prevent it. We do not take the disease voluntarily, but by infection from our proximity to, and connection with you. We can erect no barrier to its approaches—We can establish not even a QUARANTINE. You would enact for us no statute, by which the transportation of the population to the Western counties should be forbidden.[41]

In the Constitutional Convention of 1829-1830, the east proclaimed they had different interests than the west. Because of the dissimilar interests, the east claimed the west ought not to meddle with slavery. This argument did not make sense to John C. Campbell (Brooke), for while the west was told they did not have an interest in slavery, the east did not hesitate to claim that slavery was "an evil—a transcendent evil."[42] If slavery was indeed an evil, Campbell stated that it would be in the interest of the entire state to expeditiously do something about it. Prudence dictates that an evil should be removed. Bolling argued of slavery's evil effects, if it spread across the Blue Ridge Mountains, would not only introduce future violence, but corrupt western men. Therefore, western delegates believed that slavery would have a corrupting influence even on those who did not hold slaves.

The emancipationists' interest in slavery's removal was derived from the

Lockean principle *salus populi suprema lex*. As noted above, Randolph touched on this subject in his speech, but Campbell explained:

> It is the inherent right of every community to preserve itself, and to *remove* whatever may be destructive of its ends and happiness. The security and happiness of the Community are, or should be, objects of all Constitutions. The right of protection, when vitally assailed, is a right paramount to the Constitution. It is but the exercise of the undisputed principle contained in the oft repeated maxim *"salus populi suprema lex."* We claim not the right to *convert your property to the use of State*, but the right to declare that you shall not *retain*, within the territorial limits of this Commonwealth, a species of property, the possession of which endangers the safety of the State, or is destructive of her best interests.[43]

The emancipation of the slaves encouraged the health of the people, made the state more republican and removed both an immediate or future problem by securing the safety of the populace. Samuel M. Garland (Amherst) explained that *salus populi suprema lex* applied to the peculiar institution because the slaves were unlike other property:

> Let us then apply this principle to the case before us. The master has a right of property in his slave; but this right has no foundation in nature, and cannot be traced to any source higher than the laws of the land. It is then a right acquired under the laws of the Commonwealth, and held alone by the authority of those laws. But those laws guarantee the right upon condition that the safety of the community is not to be jeopardized thereby. It then follows, if the safety is endangered, the guarantee ceases; and the guarantee ceasing, and there being no other foundation on which the right can rest, it follows, as a conclusion, that, in such an event, the right of property ceases in that population.[44]

Like almost every abolitionist in the House, Garland insisted that there was no natural right in slaves. Since no right existed, the right must be positive. Therefore, what is positive may be justly removed, especially if the safety and health of the people are in danger. The principle of *salus populi suprema lex*, then, has as its foundation the equality of men. As Garland noted, this principle superseded the law and the statutes: *salus populi suprema lex* "is not for the benefit of the people, but for the preservation of its own power, and indeed for the prostration of the rights and liberties of the people." The use of the principle in fact was not the work of some extra constitutional monarch, tyrant, or despot, but was being invoked by the people themselves to protect the liberty of *all* men: "[T]here is no such danger of abuse here—no monarch declares here, when it is proper to appeal to this *suprema lex*, but it is the people themselves, or by their representatives, who are but agents or servants, when the resort should be had to this transcendent right." *Salus populi* was not an arbitrary tool, but pointed to something outside and above itself.

Since the argument on behalf of the anti-emancipationist rested on statutory law, and not the law of nature, and since the legislature had control over the creation of the statutory law, the slaveholder had no unqualified right to his slaves—especially when that property was increasingly becoming a threat to the health, safety, and welfare of the community. This was the essential meaning, or connection, between *salus populi suprema lex* and the safety of the people. According to McDowell, the east's reliance on the unequivocal right to slave property belied the proper end of government. In part, government was to protect the people. The right to private property must be concomitant to the end of politics: "the rights of private property and of personal security exist under every government, but they are not equal."[45] When property and safety come into conflict, the right to property becomes a secondary concern. Randolph's emancipation proposal was not an arbitrary act wresting property from its owner: "a State cannot arbitrarily cancel a private property when its uses are salutary without committing injustice to private rights: an individual cannot hold a property when its general qualities are dangerous or baneful without doing equal injustice to the rights which are public."[46] It was in the best interest of Virginians to preserve their lives from violence and end slavery, especially considering that the slave population was increasing at a clip faster than the increase of whites. The slaveholder's interest in keeping his slaves because the financial burden to the plantation owner would be destructive is not as strong as the argument for emancipation to save lives. Assuming a race war is in the offing, the prudent time to arrest it is when it is preventable, or manageable, than after such a catastrophic event has occurred. *Salus populi* was invoked by the emancipationists in terms of justice; it was not only just to secure the safety of the people, but to secure the rights of all men. Securing safety means little to nothing if it is not in the service of securing the rights of all men.

The most practicable plan for implementing that kind of policy is the gradual liberation and removal of the slaves. The reasonableness of the plan though was overshadowed by the increasing self-interest in slaves however—in particular, the potential slaves yet to be born. Henry Berry (Jefferson) explicated the indefensible position of the pro-slave interest regarding the right to slaves *in esse*:

> Can we not declare that the children of slaves born twenty, or fifty years hence, shall not be slaves, but shall be free? If we cannot do this, then indeed our statute is perpetual, and the present owner of a female slave has an indefensible estate in her descendents for one hundred generations to come—in fact forever. This is absurd. The right to slaves *now* in being is vested; the right to those *to be* born, is a mere possibility; if the law remains as it now is, the right may vest; if it is altered, the right will not vest.[47]

The practical problem with believing that the slave-owner has a right to the natural increase, or the offspring, of the slave, is that it makes compensated emancipation problematical, if not impossible. According to Berry, it would be very difficult to calculate the individual compensation an owner might require of the state if a compensated emancipation plan was passed. However, he asserted even if the positive law granted the owners the right to some compensation, it cannot, and does not, extend to potential human beings. McDowell concluded that *salus populi* was enough for the legislature to deny to the slave-owner the right to the increase. Ultimately the emancipationists suspected that the aim of the slaveholder was not compensation, but the perpetuation of the slave institution. The slave-owner was so attached to his property that he would never relinquish his control over it.

This attachment as expressed in the House lent evidence to the corrupting nature of slavery. Emancipation advocates asserted that slavery was harmful to both the master and slave. Recall that Chandler asserted that slavery not only affected the safety of the people, but also their happiness. Summers stated how this is so: slavery corrupts the community—it makes the master lazy and it forces the slave to work for fear of punishment if he does not. In language reminiscent of Query XVIII of Jefferson's *Notes on the State of Virginia*, slavery teaches the master, and slave, bad habits: "A slave population, exercising the most pernicious influence, upon the manners, habits, and character, of those among whom it exists. Lisping infancy learns the vocabulary of abusive epithets, and struts the embryo tyrant of its little domain."[48] There was widespread belief among many of the anti-slave delegates that slavery corrupted men, and undermined a foundational teaching of Christianity:

> When in the sublime lessons of christianity [sic], he is taught to "do unto others as he would have others do unto him" he never dreams that the degraded negro is within the pale of that holy canon. Unless enabled to rise above the operation of powerful causes, he entered the world with miserable potions of self-importance, and under the government of an unbridled temper.
>
> Habits of idleness, and their usual accompaniment, dissipation, are seldom avoided in a slave-holding community. Men in all ages have been found to seek sensual indulgences and to acquire a fondness for luxuries, whenever placed within their reach.

Slavery blights man's faith by encouraging him to forget the Golden Rule. He thinks he is above the slave and is his superior. Slavery thus corrupts the pureness of Christianity where one of the two central tenets is the equality of men—the most authoritative principle governing relationships between human beings. In the opinion of Jefferson, God would not take the side of Virginians in a contest between the two races should there be violence. God was just and He desired that the "due posterity" of the state demands some provision "for the removal of this evil."[49] The slaveholder who baulked at emancipation was more concerned with his prosperity—his luxuries—than the effect such a lifestyle had on his family and his community. The east, then, was less concerned with the community than the west. The abolitionists were more concerned with the health of Virginia than the anti-emancipationist, who was more concerned with what is his own.

Bolling agreed with Summers that the practice of slavery was injurious to the morals of the master because it instructed generations in the arts of idleness and vice. He concluded that slavery taught a master's children that they did not have to work, that they could live off the labor of another and this practice was perfectly normal. This taught the community to care not for the natural rights of others. It encouraged the passion of the master and did not cultivate his reason. These were additional justifications why ending slavery was ripe because despite the evil effects on the rights, habits, and moral of the populace, he hoped that the institution had not corrupted the entire people to such an extent that they did not want to do anything about it.[50] However, since slavery induced ill effects on the morals of the people, it made emancipation an expedient matter. The effect on the slave and the master is in part what they meant when the emancipationists claimed slavery was an evil.

In this vein, Samuel McDowell Moore (Rockbridge) spoke on the "monstrous consequences which arise from the existence of slavery."[51] The evil of slavery, he said, "may be regarded as the heaviest calamity which has ever befallen any portion of the human race." It had the "irresistible tendency . . . to undermine and destroy everything like virtue and morality in the community." In this sense, the effect is both to the slave and to the free. The slave society is more or less a closed society. As a consequence, the people are more ignorant as to their rights compared to more free societies. Since "the policy of the master" is the "ignorance of his slaves," the inculcation of enlightened morality is difficult if not impossible. The slave's habits, pursuits, and associations are less virtuous than they otherwise would be if the slave received an education, and became enlightened. This system reinforces white prejudices of blacks, but also keeps the slaves in moral darkness, ensuring their failure should they ever be freed. Indeed, it encourages unjust actions as the slave sees, and is told, that he is a lowly creature.

The Slave's inchoate mind, however, also understands in some way that his natural rights are being violated. Recall, that the pro-abolitionist delegates asserted that nature had sown into all men the desire for freedom. According to Preston, the natural desire for liberty is a part of the natural desire to be happy. For man to be happy, he must have liberty. Since enlightenment as to the natural rights of men was considered a danger to the community, the slaveholder dispenses with it. Enlightenment is an indispensable link to happiness. Without it, liberty is unstable. This ignorance "renders [the slave] incapable of deciding between right and wrong, of judging of the enormity of crime, or of estimating the high satisfaction which the performance of an honorable act affords to more intelligent beings." Slave society had an evil consequence on the slave and free alike:

> Far be it from me, Mr. Speaker, to assert, that virtue and morality cannot at all exist among the free, where slavery is allowed, or that there are not many high-minded, honorable, virtuous and patriotic individuals even in those parts of the State, where the slaves are most numerous. I know there are many such. I only contend, that it is impossible in the nature of things, that slaves can be virtuous and moral, and that their vices must have to some extent, an injudicious influence upon the morals of the free.

As we have noted, Jefferson also believed that both the master and slave were harmed by slavery. Both the abolitionists in the House, and Virginia's most prominent statesmen, understood that the success of the Founding depended on whether the people would continue to look up to that thing which was higher than mere Union, or defined that Union: that which is regarded as the highest gives a people its character.[52] In this way, the debate over the effects of slavery turned on the interpretation of the Founder's understanding of the Founding.

In the early part of the debates, Moore articulated a vigorous defense of the meaning of the American Founding:

> In reply to this assumption that, our ancestors boldly asserted, that all men were by nature equally free and independent and that they have certain inherent rights, of which, then they enter into society, they cannot, by any compact, deprive or divest their posterity. And among these unalienable rights, they enumerated those of life, liberty and the uninterrupted pursuit of happiness. The very language used by our ancestors shows that they considered the principles which they asserted, as applicable to people of color as well as those who were white.[53]

And this from Faulkner:

> The idea of a gradual emancipation and removal of the slaves from this commonwealth, is coeval with the declaration of your own independence from the British yoke. It sprang into existence during the first session of the general assembly, subsequent to the formation of your republican government. It was proper—there was a fitness of things in the fact, that so beneficent an object, as the plan for the gradual extinction of slavery in this state, should have been the twin offspring of that mind, which gave birth to the bill of rights, and to the act for religious freedom.[54]

As the western delegation noted, Virginia had an illustrious history dedicated to abolition. Faulkner held out for special mention Edmund Pendleton, George Mason, Richard Henry Lee, George Wythe, and the "all comprehensive genius of Thomas Jefferson." Gradual emancipation (*post nati*) had been successful in New York and Pennsylvania and was evidence that such a plan could succeed in the South. Jefferson once remarked that a future generation should secure emancipation. According to Preston, those serving in the 1831-1832 legislature were that generation. While the Sage and the Founders set the goal and urged emancipation, it was incumbent upon the delegates to fulfill it. Berry concurred: "I admit that we are not to be blamed for the origin of this evil among us; we are not to be blamed for its existence now, but we shall deserve the severest censure if we do not take measures as soon as possibly [sic], to remove it . . . every obligation of justice and humanity demands it."[55] If Old Dominion failed to remove slavery, then her citizens, and not the British, would be responsible for its effects in the future. They could not blame their ancestors for introducing the institution in order to deflect responsibility for its continuance as easterners were wont to do. Old Dominion's most prominent statesmen thus left a legacy of human freedom and as Faulkner contended, "it is for *us* to say whether we will carry it out or not."[56] It was the duty and responsibility of the present House to decide the question of slavery: "necessity compelled us to continue them as slaves: that necessity alone justifies their present condition—yet as men, as statesmen, as christians [sic], we should ever bear in mind, that every consideration of justice, policy, and humanity, demand us to extinguish that necessity as promptly as possible."[57]

Those who articulated a case for keeping the slaves were fashioning a new understanding. The abundant evidence suggests that all men were included in the corpus of rights. According to Virginia's most prominent statesmen, the slave had the same right to liberty as any white man:

> If they had meant to assert the doctrine of the natural equality of men, as applicable only to men in the state of nature, they would have said, that all *white men* are by nature equally free and independent, and not as they did do, that *all men* are so. The only possible way in which it could be shewn that this principle was not applicable to negroes, would be by proving that negroes were not men. An attempt too absurd to be made by any man.[58]

What makes the argument so absurd is that if any man did make that case, he would be arguing against the very rights he claimed for himself—it would be the undoing of his own argument. Moore then proceeds on a history lesson of the Founding whereby he catalogs the argument against the British King who rejected several attempts to rid the colonies of the slave trade and slavery itself. It was the King who prevented emancipation in the colonies. The only thing that prevented abolition was the necessity of impending Revolutionary war. The colonists could not extinguish the institution and conduct a war, much less win the war, as a divided nation. This is why slavery was considered a necessary evil. However, in 1832, Moore and many emancipationists believed the time had arrived to finally put the evil on the road to extinction. This the eastern, anti-emancipation, representatives would not accept.

Pro-Slavery Conservatives: From Property to Perpetuation

At the start of the session, pro-slavery advocates tried to quash any debate on emancipation because the question was deemed too dangerous to consider. We might say they attempted to effect a gag rule on the House.[59] Some argued that slavery was not wrong in the abstract, and most believed that abstract considerations were irrelevant anyway because slavery had existed in the past. If slavery was wrong, it would not be found in almost every civilization in time. Slavery was no anomaly. It was normal. While some would go on to claim that the very existence of liberty depended on slavery, others questioned the natural equality of men and attacked Jefferson's commitment to emancipation because he never formally proposed it when he served in public office.[60] Ultimately, the primary function of government was the protection of property, and the slaves were property that deserved protection.

In order to defend their position, the pro-slave delegation presented a united front on the question of abstract rights. They generally thought it had no place in the debate. Therefore, they avoided engaging their opponents on that question. Some like James H. Gholson (Brunswick) stated that he would not speak about the "abstract question of slavery" or address its "morality or immorality."[61] William Daniel (Campbell) concurred: the debate had nothing to do with the abstract question of whether it was *right* for one person to enslave another. Williams thought that the question of whether a person could own another was based on sectional "principles." What was "correct and orthodox" for one section of the Union was not for another. An abstract truth applicable to all men at all times did not matter, but a "geographical location" or "conventional prejudice" often "decides" the "correctness" of a principle.[62] The slave question was more practical than theoretical. John S. Gallaher (Jefferson) asserted that the abstract truth of equality did not pertain because "whatever may be thought of slavery in the abstract, men *will* hold on to this species of property as long as their *safety* and *interest* will permit them to do so." The pro-slave conventioneers attacked both Declarations on the ground of the unknowability of abstract truths. Since these truths were not plainly evident to men, they had no practical role in setting policy. Strictly speaking, the pro-slave delegation was correct—if one looks only at the positive law, the slaves were in many ways considered property. In other words, not all men were equal in every way. For example, Knox rejected the importance of natural rights and contended that some men were born, whether by fortune or power, to be ridden and others to ride. Empirically, this appeared true. Since the question of abstract rights had no place in the debate, a discussion about natural rights was pointless. Their focus was on reality, or the *is*, not the *ought*. This seemed to make emancipation an impossible alternative. Gholson claimed what was an almost universal sentiment in the House, that the existence of slavery was not the fault of the Americans, but the fault of the mother country—Britain. As a result, slavery should remain untouched. He rejected the claim that something must be done about the institution by deriding those who believed that, "it is the duty of a just, wise and virtuous people to mitigate its evil to the utmost extent of their ability, and to make it subservient to the best purposes of society; and on this ground, I challenge investigation."[63] Further, he disputed the belief that slavery had ill effects on the "morality," "character," "chivalry," and "honor" of the master. In other words, the Declaration of Rights did not obligate society to follow its precepts.

John Thompson Brown (Petersburg) was one of the most vigorous defenders of slavery in the House. He remarked that he had heard many speeches regarding the evils of slavery leading to impoverished souls and immoral character, but that the evil of the institution was exaggerated. He considered any plan to emancipate the slaves "visionary and impracticable."[64] Like Gholson and Daniel, he rejected abstract theories and thought a discussion about the evil of slavery was a waste of time: "many think it a bad investment— an unprofitable investment—an *unrighteous* investment. But whether it be for good or evil, the investment is made." The pro-slave master had a personal interest in slave property and that reality trumped abstract guidance on the question. Brodnax, and other property rights slave-owners, asserted that the right to their slave property was inviolable. Daniel insisted in no uncertain terms: "you may prove if you can that slavery is immoral, unjust and unnatural, that it originated in avarice and cruelty, that it is an evil and a curse, and you still do not convince me that our slaves are not property, and as such protected by our Constitution."[65]

What was only hinted at by the easterners in the Constitutional Convention of 1829-1830, was made explicit by the pro-slave faction in the House. The debate was not over real property per se, but the slaves and those in bondage are an extension of property: "take from us these slaves without compensation and what do we have left? Our land 'tis true—but even that would be depreciated to a great and incalculable extent. By depriving us of our labourers, and leaving us destitute of the means of procuring others, you throw out of cultivation a proportionate part of the soil."[66] Indeed, the pro-slave advocates asserted that the convention basically settled this matter—if the slaves were property then the ownership of them ought to be protected: "every species of property, personal, real, or mixed, over things or persons, is . . . protected by the Constitution, no matter from what title it may be deduced."[67] Even if an abolition plan were to pass the legislature and become law, it did not matter when emancipation took effect, the master would be deprived of his economic gain and be reduced to a beggar. This fear prompted a reiteration of the argument made in the convention that property deserved special representation in the state government.[68] We shall consider the argument that the slave-owner made in regard to the right to the profits of the unborn, but at this point Brown asserted that any emancipation scheme represented a taking, and that seizing of property should follow with millions in compensation. The Randolph plan provided nothing by way of monetary compensation of lost property.

Not every pro-slave advocate completely disregarded the natural rights of the slaves. Some understood, and did not try to dispute, their rights, but they strongly asserted that the property right should be protected. For instance, Brown thought his right to property in slaves was conventional, but contended that the state constitution and the statutes made the slaves property. The positive law trumped the law of nature and nature's God. While it is true that in other states slaves may not be considered mere property, they were considered such in Virginia, and that is all that should matter to the state legislature. Whatever property one owns ought to be protected because the positive law in Virginia decided the matter. If the legislature changed the status of slave property, that would be immoral. The only thing that may constitutionally prompt a regulation, or taking, of property is imminent danger.[69]

The question of the hazard of slavery put eastern slaveholders in a difficult position. They asserted that the slaves did not present a danger because the people were generally safe from insurrection. Slavery did not present a danger to the community. Ironically, the Turner affair only confirmed the people were safe. The pro-slave supporters urged their colleagues that the Southampton revolt was a petty affair and an anomaly. The response to Turner was so overwhelming that it convinced the east the slaves could never conspire successfully to plan a major coordinated attack on whites. Since there is no real short-, or long-term danger, and since the damage inflicted by Turner and his men was minimal in the grand scheme of things, it did not warrant the passage of an emancipation scheme.[70] They even invoked Jefferson to lend evidence to their position that the slaves were not a threatening force:

> Mr. Jefferson indulged the hope, that slavery might sooner or later cease to exist amongst us, it is impossible to doubt. He loved his country enthusiastically, and having assisted bringing all her institutions to the utmost attainable point of excellence, he regretted that there should remain what the most fastidious might consider a blemish on the goodly edifice. It was the day dream of the patriot and the philanthropist. Who of us, has not, at times, been beguiled into the same lovely anticipation? And yet look around on things as they are . . . Had Mr. Jefferson thought emancipation practicable, why did he never attempt its accomplishment? He spent a long and glorious life in the service of his country, and much of it, in her legislative councils—at a time, too, when this "monster" was yet in its infancy . . . Yet [he] lived and died without proposing emancipation.[71]

The argument enlisting Jefferson was meant to do two things: criticize the emancipationist's use of him as an ardent abolitionist—thus diluting his authority in favor of their cause—and, they invoked the Sage in such a way as to convert him to their side. Unlike in the Constitutional Convention of 1829-1830, the pro-slave faction did not attack Jefferson as stridently. They instead attempted to convince others that Jefferson supported slavery. Somewhat ironically, they claimed that Jefferson always maintained the right of property in slaves and that if he were alive in 1832, he would not assent to the *post nati* proposal Randolph submitted.[72] Jefferson may have articulated that the slaves ought to be free, but when he had the opportunity to free them he relented. Even in his own personal life he failed to free his own slaves. Therefore, he did not really believe that which he articulated. His actions spoke louder than his words. Jefferson was really a pro-slave Virginian! Brodnax contended that the Sage would not assent to emancipation not only for self-interested reasons stated above, but also because it was more impracticable in 1832 since more slaves existed than during Jefferson's era.

The most pervasive argument used to challenge Randolph's plan stemmed from the belief that the master had a right to unborn slaves. They readily admitted that their objection to emancipation stemmed from self-interest. Robert D. Powell (Spottsylvania), Brodnax, and other pro-slave delegates declined to support any scheme that did not recognize the "right of property."[73] Since self-interest was the ruling passion of man, the assembly should not pass any law that emancipated the slave without the consent of the specific individual owners:

> It is in vain to suppose that we can separate man from his interest. He will

pursue it, regardless of love of country or personal attachments. If you say that slaves shall not be private property within your jurisdiction, you force from you every individual whose removal will enable him to avoid operation of your law, and to enjoy, unmolested, the property which he feels to be his own. Love of country but rarely induces any man, willingly, to become a beggar—never, when his mind is deeply imbued with a sense of his country's injustice.[74]

In reality, if every slave-owner had to individually consent to such a scheme, in all practicality, abolition would never be realized. No owner would, writ large, consent to the emancipation of the slaves. In light of this argument, they maintained that the owner had a right to the increase of the slaves. Such avariciousness more and more precluded the possibility of emancipation. Someone like Gholson certainly believed that Randolph's plan would encourage those slaves not freed to rebel—such was self-preservation used as a reason to reject the bill. However, Gholson spent most of his speech decrying emancipation because it would inflict monetary harm on the slave-holder. Because the master would lose money—even if he tried to sell his slaves off before the plan took effect—the *post nati* proposal was impracticable.

Drawing on this self-interest, James C. Bruce (Halifax) held that the state constitution settled the matter:

> If we have no property in the future increase of our slaves, we certainly have none to those now in being, for the property in both must necessarily be derived in the same way . . . this property is recognized by the civil law, and runs through all our statutes, from the earliest period of our colonial existence, down to the present time. The right is there clearly ascertained and defined; "children born of slaves shall be slaves" . . . In ascertaining the rights and privileges guarantied by the Constitution, it is not necessary to resort to metaphysical subtlety.[75]

The allusion to the Constitutional Convention of 1829-1830 was hardly subtle. The pro-slave interests in the House repeated the argument by the eastern delegation in the convention that man could not really know abstract rights. In this debate, though, the pro-slave faction contended that the slaves could not be emancipated by the legislature because of "*partus sequitur ventrem*." Simply put, it meant that the increase, or offspring of the mother, is the property of the owner; the yet to be born were the property of the master. The right to slave property gave the owner an equal claim to the "future increase" of that property. Gholson expanded on this understanding:

> It has always (perhaps erroneously) been considered . . . that the owner of land had a reasonable right to its annual profits; the owner of orchards, to their annual fruits; the owner of brood mares, to their product; and the owner of female slaves, to their *increase* . . . The legal maxim of "*Partus sequitur ventrem*" is coeval with the existence of the right of property itself, and is founded in wisdom and justice. It is on the justice and inviolability of this maxim, that the master foregoes the service of the female slave; has her nursed and attended during the period of her gestation, and raises the helpless and

infant offspring. The value of the property justifies the expense; and I do not hesitate to say, that in its increase consists much of our wealth.[76]

Bruce, Brodnax, and other eastern pro-slave supporters maintained that Randolph's emancipation plan amounted to an unjust seizure of property for a public use without just compensation. The *post nati* plan not only seized property without compensation, but also did not make recompense for the increase that property would produce in the future. In the economics of buying and selling, the consideration of what a property might produce in the future is a part of the transaction and is worked out between the buyer and the seller. The anti-emancipation delegation was reasonably concerned, as were their predecessors in the convention, that all property would be insecure if the government had the authority to free the slaves outside of that negotiation process. It would have been an ambitious emancipation program and would conceivably have had to deal with hundreds of thousands of slaves. If the legislature could legislate on the "increase" of slave property, they would "have the power to attack that which is now in their possession."[77] Pro-slave interests thus viewed their slaves as similar to other forms of property. The view that the slaves were property encouraged some delegates to veer awfully close to the view of slaves as chattel.

Roane assented to Gholson's assessment of the status of slave property and added that he owned many slaves and had to correct some of them by making them feel the "impression" of his ownership. He defended the property argument thusly: "I would not touch a hair on the head of his slave [Gholson's], any sooner than I would a hair on the mane of his horse, without paying him the full and just value thereof."[78] If the slave was the same as a dog, or horse, then Roane would be correct. Despite the claims that they were going to avoid debate on the abstract question of slavery and the moral argument surrounding it, some delegates could not resist defending the institution. They also went beyond the claim that natural rights were not applicable and denied their existence:

> It is needless now to view this as an abstract question: to turn aside and enter into the metaphysical doctrines of the natural equality of man, to the abstract moral right of slavery . . . . I am not one of those who have ever revolted at the idea or practice of slavery, as many do. It has existed, and ever will exist, in all ages, in some form or degree . . . History, experience, observation, and reason, have taught me, that the torch of liberty has ever burnt brightest when surrounded by the dark and filthy, yet nutritious atmosphere of slavery.[79]

The pro-slave themes and arguments from the House certainly progressed further than the Constitutional Convention. Slavery was becoming a boon to republican government. Indeed, Knox stated that slavery was "indispensably requisite in order to preserve the forms of Republican government."[80] In similar fashion to the Easterners in the convention, who challenged on the non-existence of natural rights, Roane likewise articulated a complete denial of them:

Nor do I believe in that Fan-faronade about the natural equality of man. I do not believe that all men are *by nature* equal, or that it is in the power of human art to make them so. I no more believe that the flat-nosed, woolly-headed black native of the deserts of *Africa*, is equal to the straight-haired white man of Europe, than I believe the stupid, scentless greyhound is equal to the noble, generous dog of *Newfoundland*.[81]

The characteristics he uses to describe the slaves resembles that of a beast. Roane believed that the state existed in the service of whites. Only whites were accorded the protection of the state and it was for their happiness that it existed. If blacks had no rights the white man was bound to respect, then it called into question the Declaration of Rights itself and endorsed slavery without end. The slaves, as a lower form of animal, were thus no better than hog or dogs.

While Bruce and Roane decried abstract natural rights, Gholson specifically expounded on the illegitimacy of the Declaration of Rights:

A still stranger light has broken in upon us. The gentleman from Rockbridge (Mr. Moore,) disdaining to examine the subject *under* the Constitution and laws, has ascended to the very fountain of our political power, and rests himself upon our bill of rights. "All men, by nature, are equally free and independent." The gentleman thinks that here he has found a power sufficiently comprehensive and resistless to burst asunder the chains of slavery, and set the captive free . . . But the gentleman's construction of the Bill of Rights is not just. The section to which he has referred is only a declaration of the *natural* rights of man—not a declaration of the powers of this government, or of the social obligations or rights of *society*.[82]

If the assembly were to use the Declaration of Rights as a guide, Gholson believed it would not only destroy slavery, but every other relationship supported by the law—"the relations of husband and wife, parent and child, master and servant, governor and governed . . . ." Predictably, he believes such an understanding is the result of being attached to too much democracy, or majority government. As we noted above, Bruce adopted almost the exact language from the convention asserting that the Declaration of Rights and the idea of equality were incapable of being understood because of their metaphysical nature. Abstract rights are not esteemed like those granted by convention.

With the teaching of both Declarations called into question, it was but a small step to justify slavery. Alexander G. Knox (Mecklenburg) came the closest to asserting that slavery was a good:

But, Sir, upon what principle is it that slavery is this crying evil, this cormorant that is preying upon the vitals of the body politic, consuming all that is valuable in the principles of our Government?—I cannot force my mind even by calling to its aid, humanity, religion or philanthropy to the conclusion that slavery, as it exists in Virginia is an evil. But . . . on the contrary, I consider it susceptible of demonstration that it is to this very cause, that we may trace the high and elevated character which she has heretofore sustained; and, moreover, that its

existence is indispensably requisite in order to preserve the forms of a
Republican Government. Sir I would ask gentlemen to point to one solitary
instance of a Government, since the institution of civil society, in which the
principle of slavery was not tolerated in some form or other.[83]

Brown and William D. Sims (Halifax) also claimed that slavery in Virginia was
not "criminal or immoral."[84] It was Knox, however, who articulated three
general themes that provided a basis of the positive good argument: (1) slavery
was not an evil; (2) slavery was a prop to republican government; and (3)
slavery had always existed and is therefore not a moral wrong. Brodnax made a
positive affirmation of the right to slave property that approached the positive
good thesis as well:

> It is true, that the constitutions of both our federal and state governments, have
> erected barriers for the protection of private property, which must be prostrated,
> before such a measure as this could be carried out into effect. But what are
> charters—or constitutions—or bills of rights, on a question like this? I would
> not give a rush for them; charters and compacts can be broken or evaded. The
> charter by which we hold our slaves, is antecedent to either; it is found on the
> immutable principles of justice, which existed before the formation of political
> societies; it has received the approbation of man, and the sanction of his great
> Creator, and is written on our hearts. Under our constitutions and laws, it has
> acquired exactly the same guarantee . . . and it can now be regarded in no other
> light, legally or morally.[85]

The proximity to the positive good thesis in the above statement is
extraordinary. A justification of the peculiar institution was additionally
bolstered by Christianity. Slavery was not only just, but its justice was implanted
in us by God. Could it be that there are natural slaves? Brown concluded his
oration with a religious defense of slavery. Since there is nothing in the New
Testament condemning the practice of slavery, Brown asserted that slavery is
not inherently immoral, nor unbiblical. However, it was Goode who pursued
what would become a more familiar argument on this subject. He suggested that
the slaves were a part of the cursed race of Canaan. Since the slaves were
descendents of that cursed race, they were meant to be the servants of whites.[86]
Wood approached the good of slavery from the view of providence: "their
introduction into this land, may have been one of the inscrutable ways of
Providence to confer blessings, lasting blessings upon that race."[87] The existence
of slavery actually had benefited the United States:

> That Gentleman has discovered among our people, a deprivation of the moral
> principle; which he regards as one of the effects of slavery. It is curious to mark
> the difference between the opinions of this gentleman, and those of the great
> Edmund Burke. Burke believed that, the existence of slavery in the American
> colonies, gave to our ancestors, an early idea of importance and superiority,
> which imparted an elevation of character, rising them far above the
> commission, or toleration of littleness, or meanness.[88]

Knox went the furthest defending the peculiar institution, however, asserting that historical forces have demonstrated slavery has been tolerated throughout the ages. It has proved beneficial to many societies and civilizations. Slavery was the result of "fortune, genius, and physical power" which caused a difference in men.[89] The only line of distinction between the master and the slave is circumstances. The slave owes his services to the stronger.

If the Turner affair was not cause of alarm, it was because the anti-emancipation delegates contended that "our slave population is not only a happy one, but it is a contented, peaceful, and harmless one."[90] The Turner event was an aberration in an otherwise serene slave system. The slaves in the Union were taken care of, well fed, and well clothed. In other words, they were protected by a generous master and were happy in their condition. The feelings between the master and slave ought to be cherished and strengthened, not undermined by emancipation. For many conservative delegates the happiness of the slaves was an important defense to discourage emancipation. Daniel was one of the most brazen articulators of this position: "Show me, sir, a happier man than one of these domestics, in the possession of a kind indulgent owner. Proud of his master, he assumes his name, apes his manners, puts in his air of dignity . . . a majority of them would look upon it as an act of cruelty on our part to break asunder the ties which bind them, unprovided for, to a strange and distant land: We too, sir, are comparatively happy in the possession of them."[91] Of course, the plan would not have merely emancipated the slaves without the necessary preparation for freedom. Without some policy to prepare them for a life outside of bondage, Daniel's opinion would be in accord with Virginia's Founders that simple emancipation would be an act of cruelty.

Despite the happy state of the slaves, pro-slave supporters believed they could be prompted to rebellion. They contended that the mere discussion of the issue could not occur without jeopardizing the safety of the community because "its peculiar nature forbids it":

> But in the present case, these same speeches and essays are enlightening not only to those who are to act, but also on those who are to be acted upon. These ignorant and degraded wretches are not so entirely destitute of the means of information as not to learn the character of the public proceedings which are had respecting them. They can not long remain ignorant of the sentiments which are thus predictably expressed, . . . [92]

According to the anti-emancipationists, liberty would excite the ignorant slaves to riot. It would make them discontented, which would fester and develop into a spirit of rebellion. This duality placed the pro-slave faction in an interesting quandary—slaves were generally happy and harmless, yet they are also dangerous and might at any moment take up arms against whites. Enlightenment would be too much for them to handle. Once they understood they had rights, they would be more inclined to act to secure them.

The real fear was not slave insurrection, however, but widespread emancipation. Knox asserted the importance of the Virginia debates not just for the state, but for the entire South if it passed an emancipation plan:

> For think you, Sir, that the fanaticism of the age will confine its operations to
> Virginia? No, Sir—but emboldened by your example, it will spread its baneful
> contagion over the whole Southern country. Demagogues will rise in every
> section, proclaiming the principle of universal emancipation—and when this
> period shall arrive, the Government whose aid you would invoke, will not
> remain a silent spectator of the strife . . . but acknowledgement of its power, by
> one of the largest slave-holding States in the Union, it will erect its authority,
> and claim the privilege of deciding the contest.[93]

Knox was not the only delegate who believed this would happen if Old
Dominion passed an emancipation plan. While one might view his opinion on
this matter as mere hyperbole, judging from many of the speeches in the House,
there is considerable evidence it was not.

An Analysis of the Debates

The debates in the House of Delegates were in many ways an extension of the
debates in the Constitutional Convention of 1829-1830. The division between
the east and west was just as evident. Many of the speakers defending the right
to slave property noted the western tendency to meddle in an issue that was of
no interest to them. The same old sectional divisions in the state obdurately
remained. None perhaps stated what was at stake better than Wood: "If the West
should succeed in passing a law, unacceptable to a large part of the State, that if
any step should be taken which should destroy the tenure by which this property
was held . . . it would not only be resisted . . . [it would] divide this State [and] if
the same doctrines should be maintained elsewhere, it might sever *this Union*."[94]
Easterners believed the convention solved the conflict between representation
and the protection of property: slave property deserved special protection. It had
become a sacred right. To refer the question of slavery to the people, as
Randolph's *post nati* plan proposed, would violate the agreement of the late
convention because it placed the security of that property in the hands of the
majority. If the majority were to approve Randolph's plan, it would be similar to
the majority tyrannizing over the minority.[95] However, the submission of the
plan, if passed by the Assembly, would go to the people as a suggestion. It
would serve as a guide for the representatives in the next session. There is much
evidence that the *post nati* plan would have been received well by the people in
the state if they had a chance to vote on it.

   The eastern, pro-slave, representatives in the House exclaimed that any
proposal for emancipation was impractical. This argument is not without merit.
The amount of money it would take to colonize just the free blacks would have
been difficult to raise. However, the pro-slave supporters did not offer a
practicable plan of their own. The reason the slave supporter was able to contend
that he had a right to slave property—to another human being, and to its
increase—was because he rejected the concept of "all men are created equal."

Despite that denial, most declared that slavery was "evil," but the simple fact that many invoked the word "evil" should not distract us. There were different interpretations of what the word meant when applied to the peculiar institution. It confused the pro-emancipation delegates as to what the pro-slave side meant when they claimed slavery was an evil, but yet held that it should be protected. Faulkner understood that the pro-slave antagonists, while they were not overt advocates for slavery, were *"apologists"* of some sort.[96] Most may have claimed that slavery was an evil, but they proceeded to downplay its effects. Like Randolph, Faulkner detected a crucial turn in the opinion of slavery in Old Dominion that betrayed their opinion that the peculiar institution was evil. The debates demonstrated the problems associated with "the withering and blasting effects of slavery." Those supporting slavery claimed to be unaffected by the institution and this is why Faulkner asserted that with every passing day slavery existed it mounted more "permanency and force." In the past, the attacks on slavery came from the non-slaveholding west and the slaveholding east. By 1832, the slave-owning east had hardened their heart and rejected arguments articulated by Virginia's founding statesmen.[97] They were finding comfort in a new indulgence.

Some thought slavery was evil not because someone's rights were violated, but because slavery was inconvenient, or it harmed the economy. An evil based on the violation of rights is very different from an evil based on economics or self-interest. This opinion did not only exist on the pro-slavery side, though it was certainly more widespread. For example, Marshall (the son of Supreme Court Chief Justice John Marshall) asserted that if slavery was an evil, it was only a practical evil: "Marshall . . . felt himself at liberty to say that he was opposed to slavery as a practical evil . . . he objected to slavery, not because it implies moral turpitude, or because it is a sin to be the owner of a slave."[98] Even though he thought that slavery was indefensible, his public pronouncements on the subject were limited to its economic effects. He opposed slavery because it depressed the economy not because it was inherently wrong. Indeed, he went further asserting that if slavery was a sin, those who introduced the evil were responsible for it, not the present day slaveholder. Still, while nobody specifically described slavery as a "good," some delegates came quite close when they claimed slavery was not immoral and benefited the mind and morals of the citizen. They described slavery was something good without uttering the exact words. Couple the lack of a providential sign that slavery should end, with the Biblical imprimatur that blacks are a cursed race, and the result is an intransigent pro-slave opinion that slavery is, if not a good, a blessing from God.

As it pertained to the possibility of ending slavery, the pro-slave east balked. The opportunity had not presented itself to free the slaves. They did not offer a counter emancipation plan because many believed that providence had not provided the opportunity for men to end it. Men were powerless to end the institution because God had not seen fit to put it on the road to extinction: the "powers of man are limited—impossibilities are not expected of him, nor will he be required to sacrifice his happiness—the primary object of his existence—in the vain attempt to change the face of human affairs."[99] However, if providence means the preparation of something for future use, or foresight, it is unclear why Randolph's proposal was not evidence of God's desire to free the slaves.

When the slave debate commenced in full view of the public, the abolitionists were surprised how zealously the pro-slave interest connected property rights with slavery. William M. Rives (Campbell) criticized fellow delegates like Goode for asserting that the emancipation of the slaves amounted to a "confiscation" of property.[100] Rives objected because the word confiscation implied that the master had a right to the slaves. If the master had a right to a slave, it would probably preclude a political solution to the slave problem; it barred the legislature from doing something without compensation. McDowell claimed, "allow the private claim of property to prevail, and you authorize a progressive and indefinite increase of the slave."[101] The discord over property was even more ludicrous when considering that the slaveholders additionally believed that they had a right to the unborn. This contention would be a useful argument as the movement for compensated emancipation gained favor. When it became likely that the sale of western lands, and the monies saved up after the retirement of the War of 1812 debt, could be put to use to compensate the master for his slaves, they would object on the grounds of *partus sequitur ventrum*— which would cause the expense to be too great—natural causes, and lack of providence.[102] If there was any consensus in the House, it was over the removal of free blacks from the state. However, few free slaves were involved in the Turner plot. A preponderant majority of those who engaged in the rebellion were held in bondage.

The emancipationists were nearly united in that slavery was a moral evil, that it was economically undesirable, that it would destroy the Union and perhaps cause a servile war, that it was a danger to the public safety, and that the legislature had the authority to abolish it. To the extent that the emancipationists agreed the slaves were property, they assented that the slaveholder should receive some compensation. However, they did not claim that the slave-owner had a *right* to that compensation. The slave-owner had no legitimate claim to his slaves. Therefore, *post nati* was the best plan available because it allowed the master plenty of time to prepare for a life without that which he never rightfully owned in the first place. The plan was far from an unjust seizure of property, but was the very essence of just compensation, since it allowed the master to keep his slaves for some time. The emancipationists made clear, however, that even if slaves were property, the public welfare, or safety of the community, when threatened, subordinated property rights. The slave institution was a danger then because there was a God-given spark that existed in all men that impelled them to desire liberty, however inchoately they understood it. Therefore, given this natural desire, they thought that there would be more insurrections like that of Turner. Given the fact that blacks were increasing at a rate faster than whites (many whites were leaving the state in search of a more prosperous life), the institution of slavery would only antagonize the two races.[103] It should be no surprise that Turner and other slaves took to violence to secure their freedom.

One the one hand, the opponents of emancipation argued that the slaves were happy and were not dangerous. On the other hand, they resented the discussion and cautioned the debate over abolition because it might excite the slaves to insurrection. McDowell asserted that the fact that the pro-slave supporters worried about future slave violence demonstrated the severity of the situation. The time was ripe for gradual emancipation.[104]

The position of the emancipationists was informed by the Declaration of Independence and the Declaration of Rights: all men were endowed by God with the right to liberty. Emancipation was not only supported by Virginia's most prominent statesman, but it was also articulated in the two great Declarations.[105] All men preferred freedom to slavery and they understood that it was immoral to have slavery imposed on them. Slavery was hence, the great unnatural condition. The emancipationists politically supported a recovery of nature and natural right as a means to combat the arbitrariness of the pro-slave position. The emancipationists invoked *salus populi suprema lex* as a practical reason to end slavery. Their argument mirrored that of John Locke who, in *The Second Treatise of Government*, contended that the health and welfare of the people was the supreme law. According to Locke, the legislature should not be directed by "old custom" but by "true reason."[106] Recall that the Declaration of Rights followed almost verbatim, the maxim laid down by Locke that men are by nature equally free and independent. Slavery was not a natural condition and he considered slavery similar to a state of war. He thought that slavery should cease after the consummation of the compact, else the state of war between the enslaved and the master remained. Arbitrary rule was the antithesis of what a commonwealth, or a republic, was designed for: "*Absolute Dominion*, however placed, is so far from being one kind of Civil Society, that it is as inconsistent with it, as Slavery is with Property."[107] The east insisted that they had a right to slave property, but as Locke, and the western delegation made clear, there was no right to property in slaves.

Locke asserted that the fact that the slave was taken from his homeland did not give the master a title to that property. Chandler echoed this sentiment and found that regardless of the status of the slave property in the Constitution, no one had the right to own another man:

> What, sir, would be thought at the present day, if an elephant were taken by force or fraud from its true owner, on the coast of Africa, and brought to our country, and an individual knowledge of the circumstance were to purchase it? Would it not be said that he participated in a crime? . . . And, sir, is the reasoning different, when the subject is a human being? When a MAN has been taken by fraud or force from his native shore, and sold in your market?[108]

Since human beings are owners of their own bodies, no other person had the right to acquire another human being for the purpose of ownership. In that sense, Chandler asserts that even if the compact considered slaves as mere property, which it does not, it would be an immoral law since all men are created equal. Slavery thus violated the health and safety of the people in two ways: the people were not secure in their rights, and the possibility of servile war as a result of that fact seemed imminent.

Emancipationists contended that the slaveholder was not an absolute ruler over his property—e.g. he could not murder his slave—but in that he held another human being captive, he was responsible for him. The master did not own the slave, but was his fiduciary holder. Faulkner claimed that the master was "entrusted with their safe-keeping until an appropriate opportunity is presented of discharging ourselves of the unpleasant trust."[109] This peculiar relationship meant that the master was also responsible to see to it that the slave was fit for freedom because emancipation was the just end of that relationship: "I will not advert to the great principles of eternal justice, which demand at our hands the release of this people . . . it is due to posterity, that we should provide now for the removal of this evil."[110] Some delegates thus went beyond rights and asserted that the master had other duties toward his slave that were going unfulfilled. The slaveholder had a duty to make sure his slaves were prepared for freedom. Therefore, the damage of the slave institution was not limited to the master, but imposed consequences on the slave. The pro-emancipation delegates believed that slavery was an evil that harmed the slave and the master and this did not endear them to their eastern brethren, who became increasingly offended at the suggestion that slavery might harm the character of the master, his family, and his community.[111]

Though the pro-emancipation representatives based their arguments on abstract notions of natural right, this did not preclude their responsible statesmanship toward the practical problem at hand. They proceeded on prudential grounds: if emancipation were to be effected, the abolition wing of the House would need to persuade moderate pro-slave members of the east to support their plan:

> We have a problem, a practical problem, to discuss and to settle which demands this process of thought beyond every other one on which the mind can be employed, which takes continents and ages into its scope of operation, and which, thereby, involves an influence on the sum of happiness so immeasurably greater than any with which the results of speculative science could affect it, that all the problems of all schoolmen and philosophers seem, in comparison of this, to be little more than the day-dreams of a profitless and visionary abstraction. Let us but give our minds patiently and laboriously to some plan of gradual emancipation and removal, and we need not fear the result—need not fear but that some one will be devised which shall be just in its principle, and, for the most satisfactory in its details.[112]

They appealed to the self-interested slaveholder, and at the same time did not abandon that which was guiding them. With that in mind, the emancipationists appealed to a whole host of economic reasons to rid the state of slavery. Part of the reason the emancipation plan was so gradual was because it was understood that the master thought he had a right to his slave property. Randolph's gradual scheme effectively made the monetary sacrifice of the slaveholder minimal.

They appealed to colonization for similar practical reasons. Not only did they believe that a race war was a real possibility, even after emancipation, but they also realized prejudice existed. That is why nobody in the House considered emancipation without colonization.

Conclusion

Even though the eastern delegation wanted to avoid the debate over slavery, it lasted for over two weeks. After the dispute concluded, the gallery dwindled, attendance declined, and the debate became insipid. Nevertheless, it continued in the papers for months afterwards. Both the *Enquirer* and the *Whig* published editorials, letters to the editor, and other accounts about the House debate. No letter caused more consternation, and more debate, than the letter of "Appomattox" in the *Enquirer*. In part the author argued that the slaves must be kept in proper subordination and that the Assembly ought not debate slavery again. The pro-slave letter provoked many responses that carried on in the papers well into May of 1832.[113] Even before Appomattox reinvigorated public debate, the editorialists at the papers generally believed that the public deliberations influenced the citizens of Virginia toward emancipation while lamenting that the session ended without such a plan. After the session ended, the *Whig* continued publishing emancipation memorials and reporting on public meetings directed to the same conclusion.[114]

The *Enquirer* called Randolph's *post nati* proposal an unprecedented piece of legislation, probably the last appeal for emancipation. The result of the debate was a complete defeat for the forces of emancipation. The closest the House came to condemning slavery was via a motion offered by Bryce, which passed in the form of a preamble:

> Profoundly sensible of the great evils arising from the condition of the colored population of this commonwealth; induced by humanity as well as policy to an immediate effort for the removal in the first place, as well of those are now free, as of such as may hereafter become free; believing that this effort, while it is just in accordance with the sentiments of the community on the subject will absorb all present means; and that a further action for the removal of slaves should await a more definite development of public opinion . . .[115]

The preamble stated that the state looked forward to a future without slavery, but it rejected any immediate plan for emancipation. It indefinitely tabled emancipation until public opinion on the matter had more time to develop, yet the public was never polled in the form of a non-binding vote. The motion that emancipation was inexpedient, then, basically succeeded. Bryce then went on to propose the colonization of free blacks. While some thought that this was a first step that would end in the emancipation of the slaves, others found it wanting. This motion passed with the House allocating $35,000 for the deportation of free blacks. However, the Senate defeated this bill by one vote. In the end, the legislative session closed without anything substantive done to end slavery in

Virginia.

As far as the tone and tenor of the debate is concerned, as it continued, it increasingly became impassioned. Floyd feared that the debate was driving a wedge between those who lived east of the Blue Ridge Mountains and those who lived west of that range. The passions rose to such a level that there was talk of splitting the state into two separate entities. Some of the pro-slave faction was ready to let the west secede:

> Goode, of Mecklenburg, said to me the day the debate closed upon the "slave question" as it was called, that the Eastern and Western people were not at all the same people, that they were essentially a different people, that they did not think alike, feel alike, and had no interests in common, that a separation of the State must ensue, and rather than have the subject of abolition again debated he would be glad for a separation.[116]

The debate solidified the sectionalism of the state; the public debate seemed to foster Virginia sectionalism. Even though the debate basically ended on January 26, sporadic outbursts plagued the rest of the session. Goode even publicly stated that he hoped the state would divide: "[B]ut the spirit of candor compels me to the declaration, that I prefer DIVISION to the continued agitation of this question. And if the agitation of the question be continued, I shall, in every character which I may fill, exert myself to produce *division*."[117] Indeed, the votes in the House did fall along sectional lines. It is noteworthy that Goode publicly stated that he would pursue division of the state (and why not the Union?) over the issue of slavery. He was not alone. McDowell believed that slavery caused dissension and prophetically asserted it would be the cause of disunion. The emancipation supporters in the House came away from the debates with a belief that the slaveholder could not mingle, or coexist, with any other interest, so complete was the corruption caused by the peculiar institution. We ought not be surprised, then, that roughly thirty years later there was a division of the state. The Civil War was but the occasion for the division, but the reason for it stemmed primarily from the desire of a portion of the community to keep human beings in bondage.

According to McDowell, the gathering storm of opinion that nothing can, or should, be done about slavery necessitated the adoption of an emancipation plan: "a slight examination into the early circumstances of slavery in this commonwealth, will shew, that the change in this, which has since taken place, and upon which all legislation is now denounced, is precisely the change which justifies and requires it."[118] If slavery could not be arrested in 1832, at a moment when Old Dominion had the opportunity, in full debate, to scrutinize before the tribunal of reason an emancipation plan, then most likely the institution would never be arrested. Every day the institution survived gave it more "permanency and force."[119] McDowell asserts that since opinions were hardening concerning the institution, compared to the Founding, when sentiments were less adverse to the institution, the time to arrest it was now. He also realized that "on this interest" slavery was responsible for the geographical divide in the Union.[120]

Slavery would aggravate smaller grievances and lead the sections to greater alienation. Many recognized across party lines, that if a civil war commenced, it would conflict over slavery. McDowell was the most prescient of the speakers in the House on this question. He believed that the "gathering auguries" portended *"that the slave-holding interest of the country, will and can coalesce with no other interest* and must, as a consequence, be separate and hostile to all others."[121]

Concerning the claim by many historians that all the participants in the debate were motivated by economics or self-interest, they are only half-correct. Supporters of emancipation may have fashioned arguments derived from selfish concerns, but by and large, they began from a position of natural rights. Consideration of the ideas animated the debates and there was hardly a reference to the evil of slavery without an appeal to the natural rights of man as a basis for that opinion. In contrast, economic considerations were a vital influence of the anti-emancipationists. For example, the pro-slave faction could not understand how Randolph, who lived in the plantation-rich Tidewater region, could support emancipation. It was beyond their comprehension how a slaveholder could desire to see his property taken from him. Of the most vocal anti-slave speakers in the House, Chandler, McDowell, Bolling, Randolph, and Faulkner were slaveholders, Preston and Summers were not. Of the one hundred seventy-three representatives, ninety-one were slaveholders. Largely, the debate in the House was between those who possessed slaves.[122] However, without, first, the public attack on natural rights in the convention of 1829-1830, it would have been more difficult for the pro-slave interest to make a public defense of the slave institution in 1832. While there are similarities between the two debates, the 1831-1832 debates represented another step in the advance of the positive good thesis. In that sense, Robert's thesis explains the period more fittingly: Virginians were well on the road from Jefferson to Calhoun.

Given that the pro-slave delegation claimed a right to slaves as property, Freehling's thesis seems inaccurate. The emancipationists detected that the slave-owner was trying to make slavery perpetual. For example, the right to the increase of the slaves ensured the unremitting existence of slavery. Preston noted that the pro-slave supporters were so set on their desire to keep their slaves, they would abandon their revulsion of federal interference in state issues by invoking the central government as a defense against taking their property: "the gentlemen on the other side all admit that slavery cannot be justified on principle. They say that no man will defend the principle of slavery. But what do they mean, when they say that the Constitution, both State and Federal, protect them in their right to their property?"[123] Preston pointed out that the Federal Constitution did not secure the right to own another human being because the slaves were considered persons in that document and furthermore, in Virginia, if a master killed his slave it would be considered murder in the eyes of the law.[124]

The Virginia debates represent a turning point regarding the peculiar institution. Increasingly, slaveholders resented anyone perceived as attacking the institution of slavery, even those, in this case, who were of the same slaveholding community. Given the intense interest in the debates, it had a great influence on those outside the state. Remarkably, the Virginia debate is "the only debate on the abolition of slavery to be conducted in a southern state legislature during the ante-bellum period."[125] The debates in the House were thus of great importance. According to one historian, it "focused the nation's attention" and "revived arguments that had been raised earlier in the Constitutional Convention of 1829-1830 and suggested the outlines of the slavery debate for the next three decades."[126] In his review of the slave debates, Thomas Roderick Dew would assess the arguments made in the House and set sail for the "positive good" thesis.

Notes

1. George I. Williams, "Speech Delivered in the Virginia House of Delegates," *Constitutional Whig*, 27 April 1832, p. 4; Charles Jas. Faulkner, *The Speech of Charles Jas. Faulkner in the House of Delegates of Virginia in the Policy of the State with Respect to Her Slave Population: Delivered January 20, 1832* (Richmond, Va.: Thomas W. White, 1832), 22, or see Thomas Jefferson, "Autobiography," *Thomas Jefferson: Writings*, ed. Merrill Peterson (New York: Library of America, 1984, 44; James H. Gholson, "Speech Delivered in the Virginia House of Delegates," *Constitutional Whig*, 12 January 1832, p. 2.

2. Joseph Clarke Robert, *The Road from Monticello: A Study of the Virginia Slavery Debate of 1832* (Durham: Duke University Press, 1941), ii. Robert's book, while important in cataloguing most of the debate, did not offer a lengthy analysis of those debates. His was more a book of edited speeches from the floor of the House rather than an interpretation of those speeches.

3. Charles H. Ambler, *Sectionalism in Virginia from 1776-1861* (New York: Russell and Russell Inc., 1964), 184-185 and 197; William G. Shade, *Democratizing the Old Dominion: Virginia and the Second Party System 1824-1861* (Charlottesville: University Press of Virginia, 1996), 205.

4. Alison Goodyear Freehling, *Drift Toward Dissolution* (Baton Rouge: Louisiana State University Press, 1982), xii and xi.

5. Ibid., v.

6. "To the People of Virginia," *Constitutional Whig*, 17 November 1831, p. 2. For other examples: *Constitutional Whig*, 13 October 1831, p. 1; Common Sense, "To the People of Western Virginia," *Constitutional Whig*, 6 December, 1831, p. 4; "Slaves Free Negroes &c.," *Constitutional Whig*, 16 December 1831, p. 1.

7. "Virginia Legislature," *Richmond Enquirer*, 7 January 1832, p. 2; Ambler, *Sectionalism*, 190-191; Anthony Alfred Iaccarino, "Virginia and the National Contest over Slavery in the Early Republic, 1780-1833" (Ph.D. diss., University of California, Los Angeles, 1999), 196.

8. "Debate on Abolition," *Constitutional Whig*, 19 January 1832, p. 1; *Constitutional Whig*, 21 January 1832, p. 1; The Jeffersonian influence was obvious and selections of his letters were printed by the paper, Index, "For the Whig," *Constitutional Whig*, 26 January 1832, p. 2; Charles S. Sydnor, *The Development of Southern Sectionalism 1819-1848* (Baton Rouge: Louisiana State Press, 1948), 228.

9. Alexander Campbell, "Slavery in Virginia," *Millennial Harbinger*, 6 February 1832, 86.

10. "The Press," *Richmond Enquirer*, 19 January 1832, p. 3. The paper printed

opinions from other papers contending for the removal of the "intolerable curse" as well as for removal of freely emancipated slaves. Not everyone was happy with the public debate. One subscriber wrote to cancel his subscription, which the editors gladly accepted; Nathaniel Alexander, "Correspondence," *Richmond Enquirer*, 30 January 1832, p. 2.

11. Freehling, *Drift Toward Dissolution*, 136; Iaccarino, 209; Alex G. Knox "Speech Delivered in the Virginia House of Delegates," *Richmond Enquirer*, 14 February 1832, p. 2; Rice W. Wood, "Speech Delivered in the Virginia House of Delegates," *Constitutional Whig*, 26 January 1832, p. 4.

12. *Journal of the House of Delegates of the Commonwealth of Virginia* (Richmond, Va.: Thomas Ritchie, 1831), 10. Floyd did convey in his address that he was corresponding with other Governors in neighboring states about the events in Southampton. He promised to relay the results of the correspondence at a later date. We know from his diary entries that he was assessing the support for emancipation during this time.

13. John Floyd, Diary of John Floyd, 26 December 1831, *The Life and Diary of John Floyd*, ed. Charles H. Ambler (Richmond, Va.: Richmond Press, Inc., 1918), 172.

14. Ibid., 9-11 January 1832, 173.

15. Robert, 16; Freehling, *Drift Toward Dissolution*, 126; *Journal of the House of Delegates of the Commonwealth of Virginia*, 13 December 1831, 29. Other petitions followed regarding emancipation and some requested exploration into compensated emancipation, ibid., 16 December 1829, 34; 20 December 1829, 41; 22 December 1829, 44; 23 December 1829, 51; 29 December 1829, 54; 4 January 1832, 81; Lee Rivers Polk, "An Analysis of Argumentation in the Virginia Slavery Debate of 1832" (Ph.D. diss., Purdue University, 1967), 61-64.

16. *Journal of the House of Delegates of the Commonwealth of Virginia*, 11 January 1832, 93; Freehling, *Drift Toward Dissolution*, 128-129.

17. *Journal of the House of Delegates of the Commonwealth of Virginia*, 11 January 1832, 93.

18. Floyd, Diary of John Floyd, 12 January 1832, *The Life and Diary of John Floyd*, 174; Freehling, *Drift Toward Dissolution*, 165; Iaccarino, 200.

19. *Journal of the House of Delegates of the Commonwealth of Virginia*, 16 January 1832, 99; Robert, 19.

20. Thomas Jefferson Randolph, *Speech of Thomas J. Randolph in the House of Delegates of Virginia on the Abolition of Slavery* (Richmond, Va.: Samuel Shepherd & Co., 1832), 7.

21. Quoted in Freehling, *Drift Toward Dissolution*, 130.

22. Randolph, 15.

23. Ibid., 20. Unless otherwise noted, quotes are from this source. Coles left Virginia in 1819 in part to free his own slaves. He left even though Jefferson encouraged him to be reconciled to his state. Coles became the second Governor of Illinois. Jefferson to Edward Coles, Monticello, 25 August 1814, *The Portable Thomas Jefferson*, ed., Merrill D. Peterson (New York: Penguin Books, 1975), 547; Iaccarino, 199; Coles to Thomas Jefferson Randolph, Philadelphia, 29 December 1832, "Letters of Edward Coles to Thomas Jefferson," *William and Mary College Quarterly Historical Magazine* 7 (April 1927) : 105-107.

24. Randolph, 10.

25. Whitfield, 74; Sam McDowell Moore, "Speech Delivered in the Virginia House of Delegates," *Richmond Enquirer*, 19 January 1832, 2.

26. Randolph, 19.

27. Philip A. Bolling, *The Speeches of Phillip A. Bolling in the House of Delegates of Virginia on the Policy of the State in Relation to Her Colored Population: Delivered on January 11 and 25, 1832* (Richmond: Thomas W. White, 1832), 14.

28. Randolph, 8.

29. Ibid., 18.

30. Williams, p. 4; Henry Berry, *The Speech of Henry Berry in the House of Delegates of Virginia on the Abolition of Slavery: Delivered on January 20, 1832* (Richmond, Va.: Thomas W. White, 1832), 4.

31. William B. Preston, "Speech Delivered in the Virginia House of Delegates," *Constitutional Whig*, 28 January 1832, p. 2. Italics in the original.

32. Bolling, 6.

33. Berry, 15.

34. John A. Chandler, *The Speech of John A. Chandler in the House of Delegates of Virginia on the Policy of the State with Respect to Her Slave Population: Delivered January 17, 1832* (Richmond: Thomas W. White, 1832), 7.

35. Chandler, 8; Whitfield, 85.

36. Preston, 2. Unless otherwise noted, all quotes from this source. Italics in the original. Alexander Stephens, the vice-president of the Confederacy, removed that cornerstone of the Revolutionary Fathers and replaced it with one of their own.

37. Summers, 4; see also, Bolling 8; Berry, 3 and 8; McDowell, 19-20: "Liberty is a spark which flieth into the face of him who attempteth to trample it under foot."

38. McDowell, 19. Italics in the original.

39. We should note that an argument may be made that the more they understand their rights, the more unsettled they will become because they will be enlightened to the great wrong committed on them. To an extent, this was the argument presented by the pro-slave faction. However, to those supporting gradual emancipation, like Berry, 3, it would not matter for all the laws in the world would not suppress the natural desire for freedom (see also Preston, 28 January 1832). With increased knowledge security will increase because they will regard the rights of others as well (Moore, 19 January 1832, 1). Even if some would become unsettled like Turner, the gradual introduction of freedom would help to meliorate the situation.

40. Preston, 2.

41. Summers, 4.

42. John C. Campbell, "Speech Delivered in the Virginia House of Delegates," *Constitutional Whig*, 16 March 1832, p. 2, 20 March 1832, p. 4; William H. Brodnax, *The Speech of William H. Brodnax in the House of Delegates of Virginia on the Policy of the State with Respect to its Colored Population: Delivered January 18, 1832* (Richmond, Va.: Thomas W. White, 1832), 10; Bolling, 9.

43. Campbell, 4. Italics in the original. The emancipationists appealed to practical issues like safety of the community as often as their appeal to natural rights. Cf. Bolling, 2-4.

44. Samuel M. Garland, "Speech Delivered in the Virginia House of Delegates," *Constitutional Whig*, 2 February 1832, p. 4. Unless otherwise noted, all quotes from this source.

45. McDowell, 15.

46. Ibid., 11.

47. Berry, 5.

48. Summers, 4. All quotes, unless otherwise noted from this page and source. Summers was one of the most prolific, and consistent, debaters who referred to Jefferson.

49. Summers, 31 January 1832, 2.

50. McDowell, 4-5.

51. Moore, "Speech Delivered in the Virginia House of Delegates," *Richmond Enquirer*, 19 January 1832, pp. 1-2. Unless otherwise noted, all quotes from this source. Of all members of the House, Alexander Campbell appeared to approve of Moore the most. He published only one speech from the debates in his newspaper, and that was from Moore: Alexander Campbell, "The Crisis," *Millennial Harbinger*, 6 February 1832, 87-93.

52. Leo Strauss, "An Epilogue," *An Introduction to Political Philosophy: Ten Essays by Leo Strauss*, ed. Hillail Gildin (Detroit: Wayne State University Press, 1989), 141.

53. Moore, "Speech Delivered in the Virginia House of Delegates," *Constitutional Whig*, 28 March 1832, p. 3.

54. Faulkner, 11. Unless otherwise noted, all quotes from this source.

55. Berry, 4. The pro-slave delegation believed that since the British instituted slavery, the current generation was not responsible for it or its removal: see Wood, 2.

56. Faulkner, 12.

57. Ibid., 18.

58. Moore, 28 March 1832, p. 3. Italics in the original.

59. Freehling, *Drift Toward Dissolution*, 159-160.

60. John Thompson Brown, *The Speech of John Thompson Brown in the House of Delegates on the Abolition of Slavery* (Richmond: Thomas W. White, 1832), 15.

61. James H. Gholson, "Speech Delivered in the Virginia House of Delegates," *Constitutional Whig*, 12 January 1832, p. 2; Robert D. Powell, "Speech Delivered in the Virginia House of Delegates," *Constitutional Whig*, 12 January 1832, p. 2; Spencer M. Ball, "Speech Delivered in the Virginia House of Delegates," *Constitutional Whig*, 13 March 1832, p. 4; John S. Gallaher, "Speech Delivered in the Virginia House of Delegates," *Constitutional Whig*, 13 March 1832, p. 4.

62. George I. Williams, "Speech Delivered in the Virginia House of Delegates," *Constitutional Whig*, 24 April 1832, p. 4; William Daniel, "Speech Delivered in the Virginia House of Delegates," *Richmond Enquirer*, 31 January 1832, p. 1.

63. Gholson, 12 January 1832, 2; see also Brown, 21; Jenkins, 149; Knox, 2. It should be noted on these points, politics was ever more viewing in light of the low (interest and power) rather than viewing actions in light of the high.

64. Brown, 5. Unless otherwise noted, all quotes from this source. Italics in the original.

65. Daniel, 3.

66. Brown, 6.

67. Daniel, 3.

68. Goode, 10.

69. Brown, 11-12; Brodnax, 13. Brodnax also repeats the distinction made at the convention between minority protection and majority rule in the context of protecting slave property. Taking property without consent is akin to "absolute government" and is a politics based on "force," ibid., 18.

70. Brodnax, 23-25; John E. Shell, "Speech Delivered in the Virginia House of Delegates," *Constitutional Whig*, 16 February 1832, p. 2.

71. Brown, 15. Cf. William O. Goode, *The Speech of William O. Goode on the Abolition of Slavery Delivered in the House of Delegates of Virginia on Tuesday, January 24, 1832*, (Richmond, Va.: Thomas W. White, 1832), 33; Brodnax, 17.

72. Brown, 15; Brodnax, 17. Brown points to Jefferson's letter to Jared Sparks as evidence the Sage defended the property right in the slaves. Cf. Jefferson to Jared Sparks,

Monticello 15 February 1824, *Thomas Jefferson: Writings*, ed. Merrill Peterson (New York: Library of America, 1984), 1484-1487; Polk, 51.

73. Powell, 12 January 1832, p. 2; Brodnax, 12.

74. James H. Gholson, "Speech Delivered in the Virginia House of Delegates," *Constitutional Whig*, 26 January 1832, p. 1; Gallaher, 13 March 1832, p. 4, uttered that the slaveholder will keep his slaves as long as he has an interest in them.

75. James C. Bruce, "Speech Delivered in the Virginia House of Delegates," *Richmond Enquirer*, 26 January 1832, p. 2.

76. Gholson, 2. Italics in the original; Robert, 66; Bruce, 2; Cf. Brodnax, 13-14; Brown, 10.

77. Alexander G. Knox, "Speech Delivered in the Virginia House of Delegates," *Richmond Enquirer*, 14 February 1832, p. 2 and 1; Cf. Brodnax 14.

78. William H. Roane, "Speech Delivered in the Virginia House of Delegates," *Richmond Enquirer*, 4 February 1832, p. 1.

79. Roane, 2. Roane was particularly caustic in his comments that the debate was taking place. Like others, he thought that the public debate would cause harm to the state. He also criticized the press and wished that they were barred from reporting on the proceedings. Roane is an interesting character because he was partly responsible for the debate, having presented the Quaker memorial.

80. Knox, 2.

81. Roane, 2. Italics in the original.

82. Gholson, 12 January 1832, 2. Italics in the original.

83. Knox, 2; Robert, 24-25, 84.

84. Brown, 20; William D. Sims, *Richmond Enquirer*, 28 January 1832, p. 2.

85. Brodnax, 13.

86. Goode, 11; Brown, 9. Cf. Alexander H. Stephens, *Letters and Speeches*, ed. Henry Cleveland (Philadelphia: National Publishing Co., 1866), 723. Stephens repeated the Canaan curse in his "Cornerstone Speech."

87. Wood, 4.

88. Goode, 13-14.

89. Knox, 2.

90. Powell, 12 January 1832, p. 2; Knox, 2; Brown, 23; Brodnax, 23.

91. Daniel, 31 January 1832, p. 1.

92. Daniel, 31 January 1832, p. 1; Goode, *The Speech of William O. Goode on the Abolition of Slavery Delivered in the House of Delegates of Virginia on Tuesday, January 24, 1832*, 8-9; Roane, 1; Daniel, 1.

93. Knox, 4; Newton, 4.

94. Wood, 4. Italics in the original.

95. William O. Goode, *The Speech of William O. Goode on the Abolition of Slavery Delivered in the House of Delegates of Virginia on Tuesday, January 24, 1832* (Richmond, Va.: Thomas W. White, 1832), 10; Gholson, 12 January 1832, 2; Roane, 2; Preston, 2.

96. Faulkner, 20. Unless otherwise noted, all quotes from this source. Italics in the original.

97. Freehling, *Drift Toward Dissolution*, 145-146.

98. Thomas Marshall, *The Speech of Thomas Marshall in the House of Delegates of Virginia on the Abolition of Slavery: Delivered Friday, January 20, 1832* (Richmond, Va.: Thomas W. White, 1832), 5.

99. Brown, 21.

100. William M. Rives, "Speech Delivered in the Virginia House of Delegates,"

Richmond Enquirer, 21 January 1832, p. 3.

101. McDowell, 15.

102. Betty L. Fladeland, "Compensated Emancipation: A Rejected Alternative," *The Journal of Southern History* 42 (May 1976) : 173, 178-180. James Madison was one of the first to suggest compensated emancipation in 1819, but it was decried by pro-slave southerners who viewed it as a violation of state sovereignty.

103. Samuel M. Garland, "Speech Delivered in the Virginia House of Delegates," *Constitutional Whig*, 2 February 1832, p. 4; Berry, 3.

104. McDowell, 15.

105. Polk, 105.

106. John Locke, *Two Treatises of Government*, ed. by Peter Laslett (Cambridge: Cambridge University Press, 1988), 373. Italics in the original.

107. Ibid., 384; 284-285.

108. Chandler, 8; Locke, 385.

109. Faulkner, *The Speech of Charles Jas. Faulkner in the House of Delegates of Virginia in the Policy of the State with Respect to Her Slave Population: Delivered January 20, 1832*, 18.

110. George W. Summers, "Speech Delivered in the Virginia House of Delegates," *Constitutional Whig*, 31 January 1832, p. 2, and p. 4; Berry, 4.

111. Rives, 2-3. Summers, 2, said that slavery "diffused ignorance among those more immediately in contact with it."

112. McDowell, 6-7.

113. Appomattox was none other than Benjamin Watkins Leigh. The letter in part called slave owners to arms: Appomattox, "To the People of Virginia," *Richmond Enquirer*, 4 February 1832, pp. 2-4; *Constitutional Whig*, 7 February, 1832, p. 1; 18 February 1832, p. 1; Bacon's Quarter Branch, "The Free Negroes," *Constitutional Whig*, 21 February 1832, p. 4; Pamunkey, "For the Whig," *Constitutional Whig*, 30 March 1832, p. 2; Freehling, *Drift Toward Dissolution*, 196 and 198; Robert, 36.

114. *Constitutional Whig*, 30 December 1832, p. 2; 3 April 1832, p. 4; 21 January 1832, p. 3; Whitfield, 134-135.

115. *Journal of the House of Delegates of the Commonwealth of Virginia*, 21 January 1832, 110.

116. John Floyd, Diary of John Floyd, 3 February 1832, 177.

117. Goode, 33; Sydnor, 315, points to the caustic public rhetoric for nurturing sectionalism in Virginia.

118. McDowell, 7.

119. Faulkner, 5.

120. McDowell, 21.

121. Ibid., 23. Italics in the original.

122. Freehling, *Drift Toward Dissolution*, 274-277. Of the 133 Delegates, 33 were not slaveholders while 97 owned slaves. We are unsure whether 3 Delegates owned slaves.

123. Preston, 2.

124. Summers, 2.

125. Polk, 6.

126. Shade, 197.

Chapter 7

The Proslavery Argument Revisited: Thomas Roderick Dew and the Beginning of the Positive Good Thesis

> Now tyranny displays openly, evident for all to see, the possessions which are held to be of much value. But what is harsh hidden in the tyrants' souls, where human happiness and unhappiness are stored up.
>
> Xenophon

> Power can never be dislodged from the hands of the intelligent, the wealthy, and the courageous, by any plans that can be formed by the poor, the ignorant, and the habitually subservient; history scarce furnishes such an example.
>
> Thomas Roderick Dew[1]

There is considerable evidence that Virginians began the exodus from Jefferson to Calhoun in 1832. That excursion was not possible without Thomas Roderick Dew's *Review of the Debate in the Virginia Legislature of 1831-1832* (hereafter *Review*). The debates inspired a sympathetic pro-slave letter from Appomattox that appeared in the *Richmond Enquirer*.[2] This letter further instigated a defense of the peculiar institution. Still, a more philosophical justification was deemed necessary to protect slavery from internal and external assaults. Many of the slave apologists communicated with one another and made a concerted effort to portray their community positively as well as develop a coherent ideology. Dew was no less involved in that effort and as a result the early philosophical defense of slavery came from him. After the debates and the ensuing defense of the pro-slave argument by Dew, emancipation and colonization were rejected alternatives. Therefore, the greatest discussion on the nature and problem of slavery had the effect of strengthening the attachment to the peculiar institution. The debates led to an open defense of slavery, but also had a chilling effect on the open discussion of emancipation of the slaves. If there were any expressions in favor of abolition, they were "infrequent, cautious, and usually private."[3]

The importance of the effect of the debates falls into a larger thesis, which contends that there was a Union-wide defense of slavery that began in the late 1820s to early 1830s. This thesis has undergone some challenge since the 1980s. Some argue that proslavery literature not only grew steadily since 1808, but also that such defenses were not confined to the South. Therefore, the defense of slavery was articulated in the Union early on, not just in the 1830s. The Virginia debates are therefore not seen as a watershed moment in history where the South opted for a defense of the peculiar institution. Somewhat similar to this thesis, others contend that what was considered proslavery writing in the 1830s was really one of tone, not substance. In this way, the Virginia debates did not represent a shift in the southern approach to slavery.

Most scholars, however, accept the importance of Dew's commentary on the debates in the House. Many believe he inaugurated a new era in pro-slavery writing. For example, Eugene Genovese wrote that Dew's *Review* "altered the terms of the proslavery argument, moving it from the defense of a necessary evil to the assertion of a positive good. From the moment of its dissemination, the proslavery argument moved steadily toward higher ground."[4] Genovese continued: "Dew more than anyone, with the possible exception of John C. Calhoun, built an intellectual bridge over which southern intellectuals could cross from the world of Thomas Jefferson to that of the proslavery extremists of the 1850s." According to Genovese, "no single theorist loomed larger than [Dew]" with respect to the proslavery argument.

Another historian, Drew Gilpin Faust, described how his intellectual training might have built that bridge. She argued that Dew rejected Lockean contract theory, and the Founding, for an organic view of social order. The South, she contends, relied on positivism as a source of political wisdom. Dew was responsible for what eventually became the new dispensation of the South: the principles of the American Founding were misguided and history had revealed that man was not free and equal as Jefferson contended. Southerners even employed new methods of knowing through the discoveries of science, which determined that blacks were inferior. Therefore, Revolutionary principles were replaced by the breakthroughs made by modern science and a cacophony of other sources, whether it emanated from positivism, German idealism, or historicism. All served to legitimate southern tradition and southern conservatism.[5]

Virginia was an influential state. Old Dominion played a significant Union-wide role in the progression of the slave question: it was Virginia that led the confederate South, helping it "in formulating a rationale" for the region.[6] While, as noted above, there are some who understand that Dew's arguments offered nothing new to the pro-slave argument, others nevertheless assert he "presented the defense of slavery with a cogency and coherence never previously attained, and the essay gained added influence because of its author's position at the prestigious College of William and Mary. Widely circulated throughout the South, the essay was repeatedly quoted and paraphrased by the Southern press as abolitionist attacks mounted."[7] As the essay pertained to the slave question, Dew never addressed how the slave institution might end in Virginia. He did not confine himself, however, to just the Virginia debates, but took the opportunity to discuss slavery in general. Dew weaved together an interesting mix of free trade economics and pro-slave Hegalianism. His Hegalianism appealed to not only secular history, but the Bible for evidence that slavery was good.

Dew became a known scholar in 1829 with his publication of the economic treatise *Lectures on the Restrictive System*. As a result of that essay, he was considered a great authority and testified before the House committee on abolition during the 1831-1832 debates. His economic emphasis gave intellectual heft to the oft stated opinion in the debates that the master had a right to his slave property: "Dew provided a rationale for slavery that Tucker's liberalism rendered impotent . . . slavery's justification is implicit in the right of bargain and sale."[8] His popularity grew thereafter and at one point he was approached by a few Virginia citizens in hopes that he would become a candidate for Congress. He declined. However, much of his fame came as a result of his *Review*. The essay found its way into many pro-slave works of the era. It was widely read, and was reprinted several times. As late as 1852, it was featured in an anthology of pro-slave literature entitled *The Pro-slavery Argument as Maintained by the Most Distinguished Writers of the Southern States*. The title seems to suggest that nothing more needed to be said about the issue. It is therefore worthy to note that Dew is one of the few authors featured in that work.

Dew's influence was also felt in the intellectual trades of the day. His ability to persuade was notable. He was a featured writer in many journals like the *Southern Literary Messenger*. By 1860 the once moderate *Southern Literary Messenger* argued for secession and the perpetuation of slavery. The Charleston-based *Southern Quarterly Review* noted his importance for the South and lauded him "for the first clear and comprehensive argument on the subject of slavery."[9] J.D.B. DeBow wrote in *DeBow's Review* that "Dew's able essay on the institution of slavery entitles him to the lasting gratitude of the whole South."[10] South Carolina Governor James Henry Hammond understood Dew's *Review* as a justification for slavery and considered it the best defense of the institution at the time. By 1836, the *Review* was used to defend the institution's perpetuation and Hammond would go on to claim slavery was not evil.[11]

Dew graduated from the College of William and Mary with an A.B. at the age of eighteen and he earned an M.A. soon thereafter, graduating in 1824. After graduation William E. Dodd claimed he took a two-year trip to Europe and remained for some time in Germany to study at the universities there. In October of 1826 he was appointed a professor at William and Mary and became its president ten years later. Germany changed Dew's thinking. According to Dodd, "he had been taught that the inequality of men was fundamental to all social organization."[12] He was impressed by the open recognition of human inequality and the belief in a stratified society. Yet, this connection between Dew and Germany has undergone much scrutiny, as there is no direct evidence of Dew's trip, or his study at German universities. Nevertheless, Dodd argues: "Dew was a careful student who had spent years in Germany, where the new state philosophy of Fichte and Hegel was coming into vogue, where men were taught that duties and not rights were the fit subjects for emphasis. Whether or not the Virginia student was greatly influenced by his German masters I cannot say. But he returned to his native country and offered the South a new philosophy."[13] Dodd asserts in other places that Dew's trip to Germany brought him into contact with the greatest thinkers of the time. He continued: "The new philosophy asserted that men were not equal, but that some men were fit only for the hard toil of the field while others were plainly designed for the easier task of managing and directing the labor of others. There are no natural rights; rights were prescriptive and they implied an equivalent, a service rendered to society."[14]

Did Dew believe that inequality was the fundamental foundation for all social organization? There is evidence that Dew was enamored with the "new order of things in Europe" and he believed that the Germans were the most advanced of all Europeans.[15] Interestingly, he also admired Napoleon. Given his experience with the German landscape, it is quite possible that Dodd discovered something that has since eluded scholars. Regardless, he never conducted a careful study of Dew's *Review* in comparison to the thought of George William Frederick Hegel and Johann Gottlieb Fichte. The importance of the drift from natural rights to historical rights has not gone unmentioned in other scholarly works.[16] Therefore, it would be apropos to engage in a careful exegesis of Dew's *Review* and, if possible, substantiate the claim that Hegel and Fichte influenced him. Because there is no definite evidence that Dew was in Germany and visited the universities there, we will engage in a comparison of Dew's thoughts with the works of the two Germans.

Part of the reason Dew is so important in this study is because some scholars believe he influenced the most popular defender of the "positive good" thesis, Calhoun.[17] There are several references in Calhoun's private papers that demonstrate he was familiar with Dew's work. He thought the professor taught the proper feelings, opinions, and manners for all southern men. He therefore considered the professor a valuable asset to the South. Calhoun at one point corresponded with a friend lamenting his inability to locate some of Dew's writings.[18] Calhoun frequently passed through Richmond on his way to and from South Carolina, so it is likely that he cultivated a relationship with the professor from William and Mary, as Dew often visited the city as well. When Calhoun wrote to other acquaintances, he made a point for them to pass on to Dew his respects.[19] When the Williamsburg community decided to have a dinner in honor of Dew, they invited Calhoun to be the featured speaker. Furthermore, in some correspondence that included Calhoun, Dew's name came up as a potential contributor in a series of essays defending the institutions of the South. It is evident, then, that Calhoun respected Dew. In one letter to Calhoun at least one person referenced the college professor as a character reference. He would not have done so if Dew did not hold some influence over the Senator.[20]

Not everyone was enamored with Dew's influence, or his opinions about slavery. The grave importance of his *Review* was not lost on the likes of John Quincy Adams:

> I had my granddaughter read twice, and in the evening waded through thirty
> pages of Professor Dew's review of the debate on the project for slave

emancipation. It is a monument of the intellectual perversion produced by the existence of slavery in a free community. To the mind of Mr. Dew, slavery is the source of all virtue in the heart of the master. His argument against the practicability of abolishing slavery by means of colonization appears to me conclusive; nor do I believe that emancipation is the object of the Colonization Society, though it may be the day-dream of some of the members. Mr. Dew's argument, that the danger of insurrection among the slaves is diminished in proportion as their relative numbers increase over those of the white masters, is an ingenious paradox, in which I have no faith.[21]

Adams made a subsequent entry in his diary the next day: "I read further Professor Dew's review of the slavery debate in the Legislature of Virginia. The pamphlet deserves grave meditation, and has in it the seeds of much profitable instruction. Slavery is, in all probability, the wedge which will ultimately split this Union. It is the source of all the disaffection to it in both parts of the country—a disaffection deeply pervading Mr. Dew's pamphlet."[22] The *Review* demonstrated in a way no other pamphlet did, the divide that existed in the Union. Adams understood that Dew's essay was dangerous because it might lead—or perhaps already represented—public opinion to an apologetic position on slavery. What Adams found instructive about the *Review* was its perversion of the Revolutionary heritage and the idea of the American Founding.

Adams was not the only one who viewed Dew's essay with suspicion. When Dew sent his *Review* to James Madison, the former President of the United States sent back a cordial note of critique: "I have found much valuable and interesting information, with ample proof of the numerous obstacles to a removal of slavery from our country, and everything that could be offered on mitigation of its continuance; but I am obliged to say, that in not a few of the data from which you reason, and in the conclusion to which you are led, I cannot concur."[23] One of the chief problems he had with the essay was the fact that he downplayed the negative effects of the slave institution on the state of Virginia. According to Madison, Dew spent too much time speaking of the economic question of the tariff. It was slavery and not the tariff that was at the heart of the problem in Virginia. In his letter he also stated that the solution to the slave problem might be found in a form of compensated emancipation. As it pertained to the removal of slaves, he concluded that even when freed, they ought not be colonized by force. Madison contended that the slaves should be convinced, or persuaded, to leave—the "consent of the individuals to be removed." If they desired not to leave, then they should be allowed to remain in the Union. Nothing speaks to the humanity of the slaves more than Madison's counsel on this matter. He never wavered from his position that the foundation of the republic was one in which men possessed rights equally: "the merit of the founders of our Republics lies in the more accurate views and the practical application of the doctrines. The rights of man as the foundation of just Government had been long understood; but the superstructures projected had been sadly defective."[24] To Madison, there was no question that the slaves possessed not only the same rights, but were capable, on the account of their humanity, of making their own decisions. In his response to Dew, he seems to make clear their equality by asserting that they possessed the faculties to make a choice to remain in the Union, or leave. Madison's assertion as to the Founding falling short of its central idea of equality is instructive. He lamented that the Union was falling short of its guarantee to secure the rights of all men. Still, the effect of the Turner affair and the ensuing debate only deepened Virginia's commitment to slavery thus eliminating any possibility for emancipation. Dew's pamphlet marked an ominous shift toward the "positive good" thesis.

Dew's Review of the House of Delegates Debates

Before the conclusion of the debates, Dew began to prepare his argument in defense of the peculiar institution. The *Review* is split into three topical sections: (1) the origin of slavery and its effects on civilization, (2) the plans for the abolition of Negro slavery, and (3) the injustice and evils of slavery. Before he launches into the first section of the essay, he begins by wondering whether the two races should ever be separated, whether the blacks would ever be sent back to Africa, and whether they were capable of living in a civilization on as equal a ground as whites. The variables that must be taken into account are momentous and require,

> the most complete and profound knowledge of the nature and sources of national wealth and political aggrandizement, an acquaintance with the elastic and powerful spring of population, and the causes which invigorate or paralyze its energies, together with a clear perception of the varying rights of man, amid all the changing circumstances by which he may be surrounded, and a profound knowledge of all the principles, passions, and susceptibilities which make up the moral nature of our species, and according as they are acted upon by adventitious circumstances, alter our condition, and produce all that wonderful variety of character which so strongly marks and characterizes the human family.[25]

The project Dew sets for himself in determining if slavery may indeed be dealt with politically is quite ambitious. His approach to the question of slavery and the debates that ensued after the Turner affair suggest that his reaction to the slave dilemma will not be favorable to the abolitionists. While he seems to proceed with a view to rights, we do not get a sense that he means natural rights in the same way that Jefferson meant natural rights because, as he writes, those rights are "varying." It is more likely that he confused the "rights of man" with political rights. Dew confuses natural rights and political rights, or simply reduces everything to political right. Furthermore, his approach to the slavery question is conducted with a view to economics. Whatever is going to be done about the slave question, must take into account "national wealth."

After setting up the problem that faces Old Dominion, Dew contends that the debate was improper because the slaves, if freed, would believe that violence secured their freedom. This would cause more violence by the slaves, or former slaves, to extract other concessions. He feared that violence would then become the basis of politics. According to Dew, waiting until the next legislative session would have been more prudent for it would have allowed the passions resulting from the Turner affair to stabilize. However, he concluded that in the meantime, Virginia "could have ascertained the sentiments and wishes of other slaveholding States, whose concurrence, if not absolutely necessary, might be highly desirable, and should have been sought after and attended to, at least, as a matter of State courtesy."[26] As we noted in the last chapter, the governor did solicit the opinions of his neighbors, but even more important is that Dew is already thinking in terms of a divided Union. He believed that the South was a block, or political alliance. He did not believe that consultation with the North was necessary, but that Southern states were necessary partners. The Slave institution is the only thing all those states have in common and it is the only interest which binds them together. Slavery became an interest in which all southerners, no matter how much they disagreed on other political questions, could unite. Slavery is not a problem that afflicts the Union, but it is an interest which unites the South geographically.

This similarity of interest quite naturally prompted an hostility to anything challenging it. If anything demonstrates Dew's belief that slavery would, and perhaps should, continue indefinitely, it is the next statement:

> [W]e affirm, with confidence, that no enlarged, wise and practical plan of operations was proposed by abolitionists . . . that their arguments, in most cases, were of a wild and intemperate character, based upon false principles, and assumptions of the most vicious and alarming kind, subversive of the rights of property and the order of tranquility of society, and portending to the whole slaveholding country—if they ever shall be followed out in practice—the most inevitable and ruinous consequences.[27]

For the most part the emancipationists in the House were chastised by the professor for speaking about gradual emancipation. It is remarkable that the mere discussion of abolition was considered an intemperate activity. Yet, the reaction by Dew and the slave faction in Virginia would soon be repeated throughout the Union. To question the legitimacy of the slave institution would become a politically incorrect act. Part of the reason he objected to a discussion of emancipation was, like his allies on the pro-slave side of the debate, the slaves were considered property. They did not want to undermine their property right in their slaves. This only reinforces the conclusion that the slaves were considered as something other than human—or at least that the slaves were first property, and/or a degraded form of human. Abolition was not considered a proper policy initiative because it was an attack on property. However, what are these "false principles" and, as he added later, "imaginary good[s]" that the anti-slave delegates were erroneously speaking? Though he does not state specifically, the only principle that the emancipationists consistently referred to was the natural rights of the slaves.

If these remarks do not convey a view of slavery's perpetuity, perhaps the following statement does: "a conclusion which seems to be sustained by facts and reasoning as irresistible as the demonstration of the mathematician—that every plan of emancipation and deportation which we can possibly conceive is *totally* impracticable."[28] If emancipation is impracticable in every way imaginable, then how can slavery ever be put on the road to extinction? Is it possible that emancipation could come in the future? He does not seem to say it will always be impracticable, but if the number of slaves will never decrease, how could it ever be practicable? Dew extends the argument to state that emancipation would also be hostile to religion and morality. Dew thus begins his essay by attacking the anti-slave interest, by contending that slavery cannot end, and then concludes by asserting that ending slavery would be unjust. It would behoove us to examine why he believed these things about emancipation.

After the introduction, Dew commences the first part of his study by examining the "origin of slavery" and the effect it "has exerted on the progress of civilization."[29] His approach is historical in that he traces the origins of slavery to demonstrate that it has always existed and that the institution was beneficial and useful. To Dew, slavery was inevitable and we might say an historical inevitability. In order to argue contra those who claim slavery is wrong in the abstract, Dew states that he will demonstrate it is not wrong by appealing to reality and history. He contends that slavery is a natural condition and has prevailed in all ages. Indeed, "slavery was established and sanctioned by divine authority, among even the elect of heaven, the favored children of Israel."[30] Such divine imprint on the institution is noteworthy to the professor because, in his estimation, slaves are the most numerous in the world—there are more slaves than free men. Therefore, slavery is a natural condition for some men. In this way he placed much emphasis on the natural character of slavery. Some have been chosen for rule and others have been chosen for slavery. His historical proof did not end there.

Slavery has stymied barbarism and is an "impulse towards civilization."[31] What has impelled mankind toward civil society is the institution of property and slavery. The reason slavery is valuable for civilization is because it fixes man to the soil and civilizes him. Modern slavery is humane because instead of killing more humans in times of war, slavery salvages their lives and puts them to use: "so soon as the private right to property is established, slavery commences; and with the institution of slavery, the cruelties of war begin to diminish. The chief finds it to his interest to make slaves of his captives, rather than put them to death."[32] History demonstrates that slavery decreases the horrors of war and is actually humane. This development Dew considers more just, and milder than death. He also deemed the enslavement of men in times of war a right of the conquering nation. This right belongs to those who subdue their enemy. Could it be that he believes the master in the South has a right to his slave because of some inherited right derived from past wars? Regardless, history has demonstrated, according to the professor, that slavery is at least useful in preserving peace and inculcating mild manners in society.

Aristotle, whom Dew considers "the greatest philosopher of antiquity," noted in book one, chapter four, of *The Politics* that he was a "warm advocate of slavery" and thought that it was "reasonable, necessary, and natural."[33] Furthermore, he asserts that Aristotle contended that a healthy republic had several slaves serving few men. The definition of republic, in Dew's view, was the many serving the interests of the few, but this is little different from an oligarchy of the few rich who rule in their own interest.[34] In another work he would contend that "domestic slavery, such as ours, is the only institution which I know of that can secure that spirit of equality among freemen, so necessary to the true and genuine feeling of republicanism."[35] We have already discussed Aristotle's conception of slavery, but suffice to say that the professor applied the justice of the institution of slavery in the broadest terms possible. If Aristotle is correct, then it would seem to imply that southern slavery is natural and just. In other words, the blacks are natural slaves, and the state of Virginia is more of a republic than those states that have broader suffrage and no slavery. The free states do not have slaves and so are inferior republics than those states that do have slaves.

The central feature of republicanism, according to Dew, is the protection of private property. As noted above, he asserted property was the great moderating influence on modern civilizations and contributed greatly to peace: "It may be with truth affirmed, that the exclusive owners of the property ever have been, ever will, and perhaps ever ought to be, the virtual rulers of mankind. If, then, in any age or nation, there should be but one species of property, and that should be exclusively owned by a portion of citizens, that portion would become inevitably masters of the residue."[36] Though he does not overtly admit it, Dew seems to be an equal opportunity slave advocate. His understanding of slavery is not limited to color; under his theory it includes whites as well as blacks. Any property owner is superior to the unpropertied. His main interest, though, was to protect the property of a few in order to defend or bolster class distinctions. Majority rule would harm the societal distinctions necessary to preserve civilization. These distinctions depend almost exclusively upon the protection of property. The few who are wealthy are the owners of property and these property owners are the rulers of society. Natural rights theory was invalid because inequality was the basis of society. Slavery was so intertwined that it ought not to be separated from society. We should note that Dew seems to assert these distinctions ought to be preserved forever. The strong and able should rule their inferiors. Yet, he seems to hold open the possibility that slavery could end:

> We shall show . . . that if the slaves of our southern country shall ever be liberated, and suffered to remain among us, with their present limited wants and longing desire for a state of idleness, they will fall, inevitable, by the nature of things, into a state of slavery, from which no government could rescue them, unless by radical change of all their habits, and a most awful and fearful change in the whole system of property throughout the country. The state of property, then, may fairly be considered a very fruitful source of slavery.[37]

Not without reason, Dew contends that simple emancipation would not be beneficial because the skills and faculties of the slaves, being untrained, would make them ill-equipped to live in a civilized society. If the slaves were to develop the right habits and character, it would not happen anytime soon. Somehow the government, or political action, could not solve this problem because the very foundation of government would be disturbed in order to effect a change in the natural condition of the slaves.

In the first part of the *Review* the professor deals with the factual basis of slavery. Dew asserts that he is not looking into the justice or injustice of slavery and not passing judgment on the nature of the institution.[38] Dew does note that the rise of private property coupled with the baser parts of human nature has led inevitably and necessarily to slavery of other human beings. Far from a disadvantageous development, though, slavery is advantageous to society. Part of the reason for the inevitability of slavery was because of the generous and benevolent spirit of God who set it as a part of his design of the world that slavery was instituted *"for some useful purpose."*[39] Slavery has been an important institution impelling mankind toward civilization and it was a part of God's purpose that slavery would be used to accomplish that goal. Religion and government are thus powerful and irresistible influences on the character of nations and individuals.[40] In order to move a less advanced people from savagery to a more civilized life, they must be subdued in a certain manner. Putting those savages to work is the best method to tame the wild beast in man: "slavery . . . seems to be the only means that we know of . . . by which the ferocity of the savage can be conquered, his wandering habits eradicated, his slothfulness and improvidence . . . [and] his nature can be changed."[41] In essence, then, property cultivates peace instead of war, and slavery encourages the preservation of life not the destruction of it.

After laying the groundwork on the foundations of slavery in history, Dew prefaces the second part of his essay, which addresses the plans for abolition offered in the House of Delegates, by critiquing the value emancipationists placed on ending the peculiar institution. He considered the arguments based on the abstract truth of the equality of men as pompous and ostentatious. His rejection of natural right as a guide to political action is quite evident: "no set of legislators ever have, or ever can, legislate upon purely abstract principles, entirely independent of circumstances, without the ruin of the body politic, which should have the misfortune to be under the guidance of such quackery."[42] Of course the abolitionists in the House never argued from pure principles. They tried to act in a way that was just in light of timeless principles. They understood that emancipation must be worked out practically and in a gradual manner. Regardless, the question Dew intends to answer in the second part of the essay is whether any means might be employed to end slavery.

Appealing to the lengthy address by William H. Brodnax (Dinwiddie), Dew insists that the slaves ought not be emancipated unless the state compensates the owner the full value of the slave. In addition, he concludes that the emancipation and deportation of the slaves would be a great expense and probably outside the reach of the state to effect. Furthermore, slavery gives value to the land: "take away this, and you pull down the Atlas that upholds the whole system."[43] In other words, one part of the anti-emancipation argument is that it would be economically ruinous to Virginia. It would be ruinous because the state is the supplier of slaves to other states, and the loss of income would devastate the entire economy. Such a scheme would also be monstrous and absurd to carry out because it would harm the plantation economy. Dew thus ultimately rejected compensated emancipation. The substitution of free labor for slave labor would also not counteract the negative effects of emancipation. The reason for this is that the work of slave labor is beneath the labor of the free man. Slave labor brings the free man down to the slave's level "for the vices of the slave you may correct, by means of your authority over him, but those of the associate free laborer you cannot."[44] Dew's authority on this point is a political economist from the University of Berlin named Theodor Anton Heinrich Schmalz (1760-1831). Schmalz argued that free labor tended to be corrupted when it came into contact with servile labor.

The perceived harm caused by emancipation convinced professor Dew that if it was forced upon the slaveholder by the government it would not be beneficial to the economic well-being of Virginians. If the slaves are emancipated, it will only happen when it is in the self-interest of the master:

> Let any farmer in Lower Virginia ask himself how many he can spare from his plantation—and he will be surprised to see how few he can be dispensed with. If that intelligent gentleman, from the storehouse of his knowledge, would but call up the history of the past, he would see that *mere philanthropy*, with all her splendid boastings, has never yet accomplished one great scheme; he would find the remark of that great judge of human nature, the illustrious author of the "Wealth of Nations," that no people had generosity to liberate their slaves, until it became their interest to do so, but too true; and the philosophic page of Hume, Robertson, Stuart, and Sismondi, would inform him that serfs of Europe have been only gradually emancipated through the operation of *self-interest*, and not *philanthropy*; and we shall soon see that it was fortunate for both parties that this was the case.[45]

Dew's political science may be described as looking at the high in light of the low; he takes man as he is, and does not speak of how he ought to be. Since Thomas Jefferson Randolph's plan did not appeal to the self-interest of the slaveholder, the plan was assured failure in the mind of Dew. We can see that the professor, similar to the Tidewater and Piedmont slaveholder in the Virginia Constitutional Convention of 1829-1830, considered man a self-interested being. The problem with his analysis, however, is that Randolph, to name just one, was a slaveholder himself. How is it that he could have transcended his own personal interest in his slaves and proposed a plan for emancipation? This is something Dew indicates is impossible. Yet Randolph stands as a glaring contradiction to his opinion on the matter. Regardless, the problem with Randolph's plan is its burden placed on the master: "it proposes to saddle the slaveholder with the whole burthen; it infringes on the right of property."[46]

The use of the word saddled is perhaps ironic since it mocks the words of

Thomas Jefferson to Roger Weightman: "all eyes are opened, or opening, to the rights of man. The general spread of the light of science has already laid open to every view the palpable truth, that the mass of mankind has not been born with saddles on their backs, nor a favored few booted and spurred ready to ride them legitimately, by the grace of God." It also contradicts Algernon Sydney's famous statement similar to Jefferson's:

> Man therefore must be naturally free, unless he be created by another power than we have yet heard of. The obedience due to parents arises from hence, in that they are the instruments of our generation; and we are instructed by the light of reason, that we ought to make great returns to those from whom under God we have received all. When they die we are their heirs, we enjoy the same rights, and devolve the same to our posterity. God only who confers this right upon us, can deprive us of it: and we can no way understand that he does so, unless he had so declared by express revelation, or had set some distinguishing marks of dominion and subjection upon men; and, as an ingenious person not long since said, caused some to be born with crowns upon their heads, and all others with saddles upon their backs.[47]

Dew does not view man as inherently, or naturally, equal. He calls attention of the whole slaveholding part of the Union to the argument by the abolitionists in the House that property might be brought under the control of the legislature. This contention is the most serious to come out of the debates because such an act would be a violation of the right of property. The reason that non-slaveholders should have no interest in slavery is because they are not equal to the slaveholder. Only slaveholders are equal to each other, and therefore it seems that only slaveholders should decide whether the slaves shall be free.

In another bit of irony, he appeals to Hobbes to justify his critique of the non-slaveholders. According to Dew, Hobbes wrote in *Leviathan* that people who were overcome by their interests would "deny that 'things equal to the same are equal to each other.'"[48] Again, to Dew, slaveholders are equal to each other. Only non-slaveholders are equal to non-slaveholders. Non-slaveholders are not equal to slaveholders. The interests of one are not identical to the interests of the other:

> The fact is, it is always a most delicate and dangerous task for one set of people to legislate for another, without any community of interest. It is sure to destroy the great principle of responsibility, and in the end to lay the weaker interest at the mercy of the stronger. It subverts the very end for which all governments are established, and becomes intolerable, and consequently against the fundamental rights of man, whether prohibited by the constitution or not.
>
> If a convention of the whole State of Virginia were called, and in due form the right of slave property were abolished by the votes of Western Virginia alone, does any one think that Eastern Virginia would be bound to yield to the decree? Certainly not. The strong and unjust man in a state of nature robs the weaker, and you establish government to prevent this oppression.[49]

It is interesting how the "fundamental rights of man" becomes the "right of slave property" in the above passage. While he may be correct in asserting that the right to property is a fundamental right, he carries that right to the extreme by arguing that property may be extended to include other human beings. In probably the greatest point of irony in the essay, he likens the hypothetical abolition of slavery to rule in the state of nature. It is remarkable that abolition implies a state of nature while the subjugation of others is considered protection of the weak master. However, what Dew seems to forget is that all men are created equal in the state of nature and that the reason we move into society is not to secure our possessions of other persons, but in order to be secure in our equality and our possessions. While Dew seems to accept the Hobbesean opinion of human nature, he rejects his understanding that "men are by nature equal."[50]

Much of the inspiration of this part of the *Review* springs from the concept of the right of the minority to be free from majority rule. Unless a person has the same interest as another, that first person has no right to interfere. That this thinking began to take hold in the Union alarmed Madison, who wrote a pithy essay on majority government. According to Madison, what Dew and his allies argued was anathema:

> The patrons of this new heresy will attempt in vain to mask its anti-republicanism under a contrast between the extent and the discordant interest of the Union, and the limited dimensions and sameness of interests within its members . . . those who denounce Majority Governments altogether because they may have an interest in abusing their power, denounce at the same time all Republican Government and must maintain that minority governments would feel less of the bias of interest or the seductions of power.[51]

To attack majority rule was to attack a central feature of republicanism. Far from it being republican (as Dew would assert), it was its very opposite and hostile to republican government. Of course, Calhoun popularized the ideas expressed by Dew, and Madison could have been reacting to Calhoun, but Madison was aware of Dew's intellectual activities in the state and by 1833 thought it prudent to express an opposing view to Dew's "heresy" on one of the founding pillars of republican government.

The concluding part of the second section of the essay only solidifies the impracticability of emancipation and colonization. We have seen that it is impracticable because history demonstrates that when two races live in proximity to one another and differ in manners, customs, and other characteristics, one must rule over the other. If the races were to mix equally in society, then the inferior race would drag the higher race down to its level. In other words, a barbaric world would be the consequence. Finally, providence (or theological history/historicism) has not seen fit to impart to man that the slaves should be freed:

> And as a citizen of Virginia, we can never consent to so grand a scheme of colonization . . . until it is sanctioned by a *decree* of heaven, made known by

signs, far more intelligible than an *eclipse* and *greenness* of the sun—till manna shall be rained down for the substance of our black emigrants—till seas shall be parted, and waters flow from rocks for their accommodation—till we have a leader like Moses, who, in full confidence of all his piety and religion, can, in the midst of all the appalling difficulties and calamities by which he may be surrounded, speak forth to his murmuring people . . . "Fear ye not, stand still, and see the salvation of the Lord, which he will shew to you to-day."[52]

More so than any pro-slave member who participated in the House debates, Dew made the most unwavering argument on slavery's perpetuation when speaking of it in terms of providence. The passage above leaves no doubt that Dew did not foresee an end to the slave institution by human means, and we must conclude that unless overwhelming miracles occurred, the slaves would never be free. It is difficult to consider slavery was much of an evil if it is under divine protection. Indeed, while he rarely uses the word evil in the essay, he invokes it to describe the schemes of emancipation. Emancipation is evil because it destroys society by exciting the slaves to desire freedom. This leads to riots and revolts. Therefore, no man or men could, or should, abolish slavery unless God somehow providentially secured it.

Having addressed the origins of slavery and the plans for abolition in the House, he turns to the third and final part of the essay on the injustice and evils of slavery. In this section, he concludes the biblical reasons for forbidding emancipation and surprisingly claims that slavery is an evil. However, in what way it is evil is difficult to determine. He admits that slavery is against the spirit of Christianity, but he holds that it is not immoral to hold slaves or that there is anything mortal men can do to abolish the institution. It is rather the emancipationists who are acting contrary to the word of God because they are fomenting disobedience and rebellion. This the Bible forbids. According to Dew, the master will receive the Lord's blessing in the day of judgment because he gave to the slave what was just—emancipation would release the slaves to the care of those who do not really care for them and leave them unchecked and unrestrained, given to their passions. Therefore, Dew considers abolition an act of cruelty and a great evil. He likens emancipation to the errant physician who, while trying to kill a disease of the body, hastens the body's demise. Ultimately, then, slavery may be contrary to the spirit of revelation, but it is the actual circumstances that prohibit men from fulfilling that spirit. Circumstances determine actions. Presumably abstract considerations, whether their origin is the law of nature, or revelation, are not a guide to action. It is not merely that man should take his bearings on how to live from his present circumstances, but that God's providence has not seen fit to free the slaves.

Dew next attacks the opinions of Jefferson, who in his *Notes on the State of Virginia* asserted that the master suffered from boisterous passions and cultivated the despotic part of his soul. Dew does not concur and finds that the facts do not prove Jefferson's thesis. The master's manners are not corrupted by holding slaves. Rather, the relationship is beneficial to both. He engenders good feelings among his slaves and demonstrates to his family what it means to be kind and indulgent:

> Is it not a fact, known to every man in the south, that the most cruel masters are
> those who have been unaccustomed to slavery. It is well known that northern
> gentlemen who marry southern heiresses, are much severer masters than
> southern gentlemen. And yet, if Mr. Jefferson's reasonings were correct, they
> ought to be milder: in fact, it follows from his reasoning, that the authority
> which the father is called on to exercise over his children, must be seriously
> detrimental; and yet we know that this is not the case; that on the contrary,
> there is nothing which so much humanizes and softens the heart, *as his very
> authority*.[53]

The North without slavery is harsher than the South with slavery. The authority
of the master tames and corrects the slave in much the same way a father
corrects his child. This is quite a non-sequitur, for the relationship between a
father and his child is not the same as the relationship between the master and
slave. Nevertheless, the tie between master and slave is stronger and more
beneficial than the tie between family: "there are hundreds of slaves in the
southern country who will desert parents, wives or husbands, brothers and
sisters, to follow a kind master—so strong is the tie of master and slave."[54]

Again, we must ask ourselves: if the slave is so attached to the master, then
what prevents the perpetuation of the institution? The professor seems to be
tracking a course for just that result and adds that slavery actually contributes to
the great end of man—happiness: "Why, then, since the slave is happy, and
happiness is the great object of all animated creation, should we endeavor to
disturb his contentment by infusing into his mind a vain and indefinite desire for
liberty—a something which he cannot comprehend, and which must inevitably
dry up the very sources of his happiness."[55] Even more to the point, he claims
that the slave may be happier than free whites. Emancipation would make the
slave unhappy because he is, perhaps naturally so, incapable of comprehending
an education in liberty. The slave is incapable of living productively and
peacefully outside of bondage: "the whole population of Virginia, consisting of
three *castes*—of free white, free colored, and slave colored population, is the
soundest and most moral of any other, according to numbers, in the whole
world, as far as is known to me."[56]

The reason that Dew praises the inequality between free whites, free blacks,
and slaves is because the arrangement has done more to bolster republican
government than the liberty of all would or could. Slavery was necessary to
"keep alive the spirit of freedom." Since the peculiar institution has made men
freer, invoking Burke, he contends that the southern colonies are more attached
to liberty than the North. The enjoyment of "rank and privilege" in the South has
encouraged freedom because slavery efficiently caused a "perfect spirit of
equality" among whites in the region. Whites enjoy a higher social status than
blacks and this has caused whites to be more equal with each other. It makes
whites feel like they are a part of an upper class: "color alone is here the badge
of distinction, the true mark of aristocracy, and all who are white are equal in

spite of the variety of occupation."[57] The most remarkable thing about this understanding of republicanism is how it turns into an aristocracy. For republicanism to robustly survive, it needs an aristocracy and inequality at its foundation.

We mentioned above that Dew believed that slavery was an evil, or at least called it an evil, but did so in the context of speaking about the schemes of emancipation. He did not expound if and why the institution itself was an evil. However, near the end of his essay, he asserted that the claims of the evil of slavery were "exaggerated."[58] By 1836, Dew claimed that whatever evils came out of the system of slavery, were minor. He explained that since life was not exempt from the effects of evil there was not much that man could do to avert evil in this life. Rather, slavery had several benefits, not the least of which was the oft stated taming of barbaric man and providing for mild manners.[59] Instead of rejecting the word evil, and calling slavery a good, he examined the institution from the point of view of the slave, whom he asserted generally loved his place in society. The slaves were happy with their masters and they would only become murderers if they were exposed to "the most subtle and poisonous principles, sedulously infused into [their] mind."[60] Even though the slave was happy with his position and his master, apparently rights talk poisoned the mind of the slave and loosened the tie between him and his master. Still, because the slaves are happy with their degraded position, Dew is confident that the whites will remain in their position of superiority. He is determined to convince his readers that emancipation and colonization of the slaves is impossible: "Once more . . . do we call upon our statesmen to pause, ere they engage in this ruinous scheme. The power of man has limits, and he should never attempt impossibilities. We do believe it is beyond the power of man to separate the elements of our population, even if it were desirable. The deep and solid foundation of society cannot be broken up by the *fiat* of the legislator."[61] Since man does not have the capability to end slavery, only God does. Furthermore, he concludes that slavery was an integral part of the most glorious republics. Inequality has been a part of the development of civilization for ages. He concludes his essay noticing the effects of history in the development of republicanism in the Union. The "*lapse of ages*" has unfolded her truth to those who will but consult their own experience and contemplate the past; the "*order of nature*" has "vindicated" that relationship between the master and slave.[62]

A few years after the *Review*, Dew expanded on his view of the benefits of slavery. He objected to the interference of the slave system because it would upset the workings of the free market. He supported the free market and wished it to be unimpeded by government. The market forces worked out who would labor and who would not.[63] A free economy revealed who were equals and who were unequal. Those who did menial tasks were not the equals of those who did not do those tasks. The market, then, created a natural social hierarchy:

> The occupations which we follow, necessarily and unavoidably create distinctions in society. It is said that all occupations are honorable. This is certainly true, if you mean that no honest employment is disgraceful. But to say

that all confer equal honor, if well followed even, is not true. Such an assertion militates alike against the whole nature of man and the voice of reason. But whatever may be the vain deductions of mere theorists upon this subject, one thing is certain—Reason informed me of this truth long before experience had shown it to me in actual life—The hirelings who perform all the menial offices in life, will not and cannot be treated as equals by their employers.[64]

While his opinion does not necessarily exclude the participation of whites in the menial labors, he clearly believes that blacks will occupy those positions rather than white men. However, he seems to confound slave labor with free labor. The laborer of the North is similar, if not worse, than the slave laborer of the South in status. Dew had a disdain for the laborer of the North. According to some scholars, he wrote a "colorblind dominance" into his pro-slave argument: "wage slaves, always underpaid and often fired, would be better off as chattel slaves of protective paternalists."[65] In other words, the economic system in the North was worse off than the one in the South. Some time after the *Review*, Dew asserted that the wage slave would revolt unless slavery was allowed to save western civilization. The southern labor system had a salutary effect on the political system because it preserves distinctions and societal inequalities in ways that the northern system does not.

Slave labor not only produces benefits for the economy, but it also secures the morals of the community: "I have no hesitation in affirming that the relation between the capitalist and laborer in the South is kinder, and more productive of genuine attachment, than exists between the same classes any where on the face of the globe."[66] Slavery was so beneficial in the protection of the distinctions on society, the free market, and property in the South, that Dew boldly exclaimed "perhaps I would not hazard too much in the prediction, that the day will come when the whole confederacy will regard it as the sheet anchor of our country's liberty."[67] The professor thus believed that slavery would expand in the Union and that all the states would come to the same conclusion as those in the South: slavery was the foundation of freedom. In this way, the South was a more advanced civilization than the North. The region had come to know more than any other peoples the "spirit of freedom" and they were enlightened by the age to fervently protect that freedom.[68]

The effects of German rationalism were perhaps not as evident in the *Review* as they would become in his convocation address to the students at the College of William and Mary in 1836. In that speech, he encouraged the students to eschew abstract philosophy and pay attention to facts in their quest for knowledge. Instead of philosophizing about things not seen, he reminded them of the wisdom of the ages that had been formed long before they were born. As it pertained to the foundations of their society, he asserted that they should examine the "gathered wisdom of a thousand years" and not ignore "the whole foundation on which a great superstructure is raised."[69] Actually, he praised philosophy, but it was not the philosophy of the ancients:

It is necessary that you should examine the principles of the science of government; that you should look into the wants of our nature; examine the beautiful structure of the human mind, with all our feelings, principles, propensities and instincts. In fine you must, in the language of one who has risen to the highest eminence in the profession, "drink the lessons of the spirit of philosophy. Not that philosophy described by Milton . . . but that philosophy which is conversant with men's business and interests, with policy and welfare of nations; that philosophy which dwells not in vain imaginations and platonic dreams, but which stoops to life, and enlarges the boundaries of human happiness; that philosophy which sits by us in the closet, cheers us by the fireside, walks with us in the fields and highways, kneels with us at the altars, and lights up the enduring flame of patriotism."[70]

For Dew, the Declaration of Independence and Declaration of Rights were tantamount to an ignoble lie. The professor did not want his students to swim in the murky waters of values, but wanted them to have a command of knowledge and "generalizing facts."[71]

By 1836, Dew was convinced that there would be conflict on the battlefield over slavery. The Southern man is but one actor on the "great stage of the world" and the actors of the North are at war with the "course of life" in the South.[72] The structure of the Union, which he calls the federative system, established the beginning of a new era or epoch. A great revolution is set to take place, however, to establish more permanently that system. The conflict would be between the slaveholding (republican) defenders and the non-slaveholding (monarchists):

And you must recollect too, that you are generally members of that portion of our confederacy whose domestic institutions have been called into question by the meddling spirit of the age. You are slaveholders, or the sons of slaveholders, and as such your duties and responsibilities are greatly increased. Who governs and directs the action of others, needs especially intelligence and virtue. Prepare yourselves, then, for this important relation, as to be able discharge the duties with humanity and wisdom. Then can we exhibit to the world the most convincing evidence of the justice of our cause; then we may stand up with boldness and confidence against the frowns of the world; and if the demon of fanaticism shall at last array its thousands of deluded victims against us, threatening to involve us in universal ruin by the overthrow of our institutions, we may rally under our principles undivided and undismayed— firm and resolute as the Spartan band at Thermopylæ; and such a spirit, guided by that intelligence which should be possessed by slaveholders, will ever insure the triumph of our cause.[73]

To consider the spirit of the age as tending democratic is faulty, but those armed with a new philosophy cannot be defeated as long as they remain dispassionate about their cause. The democratic spirit appears to be a particular assessment of the age. A dispassionate philosophy understands the universal trends of history and therefore sees the spirit of the age for what it truly is. The non-slaveholder is more concerned with a narrow idea, but Dew exhorts his students to examine the entire drift of history. Those who have a grander view of time will possess a more comprehensive analysis of the great plans of history.

Dew, Fichte, and Hegel

We previously pointed out that Dodd was the first to make the contention that Dew was influenced by Hegel and Fichte after a trip to Europe in the 1820s. Dodd never noted how and where he came across such information. The question of whether Dew ever visited Germany and took classes from the leading German thinkers has been a conundrum ever since. It is possible that Dodd was mistaken. However, his academic and political experience lends evidence that he knew of that which he spoke. At the turn of the century, Dodd spent two and one half years in Germany, more specifically at Leipzig University, where he matriculated with German professors Erlich Marcks and Karl Lamprecht. His studies took him to Britain for research and to Berlin, where he continued his research in preparation for his dissertation. It is possible that he stumbled across some information that connected Dew to Germany while he was a graduate student. After his studies he returned to America and taught at many universities, including the University of Chicago, before being nominated by Franklin Delano Roosevelt in 1933 as Ambassador to Germany. He was an especially perceptive ambassador and wired the Roosevelt administration early on that Hitler did not want peace, but desired conquest. As early as 1934, Dodd reported that Hitler planned to invade and occupy Poland, Denmark, France and the Baltic regions. However, most of his reports were received coolly by the State Department, especially Secretary of State Cordell Hull. They assumed Dodd was simply a dark, negative, and gloomy man.[74] Nevertheless, Dodd appeared to understand Hitler's desires and processed the evidence he collected correctly.

Even if Dew never went to Germany and attended classes, he was aware of, and interested in, German thought. We already noted that he believed that the Germans were the most advanced of the European nations, but he also held specific praise for German universities, especially Jena, Gottingen, and Helle. Some claim that it was German thought that influenced Dew to regard duties to the state as preeminent over human rights. In 1842, when a position came open at William and Mary, he secured a position for Charles Minnegerode, a native of Hesse-Darmstadt, Germany. Dew considered his German friend a most able scholar and thought that someone as educated as Minnegerode could not have been produced by any American institution of higher learning.[75] Concerning Dew's campus presence, he became quite the icon. He was the most popular lecturer at William and Mary and his history course was the most thorough and comprehensive to be found anywhere in the country during his teaching career.[76]

To state that Dew was influenced by Fichte and Hegel is not to mean that he absorbed their arguments completely. There are some striking differences between his thought and the thought of Fichte and Hegel. However, like the two Germans, he was most interested in the philosophy of history. It is clear that he was at least influenced in the new understanding of history and philosophy and his writings reflect a fundamental agreement with German idealism. Fichte was a product of the University of Jena and taught at the college thereafter. Fichte eventually became the head of the philosophy faculty at the University of Berlin and thereafter became the school's rector. Concerning things chronologically, Fichte antedates Dew. Fichte passed away in 1814, but Hegel was Dew's intellectual contemporary, passing away in 1831.

Most unlike Dew, both Hegel and Fichte believed that the history of the world is the gradual unfolding development of human freedom. The end of human history was freedom. The state actualizes this freedom and it makes possible the further advance of the spirit of freedom. They both claimed to believe in human equality. In this vein, Fichte, at least early on in his intellectual development, was a supporter of the French Revolution and saw in it the beginning stages where freedom might be realized. He also supported democratic ideals and the French Declaration of Rights. Hegel parted from him in this matter opposing the French Revolution for its reliance on abstractions (which sounds more like Dew and will be examined below). Ultimately, both Hegel and Fichte despised slavery and in some sense they believed that all men possessed certain rights. In general, slavery was contrary to freedom.[77]

Hegel and Fichte were devotees of the historical approach to politics and this meant that they rejected the idea of an unchanging ground of experience. Nature was formerly thought to be that ground, but Hegel and Fichte replaced nature with history, thus identifying the unchanging with the changing or mutable. A politics guided by the spirit of the age is one grounded in the evolution from one historical epoch, or age, to the next. From an historical point of view there was "no meaningful distinction" between the *is* and the *ought*.[78] Fichte and Hegel agreed on a fundamental point: that history had a rationality to it and that there was a world spirit which was accomplishing its work upon the peoples of the earth. We might say that history was influencing the affairs of the world. Both Fichte and Hegel spoke of this history in terms of providence. Man could not understand the trends of history because God concealed His providence from man's mind. Providence thus guided the historical process and history was the gradual unfolding of the divine idea on earth. This is what Hegel means by a "Universal History" or what Fichte means by a "World Plan."[79] Therefore, God is at work shaping the destiny of man. He unveils to man what He desires to reveal and conceals what He wants to conceal.

Philosophy became the "*thoughtful consideration*" of history, not the contemplation of how men ought to live, or what the best regime looked like:

The insight then to which—in contradistinction from those ideals—philosophy is to lead us, is, that the real world is as it ought to be—that the truly good—the universal divine reason—is not a mere abstraction, but a vital principle capable of realizing itself. This *Good*, this *Reason*, in its most concrete form, is God. God governs the world; the actual working of his [sic] government—the carrying out of his [sic] plan—is the History of the World. This plan philosophy strives to comprehend.[80]

Hegel thought that he was giving the philosophical essence of the Christian doctrine of providence. Great philosophical questions were transformed into historical questions. Philosophy was thus transformed into the understanding of the way of history. Philosophy taught only how the State must be understood, not what the State ought to look like. The task of philosophy was to recognize the reason inherent in the present and recognize the reality of the time. It was not to criticize or contemplate on things unreal. As a result, we cannot choose the best constitution because we live in history or in time. The role of the philosopher was to clearly reveal the reason of the universe. Philosophy is therefore an attempt to account for the dialectical advance and teleological development of history. The historical philosopher claims that he has a clearer picture of history and the present time. We must therefore accept what history has made for us: "The inquiry into the best constitution is frequently treated as if not only the theory were an affair of subjective independent conviction, but as if the introduction of a constitution recognized as the best—or as superior to others—could be the result of a resolve adopted in this theoretical manner; as if the form of a constitution were a matter of free choice, determined by nothing else but reflection."[81] The form of politics is determined by history more than by philosophical inquiry. Choice has little to do with the formation of constitutions. What a state, or a people, lives under is more the work of history's divine providence: "It is absolutely essential that the constitution should not be considered as something made, even though it has come into being in time. It must be regarded rather as something simply existent in and by itself, as divine therefore, and constant, and so as exalted above the sphere of things that are made."[82] The form of government does not emanate from abstract notions of right, but from something real, or rather, from what history has made for man.

History is unfolded in various epochs or eras. Each age had its own morality or spirit. History progresses from epoch to epoch. Each age is different from the one that went before it, and the latest epoch is more advanced over the one that went before. Both Hegel and Fichte—despite their affinity for freedom being the end of man, and that man should not be enslaved—leave the occurrence of slavery to history: "While men are what they are—we must be satisfied with less freedom; the monarchical constitution—under the given circumstances, and the present moral condition of the people—being even regarded as the most advantageous."[83] This meant that slavery could and did exist in certain ages because history had not progressed, or it had not revealed, its will to man that he was meant to be free. There are times when we must be content with less freedom:

The consequence of this dialectical process of historical advance is that progress is based upon peoples or races. Advanced races come into conflict with inferior ones, defeating them and either leaving them behind or assimilating them. This is why, for example, Hegel contends that the slave trade was truly liberating for Africans. Slavery may have meant defeat and subjugation on one level, but to Hegel it marked historical progress because it brought the African race into contact with more advanced civilization.[84]

Enslaving blacks by whites could be considered as a positive development because they were being freed from their historical backwardness. For Hegel, a people are either on the forefront of history or they are not; they are either with the times or behind the times. The most progressive thing that can happen to a people behind the times is for them to be defeated by a more advanced people. Conquering such a people would represent the progress of the historical spirit.

According to Hegel, the African was wild and beast-like. He found "nothing harmonious with humanity to be found in this type of character."[85] In a particular historical sense they are in the state they are supposed to be in. However, they are far behind other particular histories represented in the western world. Therefore, to enslave the Africans would remove their particular anachronistic place in history:

> Negroes are enslaved by Europeans and sold to America. Bad as this may be, their lot in their own land is even worse, since there a slavery quite as absolute exists; for it is the essential principle of slavery, that man has not yet attained a consciousness of his freedom, and consequently sinks down to a mere Thing— an object of no value. Among Negroes moral sentiments are quite weak, or more strictly speaking, non-existent.[86]

Slavery gives the Negro humane feelings. It has humanized them to the extent where they realize the humanity of not only their master, but the human character of their fellow slave. While Hegel believes that slavery in and of itself is unjust, he believes that the epochs where slavery has existed—in Greece, Rome, and the feudal period—have been beneficial because they represent stages in the advance of universal history. However, if slavery is to end, Hegel ultimately prefers gradual abolition, not because emancipation is a recognition of natural rights, but because it will allow those human feelings to further ingratiate into the character of the Negro.

In like manner, Fichte believed that the progress of history leading to freedom was spurred by the Christian Religion and God's providence. However, he also believed that there were "wild and savage Races" that were barbaric, "corrupt and depraved."[87] According to Fichte, these races may be enslaved because they have not the character of Christianity:

> With respect to Civil Rights:—Before God all men are free and equal;—in every Christian State all men without exception must have the means and opportunity conceded to them of devoting themselves to God, and in this respect at least be assured of Personal Freedom; and from this there readily follow complete Personal Freedom, and the principles that no Christian can be a slave and that a Christian soil confers Freedom. On the other hand, according to the same principle, the Non-Christian or Heathen, may legitimately be made a slave.[88]

And this:

> Barbarism stands directly opposed to the purposes of this Culture whenever it

comes in contact with them, and constantly threatens the existence of the State; which this finds itself, even by necessity of its own preservation, placed in natural war with the surrounding Barbarism, and is compelled to use every effort for its overthrow,—which latter, indeed, can only be thoroughly accomplished by bringing the Barbarians themselves under the dominion of law and order, and in so far, cultivating them.[89]

The progress of freedom has manifested itself most greatly with the advent of Christianity. The Christian faith was a determined part of universal world history and its role in the development of the state was an important part of the development of freedom, and the political equality of all men. Yet, depending on the spirit of the age, Fichte asserted that men should be content with the advantages or distinctions conferred by that age. Though men should relinquish any privileges if the age did not support antiquated class differences, Fichte holds open the possibility that even such things as slavery are necessary if the time one lives in does not allow its prohibition. In order to correct various anachronisms there is political room for placing in bondage other humans. The State must become directly involved in promoting the "higher purpose" of developing the human race; the German thinker did not appreciate what he considered the "cold individualism" and the rights that flowed from such mechanical or Newtonian considerations of statecraft.[90] Indeed, his entire political thought represented a rejection of abstract natural rights: "I declare the very innermost spirit and soul of my philosophy to be, that he obtains all that he has, from experience, from life only. All his thinking, whether vague or scientific, whether popular or transcendental, proceeds from experience and concerns nothing but experience."[91] It was not up to philosophy to discover any great truths, but to explain experience. Philosophy was the re-thinking of experience and the explanation of history.

The historicism of Hegel and Fichte depreciated fixed universal moral principles in favor of a free development of human nature. They believed that the self was developing in history according to the values associated with the spirit of the age. This organic notion of politics extended to their understanding of constitutionalism and abstract philosophical notions of right. The mechanistic conception of the state which views the state as an enforcer or protector of abstract rights is an enemy of freedom. Eventually, both Fichte and Hegel place their faith in the organic and evolutionary state. Rather than individual rights, though, it was Fichte more than Hegel who emphasized societal morality. Man was not considered an individual as such, but as a part of a whole. According to Fichte, "individuals disappear altogether from the view of the philosopher, and are lost in the one great commonwealth:"

It is the greatest error and the real basis for all other errors which are befuddling this age, when an individual imagines that he can exist, live, think, and act for himself, and when he believes that he himself, his own person, is the object of his thought, since he is but a single unit—the general and necessary thought. Looking at the thing as it is in truth we find that the individual does not exist; that he cannot count for anything but must disappear completely; and that the group alone exists and it alone must be considered as existent.[92]

If people insisted too much on their rights, they would become disconnected from society. Meaning comes from the community and is not found in individuality. The individual does not become a person, or a real being, but through society. Humanity's identity is actualized through the community and its institutions. The community and its institutions are a part of the person and determine personhood. The individual must forget himself and his particular identity and place his individual identity in a concept of the human race as a whole. The individual is subordinate to society as a whole. Society, coupled with the progress of time, means that law and rights are judged not by a fixed standard of right and wrong, or good and evil, but with reference to the various stages of culture which history has revealed. The common good might require a curtailment of rights even as the universal history or world spirit is striving for a mankind in complete freedom and independence. However, this is not the kind of freedom that the Founders understood.

Freedom in the historical sense is found in and through the State. The State provides the atmosphere where freedom may be exercised. The State is an organic unity which exists through particulars that are distinct and one at the same time. Fichte goes so far as to assert that at one point in the future, or in a future epoch, the State will have to coerce the people to be moral. As such, Fichte may be one of the first German socialist writers. Probably more than Hegel, Fichte believes that the State could be a powerful ally in the service of freedom. Hegel however, no less viewed the State in positive terms, at one point calling it a God. The reason that the individual is devalued over the State is because that entity is like an ethical being which, with the world spirit, has its own ends and pursues those ends. The State, then, is the actuality of the rational will and the political rights protected in the State are an expression of that will. The rights and duties of man in the State are determined by his position in that social organism. Ultimately, according to one political historian, what is missing in both Fichte and Hegel is a clear "theory of absolute moral values."[93]

As noted above, Hegel frowned on the abstract notions of the enlightenment. His efforts to emphasize the concrete, the visible, and the tangible, led him to these conclusions. Hegel noted that, "for such an abstraction as 'good for its own sake,' has no place in living reality. If men are to act, they must not only intend the Good, but must have decided for themselves whether this or that particular thing is Good. What is the course of action, however, is good or not, is determined, as regards the ordinary contingency of private life, by the laws and customs of a State."[94] In an essay titled "Who Thinks Abstractly?" Hegel tried to show that the average person's appeal to abstract ideas was faulty because it lacked the important acknowledgement of real circumstances, or historical factors. For example, he believed that commonly when people hear or see a murderer, they do not take into account his history or his past—those things that might have contributed to his criminal mind: "this is abstract thinking: to see nothing in the murderer except the abstract fact that he is a murderer, and to annul all other human essence in him with his simple quality."[95] The forces of reality on the murder are what matters most, not that he has murdered. The history of the murderer's life, his education, his family relationship with father and mother, and/or other harsh facts about his existence ought to be taken into account.

Rather than construct the political life as it ought to be, Hegel rejected the thought that philosophy could be abstract or definitively express abstract truths. To the German thinker, "what is rational is actual and what is actual is rational."[96] What is real is what is most important in the direction of politics, not the ought:

> This book, then, containing as it does the science of the state, is to be nothing other than the endeavor to apprehend and portray the state as something inherently rational. As a work of philosophy, it must be poles apart from an attempt to construct a state as it ought to be. The instruction which it may contain cannot consist in teaching the state what it ought to be; it can only show how the state, the ethical universe, is to be understood.

The ability of philosophy to transcend its own time and understand anything outside that time is impossible. Hegel continues: "To comprehend what is, this is the task of philosophy, because what is, is reason. Whatever happens, every individual is a child of his time; so philosophy too is its own time apprehended in thoughts. It is just as absurd to fancy that a philosophy can transcend its contemporary world as it is to fancy that an individual can overleap his own age, jump over Rhodes."[97] He asserts that if anyone invokes an idea that appeals to standards beyond his own age, then this is mere unsubstantiated opinion. Opinion, says our thinker, is the realm of fancy and speculation. Philosophy is not to invent new ideas nor criticize the times, but to explain the reality, or truth, of the age.

The ultimate goal of history (freedom) might seem to confirm the counterargument that Dew could not have been influenced by the German historicists. That would be a shortsighted conclusion. We noted above that Dew used similar reasoning to contend that abstract thought was not applicable to real world circumstances. The professor reflected the influence of such ideas in other ways. Dew was instrumental in forming a history course at William and Mary and was working on a book of history before his death. After his death, his lecture notes were gathered, and the book was completed and published in 1852 as the *Digest of the Laws, Customs, Manners, and Institutions of the Ancient and Modern Nations* (hereafter *Digest*). The intent of the work was to be used in classrooms across the country as a comprehensive course in history. He stated before his death that the point of the work was to explain his philosophy of history.

When comparing Dew's history with Hegel's *Philosophy of History*, there are many similarities. First and foremost is the breakdown of the history of the world into nearly identical epochs. Both have chapters on early history and identical chapters dealing with Greek and Roman history. Dew's history begins earlier and includes more categories in the sections on modern history than does Hegel's. However, the similarities are striking. For example, both include a section on the Reformation and both begin with a consideration of the sale of indulgences as a primary cause for the Reformation. Furthermore, both consider the Reformation "itself the result in a great measure of the progress of civilization and knowledge . . . a most powerfully operating cause on their onward march."[98] There is no formal link between Hegel's history and Dew's *Digest*, but there is no doubt as to the connection between Hegel and Dew in terms of the importance of history. Even though Dew does not specifically reference Hegel in any of his works, he expressed interest in every sort of German literature (especially philosophy, history, and economics), and desired to see German works translated into English for the college library.

As it pertains to the *Review*, Dew made it clear that slavery contributed to the progress of civilization. Similar to Hegel's exception allowing barbaric races to be enslaved, Dew also asserts that slavery was necessary to tame the savage temper of those who had not become civilized. Indeed, he remarks in similar tones that the African race suffered from their backwardness and that their enslavement had made the wars in Africa milder because of the moderating effects of the slave trade. When there are wars in that continent, instead of slaughter at the hands of the conquering people, they enslave those captured for sale to the slave trader. This, according to Dew, has made war less bloody and more moderate. When enslaved, the African learns to adapt to the mores of his new community. He is converted from a savage to productive creature. Dew goes so far as to state that his nature is changed by the conquering race, or the master. The moderation of the African into a productive and gentle mannered creature is what Dew calls the "historical view" of slavery.[99] This historical view of politics leads Dew to consider that the proposal by the emancipationists in the Virginia House of Delegates is "very unphilosophical."[100] The reality of the institution is that the slave has not been held in captivation long enough to change the child-like development of their mind into those who exhibit a more advanced view of civilization. To emancipate the slaves would be to act in a way as to destroy the foundations of civilization and cause a barbaric age. He thus seems to justify slavery in terms of history; slavery cannot end because "experience" and the evolution of "society" has culminated over a long "*lapse of ages*" to determine that the institution cannot end in the near future.[101]

Dew's defense of the slave institution is an historical defense. He begins his *Review* by noting that history defends the use of slavery in the development of civilization. On similar grounds he follows Hegel in defending the enslavement of certain races that are historically backward. In addition, he also appears to justify slavery on the grounds that the Virginia Constitution has, in reality, sanctioned the institution. What is real in the state constitution determines a certain kind of morality for those living in the present age. This is comparable to Hegel, who understood that the state "is the actuality of the ethical idea . . . [it] exists immediately in custom, mediately in the individual self-consciousness, knowledge, and activity."[102] The authority of the State is paramount and it is through the State and its constitution that Hegel asserts freedom is realized. The particular interests are developed and recognized in the laws of the state and the universal will of the people prevails only along with the particular interests of the people. In this way, the people do not live as private persons, but are reflective of the entire community; they do not act for their own interest, but for the interest of the whole. The State is the combination of individuals in a community by and through its traditions, religion, and moral convictions instituted by the laws of the State.[103] The laws actualize freedom, and represent the development of the world spirit. Dew no less understands the state of Virginia in terms of its history, its particular interests, its traditions, and in terms of religion. Virginia is not ready for change because of the interests of the community and its religious historical development. However, we should not conclude that Dew believed similarly in the overarching reach of the State as did Hegel and Fichte.

Dew despised what he called consolidated government, but we should note that he opposed it in terms of its interaction with the demise of slavery. He was concerned about the Union's growth and influence over the individual states. It is clear he thought that Union was not on the right path, while Virginia and the South represented a dispassionate view of the spirit of the age. There is evidence that he believed that the South would be successful in exporting its way of life. It would place on firm ground its institutions and that would in turn influence the entire North. His influence was notable and extended to such journals as *DeBow's Review*, which concluded in 1862 that, "every man should feel that he has an interest in the State and that the State in a measure leans on him; and he should rouse himself to efforts as bold and heroic as if all depended upon his single right arm . . . It is implied in the spirit which times demand, that all private interests are sacrificed to the public good. The State becomes everything, and the individual nothing."[104] This sentiment is not too dissimilar from Hegel's conception of the politics where he asserted that the highest form of freedom was membership in the State. He despised, along with Fichte, too much individuality.[105] It is the State that is the fundamental vehicle or expression of world history and it is in that entity that individuals should place themselves above their personal interests.[106] A type of southern nationalism rose out of this development: "Since one cannot have abstract rights against the historical state, there is no effective boundary that the state cannot cross."[107] From Hegel and Fichte, the State becomes a leviathan, which can have no limits placed on it. Dew holds the important position of forwarding an early version of this kind of historicism on behalf of the South's slave interest. According to some historians, Dew made a real contribution to the proslavery cause and "it is possible to see him as creating a model for virtually all the proslavery writing published after 1832."[108]

Conclusion: The Positive Good Thesis Is Born

Dew's *Review* was accepted by Governor John Floyd, who considered the professor's treatise the final word on the subject of slavery. There is some evidence that Floyd encouraged Dew to take up the writing of the essay. However, he certainly approved of Dew's project, writing that nobody could be as thorough, nor as skillful, in writing the *Review* as the professor. Dew admired Floyd, and the Governor relied on him for advice on several matters concerning the state. They were warm friends and Dew often stopped off at the Governor's house to visit when he traveled through Richmond.[109]

In his *Lectures on the Restrictive System*, Dew argued that classical economic theory stressed the preeminence of natural laws. However these laws were not the same natural laws of the Founders which informed them of man's inherent natural rights. Natural law to Dew meant that things should evolve absent of man's interference. Left to themselves, states would develop an economic system that best suited them. Any interference by men would upset the natural evolution of things and retard progress.[110] There were some things that Virginia could do to encourage economic growth, however. He favored internal improvements (roads, rail, and canals, for instance) to the state to assist her economic growth, but for government, state or federal, to meddle in the foundation of her economic system was anathema.

Part of the great plan of history was under the control of the divine providence. The divine and experience showed humans that the division of labor was inherent in the human condition and it rested upon inequality. The progress of mankind rested on the great talents of great individuals—like his students at William and Mary—who have the "leisure and freedom from drudgery"; for Dew, western civilization "was the unfolding story of the glories of human freedom and of the beauties of the human spirit when liberated from the torpor of oppression and despotism."[111] Every human plan for emancipation and deportation was impracticable and subversive to human happiness; for slavery was sanctioned by God for some useful purpose. That purpose was to soften the morals of man and decrease the violent nature within barbarian man. Societies evolved through stages and moved from a primitive stage to a civilized stage. Although he was careful not to implicate whites in this historical narrative of slavery, it was implicit that whites were not completely excluded from it. He rejected natural rights theory as visionary and chimerical and therefore denied that slavery could be questioned in the abstract. In this way, he challenged the very foundations of the anti-slave argument presented in the House.[112] Dew's notion of Christianity's place in history, and as a force in time, is perhaps the most similar to the thought of Fichte and Hegel. Fichte asserted that Christianity "with the whole History of Modern Times, [was] the true principle of which is the manifestation of Christianity."[113] Likewise, Hegel believed that the Holy Spirit was at work shaping the destiny of man. Providence is manifesting itself, revealing itself, to mankind through history. God was thus personally at work in the affairs of man and directing the progress of history.

If the laws and customs are the primary guides to action in a state, then what is to prevent slavery from being protected in any given age? Dew justifies his defense of slavery on just such grounds. The history and customs of Virginia along with her constitution have determined the best cause of action. In 1830s Virginia, the just action regarding slavery was to let it alone until such a time as providence saw to its abolition. Abstract right was no guide to the statesman. In this way Dew was influenced by German historicism. His political remedy for slavery was to wait for history. However, with the notion of abstract rights suspended from political consideration, there was no reason for those interpreting their age to prefer a different end to history. Claims of justice were traditionally considered accessible to man, but the historicist claimed that it was not knowable. It is a consequence, then, that different men may interpret history in different ways. History demonstrates that there are no immutable or timeless principles of justice. Rather, principles are mutable. There was no reason why Hegel's notion of historic rights could not be used to justify slavery in one's own time, and perhaps even forever, since there was no rational foreknowledge of history: "reason was truly manifest in the absolute moment wherein history as progress was revealed."[114] If the standard of one's time is the actual, or real, then transcendent standards are no longer necessary.

Dew's *Review* placed great emphasis on the present age, or the current political situation of his time. Questions of justice for him were not as important as reality. If there was a good life, it was contained in the traditions of the culture: "The most common form of historicism expresses itself in the demand that the questions of the nature of political things, of the state, of the nature of man, and so forth, be replaced by the questions of the modern state, of modern government, of the present political situation, of modern man, of our society, our culture, our civilization, and so forth."[115] Both Hegel's and Fichte's understanding was that political philosophy should not engage in reflection of how the government should be, or ought to be, constructed. They rejected the faith in reason's ability to know what is right and wrong, or good and bad. It was a waste of time to philosophize about such matters. They would rather try to understand the present and actual time one lives. This concern with the present is a rejection of classical political philosophy and the Founders' understanding of the ends of politics. Herein is the problem with the thought of Hegel and Fichte: they taught that every philosophy is the conceptual expression of the spirit of its time, and yet they maintained the absolute truth of their own system. If one cannot transcend his own time, how is one able to expound on a philosophy that is not affected by their time?

Dodd believes that this rationalist and historical direction was present in the thought of Dew. The subjugation of other races as a necessary event to bring certain races out of their anachronistic behaviors, made the professor believe that inequality was essential to progress: "These are the views to which the people of the lower South were being converted. The adoption of this point of view marks a revolution in southern thought quite as remarkable as the revolution which took place in German thought under the leadership of Bismark during the second half of the nineteenth century."[116] The South would not have come under the spell of German rationalism had it not been for Dew. He was widely read and influential in the early part of the nineteenth century and hence paved the way for the acceptance of slavery as a perpetual institution that would bolster the development of freedom and republicanism.

The *Review* marked a definite defense of the slave system and it was received that way by sympathetic partisans in the South. Abel P. Upshur, one of the major pro-slave voices in the Constitutional Convention of 1829-1830, asserted that Dew had traced slavery to its true source and defended it on the correct principles. According to *DeBow's Review* in 1859,

> the great book on slavery has yet to be written . . . None but a Southern author of rare abilities and calm philosophic temper can do it justice. If Prof. Dew were yet living, with ripened experience he would have acquired, and with the light furnished by the incessant discussion of the past fifteen years, he might have written the great treatise. As it is, his essay, making the proper allowances for the early period of its appearance, is probably the best which has yet been published.[117]

Dew was one of the first intellectuals to publicly proclaim that the slave system did not need apology and that the system was beneficial. If *DeBow's* is any indication, Dew's *Review* and his subsequent writings provided a foundation for the pro-slave argument. His opinion about slavery only further crystallized years after the *Review* was published. In a letter to William H. Harrison Dew wrote: "Glad you agree with me on the subject of slavery. Every day convinces me of the blessings in southern latitudes. I think you are right in regard to Liberia— Man cannot be uplifted from barbarism to civilization without the aid of slavery.—All history demonstrates this proposition."[118] If slavery was a blessing, it could not have been much of a leap to consider it a good. This is why some have claimed that "the acceptance of slavery was the idea that the owners of property should be the rulers of men shows how far Dew and his associates had departed from the democratic ideals of the Declaration of Independence."[119] Dodd understood that few had the impact that Dew's writings did in striking a blow at equality and republican government. The professor's influence was great and his participation in the development of the "positive good" thesis had the effect of positioning Virginia favorably toward slavery. The German influence on Dew convinced Old Dominion to turn its back on Jefferson and the idea "all men are created equal."

Notes

1. Xenophon, *On Tyranny*, in Leo Strauss *On Tyranny*, ed. Victor Gourevitch and Michael S. Roth (New York: Free Press, 1991), 8; Thomas Roderick Dew, "Review of the Debate in the Virginia Legislature, 1831-1832," *The Proslavery Argument* (New York: Negro Universities Press, 1968), 444.

2. Appomattox, "Communicated to the People of Virginia," *Richmond Enquirer*, 4 February 1832, 2-3. Among the many things that Appomattox contended was that blacks were a "slave race." According to many scholars, the author of the letter is none other than Benjamin Watkins Leigh, one of the pro-slave promoters in the Constitutional Convention of 1829-1830.

3. Joseph Clarke Robert, *The Road from Monticello: A Study if the Virginia Slavery Debate of 1832* (Durham: Duke University Press, 1941), 53. Appomattox encouraged his colleagues in the Tidewater and Piedmont to silence the press by canceling their subscriptions and censuring them. While he did not favor sedition laws, he desired to see all debate in favor of emancipation halted; Alison Goodyear Freehling, *Drift Toward Dissolution: The Virginia Slavery Debate of 1831-1832* (Baton Rouge: Louisiana State University Press, 1982), 202; Dickson D. Bruce, *The Rhetoric of Conservatism: The Virginia Convention of 1829-30 and the Conservative Tradition in the South* (San Marino, Ca.: The Huntington Library, 1982), 177, 185; Drew Gilpin Faust, ed., *The Ideology of Slavery* (Baton Rouge: Louisiana State University Press, 1981), 10; Charles S. Sydnor, *The Development of Southern Sectionalism 1819-1848* (Baton Rouge: Louisiana State Press, 1948), 95; Stephen Mansfield, "Thomas Roderick Dew: Defender of the Southern Faith" (Ph.D. diss., University of Virginia, 1968), 64.

4. Eugene Genovese, *Western Civilization through Slaveholding Eyes: The Social and Historical Thought of Thomas Roderick Dew* (New Orleans: Graduate School of Tulane University, 1986), 1. Subsequent quotes from this source.

5. Faust, *The Ideology of Slavery*, 2-12, 22-23; William W. Freehling, *The Road to Disunion: Secessionists at Bay 1776-1854* (New York: Oxford University Press, 1990), 190; Lee Rivers Polk, "An Analysis of Argumentation in the Virginia Slavery Debate of 1832" (Ph.D. diss., Purdue University, 1967), 4. Faust argues that Dew's influence was delayed as there was not a flood of pro-slave defenses until after 1835.

6. James C. Hite and Ellen J. Hall, "The Reactionary Evolution of Economic Thought in Antebellum Virginia," *Virginia Magazine of History and Biography* 80 (October 1972) : 476.

7. John McCardell, *The Idea of a Southern Nation* (New York: W.W. Norton and Company, 1979), 56.

8. Hite and Hall, 483.

9. McCardell, 57.

10. H. Marshall Booker, "Thomas Roderick Dew: Forgotten Virginian," *Virginia Cavalcade* 19 (Autumn 1969) : 27.

11. Drew Gilpin Faust, *James Henry Hammond and the Old South* (Baton Rouge: Louisiana State University Press, 1982), 162 and 176.

12. William E. Dodd, *The Cotton Kingdom: A Chronicle of the Old South* (Toronto: Glasgow, Brook and Co., 1919), 49.

13. William E. Dodd, "The Social Philosophy of the Old South," *American Journal of Sociology* 23 (May 1918): 736. Cf. Mansfield, "Thomas Roderick Dew: Defender of the Southern Faith," 14. In the 1960s, Stephen Scott Mansfield, in researching for his dissertation, stumbled upon Dew's diary which thereunto was not known to exist. In that source, Dew never mentions a trip to Germany. However, Dodd was not unfamiliar with Germany. He eventually became an Ambassador to the country in the Franklin D. Roosevelt administration. Even though he claimed Dew was influenced by Germans there is no direct evidence Dew visited Germany. There is abundant evidence that he visited France, Switzerland, and Italy, but it remains a mystery where Dodd derived his evidence.

14. Dodd, *The Cotton Kingdom*, 51.

15. Mansfield, "Thomas Roderick Dew: Defender of the Southern Faith," 19; Thomas Roderick Dew, "An Address on the Influence of the Federative Republican System of Government upon Literature and the Development of Character," *Southern Literary Messenger* 2 (March 1836) : 268 and 269.

16. Harry V. Jaffa, *A New Birth of Freedom* (Lanham, Md.: Rowman & Littlefield,

2000), 85.

17. William E. Dodd, *Statesmen of the Old South* (New York: The MacMillan Co., 1911), 137. See also Faust, "A Southern Stewardship: The Intellectual and the Proslavery Argument," *American Quarterly* 31 (Spring 1979): 67; Carl L. Becker, *The Declaration of Independence: A Study in the History of Political Ideas* (New York: Vintage, 1942), 255.

18. Calhoun to Francis W. Pickens, 2 March 1832, *The Papers of John C. Calhoun*, ed. Clyde Wilson, vol. 11 (Columbia: University of South Carolina Press, 1980), 558-559; Calhoun to John Bauskett & Others, 3 November 1833, ibid., vol. 13, 641; Calhoun to Samuel D. Ingham, 23 April 1829, ibid., vol. 11, 545; Calhoun to Lt. James Edward Colhoun, 1 April 1833, ibid., vol. 12, 155.

19. Nathaniel Beverly Tucker to Calhoun, 23 January 1846, ibid, vol. 22, 502; Calhoun to Nathaniel Beverly Tucker, 2 February 1846, ibid., vol. 22, 563.

20. Joseph Walker to Calhoun, 13 February 1846, ibid., vol. 22, 588-589; David A. Street to Calhoun, 25 May 1844, ibid., vol. 18, 620; Thomas R. Dew to Calhoun, 26 January 1846, ibid., vol. 22, 512; Robert McCandlish to Calhoun, 28 October 1845, ibid., vol. 22, 243.

21. Charles Francis Adams, ed., *Memoirs of John Quincy Adams*, vol. 9 (Freeport, New York: Books for Libraries Press, 1969), 13 October 1833, 23.

22. Ibid., 14 October 1833.

23. Madison to Dew, 23 February 1833, *The Mind of the Founder*, ed. Marvin Meyers (Hanover: Brandeis University Press, 1981), 333.

24. James Madison, Madison to N.P. Trist, February 1830, *Letters and Other Writings*, vol. 4 (New York: R. Worthington, 1884), 58.

25. Thomas Roderick Dew, "Review of the Debate in the Virginia Legislature, 1831-32," *The Proslavery Argument* (New York: Negro Universities Press, 1968), 288.

26. Ibid., 291. Years later, Dew would contend that a debate over emancipation would not only be imprudent in the South, but approvingly asserted that it ought not be conducted. Indeed, he claimed it would never be conducted because the entire South was of one mind about abolition: Thomas Roderick Dew, "Ancient and Modern Eloquence," *Southern Literary Messenger* 8 (March 1842) : 185.

27. Dew, "Review of the Debate in the Virginia Legislature, 1831-32," 292.

28. Ibid. Italics in original.

29. Ibid., 294.

30. Ibid., 295.

31. Ibid., 300.

32. Ibid., 300-301, and 303. The Romans and Greeks used their slaves for agricultural purposes and this made those nations more mild and less savage because they did not destroy their enemy as much as they enslaved a good portion, sparing their lives.

33. Ibid., 306.

34. Aristotle, *The Politics*, 126-127, 96; or 1292b1, 1279b1.

35. Dew, "An Address on the Influence of the Federative Republican System of Government upon Literature and the Development of Character," 277.

36. Dew, "Review of the Debate in the Virginia Legislature, 1831-32," 312.

37. Ibid., 315.

38. Ibid., 335 and 316. This is an unconvincing statement since he does not address the negative effects of slavery and only speaks about its positive effects. The fact that he believes there is something positive about slavery means he has passed some judgment upon the institution.

39. Ibid., 325. Italics in the original.

40. Michael O'Brien, ed., *All Clever Men who Make their Way: Critical Discourse in the Old South* (Fayetteville: University of Arkansas Press, 1982), 128.

41. Dew, "Review of the Debate in the Virginia Legislature, 1831-32," 333.

42. Ibid., 354-355.

43. Ibid., 358.

44. Ibid., 364.

45. Ibid., 380. Italics in the original.

46. Ibid., 381.

47. Algernon Sydney, *Discourses Concerning Government*, ed. Thomas G. West (Indianapolis: Liberty Classics, 1990), 510-511; Jefferson to Roger C. Weightman, Monticello, 24 June 1826, *The Portable Thomas Jefferson*, ed. Merrill Peterson (New York: Penguin Books, 1975), 585.

48. Dew, "Review of the Debate in the Virginia Legislature, 1831-32," 385.

49. Ibid., 389.

50. Thomas Hobbes, *Leviathan*, ed., Michael Oakeshott (New York: Collier Books, 1962), 98-105; Cf. John Locke, *Two Treatises of Government*, ed. Peter Laslett (Cambridge: Cambridge University Press, 1988), 269-272, 283-284, and 330-331.

51. Madison, [Majority Governments], 1833, *Mind of the Founder*, 411, and 412-413.

52. Dew, "Review of the Debate in the Virginia Legislature, 1831-32," 413, and see 390-391, and 410. Italics in the original. We should note that Dew did not hold a high regard for free blacks either. While he does not contend they should be deported—indeed colonization is impossible—he does seem to place them in a second class of citizen, below that of whites.

53. Ibid., 456. Italics in the original.

54. Ibid., 457. Cf. Jefferson to Chastellux, Paris, 2 September 1785, *Thomas Jefferson: Writings* (New York: Library of America, 1984), 827. Jefferson considered those of the North to be cool, sober, laborious, and jealous of not only their own liberties, but their fellow man's. Those of the South were fiery, indolent, unsteady, and only zealous for their own liberties while trampling on the rights of others.

55. Ibid., 459-460.

56. Ibid., 460-461.

57. All quotes in this paragraph are from ibid., 461-462.

58. Ibid., 462.

59. Dew, "An Address on the Influence of the Federative Republican System of Government upon Literature and the Development of Character," 279.

60. Dew, "Review of the Debate in the Virginia Legislature, 1831-32," 463.

61. Ibid., 490.

62. Ibid. Italics in the original.

63. Dew, "An Address on the Influence of the Federative Republican System of Government upon Literature and the Development of Character," 277 and 278.

64. Ibid., 277-278.

65. Freehling, *The Road to Disunion*, 191.

66. Dew, "An Address on the Influence of the Federative Republican System of Government upon Literature and the Development of Character," 277 and 278.

67. Ibid., 279.

68. Ibid., 280. We ought not overlook Dew's stark warning in the same essay that if the North was not enlightened to the benefits of slavery and tried to impose their way of life on the South, that the South would resort to arms to protect their position. He thought that there were unphilosophic sentiments in the North that tended to monarchy (or the

consolidation of federal power). Emancipation, then, was a regression of history, not a part of its progress.

69. Thomas Dew, *An Address Delivered before the Students of William and Mary at the Opening of the College on Monday, October 10, 1836* (Richmond: T.W. White, 1836), 9-10.

70. Ibid., 10.

71. Ibid., 13.

72. Ibid., 14 and 15.

73. Ibid., 21.

74. The best biography on Dodd was written by Fred Arthur Bailey, *William Edward Dodd: The South's Yeoman Scholar* (Charlottesville: University Press of Virginia, 1997), ix, 17-18, 20, 141, 157-159, 161-162; Stephen Mansfield, "Thomas Roderick Dew at William and Mary," *Virginia Magazine of History and Biography* 75 (1967) : 429.

75. Thomas Roderick Dew, William and Mary College, Letter to Benjamin F. Dew, 12 July 1842, Dew Family Papers, Earl Gregg Swem Library, College of William and Mary, Williamsburg, Virginia.

76. Mansfield, "Thomas Roderick Dew: Defender of the Southern Faith," 431-433, 435; O'Brien, 16, 125; Lowell Harrison, "Thomas Roderick Dew: Philosopher of the Old South," *Virginia Magazine of History and Biography* 57 (October 1949) : 391, 401.

77. G.W.F. Hegel, *The Philosophy of History*, with an Introduction by C.J. Friedrich (New York: Dover Publications, 1956), 18-19; Fichte, "Characteristics of the Present Age," *The Popular Works of Johann Gottlieb Fichte*, vol. 2, trans. William Smith (London: Trübner and Co., 1889), 162-165; Walter Kaufmann, *Hegel: Reinterpretation, Texts, and Commentary* (Garden City, N.Y.: Doubleday and Company, 1965), 255 and 268; H.C. Engelbrecht, *Johann Gottlieb Fichte: A Study of his Political Writings with Special Reference to his Nationalism* (New York: AMS Press, 1968), 18, 25-26; Dante Germino, "Hegel as a Political Theorist," *The Journal of Politics* 31, no. 4 (November 1969) : 889.

78. Jaffa, *A New Birth of Freedom*, 84-85.

79. Hegel, *The Philosophy of History*, 4, 13, and 15; Ronald J. Pestritto, *Woodrow Wilson and the Roots of Modern Liberalism* (Lanham: Rowman and Littlefield Publishers, Inc., 2005), 16. Because the future was obscure, Hegel did not engage in much prediction of the future. This was not the case with Fichte, who laid out before his audiences the progression of history explained not only in the past, but what would happen in the world to come: Fichte, "Characteristics of the Present Age," 4 and 9.

80. Hegel, *The Philosophy of History*, 36 and 8. Italics in the original.

81. Ibid., 45; Strauss, *What is Political Philosophy?*, 59.

82. G.W.F. Hegel, *Philosophy of Right*, trans. T.M. Knox (London: Oxford University Press, 1977), 178, or §273; Pestritto, 17.

83. Hegel, *The Philosophy of History*, 45; Pestritto, 15.

84. Pestritto, 15.

85. Hegel, *The Philosophy of History*, 93.

86. Ibid., 96.

87. Fichte, "Characteristics of the Present Age," 220, and 192-193.

88. Ibid., 220-221.

89. Ibid., 181.

90. Robert Adamson, *Fichte* (Freeport, New York: Books for Libraries Press, 1969), 80; Fichte, "Characteristics of the Present Age," 235 and 185.

91. Quoted in Adamson, 108 and 122; Tom Rockmore, *Fichte, Marx, and the*

German Philosophical Tradition (Carbondale: Southern Illinois University Press, 1980), 10.

92. Quoted in H.C. Engelbrecht, *Johann Gottlieb Fichte*, 85; Fichte, "Characteristics of the Present Age," 12. We should note that Hegel did not view things in this way. As previously noted, he despised slavery. Hegel thought the truly modern state was based on the right of each individual. Leo Strauss noted Hegel's preoccupation with the "I" self: "everything objective—the gods, the city, the family, justice—has become dissolved into the self-consciousness or taken back into it." See Leo Strauss, *The Rebirth of Classical Political Rationalism*, intro. Thomas L. Pangle (Chicago: University of Chicago, 1989), 116, and 117-118.

93. Frederick Copleston, *A History of Philosophy: Modern Philosophy*, vol. 7 (New York: Doubleday, 1963), 29, see also 14, 16, 60-61, 71-72, 74, and 212-213; Fichte, *Addresses to the German Nation*, xx-xxi; Fichte, "Characteristics of the Present Age," 35-38; Engelbrecht, 30-31; Wm. A. Dunning, "The Political Theories of the German Idealists II," *Political Science Quarterly* 28, no. 3 (September 1913) : 486.

94. Hegel, *The Philosophy of History*, 29.

95. Kaufmann, *Hegel: Texts and Commentary*, 116-117.

96. Hegel, *Philosophy of Right*, 10. Some translate "real" for "actual."

97. Ibid., 11. This quote and the one above from same source and page.

98. Dew, *Digest*, 437. Cf. Hegel, *Philosophy of History*, 416-417. Hegel sees the Reformation as important for its exclusion of external authority. Man's moral compass comes from within, than from without. In other words, he praises the Reformation for bringing about the secularization of Christianity.

99. Dew, "Review of the Debate in the Virginia Legislature, 1831-32," 355, see also 294, 300-301, 303, 325-327, 333-334.

100. Ibid., 453 and 454.

101. Ibid., 490 and 450. Italics in the original.

102. Hegel, *Philosophy of Right*, 155, or §257.

103. Ibid., 163, or §267, and 364, note 9.

104. "Our Danger and Our Duty," *DeBow's Review* 33 (May-August 1862) : 238.

105. Dew, *Digest of the Laws, Customs, Manners, and Institutions of the Ancient and Modern Nations*, 210; Fichte, "Characteristics of the Present Age," 38-39; Kaufmann, *Hegel: Reinterpretation, Texts, and Commentary*, 269. We should note that Dew states at this part of the *Digest* that the Germans have understood ancient history better than any other race in the modern age, see *Digest of the Laws, Customs, Manners, and Institutions of the Ancient and Modern Nations*, 209. It is difficult to see how—even if Dew did not visit Germany and attend the universities there—that he was not at least influenced by the ideas emanating from that region.

106. Allen W. Wood, ed., *Elements of the Philosophy of Right*, trans. H.B. Nisbet (Cambridge: Cambridge University Press, 1991), xxv; Hegel, *Philosophy of Right*, 155-157, or §258, 212-213, or §331, and 217, or §344.

107. Pestritto, 17.

108. Bruce, *The Rhetoric of Conservatism*, 180.

109. Mansfield, "Thomas Roderick Dew: Defender of the Southern Faith," 48-50; Harrison, 402-403. Recall in chapter five that Floyd wrote in his personal diary that he desired to see the end of the slave institution in Virginia. What caused him to back off that desire is a mystery.

110. Mansfield, "Thomas Roderick Dew: Defender of the Southern Faith," 34; Dew, *Lectures on the Restrictive System*, preface, n.p.

111. Genovese, *Western Civilization through Slaveholding Eyes*, 3 and 2. Dew

appealed to the great thinkers and philosophers in history to demonstrate his point that history tended toward liberty. Each authority whether Socrates or Jefferson were representative of this evolution, see Dew, *An Address Delivered before the Students of William and Mary at the Opening of the College on Monday, October 10, 1836*, 30-33.

112. Kenneth M. Stampp, "An Analysis of T.R. Dew's Review of the Debates in the Virginia Legislature," *Journal of Negro History* 27 (October 1942) : 384; McCardell, 55; Bruce, *The Rhetoric of Conservatism*, 180; Genovese, *Western Civilization through Slaveholding Eyes*, 8.

113. Fichte, "Characteristics of the Present Age," 209.

114. Jaffa, *New Birth of Freedom*, 94-95.

115. Strauss, *What is Political Philosophy?*, 59.

116. Dodd, *Cotton Kingdom*, 59-60; cf. Dodd, "The Social Philosophy of the Old South," 741.

117. Quoted in Harrison, 403.

118. Thomas Roderick Dew, William and Mary College, to William H. Harrison, 18 October 1838, Dew Family Papers, Earl Gregg Swem Library, College of William and Mary, Williamsburg, Virginia.

119. Stampp, 387, 386, and 382; Harrison, 403.

Chapter 8

Conclusion: Virginia and the Positive Good Thesis

Of *this* I am very sure, that the difference—nothing short of frightful—
between all that exists on one side of the Potomac, and all on the other, is
owing to *that cause alone.*—The disease is deep-seated—it is at the
heart's core—it is consuming, and has all along been consuming our
vitals, and I could laugh, if I *could* laugh on such a subject, at the
ignorance and folly of the politician, who ascribes that to an act of the
government, which is the inevitable effect of the eternal law of Nature.
What is to be done? Oh! My God—I don't know, but something must be
done.

Richmond Enquirer

As I would not be a *slave*, so I would not be a *master.*

Abraham Lincoln

Jefferson knew perfectly well that the concept "slave" excludes by definition that of "citizen" and *vice versa* . . . Slavery, he says, makes men enemies; that is, it alienates them from one another. It destroys the bonds
which *should* link them in mutual regard for their rights as men, and make
it possible for them to become fellow citizens.

Harry V. Jaffa[1]

Although in 1823, there was one anti-slavery society in Virginia, four years later
one hundred six of the one hundred thirty of such societies in the Union were
located in the South. Many of those societies were located in the western part of
the southern states.[2] Unlike the Constitutional Convention of 1829-1830, the
debates in the House were decidedly over the question of emancipation. There
was no veiled discussion in 1832 as there was two years earlier. Virginians
engaged in a unique discussion, yet "never again would a Southern state so
openly and so seriously consider the possibility of ending slavery."[3] The forces
of emancipation had a unique opportunity to end the peculiar institution. By the
close of 1832, however, the possibility that emancipation could be effected for
the Union, much less Virginia, closed. Southerners came to see themselves as
constituting a separate nation bound together by the interest they had in slavery.

Few were surprised by the geographical division caused by the peculiar institution. John Quincy Adams conceived slavery would divide the Union when he wrote in his diary that "if the Union must be dissolved, slavery is precisely the question upon which it ought to break."[4] Slavery was a decisive factor causing the Civil War, and the coming war appeared to be a surety as the "positive good" thesis found its moorings in Virginia.

Thomas Roderick Dew's *Review of the Debate in the Virginia Legislature of 1831-1832* (hereafter *Review*) represented a "flank attack on Jefferson" and the American Founding by representing a defense of the virtues of a slaveholding society.[5] Even though there was a lengthy response to Dew in the likes of Jesse Burton Harrison in 1832 with a counter review of the debates, Dew's *Review* exerted much influence on Southern thought. Carl L. Becker noted in his history of the Declaration of Independence that Dew's historical sense, reflected through the providential influence of God, permitted him to believe that "slavery must be in accord with the nature of man."[6] He explained that if God is perfect and is unfolding His perfect will gradually before us, that any evil in the world is incidental to some universal plan and some universal good. If slavery existed by some universal purpose, then superior men subjugating inferior men is decreed by God. Dew thus saw an historical spirit in the natural law. This meant that if there was a law of nature it was subject to the will of God. If God willed for some men to be ruled by others, then the concept all men are created equal was a lie. Becker concluded as much when he wrote that, "Hegel's notion that the Transcendent Idea was working steadily toward Freedom. Yet it left the individual more diminished than ever, and more helplessly bound."[7]

Since man possessed no rights by nature, he was bound by history. Dew's interest in German thought, even if he was not directly influenced by Hegel or Fichte, was pronounced. While he did not absorb everything from those German thinkers, he certainly adopted their opposition to natural rights, and their appreciation for history. Since universal principles were not discernable by human reason, one is left with a form of conventionalism. What was right and just had no basis in nature but was grounded in tradition or in the decisions made by one's community. Since universal principles had no place in politics, historical principles filled the void and thus the real and actual took the place of the transcendent. This presents a problem for politics. If changes are made, the historical school "does not teach us whether the change was sound or whether the rejected view deserved to be rejected."[8] In other words, there was no standard by which to judge whether a particular choice was good or bad since universals were suspended in favor of historical realities. Absent natural rights, the spirit of the age might justify slavery. If slavery was the work of God, then slavery was just. Dew's intellectual defense of slavery from a religious perspective made the defense of slavery in Christian terms palpable. After 1832, the religious justification for slavery seized the South in part because of the professor's arguments. Therefore, the *Review* has been received by many as a defense of slavery. It marked a turn in the prevailing southern opinion on slavery to one more accepting of the institution. Some believe that his views had such an influence that they prompted the Virginia legislature to pass stricter laws regarding slavery—restricting the slaves' ability to assemble and to preach. In addition, the Virginia House and Senate passed a law denying free blacks jury trials. According to one scholar, the *Review* became the manual for Virginia conservatism for one-third of a century.[9] Virginia could boast of a long line of those from the state who decried slavery and human bondage. By 1832, pro-slave supporters were replacing the anti-slave fathers as the most influential voices in the state. For example, Benjamin Watkins Leigh became an ardent defender of slavery as an integral part of the southern way of life, and Abel Upshur wrote that the natural rights of man were a menace to free institutions. St. George Tucker's son, Beverly Tucker, argued that inequality was a "self-evident fact."[10] Another rising intellectual was Thomas Cooper, who asserted that "rights are what society acknowledges and sanctions, and they are nothing else."[11] This rejection of natural rights as a basis for good government could not have come about had it not been for the convention in 1829-1830. That event represents the first major public abandonment of the teachings of the Revolution where property rights superseded all other rights.

Perhaps the greatest contribution of this work is that the influence of German rationalism on American thinkers, like Dew, became publicly visible earlier than in John C. Calhoun. Before Calhoun popularized his politics and raciology, German thought was already at work in the psyche of southern intellectuals. These intellectuals in turn influenced Calhoun. The irony is that German thinkers like Hegel and Fichte, who believed in freedom, contributed to the "positive good" thesis and the entrenchment of slavery in America.

As 1832 came to a close, the opinion that slavery was a moral evil was in retreat. The Constitutional Convention of 1829-1830, the slave debates of 1831-1832, and the intellectual defense of those debates by Dew, sowed the seeds of what would later become the "positive good" thesis. Men like Calhoun built upon the foundations that Dew had poured. By 1837 Calhoun openly declared that slavery was a "positive good." Interestingly, Dew's influence is present in much of today's political thought. He can be considered an early American founder of the more modern conservative, paleo-con, movement represented by Russell Kirk. Kirk views politics not in terms of natural rights, but in terms of community interest. He prefers inequality and fears majority rule. Furthermore, he is suspicious of modern industrialism and its effects on community. Kirk rejected rights talk and criticized the Declaration as essentially a meaningless document meant only to persuade the court of France. Kirk praised a conservatism that had no esteem for the American Founding; Christian doctrines of submission and tradition should be more authoritative than natural right.[12] As a result, he often found much to praise in the conservatism of John Randolph and Calhoun. According to Kirk, they were both men of principle who articulated, better than any other, the doctrine of conservatism. If Calhoun is a guide for modern conservatives, we must wonder if Kirk found the South Carolina native a guide in all political matters. Consider these public statements from Calhoun on the reception of the abolition petitions, which are the basis of the "positive good" thesis: "But let me not be understood as admitting, even by implication, that the existing relations between the two races in the slaveholding States is an evil: —far otherwise; I hold it to be a good, as it has thus far proved itself to be both, and will continue to prove so if not disturbed by the fell spirit of abolition."

And this:

> But I take a higher ground. I hold that in the present state of civilization where two races of different origin, and distinguished by color, and other physical differences, as well as intellectual, are brought together, the relation now existing in the slaveholding States between the two, is, instead of an evil, a good—a positive good.

And finally: "Abolition and Union cannot coexist . . . We of the South will not, cannot surrender our institutions."[13] Both Calhoun and Dew created a new set of values for the Union. By 1835, the most important person responsible for recasting the American Founding was Calhoun, but Dew's *Review* was responsible for the early phases of this transition from a belief in the Declaration of Independence and Declaration of Rights to a belief in historical rights.

Since abstract rights were rejected, man was almost entirely a creature of circumstances. In his diary in 1820, John Quincy Adams noted the problems associated with the slave institution and the corruption infected upon the manner of men. Recounting a conversation he had with Calhoun, Adams made the argument that justice ought to be the end of government. Calhoun rejected such sentiments and asserted that justice and equality only applied to white men:

> Domestic labor was confined to blacks, and such was the prejudice, that if he, who was the most popular man in his district, were to keep a white servant in his house, his character and reputation would be irretrievably ruined.
>   I said that this confounding of the ideas of servitude and labor was one of the bad effects of slavery: but he thought it attended with many excellent consequences . . . .It was only manual labor—the proper work of slaves. No white person could descend to that.

Calhoun asserted that not every form of labor was improper for white men; he approved of farming and mechanical labor for whites. However, other forms of labor would corrupt whites if blacks did not engage in that form of work. Manual labor, for example, was reserved for blacks. It produced equality among whites and secured inequality among the races. To this, Adams responded:

> I told Calhoun I could not see things in the same light. It is in truth, all perverted sentiment—mistaking labor for slavery, and dominion for freedom. The discussion of the Missouri question has betrayed the secret of their souls. In the abstract they admit slavery is an evil, they disclaim all participation in the introduction of it, and cast it all upon the shoulders of our Grandam Britain.

But when probed to the quick upon it, they show at the bottom of their souls pride and vainglory in their condition of masterdom. They fancy themselves more generous and noble-hearted than the plain freemen who labor for subsistence. They look down upon the simplicity of a Yankee's manners, because he has no habits of overbearing like theirs and cannot treat negroes like dogs. It is among the evils of slavery that it taints the very sources of moral principle.[14]

Even as early as 1820, Adams understood where the heart of the southern slaveholder was tending. He saw privately in Calhoun some of the same sentiments that Dew developed and then articulated openly in 1832. As we have read, the Founders did not think about slavery in these terms, and they thought that it was ultimately a corrupting institution.

The Virginia debates demonstrated the difficulty of enacting an emancipation plan. Speaking of Jefferson, Herbert Storing noted that the obstacles to slave integration into American society were threefold: (1) the race prejudice of whites, (2) blacks' sense of injustice, and (3) the perceived natural and probable inferiority of blacks. These issues did not disappear in 1830s Virginia. Storing notes of the first two impediments that it would be nearly impossible to craft a peaceful civil society—the political bonds necessary for such a society depend on mutual trust and obligation. However, a political society with strong bonds that tie a people together needs the mutual recognition of rights.[15] The Founders were not unaware of the problems associated with abolition. They believed, generally, that slavery destroyed the possibility of such a union of the races in a tranquil polis. Jefferson stated it similarly in Query XVIII of his *Notes* when he opined that the moral foundations of society are destroyed, or corrupted, absent the mutual recognition of each and every man's liberty. Prejudice on the one hand, and black animosity, on the other hand, prevented peaceful coexistence, he thought. Furthermore, the inferiority of the slaves, whether natural or caused by their degraded state, contributed to the difficulty of passing an emancipation plan. Storing concluded: "The American founders and their immediate descendants North and South, not only believed in but emphasized the wrongness of slavery, at the same time that they wrestled with the fact of slavery and the enormous difficulty of getting rid of it. It was a fact; it seemed for the time being a necessity; but it was a curse—the curse of an unavoidable injustice."[16] If Virginia was making any progress toward emancipation before 1830, that sentiment evaporated after the Nat Turner insurrection. The debates that followed Turner in the House of Delegates and the rejection of emancipation reflected that evaporation.

Coincidentally Alexis de Tocqueville happened to be in America during the Virginia slave debates. He spent the better part of 1831-1832 in America conducting research for his book *Democracy in America*. The Virginia debates of 1831-1832 were of such importance, that he made special note of it.[17] According to Tocqueville, "the mere desire for the mastery over subjects (or slaves) debases master as well as subject, for when the master denies the humanity common to both, he loses his own and lets himself be ruled by his passions."[18] The effects of slavery are not necessarily readily seen. Slavery "enters the world furtively so that the abuses of power are not evident until it spreads and grows."[19]

In that slavery is bad for the slave, Tocqueville asserts that servitude makes his thoughts and his ambitions slavish. It encourages him to admire tyrants. In this way, it debases the slaves' intellect and reason. The lack of education prevalent in slave society—in terms of his reason and his soul—makes him susceptible to unreasonable ideas and less apt to be able to succeed and live well, should he gain his freedom. Without education, the slave could not appreciate moral principles, or judge the wrongness of a crime. He needed that education so that he might be able to live peaceably with his fellow men. Slavery is especially evil because it stealthily grows until it cannot be controlled. By then the mores of the populace regard the institution as normal and hardly want to let it die. The effect on society is fatal, for once men reject "nature and humanity" they will be given to the "excesses of tyranny."[20]

Tocqueville does not limit his observations to the harm slavery causes to the slave. He also considers what the institution does to the master. Slavery is bad for the master because the lifestyle "penetrates [his] very soul and impresses a particular direction on his ideas and tastes."[21] It emphasizes the master's passions over his reason and makes him an idle man. The master "scorns not only work, but all undertakings that work makes successful; living in idle ease, he has the tastes of idle men; money has lost a part of its worth in his eyes; he pursues fortune less than *agitation* and *pleasure*, and he applies in this direction the energy that his neighbor deploys elsewhere; he *passionately* loves hunting and war; he pleases himself with the most violent exercises of the body."[22] Slavery not only affects material prosperity, but it also has deleterious effects on the manners of the master. Tocqueville asserts that the effects of slavery on the character of the master leads to another consequence: the decline in material prosperity. The slaveholder and his family grow so accustomed to the lifestyle they develop into petty tyrants. The master becomes a passionate ruler, more attached to his own idleness, and his own rights, at the expense of others. What Tocqueville observed during his time in America, was therefore similar to what Jefferson wrote in Query XVIII of his *Notes* some fifty years earlier.[23]

The Frenchman's description of slavery in 1830s Virginia is quite striking in that it seems to lend evidence to the validity of Jefferson's claims in the *Notes*. Slavery's corrupting influences were already being seen in the 1830s. Constitutional protections confounded southern intellectuals who confused the slave compromises in the Constitution with constitutional principle itself. Their hostility to a shared humanity made it more difficult to build a society based on friendship in which our reason informs us that inflicting injury on another is against the law of nature. Certainly, there were compromises in the Founding, but the Union's Founding principles were opposed to slavery. Regarding the Founding, Jefferson, and the Declaration, John Quincy Adams wrote this in his memoirs:

Jefferson is one of the great men which this country has produced, one of the men who has contributed largely to the formation of our national character . . . his Declaration of Independence is an abridged Alcoran of political doctrine, laying open the first foundations of civil society . . . It also laid open a precipice into which the slave-holding planters of his country sooner or later must fall . . . Jefferson has been himself all his life a slave-holder, but he has published opinions . . . blasting the very existence of slavery . . . The seeds of the Declaration of Independence are yet maturing. The harvest will be what West, the painter, calls the terrible sublime.[24]

While Jefferson and the anti-slave conventioneers and Delegates in the Virginia House were opposed to slavery, they also understood that the choices in political life often require choosing the lesser of two evils. The lesser evil is preferred in the pursuit of some greater good. Therefore, for Jefferson, slavery could be temporarily tolerated in the Constitution because the Union was founded on principles hostile to slavery. Virginia's most prominent statesmen believed that it would eventually come to an end. The problem is that the slave interest was becoming increasingly hostile to those principles.

Southern intellectuals were progressively alienated from the "unrealistic" and "abstract" concepts of the Revolution—the natural rights that the Union and Virginia proclaimed every human possessed. The South, however, increasingly compared the invocation of natural rights to the French Revolution in terms of its bloody lawlessness. They abandoned rights for "tradition," "experience," "prescription," and institutions as more able to secure a peaceful politics.[25] The consequences of this thought are dramatic. Some scholars believe that the abandonment of human equality for historical rights ends in nihilism. Others see a link between the southern cause and Hitler.[26] The raciology of the pro-slave movement that culminated in Calhoun has some similarity to Hitler's Germany. This is not to say that Hegel is responsible for Hitler, or that Hegel *is* Hitler. As Carl Schmitt noted, when Hitler came to power Hegel's spirit departed for Moscow.[27] Still, Calhoun would not have entertained the ideas of collective and historical rights—and he defended the rights of the minority slave holder as well as the group rights of the South—if he had not come under the influence of Hegelian ideas. The abandonment of natural rights for an historical interpretation of politics had other consequences. Randolph reveled in the emotionalism of the romantics: "the necessity of *loving* and *being be-loved* was never felt by the imaginary beings of Rousseau and Byron's creation more imperiously than by myself."[28] This emotive view of his life and his longing for a past escaping modernity led him to a sort of estrangement and alienation toward the Union. This is why he was a vigorous defender of the more simpler, aristocratic, southern way of life.[29]

A transition took place in the South, rejecting enlightenment thought for sentimentality. Virginia in 1832 went from rationalism, or a belief in the power of reason, to a form of romanticism. John Randolph, while never claiming to be a "romantic" was quite taken with the romantic poets. He thought that Lord Byron was the best poet of his lifetime. The historicism of Hegel and Fichte had other effects. It caused many to identify with the Romantic Movement, which repudiated reason or rationalism because "the heart had its reasons which reason did not know."[30] In this way, the historical school, pro-slave interests, and paleocons have something in common: they believe in the ascendancy of sentiment over reason. Scholars have observed that there was a growth of romanticism in the 1830s. Southern intellectuals began to look to the past for political inspiration. While Dew is not necessarily representative of romantic thought, he did espouse elements of romanticism. In his 1836 address to the students, Dew said that statesmanship involved a "generous exercise of the feelings of the heart."[31] Dew's later connections to those who promoted the romantic elements of southern thought are quite extensive. Interestingly enough, the South's pro-slave intellectual defenders were not the largest slaveholders. Most of them were college professors (like Dew), or ministers, writers, and journalists. The ties among the pro-slave apologists were extensive and great and they found a receptive audience in the slaveholder.

Dew had personal interactions with Nathaniel Beverly Tucker, the son of St. George Tucker. Privately, St. George struggled with his sons over the role of natural rights and the role of reason in politics. His sons, Henry St. George and Beverly, eventually rejected natural rights because they believed that "speculative opinion" had no place in politics.[32] Beverly Tucker in turn had personal interactions with Calhoun, John Henry Hammond, Edmund Ruffin, George Fredrick Holmes, and other influential pro-slave apologists. Most of these people were either acquainted with one another directly or through mutual friends. These thinkers endeavored to create an authentic southern idea, and a body of knowledge, that would define a southern identity and support the region's institutions. The personal ties among the proslavery writers arose in large part because of the small size of the intellectual class. This intellectual relationship and the discussion that flowed from these interactions led to a particular promulgation of three modes of thought: historicism, romanticism, and the belief that science could solve the world's problems or provide new insights into complex issues of the day. We have spent much time considering the historical presence of Dew's political thought. Similar to Dew, almost all the apologists for slavery between 1832 and 1850 defended slavery on the grounds that it was a part of some divine purpose. As Holmes observed, "by examining the progressive revelation of God's designs in history, [it] would . . . provide the needed 'basis of our inductions about the proper social order.'"[33] This approach represented an attack on natural law and American Founding. Therefore, it should come as no surprise that Beverly Tucker would utter that slavery was "the basis of all our institutions."[34]

Dew exercised great influence over the likes of Beverly Tucker convincing many in the South of the inapplicability of abstractions. Building on Dew's attack of the Founding, these romantic southerners became "realists [who] appealed to the trustworthiness of man's senses, placed credence in 'facts' as opposed to the recondite, and assumed that 'first principles' found in all men made their good sense and intuition philosophically reliable."[35] This is how historicism and romanticism coincided. Reason was devalued in place of feelings and facts. Because reason cannot overcome instinct, the institutions that have arisen in time ought to be the guide; these institutions, which find their legitimacy in the State, are better protectors of society than abstract reasoning. The movement of the Tucker family from the head (reason) to the heart (romanticism) culminated in Beverly Tucker, who concluded that "non-rational qualities of emotion and impulse as genuine, as naturally good."[36]

As this development pertains to Hegel and Fichte, they had barely a kind word for the romantics. However, that is not to say that they did not have similar ideas about politics. The romantics emphasized not what was common to all men, but what was original in each human person. Each person has his own creative imagination and his own feelings and intuition. According to Frederick Copleston, like Hegel and Fichte, the romantics had a tendency "to depreciate fixed universal moral laws or rules in favour of the free development of the self in accordance with values rooted in and corresponding to the individual personality."[37] They emphasized the freedom of the individual to pursue his own morality rather than to habituate himself to some notion of a universal law dictated by their dispassionate reason. They believed in an instinctive morality rather than an enlightened morality. Yet, Hegel and Fichte have something else in common with the romantics—their concept of nature. Instead of viewing nature as a mechanical system, they viewed nature as part of an organic whole. Like the two Germans, romantics in general viewed nature as a spirit that is cloaked in mystery. This is not altogether different from the historicist understanding of the spirit of the age. While some romantics found in nature a form of divination, they agreed that nature and the historical influences of the world were gradually unfolding. Human history interacts with nature and our personality finds its utmost potential in nature. However, they tended to view nature a bit differently than their historicist counterparts in that they longed for a simpler time. This is why the romantics idealized certain epochs or ages like classical Rome and Greece and why they found agreement with the historicist idea of the spirit of a people or *volkgeist*. They found in the simple spirit of the people a sense of the infinite spirit of nature.

Looking for an ever certain basis to build political science, or a southern nation, Calhoun asserted that his political system of concurrent majorities was founded on the same principles as "astronomy."[38] Alexander Stephens similarly placed his political science on a scientific foundation. In his "cornerstone speech" he claimed that the foundation of the Union was based on Jefferson's understanding of equality: "the prevailing ideas entertained by him and most of the *leading statesmen at the time* of the formation of the old constitution, were that the enslavement of the African was in violation of the laws of nature; that it was wrong in *principle*, socially, morally, politically."[39] Stephens continued to claim that the Founders believed at the time of the Founding that the slaves were meant to be free. Slavery was an evil that they did not know how to abolish, but they expected it to somehow come to an end. However, according to Stephens, the Founders were incorrect: "Those ideas, however, were fundamentally wrong.

They rested upon the assumption of the equality of the races . . . Our new
government is founded upon exactly the opposite idea; its foundations are laid,
its corner-stone rests upon the great truth, that the negro is not equal to the white
man; that slavery—subordination to the superior race—is this natural and
normal condition."[40] Why would Stephens contend that the slave was in his
natural position? Because science demonstrated the Declaration of Independence
was wrong; science had confirmed the inequality of the races. Like a scientist,
Calhoun and his supporters view politics in an empirical fashion. Wisdom came
from experience not speculation. As it pertains to politics, the scientific
foundation to politics left little room for prudence, or practical wisdom. History,
or Providence, had conspired with science to reveal the truth of the world, which
was that the slaves deserved their enslavement.[41] Dew's influence on the
intellectuals of his day convinced scholars that Virginia "produced the most
articulate and most widely read defenders of slavery in antebellum America."[42]
The professor not only made an impact on those inside Old Dominion, but he
made an impression on those outside the state. Therefore, Dew is important in a
larger context because his thought reached beyond Virginia's borders.

Virginia Slavery, the Slave Debates, and the Civil War

The Virginia debates and Dew's ensuing *Review* are of interest because recent
scholarship has downplayed the importance of the slavery issue both leading up
to the Civil War, and as a predominant cause of the war itself. Proponents of this
view run the scale from partisan rhetoricians to serious academicians. A
scholarly treatment of this line of thought is noted in *The Myth of the Lost Cause
and Civil War History* by Gary W. Gallagher and Alan T. Nolan. Arguments on
behalf of the confederacy were advanced, in many ways successfully, by
partisans after the war in what the authors label the "lost cause" thesis: "slavery
was trivialized as a cause of the war in favor of such things as tariff disputes,
control of investment banking and the means of wealth, cultural differences, and
conflict between industrial and agricultural societies. In all events, the South had
not seceded to protect slavery."[43] Soon after the war, Jefferson Davis asserted
that slavery had nothing to do with the conflict. Yet, as noted above, in 1861
Confederate Vice-president Alexander Stephens said that slavery was the
"corner-stone" of the confederate government. After the war he contended it
"was not a contest between the advocates or opponents of that peculiar
institution."[44] We can see that the "lost cause" thesis nascently percolated from
the progenitors of the confederacy.

    Some demote the importance of slavery by asserting that the peculiar
institution would have withered away because there were "natural limits" to
slavery expansion. One of the typical revisionists proffering this argument is
Charles Ramsdell. In "The Natural Limits of Slavery Expansion," which
appeared in *The Mississippi Valley Historical Review* in 1929, he stated that
there was a geographic limit with which cotton, and other farming staples, could
be profitable under slavery.[45] By 1860, the land with which to cultivate crops

declined as did the profits of the plantation owner. Therefore, slavery was destined to collapse.[46]

Jeffrey Rogers Hummel weaves historical narrative and economic statistics to offer a variation on the "lost cause" hypothesis. In *Emancipating Slaves, Enslaving Free Men*, Hummel rejects the claim that slavery was the root cause of the Civil War. He concedes that slavery explains why Southerners wanted to secede, but it does not explain why the North did not allow them.[47] According to the author, allowing the South to secede was a viable option to ending slavery. However, according to Hummel the North did not let them go because they wanted to preserve the Union. The North fought to build a federal hegemony, not end slavery. However, the author interestingly contends that the confederacy ultimately failed, not because of "natural limits," but because the war confederacy organized as a socialist state. Economic data suggests that up to the Civil War slavery was thriving and not destined to fail. However, he notes that the confederacy's central planning caused economic stress which had devastating effects on the South's war effort. The burden of a welfare state— which is what slavery most resembled—would have had a significant impact on the South eventually.

As it pertains to the 1831-1832 Virginia legislative session, Hummel notes that it was the last official body in a slave state to debate gradual and compensated emancipation. For all the discussion of the unjust seizure of slave property without compensation in Virginia between 1829-1832, when there was serious discussion of accomplishing just that, the pro-slave South balked. Before the Civil War compensated emancipation was a rejected alternative. Even Dew expressed hostility to that kind of emancipation, believing it was a corrupting scheme. Calhoun agreed: "It is to us a vital question . . . The relation which exists between the two races in the slaveholding States has existed for two centuries. It has grown with our growth, and strengthened with our strength. It has entered into and modified all our institutions, civil and political. None other can be substituted. We will not, cannot permit it to be destroyed."[48]

Because of the growing importance of slavery, the South effectively eliminated compensated emancipation as a viable option by the end of 1832. Virginia played an important role rejecting that practical end to the peculiar institution. The pro-slave faction killed compensation before the growth of the anti-slavery societies and well before the militant anti-slavery position proliferated. Some contend that compensated emancipation was not seriously debated before the Civil War, but the House of Delegates spent considerable time deliberating precisely the issue of compensated emancipation. Providing the slaveholders with some form of monetary compensation was also part of Thomas Jefferson's *post nati* proposal in Query XIV of his *Notes*.[49] Virginians in 1831-1832 debated the merits of Jefferson's emancipation scheme at length. Furthermore, compensated emancipation was discussed several times to no avail in the South, not just Virginia. Each time, proposals advancing gradual emancipation were unsuccessful.[50] According to historian Betty Fladeland, "it seems clear that down through the years the proslavery adherents viewed the idea of compensated emancipation as a radical rather than as a moderate or reasonable solution to the slavery problem and that they were prepared to resist any plan based on it."[51]

Other scholars argue that the Founders, as well as Lincoln, were not serious about the eradication of slavery and/or believed that the Declaration of Independence applied only to white men because, generally, their actions contradicted the principles stated in the document.[52] The most compelling piece of evidence for this assertion is that the Founders did not ban slavery outright when framing the Constitution. Because they did not ban slavery, they must have meant that equality only applied to white men. The Virginia debates challenge that opinion. Not only did the anti-slave supporters make a case for equality based on the Declaration of Independence—that slavery was wrong. The Virginia experience between 1829-1832 also contests the theory that slavery was a secondary war issue because pro-slave advocates alluded to a coming war over slavery. The pro-slave side of the debates raised the concept of disunion thirty years before the Civil War.

The fact that pro-slave Virginians veered toward a positive defense of slavery raises the possibility that self-interest overcame principle. Thomas G. West noted this contention in *Vindicating the Founders*. According to West, "there will always be a gap between moral principles and actions."[53] West points out that it is easy to confuse principles with interest:

> Selfish interest sometimes led men to misunderstand their own principles. In 1785 six Virginia counties petitioned the state legislature, objecting to any emancipation of slaves "on the ground that the Revolution had been fought to preserve liberty and property." These Virginians, and other slaveholders who shared their view, forgot that the right to property flows from—is part of—the natural right to liberty. If there is no natural right to liberty, there can be no natural right to property. If men are rightfully free, they all may keep the bread they earn with their own hands. Therefore, there can be no right to property *in slaves*.[54]

Abraham Lincoln also articulated the gap between principle and interest. During the "house divided" speech, he argued that only one side in the debate would win. The house was divided because self-interest clouded reason. In his second inaugural address, Lincoln stated that slavery "constituted a peculiar and powerful interest. All knew that this interest was, somehow, the cause of the war."[55] According to Lincoln, there was no way to keep together liberty and slavery. Those who wanted slavery had to develop a new philosophy to justify holding men in bondage.

Economic scholarship seems to confirm the arguments forwarded by Lincoln and West. Robert W. Fogel and Stanley L. Engerman provide evidence that slavery was expanding and was in no danger of disappearing. They challenged the Ramsdell thesis by finding that slavery was thriving up to the Civil War. In *Time on the Cross*, the authors argue that slaveholders acted in their "best economic interests."[56] Slavery was a profitable investment. Fogel and

Engerman find no evidence that the institution of slavery was on the verge of collapsing, or that the institution was only suited to farming. Rather, they demonstrate that slavery could profitably adapt to the industrial system. Finally, the authors unearth data suggesting that the slave system was highly efficient. Compared to farming in the North, and controlling for a number of factors like soil conditions, size of farms, etc., they contend that slave agriculture was 35 percent more efficient. Therefore, extending slavery westward was a lucrative investment, especially given the increased demand for cotton.

Cotton production increased from under 800,000 bales in 1830 to over 4,000,000 by 1860 with no signs of slowing. Cotton farming expanded into other states to meet that demand and slavery expanded westward with it.[57] Per capita income was also on the rise in the South during the antebellum period. Far from a poverty stricken region, the South stood as the "fourth richest nation in the world in 1860. The South was richer than France, richer than Germany, richer than Denmark, richer than any of the countries in Europe except England."[58] Therefore, the South exhibited personal economic interests in not only sustaining the peculiar institution, but expanding it.

The 1829-1832 period of Old Dominion's history has been neglected over the years. While we might examine larger trends in the history of the United States, it seems that Virginia's specific political contribution to those trends has been somewhat forgotten, or overlooked.[59] Nevertheless, there are some worthy studies of the era. Historians generally fall into three categories regarding the significance of the Virginia slavery debates and the review of those debates by professor Dew. Generally, historians agree on the importance of the debates but disagree on what the debates symbolize in the larger historical context. Some argue that in the late 1820s through early 1830s Virginia, the "positive good" thesis took its initial shape. The Virginia debates were thus a defining moment in history. Some scholars go further and hold that Virginia, and the South in general, was consumed with the defense of the peculiar institution. Others contend that a definitive "positive good" argument did not occur until much later after the debates—for example when Calhoun declared on the Senate floor in 1837 that slavery was a "positive good." Those who argue that the 1829-1832 period did not represent an ideological affirmation of the "positive good" thesis generally place greater emphasis on economic arguments, or geographical factors, which divided the state. Finally, there are those who contend that the "positive good" argument was always present in American history and was hence plainly evident at the time of the Founding. Forebears of this argument assert that Calhoun's pro-slave position was a commonly held opinion in 1776. While certainly there were people who held that slavery was a "positive good," historians in this camp have failed to make a distinction between privately held opinion of a few and the publicly spoken opinion of politicians who represent many.[60] Indeed, it was John Randolph who came to the constitutional convention with the opinion that the notion "all men are created equal" was a "pernicious falsehood."[61] In such instances the significance of such publicly held opinions—the very real rejection of the natural rights proclaimed in the

Declaration—are overlooked. The ideological departure of the pro-slave faction from the Founding could lead one to conclude erroneously that the Virginians at this time did not further the "positive good" thesis. Of the several histories written about the Virginia Constitutional Convention of 1829-1830 and the slavery debates of 1831-1832, with a few exceptions, most of these accounts are included in larger historical works. Of these larger works, much of the material concerning this topic is limited to a chapter. However, of all the literature written on this subject, none has approached those debates, and the ensuing review of those debates, from the standpoint of political philosophy. Historians have noted certain speeches and other public documents pertaining to the debates, but they have not spent the necessary time examining these documents closely. One historian acknowledged this gap:

> We need more research into topics that appear to offer new and useful insights into previously neglected subjects . . . Drew Gilpin Faust's collective study of southern conservatives contains extended treatments of the role that Thomas R. Dew, initially of the College of William and Mary, played in defining what became the Virginia contribution to the emerging southern pro-slavery argument, but we still await a full study of Dew.[62]

If anything, this book has been an attempt to try to consider Dew in light of his ideas. Other than a few doctoral dissertations with interest in Old Dominion between 1829-1832, there has not been a major published work on the topic in over twenty years and the majority of published works are over forty years old. Only one history, published in 1930, was dedicated to mapping out the similarities between the Virginia Constitutional Convention of 1829-1830 and the Virginia slavery debates of 1831-1832. A full biography on Dew is still needed. However, this work has endeavored to fill an important gap: examine Dew's connection to German political thought.

Conclusion

This book has attempted to revive interest in an important event in American history. It has attempted to build upon prior historical works by seeking to undertake something that has not been accomplished to date—write a work that is more concerned with the *ideas* than the historical events of slavery in 1829-1832 Virginia. Though there have been some works noting the importance of the debates in Virginia and the ensuing *Review* by Dew, none have engaged in an analysis of the entirety of the debates which spanned this four year period. Joseph Clarke Robert declared that the debates were the "final and most brilliant of the Southern attempts to abolish slavery" and it "represents the line of demarcation between a public willing to hear the faults of slavery and one intolerant of criticism."[63] The debates spurred pro-slavery conservatives to defend the peculiar institution. That argument was best articulated by Dew's widely circulated review of the debates which "for a third of a century . . . was the manual of Virginia conservatism."[64]

The purpose of this book was to elucidate the moral controversy over slavery between the Founding and the Civil War, focusing in particular on the Virginia slavery debates that occurred between 1829 and 1832. It examined the historical events that led up to the debates as well as the ideological development of one of the earliest public articulations of the "positive good" thesis. Here is a recap of the four questions this book sought to address and answer: (1) What was the importance of the slavery issue in the United States at about the midway point between the Founding and Civil War? (2) How did the participants in Virginia slavery debates understand the principles of the Founding and how did they seek to apply those principles practically? (3) How should we understand the principles of the Declaration in light of the arguments raised during the debates? (4) How did the advance of the "positive good" thesis change the understanding of the Founding?

Essentially, concerning the first question, we have demonstrated that slavery was an important, if not consuming, interest in Virginia at roughly the halfway point, between the Declaration and the Civil War. Second, the problems of slavery led many of Old Dominion's statesmen to try to find some way to rid the peculiar institution from her soil. More importantly, their dedication to the idea that "all men are created equal" or "all men are by nature equally free and independent" guided them. Many concluded that Virginia's most prominent fathers like Jefferson, Tucker, Madison, Wythe, and Mason were correct that slavery should be abolished gradually. Third, this in turn led them to understand both Declarations as applying to all men, not a certain few. Slavery was not just and it was unnatural for Negroes to be held in bondage. Finally, the rejection of those principles starting with the Virginia Constitutional Convention of 1829-1830, and continuing with the House of Delegates debates of 1831-1832, prepared the ground for an intellectual defense of the institution by Dew in 1832. Dew more than any other Virginian, is responsible for the promotion of the idea of perpetual slavery. While in the eighteenth century human equality was widely held to be true, by the close of 1832, there were many public voices either claiming it was not true, or that its truth did not apply to Negroes.[65]

The 1829-1832 slave debates in Virginia are significant because of the influence the state had on the rest of the country. For a state where four of the first five presidents were from Virginia, the political weight of the state is undeniable. Even in the 1830s it was one of the most important and influential states in the Union. The political direction of Old Dominion was a bellwether for the Union. Virginians had an opportunity to reaffirm the principles of liberty, but ultimately that argument lost. The forces of self-interest defeated those who articulated the principles expressed in the Declaration of Independence. Virginians debated the slave issue essentially for four years. By the end of 1832, it was clear that the state had abandoned her revolutionary heritage; slavery was no longer a "great and foul stain" on the Union and Dew represented that broad shift in public opinion.[66]

We have tried to persuade the reader that every leading Founder believed, or "acknowledged," that slavery was wrong.[67] The Founding was incomplete because slavery was allowed to continue. The Constitution, and the Virginia Constitution, was inconsistent with the principles of the Declaration of Independence and the Virginia Declaration of Rights respectively. According to historian Edmund Morgan, it is "tempting to dismiss Jefferson and the whole Virginia dynasty as hypocrites. But to do so is to deprive the term 'hypocrisy' of useful meaning. If hypocrisy means, as I think it does, deliberately to affirm a principle without believing it, then hypocrisy requires a rare clarity of mind combined with an unscrupulous intention to deceive."[68] Hypocrisy, understood correctly, is not a quality Jefferson or any of his anti-slave contemporaries in Virginia seemed to share. Modern scholars have difficulty when studying Jefferson because they cannot separate themselves from the imprint of historicism. They attempt to understand the past better than those in the past understood themselves. They think they understand Jefferson better than he understood himself and reject approaching the Sage as he understood himself. They condemn Jefferson, and the other Founders, because they were representative of a more unenlightened time and place. As a result, they misunderstand Jefferson and construe his opinions as racist. However, Jefferson never asserted privately or publicly that blacks deserved their enslavement; nobody was naturally meant to serve a master. Unlike Dew, the Founders never thought that providence sanctioned slavery. To the contrary, both Jefferson and Mason believed that God would be on the side of the slave, not the master. Mason in particular thought that God would punish national sins with calamity. Whether he would have believed that such an event as the Turner insurrection was just such a calamity is difficult to determine. However, the Founders' opinion of the injustice of the peculiar institution is difficult to mistake.

Scholars who claim the Founders were hypocrites make that charge because they do not understand that justice is eternal, but the way in which justice is implemented depends on circumstances. Political choices of the statesman are thus changed or altered in consideration of that end. Jefferson at first tried to abolish slavery in the territories and then tried to articulate a way for slavery's eradication. He and Madison may be criticized for their diffusionist argument, but the end they had in mind was the emancipation of the slaves. Though Jefferson and the rest of Virginia's most prominent statesmen never accomplished their goal, we cannot fault Jefferson for the articulation of such a goal. His caution later in life does not necessarily convict him of hypocrisy. A recent article by Sean Wilentz responded to critics of Jefferson's public silence on the issue of slavery while he was President: "in part, his silence was politically expedient. Not only would attacks on slavery endanger both his party and the Union; but he had learned from hard personal experience in his younger days that anti-slavery sentiments could be politically disastrous in Virginia."[69] Jefferson surmised that his public pronouncement on the subject would actually cause a regression in the progress of emancipation. Therefore, he had to work stealthily concerning the subject. Nevertheless, his public record was known and he never repudiated it. Yet to agitate the issue would have detrimental effects on the progress of abolition. The same criticisms exist concerning the Founders and their position on colonization. However, it is not like the issue was far from the mind of the Founders. It seemed to be at the forefront of their mind. For instance, in 1832 Harriet Martineau visited the Madison home and observed of the former President:

> He talked more on the subject of slavery than on any other, acknowledging, without limitation or hesitation, all the evils with which it has ever been charged. He told me the black population increases far faster than the white; and that the licentiousness only stops short of the destruction of the race; every slave girl being expected to be a mother by the time she is fifteen. He assumed from this, I cannot make out why, that the negroes must go somewhere, and pointed out how the free states discourage the settlement of blacks; how Canada disagrees with them; how Hayti shuts them out; so that Africa is their only refuge. He did not assign any reason they should not remain where they are when freed . . . . He had parted with some of his best land to feed the increasing numbers, and yet been obliged to sell a dozen of his slaves the preceding week. He observed the whole Bible is against negro slavery; but the clergy do not preach this, and the people do not see it . . . He accounted for his selling his slaves by mentioning their horror of going to Liberia, which he admitted to be prevalent among the blacks, and which appears to me decisive as to the unnaturalness of the scheme.[70]

The truly complicated results of abolition are evident in this account. Madison's lament was evident. He emerged from the Virginia Constitutional Convention a disillusioned man in part because slavery was burrowing itself in society ever more solidly.[71] While we might criticize Jefferson, Madison, and other Founders for falling short of their political goal, or living up to their own political ideals— even to the point of not freeing their own slaves—we have much to be thankful for that a nation of slaveholders articulated a principle against their own personal interest, that "all men are created equal."

If it were not for the Sage, the anti-slave promoters would not have had ample material from which to draw. Thanks to the Founders' public and private (many of which were eventually made public) opinions on the nature of slavery, the generation on the side of equality could, and did, appeal to the Revolutionary generation when the opportunity arose. Following Jefferson, the anti-slave advocates in 1829-1832 Virginia asserted that there was no human being naturally superior to another. In that sense, they remained dedicated to the idea that "all men are created equal." However, this argument ultimately lost. The public arguments on behalf of slavery were a far cry from the public and private writings of Virginia's most important statesmen. Though there have been many criticisms of the Founders as to their failure to secure the abolition of slavery, those critics never ask whether what the Founders wrote and spoke was true. In order to pursue a serious study of the Founders we must be open to the possibility that they believed in equality and that it applied to all men.

The debates demonstrate the very real quandary over slavery. The aftermath of the debates did not bode well for public discussion of the issue. Concerning the press, the 1831-1832 debates represented one of the greatest moments of freedom of the press in the South. However, since both the *Whig* and the *Enquirer* were supportive of emancipation, many eastern Virginians held public meetings to condemn the papers for their open support of gradual emancipation. They believed that the press could stir the slaves to revolt if they printed anything concerning emancipation. Thomas Ritchie, of the *Enquirer*, especially faced some pressure to quit agitating in favor of the issue. Both the *Whig* and *Enquirer* received many letters condemning them for publishing arguments, or taking editorial stances, that favored abolition. The papers' appeal to freedom of the press was unpersuasive. The effect was that the papers eventually grew silent on the question of slavery. Even Tocqueville noted that preserving a free press in the South was difficult, in part because of the great fear of another insurrection. During the later part of the ante-bellum period, even college professors, and presidents of collegiate institutions, could not express sympathy for the antislavery movement because they feared losing their jobs. From 1835 to 1861, the South generally pursued a policy of silence in regard to emancipation.[72] The slave debate thus had a chilling effect on the deliberation of slavery's eradication. Eighteenth century political thought thus went from an appeal to reason to one where criticism of anything hostile to traditional southern institutions was suppressed.

There was one exception to the pressure felt by the press in the Tidewater and Piedmont region. Alexander Campbell, who was such a force on behalf of natural rights in the Constitutional Convention, retired from political life to pursue a career as a preacher. Toward that calling, he founded a religious publication called the *Millennial Harbinger*. From 1830 until 1850, he wrote about slavery and defended his position on emancipation. He became an ardent defender of colonization and urged his readers to petition Congress to make it a national affair in order to more quickly "extirpat[e] the evil."[73] Nevertheless, Virginians ended up departing ideologically from the Declaration of Independence, and the Virginia Declaration of Rights.

Abraham Lincoln understood the reason for this departure. He wrote to Henry Pierce in 1859 and explained this devolution:

> Bearing in mind that about seventy years ago, two great political parties were first formed in this country, that Thomas Jefferson was the head of one of them, and Boston the head-quarters of the other, it is both curious and interesting that those supposed to descend politically from the party opposed to Jefferson should now be celebrating his birthday in their own original seat of empire, while those claiming political descent from him have nearly ceased to breathe his name everywhere.
> Remembering too, that the Jefferson party were formed upon its supposed superior devotion to the personal rights of men, holding the rights of property to be secondary only, and greatly inferior, and then assuming that the so-called democracy of today, are the Jefferson, and their opponents, the anti-Jefferson parties, it will be equally interesting to note how completely the two have changed hands as to the principle upon which they were originally supposed to be divided.
> The democracy of today holds the liberty of one man to be absolutely

nothing, when in conflict with another man's right of property. Republicans, on the contrary, are for both the man and the dollar; but in cases of conflict, the man before the dollar.

It is worthy of note that Lincoln understood the connection between the opinion that mankind had no inherent nature and the possession of men as property. He, like the anti-slave reformers in the debates, put the nature of man above all other considerations; man ought not be degraded to a state of slavery. Lincoln continued in the same letter to note how natural rights had come under intense scorn and ridicule:

> One would start with great confidence that he could convince any sane child that the simpler propositions of Euclid are true; but, nevertheless, he would fail, utterly, with one who should deny the definitions and axioms. The principles of Jefferson are the definitions and axioms of free society.
> And yet they are denied and evaded, with no small show of success.
> One dashingly calls them "glittering generalities"; another bluntly calls them "self evident lies"; and still others insidiously argue that they apply only to "superior races."
> These expressions, differing in form, are identical in object and effect—the supplanting the principles of free government, and restoring those of classification, caste, and legitimacy. They would delight a convocation of crowned heads, plotting against the people. They are the vanguard—the miners, and sappers—of returning despotism.
> We must repulse them, or they will subjugate us.
> This is a world of compensations; and he who would be no slave, must consent to have no slave. Those who deny freedom to others, deserve it not for themselves; and, under a just God, can not long retain it.
> All honor to Jefferson—to the man who, in the concrete pressure of a struggle for national independence by a single people, had the coolness, forecast, and capacity to introduce into a merely revolutionary document, an abstract truth, applicable to all men and all times, and so to embalm it there, that today, and in all coming days, it shall be a rebuke and a stumbling-block to the very harbingers of re-appearing tyranny and oppression.[74]

By Lincoln's time, many of the arguments championed by the Virginia pro-slave faction were commonplace. To Jefferson belongs much honor because he was among the first to prohibit slavery in the territories. Yet, it was Lincoln who would finally embody the ideal of the Declaration of Independence and the Virginia Declaration of Rights. Lincoln articulated that Jefferson and the Founders built a nation that was a bulwark of liberty and freedom against tyranny and despotic government. We might claim that Lincoln represented the completed Jefferson righting the American ship on the unchanging ground of liberty which rests on the truth "all men are created equal."

Notes

1. "Virginia Legislature," *Richmond Enquirer*, 7 January 1832, p. 2; Abraham

Lincoln, "On Slavery and Democracy," 1 August 1858, *Abraham Lincoln: Speeches and Writings, 1832-1858*, ed. Don E. Fehrenbacher (New York: Library of America, 1989), 484; Harry V. Jaffa, *How to Think about the Revolution* (Durham: Carolina Academic Press, 1978), 65. All italics in the original.

2. Stephen Mansfield, "Thomas Roderick Dew: Defender of the Southern Faith" (Ph.D. diss., University of Virginia, 1968), 60.

3. Ibid., 61.

4. John Quincy Adams, Diary, 2 March 1820, *The Diary of John Quincy Adams: 1794-1845*, ed. Allan Nevins (New York: Charles Scribner's Sons, 1951), 232.

5. Joseph Clarke Robert, *The Road from Monticello: A Study of the Virginia Slavery Debate of 1832* (Durham: Duke University Press, 1941), 48.

6. Carl L. Becker, *The Declaration of Independence: A Study in the History of Political Ideas* (New York: Vintage Books, 1942), 247. Concerning the counter review see, Jesse Burton Harrison, *Review of the Slave Question* (Richmond, Va.: T.W. White, 1833).

7. Ibid., 276.

8. Leo Strauss, *Natural Right and History* (Chicago: University of Chicago Press, 1965), 19, and 9-17.

9. Lowell Harrison, "Thomas Roderick Dew: Philosopher of the Old South," *Virginia Magazine of History and Biography* 57, no. 4 (October 1949) : 392, and 404; Anthony Alfred Iaccarino, "Virginia and the National Contest over Slavery in the Early Republic, 1780-1833" (Ph.D. diss., University of California, Los Angeles, 1999), 213; Eugene Genovese, *"Slavery Ordained of God": The Southern Slaveholders' View of Biblical History and Modern Politics* (Gettysburg: Gettysburg College, 1985), 7.

10. Robert J. Brugger, *Beverly Tucker: Heart Over Head in the Old South* (Baltimore: Johns Hopkins University Press, 1978), 106; Kermit L. Hall and James W. Ely, Jr., eds., *An Uncertain Tradition: Constitutionalism and the History of the South* (Athens: The University of Georgia Press, 1989), 165; W.G. Bean, "Anti-Jeffersonianism in the Ante-Bellum South," *The North Carolina Historical Review* 12 (April 1935) : 110.

11. Clement Eaton, *Freedom of Thought in the Old South* (Durham: Duke University Press, 1940), 27-28. Cooper was part of a small band of intellectuals who corresponded with either Dew or his friends. Therefore, he was associated with many of the rising generation of pro-slave voices in Virginia.

12. Russell Kirk, *John Randolph of Roanoke* (Indianapolis: Liberty Press, 1978), 218-219. Kirk believes that Randolph influenced Calhoun more than anyone else. In this book, Kirk features prominently Randolph's speeches and political actions during the Constitutional Convention of 1829-30. On the influence Calhoun has had on modern political science, see Harry V. Jaffa, *A New Birth of Freedom* (Lanham, Md.: Rowman and Littlefield, 200), 429.

13. All quotes from Calhoun taken from Richard K. Crallé, ed., "Speech on the Reception of Abolition Petitions, delivered in the Senate, February 6, 1837," *The Works of John C. Calhoun*, vol. 2 (New York: D. Appleton and Company, 1855), 629-630; see also Calhoun's denunciation of the Declaration of Independence as a "delusion" in Bean, 103; On Kirk's positive view of Calhoun and Randolph see Russell Kirk, *The Conservative Mind: From Burke to Eliot* (Chicago: Regnery Books, 1986), 152, 154-155; On Kirk and Calhoun see Harry V. Jaffa, "The False Prophets of American Conservatism" (Paper delivered at the Claremont Institute's Lincoln Day Conference, Washington, D.C., February 12, 1998), 18-20; Jaffa, "The Decline and Fall of the American Idea: Reflections on the Failure of American Conservatism" (Paper presented for the 25th Anniversary Symposium of the Henry Salvatori Center for the Study of

Individual Freedom, Claremont, Ca., April 18-20, 1996), 23.

14. John Quincy Adams, *The Diary of John Quincy Adams*, 231-232.

15. Herbert J. Storing, *Toward a More Perfect Union: Writings of Herbert J. Storing*, ed., Joseph M. Bessette (Washington, D.C.: AEI Press, 1995), 146; Jaffa, *How to Think about the American Revolution*, 65.

16. Bessette, ed., 137.

17. Alexis de Tocqueville, *Democracy in America*, trans. Harvey C. Mansfield and Delba Winthrop (Chicago: University of Chicago Press, 2000), 334.

18. Ibid., xxiv.

19. Ibid., 326.

20. Ibid.; Theodore M. Whitfield, *Slavery Agitation in Virginia, 1829-1832* (New York: Negro University Press, 1930), 76-77.

21. Tocqueville, 333.

22. Ibid., 333. Emphasis added.

23. Jefferson, *Notes on the State of Virginia, The Portable Thomas Jefferson*, ed. Merrill D. Peterson (New York: Penguin, 1875), 214-215; Tocqueville, 346-348: Like Jefferson, Tocqueville thought that a race war was very possible as well; George Mason, "Speech before the Federal Convention," 22 August 1787, *The Records of the Federal Convention of 1787*, vol. 2, ed., Max Farrand, (New Haven: Yale University Press, 1966), 370; Robert E. Shalhope, "Thomas Jefferson's Republicanism and Antebellum Southern Thought," *The Journal of Southern History* 42 (November 1976) : 539.

24. From Adams' Memoirs, 27 December 1819, quoted in Gary Wood, *Heir to the Fathers: John Quincy Adams and the Spirit of Constitutional Government* (Lanham, Md.: Lexington, 2004), 51.

25. Theodore Dwight Bozeman, "Joseph LeConte: Organic Science and a 'Sociology for the South,'" *The Journal of Southern History* 39, no. 4 (November 1973) : 565.

26. Edward J. Erler, "Philosophy, History, and Jaffa's Universe," *Interpretation* 28, no. 3 (Spring 2001) : 245 and 253; Jaffa, *A New Birth of Freedom*, 73; Jaffa, "The False Prophets of American Conservatism," 14-15; Thomas G. West, "Jaffa's Lincolnian Defense of the Founding," *Interpretation* 28, no. 3 (Spring 2001) : 286, argues that "the historicism of which Becker is a gentlemanly academic representative was also the basis of the Marxist Soviet Union and Hitler's Germany." Eugene Genovese, *The Southern Tradition* (Cambridge, Mass.: Harvard University Press, 1994), xi, and 124-125, asserts that the South has been wrongly accused of such connections: as a whole the South is not responsible for racism and white supremacy because many of those characteristics have existed in other democracies.

27. Carl Schmitt, *The Concept of the Political* (Chicago: University of Chicago Press, 1996), 63.

28. Quoted in Robert Dawidoff, *The Education of John Randolph* (New York: W.W. Norton and Company, 1979), 265.

29. Ibid., 292.

30. Jaffa, *A New Birth of Freedom*, 329; West, "Jaffa's Lincolnian Defense of the Founding," 288; Steve Sorenson, "My Country, 'Tis of Thee: Jaffa's Defense of the Noble, the Holy, and the Just," *Interpretation* 28, no. 3 (Spring 2001) : 270-271; Vernon Louis Parrington, *The Romantic Revolution in America, 1800-1860* (Norman: University of Oklahoma Press, 1927), xv, asserts that no other ideal shaped early America more than romanticism.

31. Quoted in Brugger, 133.

32. Hamilton, 550.

33. Drew Gilpin Faust, "A Southern Stewardship," *American Quarterly* 31 (Spring 1979) : 71-72. In another work, Faust noted that those like Tucker and Dew wanted to create a "sacred circle" where their single most important effort was the perpetuation of slavery, see Faust, *A Sacred Circle: The Dilemma of the Intellectual in the Old South* (Baltimore: Johns Hopkins University Press, 1977). Cf. John McCardell, *The Idea of a Southern Nation* (New York: W.W. Norton and Company, 1979), 7, who emphasizes the same theme.

34. Quoted in Faust, "A Southern Stewardship: The Intellectual and the Proslavery Argument," 74.

35. Brugger, 17-18.

36. Ibid., 41; Eaton, 48, argues that the romantic impulse came into vogue in part because the masters were idle and this allowed them to pursue matters of the heart over the head. Because they were free from drudgery, the sons of the planters indulged their romantic fancies.

37. Frederick Copleston, *A History of Philosophy: Modern Philosophy*, vol. 7 (New York: Doubleday, 1963), 14. Ironically enough, Copleston asserts that Fichte influenced the romantics in his early years. Similarly, Strauss noted the connection between romanticism (Rousseau) and German idealism in his "Three Waves of Modernity." See in particular, Strauss, *An Introduction to Political Philosophy: Ten Essays by Leo Strauss*, ed. Hillail Gildin (Detroit: Wayne State University Press, 1989), 91-93.

38. Ross M. Lence, ed., *Union and Liberty: The Political Philosophy of John C. Calhoun* (Indianapolis: Liberty Fund, 1992), 5.

39. Alexander H. Stephens, *Alexander H. Stephens in Public and Private with Letters and Speeches, Before, During, and Since the War*, ed. Henry Cleveland (Philadelphia: National Publishing Company, 1866), 721. Some emphasis added: The word principle in the original italics.

40. Ibid.

41. For an extended discussion of these ideas, see Jaffa, *A New Birth of Freedom*, 92-93, 222-224, 429, 431, and 440-441; Brugger, 108; Sorenson, "My Country, 'Tis of Thee: Jaffa's Defense of the Noble, the Holy, and the Just," 271.

42. Shade, 205.

43. Gary Gallagher and Alan T. Nolan, eds., *The Myth of the Lost Cause and Civil War History* (Bloomington: Indiana University Press, 2000), 15. For a partisan example see Thomas DiLorenzo, *The Real Lincoln* (New York: Prima Publishing, 2002), ix, 2-3, 56; and Charles Adams, *When in the Course of Human Events: Arguing the Case for Southern Secession* (New York: Rowman and Littlefield, 2000). The relationship between the tariff and slavery is complex. Jaffa suggests that the South worried that the federal surplus from the tariff could be used to finance a compensated emancipation scheme—one which Jefferson, Madison and Monroe had all endorsed, see *How to Think About the American Revolution*, 69.

44. Stephens, 721; Gallagher and Nolan, 15.

45. Charles Ramsdell, "The Natural Limits of Slavery," *The Mississippi Valley Historical Review* 16 (September 1929): 155.

46. Ibid., 171. The Ramsdell thesis, though dated, remains popular. Harry V. Jaffa noted his influence in *Crisis of the House Divided* (Chicago: University of Chicago Press, 1982), 387-399.

47. Jeffrey Rogers Hummel, *Emancipating Slaves, Enslaving Free Men* (Chicago: Open Court, 1996) 3 and 8.

48. Quoted in Betty L. Fladeland, "Compensated Emancipation: A Rejected Alternative," *The Journal of Southern History* 42 (May 1976): 186. See also, ibid., 179-

180; Hummel, 22.

49. Thomas Jefferson, *Notes on the State of Virginia* in *The Portable Thomas Jefferson*, 185-186; "A Bill Concerning Slaves," *The Papers of Thomas Jefferson*, ed. Julian P. Boyd, vol. 2 (Princeton: Princeton University Press, 1950), 471-473.

50. Fladeland, 170. Fladeland focuses on the formal debates and votes in Congress during the early to mid 1800s. There were discussions in the states that occurred through various local representatives who wrote opinion pieces in newspapers. By 1849 congressmen from all of the seceding states rejected compensated emancipation and considered it a "radical" solution. Of course, there were practical considerations over what to do with emancipated slaves, how much would it cost to colonize them, and who would work the plantations, etc., but the author argues the South believed such federal plans to be unconstitutional and interfered with states' rights. Yet, on the state level, such schemes interfered with the property owner's right of consent.

51. Fladeland, 185.

52. William W. Freehling, "The Founding Fathers and Slavery," *The American Historical Review* 77 (February 1972): 81. Freehling endeavors to refute somewhat the argument that the Founders meant only white men. Some authors who believe the Founders were disingenuous are: Robert McColley, *Slavery and Jeffersonian Virginia* (Urbana: University of Illinois Press, 1964; William Cohen, "Thomas Jefferson and the Problem of Slavery," *Journal of American History* 56 (December 1969); Connor Cruise O'Brien, *The Long Affair*, Chicago: University of Chicago Press, 1996; Thurgood Marshall, "Reflections on the Bicentennial of the United States Constitution," *Harvard Law Review* 101 (November 1987): 1-5; and recently Dilorenzo, *The Real Lincoln*, x.

53. Thomas G. West, *Vindicating the Founders: Race, Sex, Class, and Justice in the Origins of America* (Lanham, Md.: Rowman and Littlefield, 1997), 21.

54. Ibid., 23.

55. Abraham Lincoln, "Second Inaugural Address," 4 March 1865, *Abraham Lincoln: Speeches and Writings 1832-1858*, Edited by Don E. Fehrenbacher, (New York: Library of America, 1989), 686.

56. Robert William Fogel and Stanley L. Engerman, *Time on the Cross* (Boston: Little, Brown, and Co., 1974), 4. See also Alfred H. Conrad and John R. Meyer, "The Economics of Slavery in the Antebellum South," *The Journal of Political Economy* 66 (April 1958): 95-130; and Harold D. Woodman, "The Profitability of Slavery: A Historical Perennial," *The Journal of Southern History* 29 (August 1963): 303-325.

57. Fogel and Engerman, 44-45. The authors argue that only a small portion of this expansion resulted from illegal importations into the United States. Most of the increase in the slave population derived from natural increase.

58. Ibid., 249.

59. This is especially particular to works examining the history of state constitutions. See G. Alan Tarr, *Understanding State Constitutions* (Princeton: Princeton University Press, 1998); Laura J. Scalia, *America's Jeffersonian Experiment: Remaking State Constitutions 1820-1850* (DeKalb: Northern Illinois University Press, 1999); Don E. Fehrenbacher, *Constitutions and Constitutionalism in the Slaveholding South* (Athens: University of Georgia Press, 1989).

60. Some who fall into the above categories are Theodore Whitfield, *Slavery Agitation in Virginia, 1829-1832*, contends that that by 1835, anti-slavery sentiment underwent a "profound change" and receded (vii), but he largely ignores the important rejection of natural rights in the 1829-30 convention. Whitfield's work is certainly valuable as it is the only book that recognizes the importance of both the Virginia Constitutional Convention and the debates in the House of Delegates. But it is only a

general overview of the period. Like other historical works, Whitfield does not analyze political speeches to any great extent nor does he probe the importance of Dew's contribution to the development of the proslavery argument; Dickson D. Bruce, *The Rhetoric of Conservatism: The Virginia Constitutional Convention of 1829-1830 and the Conservative Tradition in the South* (San Marino, Ca.: The Huntington Library, 1982), examines the eastern Virginia plantation representatives, or "conservatives," who did not want to amend the constitution. Since his is primarily an intellectual history he includes in his analysis liberal doses of the speeches made during the convention. He argues that Virginia's history has always been dominated by conservative thought. Conservative ideology rejects natural rights as a basis for just government for one that springs from history and experience. He does not argue that slavery was a significant part of the debate. Even though he admits it might have been an underlying issue, he rejects the argument that conservatism was synonymous with pro-slavery thought in 1830. He also argues that the reformers did not make a serious attack on slavery and he downplays a contention made by other authors that the extension of suffrage, as well as greater western representation in the Virginia legislature, was a means to the end of gradual emancipation (175-176). Cf. Fehrenbacher, *Constitutions and Constitutionalism in the Slaveholding South*, 14; William E. Dodd, "The Social Philosophy of the Old South," *American Journal of Sociology* 23 (May 1918): 735-736. Bruce asserts, "it was possible, in 1829, to be both conservative and antislavery" (176). He also downplays political speech: economic and social interests are clearer or more easily defined than the "words politicians use" (vii); For a more favorable view to the general thesis of this book, but in a very limited sense, see Robert, *The Road from Monticello*; Some conclude that Dew's essay was not representative of the pro-slave argument, see Tise, 71 and 316; In his *Road to Disunion*, William Freehling asserted in a chapter on Virginia that Dew did not lead Old Dominion and the rest of the South into war. He was no transitional figure. Therefore, he does not represent a turn to slave ideology, Freehling, *Road to Disunion*, 190-191 and 193; Freehling, *Drift Toward Dissolution*, challenges Robert's 1941 conclusion that the debates represented a major turning point, not only for Virginia, but for the entire South. While she disagrees with that conclusion, she nevertheless notes the significance of Virginia's place in the Union: "That Virginians should so publicly and vigorously weigh emancipation was a momentous historical event, for Virginia in 1832 was not only the nation's largest slaveholding state, but one whose preeminence during the American Revolution and early decades of the republic still carried singular influence and prestige" (xi). She also challenges the view that Dew was as pro-slave as others have concluded. Freehling concludes that at the close of 1832, Virginia was what it always had been—a "house divided." Virginia was incessantly irresolute as to what to do about her peculiar institution for she had both northern anti-slavery and southern pro-slavery sympathies.

61. Alison Goodyear Freehling, 63.

62. Brent Tarter, "The New Virginia Bookshelf," *The Virginia Magazine of History and Biography* 104 (Winter 1996): 7 and 46.

63. Robert, *The Road from Monticello: A Study of the Virginia Slavery Debate of 1832*, v.

64. Ibid., 46.

65. Becker, 24; Adair, 236, asserts that by the 1830s the South turned to Calhoun finding Jefferson's majority rule and anti-slave sentiment increasingly distasteful.

66. John Quincy Adams, *The Diary of John Quincy Adams: 1794-1845*, 228; McCoy, *The Last of the Fathers*, 300.

67. West, *Vindicating the Founders*, xiii.

68. Edmund S. Morgan, "Slavery and Freedom: The American Paradox," *The Journal of American History* 59, no. 1 (June 1972) : 7.

69. Sean Wilentz, "The Details of Greatness," *The New Republic*, 29 March 2004, 34.

70. Harriet Martineau, *Retrospect of Western Travel*, 2 vol. (London: Saunders and Otley, 1838; reprinted 1948), 191-2.

71. McCoy, 249; Madison to General Lafayette, 1 February 1830, *Letters and other Writings*, vol. 4 (New York: R. Worthington, 1884), 60; Madison to R.R. Gurley, 28 December 1831, ibid, 214.

72. Eaton, *Freedom of Thought in the Old South*, 89, 95, 167, 169, 171-172, 174, 202, 479-480, and 485-486; Ambler, *Thomas Ritchie: A Study in Virginia Politics* (Richmond: Bett Book and Stationary Co., 1913), 166-167; The *Whig* was more ardently pro-abolition than the *Enquirer*, see Shade, 196.

73. Alexander Campbell, "Slavery and Antislavery," *Millennial Harbinger* (December 1835) : 589. Some have accused Campbell of moderating his position in the years hence the convention, but his opinions expressed in the *Harbinger* focus more on the radicalism of the religious anti-slavery movement and the pro-slavery movement. He decried both positions as being unchristian because of their passionate arguments and their appeals to lawlessness.

74. Abraham Lincoln, "Letter to Henry Pierce and others, April 6, 1859" in *Abraham Lincoln: Speeches and Writings 1859-1865*, 18-19.

Bibliography

Adair, Douglass. *Fame and the Founding Fathers*. Edited by Trevor Colbourn. New York: W.W. Norton and Company, 1974.

———. "James Madison's Autobiography." *The William and Mary Quarterly* 2, no. 2 (April 1945): 191-209.

Adams, Charles. *When in the Course of Human Events: Arguing the Case for Southern Secession*. New York: Rowman and Littlefield, 2000.

Adams, Charles Francis, ed. *Memoirs of John Quincy Adams*. Vol. 9. Freeport, New York: Books for Libraries Press, 1969.

Adamson, Robert. *Fichte*. Freeport, New York: Books for Libraries Press, 1969.

Allen, W.B., ed. *George Washington: A Collection*. Indianapolis: Liberty Classics, 1988.

Ambler, Charles H. *Sectionalism in Virginia from 1776-1861*. New York: Russell and Russell Inc., 1964.

———. *A History of West Virginia*. New York: Prentice-Hall Inc., 1933.

———, ed. *The Life and Diary of John Floyd*. Richmond, Va.: Richmond Press, Inc., 1918.

———. *Thomas Ritchie: A Study in Virginia Politics*. Richmond, Va.: Bell Book and Stationary Co., 1913.

———. "The Cleavage between Eastern and Western Virginia." *The American Historical Review* 15 (July 1910): 762-780.

Anderson, D.R. "Jefferson and the Virginia Constitution." *The American Historical Review* 21, no. 4 (July 1916): 750-754.

Aristotle. *Nicomachean Ethics*. Translated with an Introduction by Martin Ostwald. New York: Macmillan, 1986.

———. *The Politics*. Translated with an Introduction by Carnes Lord. Chicago: University of Chicago, 1984.

Bailey, Fred Arthur. *William Edward Dodd: The South's Yeoman Scholar*. Charlottesville: University Press of Virginia, 1997.

Ball, Spencer M. "Speech Delivered in the Virginia House of Delegates." *Constitutional Whig*, 13 March 1832, p. 4.

Ballagh, James Curtis, ed. *The Letters of Richard Henry Lee*. 2 vols. New York: DeCapo Press, 1970.

———. *A History of Slavery in Virginia*. Baltimore: Johns Hopkins Press, 1902.

Barlow, J. Jackson, Leonard W. Levy, and Ken Masugi, eds. *The American Founding*. New York: Greenwood Press, 1988.

Barthelmas, Della Gray. *The Signers of the Declaration of Independence*. With a Foreword by Frank Borman. Jefferson, N.C.: McFarland and Company, 1997.

Bean, W.G. "Anti-Jeffersonianism in the Ante-Bellum South." *The North Carolina Historical Review* 12 (April 1935): 103-124.

Becker, Carl L. *The Declaration of Independence: A Study in the History of Political Ideas.* New York: Vintage, 1942.

Bergh, Albert Ellery, ed. *The Writings of Thomas Jefferson.* Washington, D.C.: The Thomas Jefferson Memorial Association, 1907.

Berry, Henry. *The Speech of Henry Berry in the House of Delegates of Virginia on the Abolition of Slavery: Delivered on January 20, 1832.* Richmond: Thomas W. White, 1832.

Bessette, Joseph M. *The Mild Voice of Reason: Deliberative Democracy and American National Government.* Chicago: University of Chicago Press, 1994.

Bolling, Philip A. *The Speeches of Phillip A. Bolling in the House of Delegates of Virginia on the Policy of the State in Relation to Her Colored Population: Delivered on January 11 and 25, 1832.* Richmond, Va.: Thomas W. White, 1832.

Booker, H. Marshall. "Thomas Roderick Dew: Forgotten Virginian." *Virginia Cavalcade* 19 (Autumn 1969) : 20-29.

Boyd, Julian P., ed. *The Papers of Thomas Jefferson.* 30 vols. Princeton: Princeton University Press, 1950.

———. "Thomas Jefferson's 'Empire of Liberty.'" *The Virginia Quarterly Review* 24, no. 4 (Autumn 1948) : 538-554.

Bozeman, Theodore Dwight. "Joseph LeConte: Organic Science and a 'Sociology for the South.'" *The Journal of Southern History* 39, no. 4 (November 1973) : 565-582.

Brenaman, J.N. *A History of Virginia Conventions.* Richmond: J.L. Hill Printing Co., 1902.

Broadwater, Jeff. *George Mason: Forgotten Founder.* Chapel Hill: University of North Carolina Press, 2006.

Brodnax, William H. *The Speech of William H. Brodnax in the House of Delegates of Virginia on the Policy of the State with Respect to its Colored Population: Delivered January 18, 1832.* Richmond: Thomas W. White, 1832.

Brown, John Thompson. *The Speech of John Thompson Brown in the House of Delegates on the Abolition of Slavery: Delivered on Wednesday, January 18, 1832.* Richmond: Thomas W. White, 1832.

Brown, Richard H. "The Missouri Crisis, Slavery, and the Politics of Jacksonianism." In *The Many-faceted Jacksonian Era,* ed. Edward Pessen. New York: Greenwood Press, 1977.

Bruce, Dickson D. *The Rhetoric of Conservatism: The Virginia Convention of 1829-30 and the Conservative Tradition in the South.* San Marino, Calif.: Huntington Library, 1982.

Bruce, James C. "Speech Delivered in the Virginia House of Delegates." *Richmond Enquirer,* 26 January 1832, p. 2.

Brugger, Robert J. *Beverly Tucker: Heart Over Head in the Old South.* Baltimore: Johns Hopkins University Press, 1978.

Bryce, James G. "Speech Delivered in the Virginia House of Delegates." *Constitutional Whig,* 13 January 1832, p. 1.

Burnstein, Andrew. "The Problem of Jefferson Biography." *The Virginia Quarterly Review* 70 (Summer 1994) : 403-420.

Campbell, Alexander, ed. *The Christian Baptist.* St. Louis: Christian Publishing Co., 1889.

———. *Popular Lectures and Addresses.* Philadelphia: James Challen & Son, 1863.

———. "Slavery and Anti-Slavery." *Millennial Harbinger,* December 1835, 587-590.

———. "The Crisis." *Millennial Harbinger,* 6 February 1832, 86-93.

———. "Slavery in Virginia." *Millennial Harbinger,* 2 January 1832, 14-19.

————. "Emancipation of White Slaves." *Millennial Harbinger*, 1 March 1830, 128-132.

Campbell, John C. "Speech Delivered in the Virginia House of Delegates." *Constitutional Whig*, 16 March 1832, p. 2, 20 March 1832, p. 4.

Cappon, Lester J., ed. *The Adams-Jefferson Letters*. New York: Simon and Schuster, 1971.

Catterall, Helen Tunnicliff, ed. *Judicial Cases Concerning American Slavery and the Negro*. Vol 1. Washington, D.C.: Carnegie Institution of Washington, 1926.

Chandler, John A. *The Speech of John A. Chandler in the House of Delegates of Virginia on the Policy of the State with Respect to Her Slave Population: Delivered January 17, 1832*. Richmond, Va.: Thomas W. White, 1832.

Chandler, Julian A.C. *The History of Suffrage in Virginia*. Baltimore: The Johns Hopkins University Press, 1901.

————. *Representation in Virginia*. Baltimore: The Johns Hopkins University Press, 1896.

Chitwood, Oliver Perry. *Richard Henry Lee: Statesman of the Revolution*. Morgantown: West Virginia University, 1967.

Cleveland, Henry, ed. *Alexander H. Stephens Public and Private Letters and Speeches*. Philadelphia: National Publishing Co., 1866.

Clough, A.H., ed. *Plutarch's Lives*. Boston: Little, Brown, and Company, 1876.

Cohen, William. "Thomas Jefferson and the Problem of Slavery." *The Journal of American History* 56, no. 3 (December 1969) : 503-526.

Coles, Edward. "Letters of Edward Coles: Edward Coles to Thomas Jefferson." *William and Mary College Quarterly Historical Magazine* 7, no. 2 (April 1927) : 97-113.

————. "Letters of Edward Coles." *William and Mary College Quarterly Historical Magazine* 7, no. 1 (January 1927) : 32-41.

————. "Letters of Governor Edward Coles Bearing on the Struggle of Freedom and Slavery in Illinois." *The Journal of Negro History* 3, no. 2 (April 1918) : 158-195.

Conrad, Alfred H., and John R. Meyer. "The Economics of Slavery in the Antebellum South." *The Journal of Political Economy* 66 (April 1958): 95-130.

Constitutional Whig (Richmond). August 1831-December 1832.

Cook, Frank Gaylord. "Richard Henry Lee." *The Atlantic Monthly* 66 (July 1890) : 23-35.

Cooper, William J. *The South and the Politics of Slavery 1828-1856*. Baton Rouge: Louisiana State University Press, 1978.

Copleston, Frederick. *A History of Philosophy: Modern Philosophy*. Vol. 7. New York: Doubleday, 1963.

Crallé, Richard K., ed. *The Works of John C. Calhoun*. Vol. 2. New York: D. Appleton and Company, 1855.

Cromwell, John W. "The Aftermath of Nat Turner's Insurrection." *Journal of Negro History* 5, no. 2 (April 1920): 208-234.

Curry, Richard O. "A Reappraisal of Statehood Politics in West Virginia." *The Journal of Southern History* 28 (November 1962): 403-421.

Curtis, Christopher M. "Can These be the Sons of their Fathers? The Defense of Slavery in Virginia, 1831-1832." Thesis, Virginia Polytechnic Institute, 1997.

Dabney, Benjamin F. "Speech Delivered in the Virginia House of Delegates." *Richmond Enquirer*, 3 April 1832, p. 4.

Daniel, William. "Speech Delivered in the Virginia House of Delegates." *Constitutional Whig*, 26 January 1832, p. 1.

Davis, Richard Beale. *Intellectual Life in Jefferson's Virginia: 1790-1830*. Knoxville: The University of Tennessee Press, 1964.

Dawidoff, Robert. *The Education of John Randolph.* New York: W.W. Norton and Company, 1979.

Dew, Thomas Roderick. *Digest of the Laws, Customs, Manners, and Institutions of the Ancient and Modern Nations.* New York: D. Appleton and Company, 1852.

———. "Professor Dew on Slavery: Review of the Debate in the Virginia Legislature, 1831-1832." *The Proslavery Argument as Maintained by the Most Distinguished Writer of the Southern States.* n.p.: Walker, Richards and Company, 1852; reprint, New York: Negro Universities Press, 1968.

———. William and Mary College, to Benjamin F. Dew, 12 July 1842. Dew Family Papers, Earl Gregg Swem Library, College of William and Mary, Williamsburg, Virginia.

———. "Ancient and Modern Eloquence." *Southern Literary Messenger.* 8, no. 3 (March 1842) : 169-185.

———. William and Mary College, to William H. Harrison, 18 October 1838. Dew Family Papers, Earl Gregg Swem Library, College of William and Mary, Williamsburg, Virginia.

———. "An Address on the Influence of the Federative Republican System of Government upon Literature and the Development of Character." *Southern Literary Messenger.* 2, no. 4 (March 1836) : 261-282.

———. *An Address Delivered before the Students of William and Mary at the Opening of the College on Monday, October 10, 1836.* Richmond, Va.: T.W. White, 1836.

———. *Review of the Debate in the Virginia Legislature of 1831-1832.* Richmond: T.W. White, 1832.

———. *Lectures on the Restrictive System.* Richmond, Va.: Samuel Sheppard and Co., 1829.

DiLorenzo, Thomas J. *The Real Lincoln.* New York: Forum Publishing, 2002.

Dodd, William E. *Jefferson Davis.* New York: Russell and Russell, 1966.

———. *The Cotton Kingdom: A Chronicle of the Old South.* Toronto: Glasgow, Brook and Co., 1919.

———. "The Social Philosophy of the Old South." *American Journal of Sociology* 23 (May 1918) : 735-746.

———. *Statesmen of the Old South.* New York: The MacMillan Co., 1911.

Drewry, William Sidney. *The Southampton Insurrection.* Murfreesboro, N.C.: Johnson Publishing Company, 1968.

DuBois, W.E.B. *The Suppression of the African Slave-Trade to the United States of America 1638-1870.* With an Introduction by Herbert Aptheker. Millwood, New York: Kraus-Thomson, 1973.

Dunning, Wm. A. "The Political Theories of the German Idealists II." *Political Science Quarterly* 28, no. 3 (September 1913) : 480-495.

Eaton, Clement. "The Freedom of the Press in the Upper South." *The Mississippi Valley Historical Review* 18, no. 4 (March 1932): 479-499.

———. *Freedom of Thought in the Old South.* Durham: Duke University Press, 1940.

"Education in Colonial Virginia: Part IV, The Higher Education." *William and Mary College Quarterly Historical Magazine* 6, no. 3 (January 1898) : 171-187.

Elliot, Jonathan, ed. *The Debates in the Several State Conventions, on the Adoption of the Federal Constitution as Recommended by the General Convention at Philadelphia in 1787.* Vol. 3. Philadelphia: J.B. Lippincott and Co., 1861.

Ellis, Joseph J. *Founding Brothers.* New York: Vintage Books, 2000.

———. "Who Owns the Eighteenth Century?" *The William and Mary Quarterly* 57, no. 2 (April 2000) : 417-421.

————. *American Sphinx: The Character of Thomas Jefferson*. New York: Alfred A. Knopf, 1997.

Eminhizer, Earl Eugene. "Alexander Campbell's Thoughts on Slavery and Abolition." *West Virginia History* 33 (1972): 109-123.

Engelbrecht, H.C. *Johann Gottlieb Fichte: A Study of his Political Writings with Special Reference to his Nationalism*. New York: AMS Press, 1968.

Erler, Edward J. "Philosophy, History, and Jaffa's Universe." *Interpretation* 28, no. 3 (Spring 2001) : 245-257.

Farrand, Max, ed. *The Records of the Federal Convention of 1787*. Three vols. New Haven: Yale University Press, 1966.

Faulkner, Charles Jas. *The Speech of Charles Jas. Faulkner in the House of Delegates of Virginia in the Policy of the State with Respect to Her Slave Population: Delivered January 20, 1832*. Richmond, Va.: Thomas W. White, 1832.

Faust, Drew Gilpin. *James Henry Hammond and the Old South*. Baton Rouge: Louisiana State University Press, 1982.

————. ed. *The Ideology of Slavery*. Baton Rouge: Louisiana State University Press, 1981.

————. "A Southern Stewardship: The Intellectual and the Proslavery Argument." *American Quarterly* 31 (Spring 1979) : 63-80.

————. *A Sacred Circle: The Dilemma of the Intellectual in the Old South*. Baltimore: Johns Hopkins University Press, 1977.

Fehrenbacher, Don E. *Sectional Crisis and Southern Constitutionalism*. Baton Rouge: Louisiana State University Press, 1995.

————. *Constitutions and Constitutionalism in the Slaveholding South*. Athens: University of Georgia Press, 1989.

————, ed. *Abraham Lincoln: Speeches and Writings*. 2 vols. New York: Library of America, 1989.

Fichte, J.G. *Foundations of Natural Right*. Translated by Michael Baur. Cambridge: Cambridge University Press, 2000.

————. "Reclamation of the Freedom of Thought from the Princes of Europe, who have Oppressed it Until Now." In *What is Enlightenment?* ed. James Schmidt. Berkeley: University of California Press, 1996.

————. *Introductions to the Wissenschaftslehre and Other Writings*. Edited and Translated by Daniel Breazeale. Indianapolis: Hackett Publishing Company, 1994.

————. *Addresses to the German Nation*. Edited with an Introduction by George Armstrong Kelly. New York: Harper Torchbooks, 1968.

————. *The Popular Works of Johann Gottlieb Fichte*. 2 vols. Translated by William Smith. London: Trübner and Co., 1889.

Filler, Louis. *The Crusade Against Slavery 1830-1860*. New York: Harper and Brothers, 1960.

Finkleman, Paul. *Slavery and the Founders: Race and Liberty in the Age of Jefferson*. Armonk, New York: M.E. Sharpe, 1996.

————. "Thomas Jefferson and Antislavery: The Myth Goes On." *The Virginia Magazine of History and Biography* 102 (April 1994) : 193-228.

Finnie, Gordon E. "The Antislavery Movement in the Upper South Before 1840." *The Journal of Southern History* 35 (August 1969): 319-342.

First Annual Report of the American Society for Colonizing the Free People of Color of the United States. Washington City: D. Rapine, January 1818.

Fladeland, Betty L. "Compensated Emancipation: A Rejected Alternative." *The Journal of Southern History* 42, no. 2 (May 1976): 169-186.

Fogel, Robert William, and Stanley L. Engerman. *Time on the Cross*. Boston: Little, Brown, and Co., 1974.

Ford, Paul Leicester, ed. *The Works of Thomas Jefferson*. 12 vols. Federal Edition. New York: G.P. Putnam's Sons, 1905.

———. *The Writings of Thomas Jefferson*. 20 vols. New York: G.P. Putnam's Sons, 1898.

Freehling, Alison Goodyear. *Drift Toward Dissolution: The Virginia Slavery Debate of 1831-1832*. Baton Rouge: Louisiana State University Press, 1982.

Freehling, William W. *The Road to Disunion: Secessionists at Bay, 1776-1854*. New York: Oxford University Press, 1990.

———. "The Founding Fathers and Slavery." *The American Historical Review* 77 (February 1972): 81-93.

Gallagher, Gary, and Alan T. Nolan, eds. *The Myth of the Lost Cause and Civil War History*. Bloomington: Indiana University Press, 2000.

Gallaher, John S. "Speech Delivered in the Virginia House of Delegates." *Constitutional Whig*, 13 March 1832, p. 4.

Garland, Samuel M. "Speech Delivered in the Virginia House of Delegates." *Constitutional Whig*, 2 February 1832, p. 4.

Genovese, Eugene. *The Southern Tradition*. Cambridge, Mass.: Harvard University Press, 1994.

———. *Western Civilization through Slaveholding Eyes: The Social and Historical Thought of Thomas Roderick Dew*. New Orleans: Graduate School of Tulane University, 1986.

———. *"Slavery Ordained of God": The Southern Slaveholders' View of Biblical History and Modern Politics*. Gettysburg: Gettysburg College, 1985.

Germino, Dante. "Hegel as a Political Theorist." *The Journal of Politics* 31, no. 4 (November 1969) : 895-912.

Gholson, James H. "Speech Delivered in the Virginia House of Delegates." *Constitutional Whig*, 12 January 1832, p. 2; 26. January 1832, p. 1.

Goldwin, Robert A., and Art Kaufman, eds. *Slavery and Its Consequences: The Constitution, Equality, and Race*. Washington, D.C.: AEI, 1988.

Goode, William O. *The Speech of William O. Goode on the Abolition of Slavery Delivered in the House of Delegates of Virginia on Tuesday, January 24, 1832*. Richmond, Va.: Thomas W. White, 1832.

Goodrich, Charles A. *Lives of the Signers of the Declaration of Independence with a Sketch of the Life of Washington*. Charlottesville, New York: Sam Har Press, 1976.

Grigsby, Hugh Blair. *The Virginia Convention of 1829-1830*. New York: DeCapo Press, 1969.

Gutzman, K.R. Constantine. "Old Dominion, New Republic: Making Virginia Republican, 1776-1840." Ph.D. diss., University of Virginia, 1999.

Hall, Claude H. *Abel Parker Upshur: Conservative Virginian 1790-1844*. Madison, Wisconsin: The State Historical Society of Wisconsin, 1964.

Hall, Kermit L., and James W. Ely, Jr., eds. *An Uncertain Tradition: Constitutionalism and the History of the South*. Athens: The University of Georgia Press, 1989.

Hamilton, Phillip. "Revolutionary Principles and Family Loyalties: Slavery's Transformation in the St. George Tucker Household of Early National Virginia." *The William and Mary Quarterly*, 3rd ser:, 55, no. 4 (October 1998) : 531-556.

Hamilton, Stanislaus Murray, ed. *The Writings of James Monroe*. Vol. 7. New York: G.P. Putnam's Sons, 1903.

Harrison, Jesse Burton. *Review of the Slave Question*. Richmond, Va.: T.W. White, 1833.

Harrison, Lowell. "Thomas Roderick Dew: Philosopher of the Old South." *Virginia Magazine of History and Biography* 57, no. 4 (October 1949): 390-404.

Hast, Adele. "The Legal Status of the Negro in Virginia 1705-1765." *The Journal of Negro History* 54, no. 3 (July 1969) : 217-239.

Hegel, G.W.F. *Elements of the Philosophy of Right*. Edited by Allen W. Wood and Translated by H.B. Nisbet. Cambridge: Cambridge University Press, 1991.

———. *Philosophy of Right*. Translated by T.M. Knox. London: Oxford University Press, 1977.

———. *The Phenomenology of Mind*. Translated with an Introduction and Notes by J.B. Baillie and with an Introduction by George Lichtheim. New York: Harper Torchbooks, 1957.

———. *The Philosophy of History*. With an Introduction by C.J. Friedrich. New York: Dover Publications, 1956.

Helderman, Leonard C. "A Social Scientist of the Old South." *The Journal of Southern History* 2 (May 1936) : 148-174.

Helo, Ari, and Peter Onuf. "Jefferson, Morality, and the Problem of Slavery." *The William and Mary Quarterly* 60, no. 3 (July 2003) : 583-614.

Hesseltine, W.B. "Some New Aspects of the Pro-Slavery Argument." *Journal of Negro History* 21, no. 1 (January 1936): 1-14.

Hill, Helen. *George Mason: Constitutionalist*. Cambridge, Mass.: Harvard University Press, 1938.

Hite, James C., and Ellen J. Hall. "The Reactionary Evolution of Economic Thought in Antebellum Virginia." *Virginia Magazine of History and Biography* 80, no. 4 (October 1972): 476-488.

Hizer, Trenton Eynon. "Virginia is Now Divided: Politics in Old Dominion 1820-1833." Ph.D. diss., University of South Carolina, 1997.

Hobbes, Thomas. *Leviathan*. Edited by Michael Oakshott. New York: Collier Books, 1962.

Hobson, Charles F., and Robert A. Rutland, eds. *The Papers of James Madison*. Vol. 12. Charlottesville: University Press of Virginia, 1979.

Holzer, Harold. *Lincoln at Cooper Union*. New York: Simon & Schuster, 2004.

Horowitz, Irving Louis. "The Hegelian Concept of Political Freedom." *The Journal of Politics* 28, no. 1 (February 1966) : 3-28.

Howe, Daniel Walker. *The Political Culture of the American Whigs*. Chicago: University of Chicago Press, 1979.

Hummel, Jeffrey Rogers. *Emancipating Slaves, Enslaving Free Men*. Chicago: Open Court, 1996.

Hunt, Gaillard, ed. *The Writings of James Madison*. Nine vols. New York: G.P. Putnam's Sons, 1900-1910.

Hutson, James H., ed. *Supplement to Max Farrand's The Records of the Federal Convention of 1787*. New Haven: Yale University Press, 1987.

Iaccarino, Anthony Alfred. "Virginia and the National Contest over Slavery in the Early Republic, 1780-1833." Ph.D. diss., University of California, Los Angeles, 1999.

Jackson, Luther P. "The Virginia Free Negro Farmer and Property Owner, 1830-1864." *The Journal of Negro History* 24 (October 1939) : 390-439.

———. "Manumission in Certain Virginia Cities." *The Journal of Negro History* 15, no. 3 (July 1930) : 278-314.

Jaffa, Harry V. *A New Birth of Freedom*. Lanham, Md.: Rowman & Littlefield, 2000.

———. "The False Prophets of American Conservatism." Paper delivered at the Claremont Institute's Lincoln Day Conference, Washington, D.C., February 12,

1998.
———. "The Decline and Fall of the American Idea: Reflections on the Failure of American Conservatism." Paper presented for the 25th Anniversary Symposium of the Henry Salvatori Center for the Study of Individual Freedom, Claremont, Calif., April 18-20, 1996.
———. *Original Intent and the Framers of the Constitution: A Disputed Question.* Washington, D.C.: Regnery Gateway, 1994.
———. *Crisis of the House Divided.* Chicago: University of Chicago Press, 1982.
———. *How to Think about the American Revolution.* Durham, N.C.: Carolina Academic Press, 1978.
———. "Equality, Liberty, Wisdom, Morality and Consent in the Idea of Political Freedom." *Interpretation* 15, no. 1 (1987) : 3-28.
———. *The American Founding as the Best Regime: The Bonding of Civil and Religious Liberty.* Claremont: The Claremont Institute, 1987.
———. *Equality and Liberty.* New York: Oxford University Press, 1965; reprint Claremont: Claremont Institute, 1999.
Jenkins, William Sumner. *Pro-Slavery Thought in the Old South.* Gloucester, Mass.: University of North Carolina Press, 1935.
Journal of the House of Delegates of the Commonwealth of Virginia. Richmond, Va.: Thomas Ritchie, 1831.
Kaufmann, Walter. *Hegel: Texts and Commentary.* Notre Dame: University of Notre Dame Press, 1977.
———. *Hegel: Reinterpretation, Texts, and Commentary.* Garden City, N.Y.: Doubleday and Company, 1965.
Kesler, Charles R., ed. *Saving the Revolution.* New York: The Free Press, 1987.
Kirk, Russell. *The Conservative Mind: From Burke to Eliot.* 7th ed. Chicago: Regnery Books, 1986.
———. *John Randolph of Roanoke.* Indianapolis: Liberty Press, 1978.
Klebaner, Benjamin Joseph. "American Manumission Laws and the Responsibility for Supporting Slaves." *The Virginia Magazine of History and Biography* 63 (1955) : 443-453.
Knox, Alexander G. "Speech Delivered in the Virginia House of Delegates." *Richmond Enquirer,* 14 February 1832, p. 1-2.
Kurland, Philip B., and Ralph Lerner, eds. *The Founders' Constitution.* 4 vols. Indianapolis: Liberty Fund, 1987.
Larson, John Laurintz. "'Bind the Republic Together': The National Union and the Struggle for a System of Internal Improvements." *The Journal of American History* 74 (September 1987) : 363-387.
Lee, Richard Henry. "Memoir of Richard Henry Lee." *The North American Review* 22, no. 51 (April 1826) : 373-400.
Lence, Ross M., ed., *Union and Liberty: The Political Philosophy of John C. Calhoun.* Indianapolis: Liberty Fund, 1992.
Levasseur, Auguste. *Lafayette in America in 1824 and 1825: or Journals of Travels in the United States.* Vol. 1. New York: White, Galaher & White, 1829.
Locke, John. *Two Treatises of Government.* Edited with an Introduction by Peter Laslett. Cambridge: Cambridge University Press, 1988.
Löwith, Karl. *From Hegel to Nietzsche: A Revolution in Nineteenth-century Thought.* Translated by David E. Green. New York: Holt, Rinehart and Winston, 1964.
Ludlum, Robert P. "The Antislavery 'Gag Rule': History and Argument." *Journal of Negro History* 26, no. 2 (April 1941): 203-243.

Lunger, Harold Lehman. *The Political Ethics of Alexander Campbell.* St. Louis: Bethany Press, 1954.

Malone, Dumas. *Jefferson and His Time.* 6 vols. Boston: Little, Brown and Company, 1948-1981.

Mansfield, Stephen. "Thomas Roderick Dew: Defender of the Southern Faith." Ph. D. diss., University of Virginia, 1968.

———. "Thomas Roderick Dew at William and Mary." *Virginia Magazine of History and Biography* 75, no. 4 (1967): 429-442.

Marshall, Thomas. *The Speech of Thomas Marshall in the House of Delegates of Virginia on the Abolition of Slavery: Delivered Friday, January 20, 1832.* Richmond, Va.: Thomas W. White, 1832.

———. *The Speech of Thomas Marshall (of Fauquier) in the House of Delegates of Virginia on the Policy of the State in Relation to Her Colored Population: Delivered Saturday, January 14, 1832.* 2nd ed. Richmond: Thomas W. White, 1832.

Matison, Sumner Eliot. "Manumission by Purchase." *The Journal of Negro History* 33, no. 2 (April 1948) : 146-167.

Matthews, Albert. *Notes on the Proposed Abolition of Slavery in Virginia in 1785.* Cambridge: John Wilson and Son, 1903.

Mayer, Henry. *A Son of Thunder: Patrick Henry and the American Republic.* New York: Franklin Watts, 1986.

McCardell, John. *The Idea of a Southern Nation.* New York: W.W. Norton and Company, 1979.

McColley, Robert. *Slavery and Jeffersonian Virginia.* Urbana: University of Illinois Press, 1964.

McCoy, Drew R. *The Last of the Fathers: James Madison and the Republican Legacy.* Cambridge: Cambridge University Press, 1989.

McDowell, James. *The Speech of James M'Dowell Jr. in the House of Delegates of Virginia on the Slave Question.* 2nd ed. Richmond, Va.: Thomas W. White, 1832.

Meyers, Marvin, ed. *The Mind of the Founder.* Hanover: Brandeis University Press, 1981.

Middlekauff, Robert. *The Glorious Cause.* New York: Oxford University Press, 1982.

Millennial Harbinger, 1830-1857.

Miller, Helen Hill. *George Mason: Gentleman Revolutionary.* Chapel Hill: The University of North Carolina Press, 1975.

Miller, William Lee. *Arguing About Slavery.* New York: Alfred A. Knopf, 1996.

Moore, Glover. *The Missouri Controversy 1819-1821.* Lexington: University of Kentucky Press, 1953.

Moore, Sam McDowell. "Speech Delivered in the Virginia House of Delegates." *Richmond Enquirer*, 19 January 1832, pp. 1-2.

———. "Speech Delivered in the Virginia House of Delegates." *Constitutional Whig*, 28 March 1832, p. 3.

Moorhouse, William M. "Alexander Campbell and the Virginia Constitutional Convention of 1829-1830." *Virginia Cavalcade* 20 (Spring 1975): 184-191.

Morgan, Edmund S. *American Slavery, American Freedom: The Ordeal of Colonial Virginia.* New York: W.W. Norton and Company, 1975.

———. "Slavery and Freedom: The American Paradox." *The Journal of American History* 59, no. 1 (June 1972) : 5-29.

Munford, Beverly B. *Virginia's Attitude Toward Slavery and Secession.* Richmond, Va.: L.H. Jenkins Inc., 1915.

Nevins, Allan, ed. *The Diary of John Quincy Adams: 1794-1845.* New York: Charles

Scribner's Sons, 1951.

Newton, Willoughby. "Speech Delivered in the Virginia House of Delegates." *Constitutional Whig*, 14 February 1832, p. 4.

Nye, Russell B. *Fettered Freedom: Civil Liberties and the Slavery Controversy.* East Lansing, Mich.: State College Press, 1949.

Oakes, James. "From Republicanism to Liberalism: Ideological Change and the Crisis of the Old South." *American Quarterly* 37, no. 4 (Autumn 1985) : 551-571.

Oates, Stephen B. *The Fires of Jubilee: Nat Turner's Fierce Rebellion.* New York: Harper and Row, 1975.

O'Brien, Connor Cruise. *The Long Affair: Thomas Jefferson and the French Revolution, 1785-1800.* Chicago: University of Chicago Press, 1996.

O'Brien, Michael, ed. *All Clever Men Who Make their Way: Critical Discourse in the Old South.* Fayetteville: University of Arkansas Press, 1982.

Onuf, Peter. *Jefferson's Empire: The Language of American Nationhood.* Charlottesville: University Press of Virginia, 2000.

———. "The Scholars' Jefferson." *The William and Mary Quarterly* 50, no. 4 (October 1993) : 671-699.

Padover, Saul K. *Jefferson: A Great American's Life and Ideas.* New York: Mentor, 1952.

Parker, Alton B. "The Foundations in Virginia." *William and Mary College Quarterly Historical Magazine*, 3rd ser., 1, no. 1 (January 1921) : 1-15.

Parkinson, Robert G. "First from the Right." *Virginia Magazine of History and Biography* 112, no. 1 (2004) : 3-35.

Parrington, Vernon Louis. *The Romantic Revolution in America, 1800-1860.* With a foreword by David W. Levy. Norman: University of Oklahoma Press, 1927.

Patteson, William N. "Speech Delivered in the Virginia House of Delegates." *Constitutional Whig*, 28 March 1832, p. 4.

Pestritto, Ronald J. *Woodrow Wilson and the Roots of Modern Liberalism.* Lanham, Md.: Rowman and Littlefield Publishers, Inc., 2005.

Peterson, Merrill D., ed. *Thomas Jefferson: Writings.* New York: Library of America, 1984.

———. ed. *The Portable Thomas Jefferson.* New York: Penguin Books, 1975.

———. *Democracy, Liberty, and Property: The State Constitutional Conventions of the 1820's.* Indianapolis: The Bobbs-Merrill Company Inc., 1966.

———. "The Jefferson Image, 1829." *American Quarterly* 3, no. 3 (Autumn 1951): 204-220.

Peterson, Norma Lois. *Littleton Waller Tazewell.* Charlottesville: University Press of Virginia, 1983.

Pocock, J.G.A. "Virtue and Commerce in the Eighteenth Century." *Journal of Interdisciplinary History* 3 (Summer 1972) : 119-134.

Pole, J.R. "Representation and Authority in Virginia from the Revolution to Reform." *The Journal of Southern History* 24 (February 1958): 16-50.

Polk, Lee Rivers. "An Analysis of Argumentation in the Virginia Slavery Debate of 1832." Ph.D. diss., Purdue University, 1967.

Powell, Robert D. "Speech Delivered in the Virginia House of Delegates." *Constitutional Whig*, 12 January 1832, p. 2.

Preston, William B. "Speech Delivered in the Virginia House of Delegates." *Constitutional Whig*, 28 January 1832, p. 2.

Prufer, Julius F. "The Franchise in Virginia from Jefferson through the Convention of 1829." *William and Mary College Quarterly Historical Magazine* 4, no. 4 (October

1927): 255-270; 8, no. 1 (January 1928): 17-32.

Rahe, Paul A. *Republics Ancient and Modern*. Vol. 3, *Inventions of Prudence: Constituting the American Regime*. Chapel Hill: The University of North Carolina Press, 1994.

Ramsdell, Charles. "The Natural Limits of Slavery." *The Mississippi Valley Historical Review* 16 (September 1929): 151-171.

Randall, Max Ward. *The Great Awakenings and the Restoration Movement*. Joplin, Miss.: College Press Publishing, 1983.

Randolph, Thomas Jefferson. *Speech of Thomas J. Randolph in the House of Delegates of Virginia on the Abolition of Slavery*. Richmond, Va.: Samuel Shepherd & Co., 1832.

Reiss, H.S., ed. *The Political Thought of the German Romantics, 1793-1815*. Oxford: Basil Blackwell, 1955.

Rhodehamel, John, ed. *George Washington: Writings*. New York: Library of America, 1997.

Richardson, Robert. *Memoirs of Alexander Campbell*. 2 vols. Philadelphia: J.B. Lippincott, 1870.

Richmond Enquirer (Richmond). August 1831-December 1832.

Rives, William M. "Speech Delivered in the Virginia House of Delegates." *Richmond Enquirer*, 21 January 1832, pp. 2-3.

Roane, William H. "Speech Delivered in the Virginia House of Delegates." *Richmond Enquirer*, 4 February 1832, p. 1-2.

Robert, Joseph Clarke. *The Road from Monticello: A Study of the Virginia Slavery Debate of 1832*. Durham, N.C.: Duke University Press, 1941.

Rockmore, Tom. *Fichte, Marx, and the German Philosophical Tradition*. Carbondale: Southern Illinois University Press, 1980.

Rosen, Bruce. "Abolition and Colonization, the Years of Conflict: 1829-1834." *Phylon* 33 (Second Quarter 1972): 177-192.

Rossiter, Clinton, ed. *The Federalist Papers*. With a New Introduction and Notes by Charles R. Kesler. New York: Mentor, 1999.

Rowland, Kate Mason. *The Life of George Mason: 1725-1792*. Vol. 1 New York: Russell and Russell Inc., 1964.

Rutland, Robert A., ed. *The Papers of George Mason*. 3 vols. Chapel Hill: The University of North Carolina Press, 1970.

Rutland, Robert A., Thomas A. Mason, and William M.E. Rachal, et. al., eds. *The Papers of James Madison*. 17 vols. Chicago: University of Chicago Press, 1962-1991.

Scalia, Laura J. *America's Jeffersonian Experiment: Remaking State Constitutions 1820-1850*. Dekalb: Northern Illinois University Press, 1999.

Schmidt, Fredrika Teute, and Barbara Pipel Wilhelm. "Early Proslavery Petitions in Virginia." *William and Mary Quarterly* 30 (January 1973): 133-146.

Schmitt, Carl. *The Concept of the Political*. Translated with an Introduction by George Schwab. Chicago: University of Chicago Press, 1996.

Shade, William G. *Democratizing the Old Dominion: Virginia and the Second Party System 1824-1861*. Charlottesville: University Press of Virginia, 1996.

Shalhope, Robert E. *John Taylor of Caroline: Pastoral Republican*. Columbia: University of South Carolina Press, 1980.

———. "Thomas Jefferson's Republicanism and Antebellum Southern Thought." *The Journal of Southern History* 42 (November 1976) : 529-556.

Shell, John E. "Speech Delivered in the Virginia House of Delegates." *Constitutional Whig*, 16 February 1832, p. 2; 24 February 1832, p. 2.

"The Sixth Annual Report of the American Society for Colonizing the Free People of

Color of the United States." *North American Review* 18 (January 1824) : 40-90.

Smith, Richard Norton. *Patriarch: George Washington and the New Nation.* Boston: Houghton Mifflin Company, 1993.

Smith, Steven B. "What is 'Right' in Hegel's Philosophy of Right?" *The American Political Science Review* 83, no. 1 (March 1989) : 3-18.

Sorensen, Steve. "My Country, 'Tis of Thee: Jaffa's Defense of the Noble, the Holy, and the Just." *Interpretation* 28, no. 3 (Spring 2001) : 259-278.

Spalding, Matthew, and Patrick J. Garrity. *A Sacred Union of Citizens.* With an Introduction by Daniel Boorstin. Lanham, Md.: Rowman & Littlefield Publishers Inc., 1996.

Stampp, Kenneth M. "An Analysis of T.R. Dew's Review of the Debates in the Virginia Legislature." *Journal of Negro History* 27 (October 1942) : 380-387.

Stephens, Alexander H. *Alexander H. Stephens in Public and Private with Letters and Speeches, Before, During, and Since the War.* Edited by Henry Cleveland. Philadelphia: National Publishing Company, 1866.

Storing, Herbert J. *Toward a More Perfect Union: Writings of Herbert J. Storing.* Edited by Joseph M. Bessette. Washington, D.C.: AEI Press, 1995.

Strauss, Leo. *On Tyranny.* Edited by Victor Gourevitch and Michael S. Roth. New York: Free Press, 1991.

———. *An Introduction to Political Philosophy: Ten Essays by Leo Strauss.* Edited with an Introduction by Hillail Gildin. Detroit: Wayne State University Press, 1989.

———. *The Rebirth of Classical Political Rationalism.* Introduction by Thomas L. Pangle. Chicago: University of Chicago, 1989.

———. *What is Political Philosophy?* Glencoe, Ill.: The Free Press, 1959; reprint, Chicago: University of Chicago Press, 1988.

Strauss, Leo, and Joseph Cropsey, eds. *History of Political Philosophy.* 3rd ed. Chicago: University of Chicago Press, 1987.

———. *Natural Right and History.* Chicago: University of Chicago Press, 1953; reprint, 1965.

Summers, George W. "Speech Delivered in the Virginia House of Delegates." *Constitutional Whig,* 31 January 1832, pp. 2 and 4.

Sydney, Algernon. *Discourses on Government.* Edited by Thomas G. West. Indianapolis: Liberty Classics, 1990.

Sydnor, Charles S. *The Development of Southern Sectionalism 1819-1848.* Baton Rouge: Louisiana State Press, 1948.

Tarr, G. Alan. *Understanding State Constitutions.* Princeton: Princeton University Press, 1998.

Tarter, Brent. "The New Virginia Bookshelf." *The Virginia Magazine of History and Biography* 104, no. 1 (Winter 1996): 7-102.

Taylor, Alrutheus A. "Making West Virginia a Free State." *Journal of Negro History* 6 (April 1921): 131-173.

Taylor, John. *Arator.* Edited with an Introduction by M.E. Bradford. Indianapolis: Liberty Fund, 1977.

Tise, Larry E. *Proslavery: A History of the Defense of Slavery in America 1701-1840.* Athens: The University of Georgia Press, 1987.

Tocqueville, Alexis de. *Democracy in America.* Translated, Edited, and with an Introduction by Harvey C. Mansfield and Delba Winthrop. Chicago: University of Chicago Press, 2000.

Tucker, Robert W., and David C. Hendrickson. *Empire of Liberty.* New York: Oxford University Press, 1990.

Tucker, St. George. *View of the Constitution of the United States with Selected Writings.* With a foreword by Clyde N. Wilson. Indianapolis: Liberty Fund, 1999.

Vance, Joseph Carroll. "Thomas Jefferson Randolph." Ph.D. diss., University of Virginia, 1957.

Virginia. Virginia Constitutional Convention (1829-30). *Proceedings and Debates of the Virginia State Convention of 1829-1830.* 2 vols. Richmond, Va.: Samuel Shepherd and Co., 1830.

Webb, Henry E. *In Search of Christian Unity: A History of the Restoration Movement.* Cincinnati: Standard Publishing, 1990.

West, Thomas G. "Jaffa versus Mansfield: Does America Have a Constitutional or a 'Declaration of Independence' Soul?" *Perspectives on Political Science* 31 (Fall 2002) : 235-246.

———. "Jaffa's Lincolnian Defense of the Founding." *Interpretation* 28, no. 3 (Spring 2001) : 279-296.

———. *Vindicating the Founders: Race, Sex, Class, and Justice in the Origins of America.* Lanham, Md.: Rowman and Littlefield, 1997.

———. "Classical Republicanism and America." *Review of Politics* 56 (Spring 1994) : 359-363.

Whitfield, Theodore M. *Slavery Agitation in Virginia 1829-1832.* New York: Negro Universities Press, 1930.

Wiecek, William M. "The Statutory Law of Slavery and Race in the Thirteen Mainland Colonies of British America." *The William and Mary Quarterly* 34, no. 2 (April 1977) : 258-280.

Wiencek, Henry. *An Imperfect God: George Washington, His Slaves, and the Creation of America.* New York: Farrar, Straus, and Giroux, 2003.

Wilentz, Sean. "The Details of Greatness." *The New Republic,* 29 March 2004, 27-35.

———. "Life, Liberty, and the Pursuit of Thomas Jefferson." *The New Republic,* 10 March 1997, 32-42.

———. ed. *Major Problems in the Early Republic 1787-1848.* Lexington, Mass.: D.C. Heath and Co., 1992.

Williams, George I. "Speech Delivered in the Virginia House of Delegates." *Constitutional Whig,* 24 April 1832, p. 4; 27 April 1832, p. 4.

Wilson, Clyde, ed. *The Papers of John C. Calhoun.* 26 vols. Columbia: University of South Carolina Press, 1959-1998.

Wilson, Douglas L. "Thomas Jefferson and the Character Issue." *The Atlantic Monthly* (November 1992) : 57-74.

Wood, Gary. *Heir to the Fathers: John Quincy Adams and the Spirit of Constitutional Government.* Lanham, Md.: Lexington, 2004.

Wood, Gordon S. *The Creation of the American Republic, 1776-1787.* New York: W.W. Norton and Company, 1969.

Wood, Rice W. "Speech Delivered in the Virginia House of Delegates." *Constitutional Whig,* 26 January 1832, p. 4.

Woodman, Harold D. "The Profitability of Slavery: A Historical Perennial." *The Journal of Southern History* 29 (August 1963): 303-325.

Index

251

About the Author

Erik S. Root is assistant professor at West Liberty State College. He earned his Ph.D. in political science from the Claremont Graduate University in Claremont, California.